Self-Realization through *self*-Knowing

A New Hindu Enquiry into *Dharma* and *Moksha*
Sankara Bhagavadpada

Readers interested in listening to the high quality audio soundtrack of this
entire book – topic by topic, and the 14 meditations with a sublime music track,
may contact the author through his e-mail, or the two websites:
e-mail: bhagavadpada@gmail.com
websites: www.amanaska.yoga, www.tat-tvam-asi.org

Self-Realization through *self*-Knowing

First Edition, August 2016

ISBN 978-93-82742-53-1

"To understand *what is*, there must be freedom from all distraction. Distraction is the condemnation or the justification of *what is*. Distraction is comparison; it is resistance or discipline against the actual. Distraction is the very effort or compulsion to understand. All distractions are a hindrance to the swift pursuit of *what is*. *What is*, is not static; it is a constant movement, and to follow it the mind must not be tethered to any belief, to any hope of success or fear of failure. Only in passive, yet alert awareness can that *which is* unfold. This unfoldment is not of time."

- J. Krishnamurti. *Commentaries on Living*. Ed. by Rajagopal, D.
Page 127. Victor Gollancz Ltd. London. Seventh Impression, 1976.

Na tatra cakṣur gacchati na vāggacchati no manaḥ |
Na vidmo na vijānīmo yathai tadanuśiṣyāt ||

"There, the eye does not reach, nor speech, nor the 'knowing consciousness'.
We do not know, we do not understand, how one can teach this."

- Kena Upanishad, I.3,
Swami Lokeswarananda's English Translation.2003.
The Ramakrishna Mission Institute of Culture, Kolkata, India, Third Impression.

Front cover: Image of *Siva and Sakti* (*Uma Maheswara murti*)

This image is of a sculpture of *Siva and Sakti*, originally from a *Siva* temple in Kalinga, Odisha, India (10th to 13th century CE). This masterpiece of sculpture is presently conserved at the British Museum. According to the author, it signifies the 'homecoming' of *Sakti* (consciousness), after the end of all Her infatuation with *maya*, and Her boisterous 'roaming' in the world.

This union of *Siva and Sakti* is a mythic portraiture of a 'calmed and silenced *self*,' of the *sthitha prajnya* and His awakened state in which awareness *(chit)* and *prajnya* (*Atmic* intelligence) have become manifest. This image is used as an important metaphor in the teaching in Ch. III, topic 35, and in Ch. V, topic 8.

It is unfortunate and tragic that casual observers, because of their spiritual inability to decipher the profound inner meaning of this very sublime work of religious art, may instead give it a deluded erotic interpretation.

Sources: *'Uma Maheswara murti'* as image # EG5B81 at www.alamy.com.
Zimmer, Heinrich. *Myths and Symbols in Indian Art and Civilization*, 1972. Plate 34. Bollingen Series/Princeton, USA.

C. Rajan Narayanan, PhD
Executive Director, Life in Yoga Institute & Foundation
General Secretary, Council for Yoga Accreditation International
1111 University Blvd West, #1306
Silver Spring, MD 20902

<u>Clinic:</u> Clarksburg Medical Center
22616 Gateway Center Drive, Suite 600
(Adventist Healthcare)
Clarksburg, MD 20871
301-328-3845 - Desk; 301-526-8308 - Mobile
<u>www.cyai.org</u>; <u>www.lifeinyoga.org</u>
<u>narayanan@lifeinyoga.org</u>

Foreword

This book, serving also as an educational tool for the seeker, is the expression of a Realized Master, Dr. Sankara Bhagavadpada. Given his background of devotion and dedication to Masters like Sri J. Krishnamurti, Sri Nisargadatta Maharaj; and also to the traditions of *Advaita Vedanta*, the *Saiva* tradition of Adi Sankaracharya and to Sri Ramana Maharishi; he seeks to highlight and bring home the importance of *self* - Knowing (as meant by Sri J. Krishnamurti) in relationship to traditional Self - Realization. He also seeks to explain his philosophical disagreement with Sri J. Krishnamurti and Sri Nisargadatta Maharaj, regarding the value and wisdom of the ancient traditions of India, which the two great masters seem to have ignored.

Thus, this book intended for the seeker of the True Reality of existence; is most relevant for those who share a background either in *Advaita Vedanta* or in the *advaitic* teachings and philosophies of Sri J. Krishnamurti, or Sri Nisargadatta Maharaj. They will find herein resonance with many of their unanswered questions.

A Self - Realized Master needs no background to relate to. It is well exemplified by the many examples Dr. Bhagavadpada provides in this book. However, finding meaning in other structures of thinking in traditional knowledge, and in the literature of past giants and Realized Masters, is mindful, as opposed to the purely intuitive and mindless state. Depending on the background (other than *Advaita Vedanta*) one comes from, this book may suffer from the same criticism that Dr. Bhagavadpada notes in the approaches of Sri J. Krishnamurti as well as Sri Nisargadatta Maharaj. If the standpoint of the background was not post-Adi Sankaracharya, but rather pre - Vyasa and before the compilation of the *Vedas* (pre *Vedanta*), the view may have been yet different.

It is my view that language and perspective, frame of reference of expression is the barrier, and not any deficiency in Realization.

Being a *Yogi* myself, I am a poor reader. I prefer not to read, unless I have to, and just prefer to imbibe. In the journey of this body and spirit, somehow all the giants referred in this book have crossed my path without really reading much. *Thus my expressions don't have to rely on the structure of any of the others. A brief overview of the Yoga approach may shed some new important light on the differing themes of self - Knowing and Self - Realization, and my perspective is purely from the ancient Yoga traditions of India, which predate Vyasa.*

The most ancient tradition of *Yoga* comes from the spiritual practices of India even before the coming of Vyasa - probably between 15,000 and 5,000 years ago. The practices can be summarized in three categories: *Bhakti Yoga, Hatha Yoga and Tantra Yoga.* The common principle of these approaches were later summarized by Maharishi Patanjali in his *Yoga Sutras.* Our best assessment at this time is that it was written around 5,100 years ago (even though the earlier Oxford approach dates it only about 2,000 years ago). The concept of the four *Yogas - Bhakti, Karma, Jnana and Raja* - is a Vivekananda construct based on his *Advaita* view, and in my view, a mistaken understanding. *However, each of the three systems of practices and Patanjali's summarized expression, provide insights that can give some illumination on the distinction between self - Knowing and Self - Realization.*

It is important to realize that none of these three systems were outside the perspective of religious and cultural systems of India. And any attempt to understand this cannot be based on specific documented literature, but rather on the totality of known literature references and also on modern scientific findings.

Following are some of these linkages:

- The old debate of *Aryans* and *Dravidians* and dating of the Indus Valley culture (also called Saraswati Valley culture), now has new dimensions. Based on the work of Spencer Wells, a biologist from Stanford University, who mapped the global Y-chromosome, there is reasonable basis to understand that the roots of modern *Homo sapiens* is from the San Bushmen of East Africa, and India was the first populated country in the world about 50,000 years ago and a second wave settling in Kazakhstan about 25,000 years later, came again to India about 15,000 years back.

- There is the finding of the Saraswati River with the efforts of Kalayanaraman and validation of the dating of its disappearance (after two tectonic plate shifts) with geological studies by K.S. Valdiya, who was given Padma Bhushan in 2015.

- The availability of carbon dating of fossils and flouro-luminescence dating of pottery allows us today to recognize that wooden debris from sunken Dwaraka and pottery from Saraswati Valley show an age of 14,000 years.

- Further, the understanding from polar ice-core drilling and plankton deposit on sea-beds provide evidence of global climate changes and how the early *Homo sapiens* would have conducted the journey of migration and factors that changed the physical features.

- Spoken language is known to predate written language, and accordingly grammar came after the language came to be written and also taught. Thus the written Sanskrit language came much after the spoken language and the grammar came much after. This understanding provides much insight into concatenated format of writing in Sanskrit - suggesting writing down string of syllables with limited understanding and origins of documenting the *Vedas* - and also diversity of terms from different Indian philosophical systems.

- While there is western scholarly work that speaks of written language, starting first in Mesopotamia (Iraq) in 3, 200 BCE, it is likely that the written Sanskrit language in the Saraswati Valley preceded that period considering the writing of the Mahabharata in mature language form by Vyasa, which is now precisely dated.

- The work of Vyasa to standardize rituals as reported by K.M. Munshi in his 8 volume series, Krishna, suggests he carried on the work of his father, Parashara who had begun the work, but did not have the Hastinapur kingdom's patronage, unlike Vyasa.

- The dating of the first day of Mahabharata war as November 22, 3067 BCE by Narahari Achar, physicist from Memphis State University who used the 150 astronomical observations and the interval between each observation to reconstruct the timing, and it is consistent with the disappearance of the Saraswati River and other scientifically observed events mentioned above.

- It is documented by scholars that the earliest philosophy among the six Indian philosophies *(Shad Darshana)* was *Sankhya* and the last one was *Vedanta* (*Brahma Sutras* of Vyasa), with the one before *Vedanta,* being *Yoga.*

- There exists a commentary of Vyasa on *Yoga Sutras* - which is an inconvenient document for those fixated on *Advaita Vedanta,* who seek to claim that Patanjali came after Vyasa, and therefore it could not be that Vyasa, completely negating the accepted chronology of scholars. Vyasa is not known to have written a commentary on any document, except the *Yoga Sutras.* This speaks volumes regarding the importance of the *Yoga Sutras,* as a document.

- The presence of 28 *Shaiva Agamas,* 3 *Vaishnava Agamas* and 2 *Tantras* - total of 33 systems of worship in India - that scholars suggest, is as old as *Vedas,* but is not part of the *Vedas.*

- Thus we conclude that Vyasa found the philosophy of the *Yoga Sutras* complete, but being both a spiritual giant and politically savvy (with one anchor in the Hastinapur Royal family) completed his father's work by unifying 33 religions by taking hymns from all of them, constructing the *Vedas,* establishing fire-based *(Yajna)* worship as the standard, giving room for gods of the 33 religions in the *Puranas* and completely ignoring the 33 *Agamas* used for temple worship without condemning them, writing the *Brahma Sutras* to knit the message of philosophical hymns, called the Upanishads, from the 33 religions, and calling himself only a compiler instead of the originator of *Sanatana Dharma* (Hindu) tradition. And realizing the wonderful monstrosity he had created to unify *Bharata Varsha* since common people cannot live by philosophy alone, but rather need a religion, he needed to write the Mahabharata with the Bhagavad Gita in its core and the Bhagavatam to convey the message of the Upanishads for people who needed the faith-based prodding and simplistic sermon towards further introspection.

If one understands thus, the 196 *sutras* of the *Yoga Sutras* with the commentary of Vyasa provides a full and complete understanding, while recognizing that the approaches (including practice elements) of *Bhakti, Hatha* and *Tantra* came from these 33 religious traditions. Until Vyasa's *Brahma Sutras* were explained by Adi Sankaracharya, the idea of *Jnana Yoga* was never present, since it would be the natural outcome of the highest experience in *Yoga*, Self - Realization.

Further by usage, *Yoga* has come to mean the following:

1. The practices that lead to higher Realization
2. The state of balance that makes one a *sthitha prajnya, self* - Knowing
3. The state of cosmic union that reveals all knowledge and makes one Self - Realized

To understand the relevance of *Jnana Yoga* and its relationship to the *Yoga Sutras*, one has to look into the depths of Kashmir Shaivism, which prescribes four different approaches, for people in four different spiritual stages.

- *Shambhopaya (Shambhu-Upaaya)* or directly merging with *Siva* by mere thought or inquiry - a path available only for the most purified being. From the *Yoga Sutras* perspective, this is *Jnana Yoga* available only to the person with complete *Chitta shuddhi* by mere inquiry. In the words of Dr. Bhagavadpada, that level of purification needed for this is *self* - Knowing, that is a requirement to lead the inquiry further, to Self Realization.
- *Shaktopaya (Shakti-Upaya)* or working with the *Shakti* or *Prana* to cleanse the cloud of the *Chitta* - this is the role of *Pranayama* and is *Kriya Yoga* in the *Yoga Sutras* and *Karma Yoga* in *Vedantic* parlance, for one who needs some purification before accessing *Siva*.
- *Anvopaya (Anva-Upaya)* or the lower solution that is relevant for a person who needs to go through the wringer of life before one has base level of purification to begin the practice of *Shaktopaya*.
- *Anupaya (An-Upaya)* or no solution for the one who is deemed to have another birth.

Thus Jnana Yoga, is the final stage for a purified being that is generated by inquiry. The inquiry can be structured based on traditional literature or culture of the society, or can be unstructured and innovative like the first person seeking since there is no basis knowledge.

The lower attainments of *Yoga* are the first state of calming the mind and having an attitude of acceptance most of the time. This prepares one for *Shaktopaya* or *Kriya* practices - engaging with all activities of life with non-attachment with no sense of 'doership' - that eventually results in the *sthitha prajnya* state or *self* - Knowing. Thus *Bhakti Yoga* or faith based system that merely provides focus of the mind is the lowest in the hierarchy.

Thus understood, the four *Yogas* of Vivekananda and *advaitic* understanding are not four separate paths, but rather one building on the next. And in the *Jnana Yoga* stage, the surrender to the Divine, is called *Jnana-Bhakti* which is entirely different from faith-based *Bhakti*, which is the lowest beginning. It is the importance of *Jnana-Bhakti* in full Realization that Patanjali states that it is the *Ishvara Pranidhana* that finally leads to *Samadhi*.

The current approach by many institutions that gets people who are not yet purified to study the Upanishads is a misnomer as *Jnana Yoga*. *Jnana Yoga* is present only when one is purified enough to transcend from *self* - Knowing to Self Realization - the *Shambhopaya* of Kashmir Shaivism -and in itself is the experience rather than the path.

In the context of the *Yoga Sutras*, Patanjali explains different levels of *Samadhis*. The common element in all levels is that the natural program in a person (*Chitta*, which also includes the mind) stops in *Vairagya Bhava* without attachment to anything. This is the basis for connection into the Intelligence of the cosmic flow *(Ritambhara Tatra Pranjna)*. This connection allows one to understand ones purpose in life, *Svadharma*, which is done without mindful judgement. Being in this state of 'mindless activity' of ones duties removes all the programs within us that impel us to act. This is called *Dharma Megha Samaadhi*. It is a guarantor of *Moksha*. But it may only be *self* - Knowing and not necessarily Self - Realizing. The Self - Realized state is knowledge of everything in existence that is called *Samprajnata* state. This corresponds to Self - Realization. Patanjali goes on to make a subtle distinction in the final state. The term used is *Kaivalya* and not *Moksha*. While it may be *Moksha* (release from rebirth) for one who has no more cause for rebirth, yet *Kaivalya* has a special reference to the concept of being in *Yoga* every moment *(Kshana Prati Yogi)* even while beyond rebirth, with the *Vishishtha Advaita* view of being connected with *Ishvara*. (Such a state in *Vishistha Advaita Vaishnavism* is called *Nitya Suri*, also understood as the state of *Jnana Bhakti*.)

The Tantra Yoga approach, coming from *Siva & Shakti* worship, recognizes the concept of *Kundalini* (with *Siva & Sakti* merging at the *Sahasrara*). The merger in the *Sahasrara* is considered going beyond rebirth - *Moksha*. The concept of *self* - Knowing and Self - Realization is not clear in the Tantra literature. The concept of the *Hrth* (hidden) *eighth chakra* is not in popular *Tantra Yoga* literature but is there in other literature including the *Narayana Sooktam* and *Aruna Prashnam* of the *Vedas*. This, in the sternum, is considered the seat of *self* - Knowing, what we call *Atma Chakra*, the *eighth chakra*, that Sri Ramana Maharishi calls the Spiritual Heart. From this state, seeking to know (*Jignyasu*, as opposed to seeking to liberate – *Mumukshu*) leads to Self - Realization. The path of this connection, which is different from the *Ida-Pingala and Sushumna Nadis*, we call the *Atma Nadi*.

The Hatha Yoga approach, has the highest state of realization as *Nada Anusandhana*, or imbibing the cosmic vibration. The final states are similar to *Tantra Yoga*.

In ***Bhakti Yoga*** approach, the highest is considered *Jnana Bhakti* which in its fullest state is Self - Realization, but *Bhakti* that remains faith-based is the lowest path that provides minimal focus for the mind until spiritual maturity takes one to the next stage.

An important contribution of the *Yoga Sutras* that may tie in with what Dr. Bhagavadpada presents in his approach is the distinction between "I as the observer" *(Asmita* in the *Yoga Sutras)* and "I as the doer" *(Abhinivesha* in the *Yoga Sutras)* which in common *Vedantic* literature is bundled as ego or *Ahankara*. The separation of the two is necessary to understand the distinction between *self* - Knowing and Self - Realization.

As Dr. Bhagavadpada has observed, *self* - Knowing is a pre-requisite for approaching Self - Realization, and while his requirement is to be a *Mumukshu* (seeker of liberation), we would call it as *Jijnasu* (seeker of higher knowledge).

To reiterate the value of this book, it is important to note that the concept of higher spiritual experience has to be understood in one's own terms. Those with background in *Advaita Vedanta* or in the philosophies of Sri J. Krishnamurti or Sri Nisargadatta Maharaj, should find this book valuable - an educational and hopefully enlightening experience.

August 1, 2016

C. Rajan Narayanan

Preface

A new Hindu enquiry into Self - Realization, enshrining Sri J. Krishnamurti's *self* - Knowing as *sine qua non* and bridging the gulf between the *nascent and virgin* continent of *self* - Knowing and the *ancient and haloed* continent of Self - Realization.

The *Ancient and Haloed* Continent of Self - Realization

Though there is no difficulty in understanding the meaning and significance of *dharma*, the same cannot be said about the subtler sphere of *moksha*, for the latter term will not be intelligible in the simple way in which *dharma* has always been intelligible. This has called for a closer examination of both *dharma and moksha* in broader perspective, so as to prepare the ground for dealing with the *contrasting themes* of *self* - Knowing and Self - Realization. Obviously, these themes cannot be adequately dealt with at all, without going deeply into the intricacies of the spiritual life in the spheres of *dharma and moksha*.

For both mature seekers as well as *mumukshus* (seekers of *moksha*), who are on the *advaitic* path of Self-Realization *(Jnana yoga)*; the *upanishads*, the many *moksha shastras* in the Hindu world, the works of Adi Sankaracharya and the vast corpus of literature sourced in the life and teachings of Sri Ramana Maharshi and Sri Nisargadatta Maharaj - all of these, would have already clarified the significance of the *ancient and haloed* Self - Realization. Thus, in the present context, this theme does not really call for any further elucidation. 'Continent' came to mind naturally, in view of the vastness of the history and the corpus of this literature. It seems to convey the idea in a simple metaphoric way.

There is an unrecognized obstacle in the traditional path of Self - Realization. Though this obstacle is actually of Himalayan proportions, yet its virulence has never been exposed, muchless detected and brought under the scanner in any of the traditional *advaitic* and *Jnana yoga* teachings. Why should this be so? True *advaita* teachers, who are in the Self - Realized state, can never see what an insuperable obstacle this *self* can be, because it is an unreality and even fundamentally 'non-existent' in their state. The term *self* does not appear in the traditional *advaitic* literature. Instead *Jiva* is the term used there for signifying *self*. For our part, we shall use the two terms synonymously or interchangeably, and shall provide a justification for the same. But perceptive, honest and sincere seekers travelling in the terrain of *moksha*, in search of Self - Realization, will have no hesitation in admitting that the *self* is the greatest obstacle in their quest.

The mature seeker or *mumukshu* would qualify to pursue this Self - Realization, only if the *self* has fallen silent. Why do we say this? Only because, in truth, the *self* alone is the greatest obstacle to Self - Realization. *If there is no calming and silencing of the self, the inner thirst for moksha, does not even come into being in a natural manner.* Instead, when seekers hear it repeatedly said, that this is the highest goal, which all ought to tenaciously seek; they develop an idealistic aspiration at best, but this will not certainly be what is beloved to the heart, as the heart may still be engrossed in the pursuit of some material goal in the spheres of *artha and kama.*

The divergence between the idealistic aspiration on the one hand and the actual aspiration of the heart on the other is bound to create unending conflict in the spheres of *dharma and moksha.* This is the reason, inner purity and nobility, in the form of a calmed and silenced *self* is the true qualification for stepping into the terrain of *moksha*, in 'search' of Self - Realization.

Paradoxically, unlike the *mumukshu*, whose *self* has not fallen silent, the one whose *self* has truly fallen silent through the process of Krishnamurti's *self* - Knowing, is unlikely to even seek the grandiose Self - Realization. He will be in the state of innocence, perfectly contented and the Hindu scriptures describe such a one as a *sthitha prajnya*, that is, one in whom, *prajnya* or the intelligence, sourced in *Parabrahma*, has become steady and stabilized. The awakening to the Divine, in the wake of the awakening of *prajnya* (intelligence), is something which happens, only after a seeker has crossed the important milestone of being a *sthitha prajnya*. The vast corpus of the *advaitic* and *Jnana yoga* literature will generally touch only the heart of the *sthitha prajnya.*

In contrast to the traditional Self - Realization, Krishnamurti's *self* - Knowing, is really the only new and enigmatic term in the title. So this certainly calls for a *clear vindication,* and on two accounts. Firstly because, it is a relatively nascent teaching, which, rather than being in line with the traditional Hindu *moksha shastras, has taken an all together new course, in an entirely different direction, divergent from the traditional mainstream.* Secondly, we have to also vindicate how Krishnamurti's *self* - Knowing has a profoundity and potency that is commensurate with the corresponding virtues seen in traditional Self - Realization *(advaitic* path and *Jnana yoga).*

The *Nascent and Virgin* Continent of *self* - Knowing

The *nascent and virgin self* - Knowing, cannot be ignored, because ever since its birth, it has been intensely alive, almost like a continuous luminous thread, running through Krishnamurti's life-long teachings, which had flowed without any break for seven significant decades. Moreover, because we have juxtaposed this *self* - Knowing beside the *ancient and haloed* Self - Realization, we have unwittingly created an enigma, which we will now be obliged to address and resolve.

What indeed is *self* - Knowing and how does it differ from Self - Realization, which is already familiar to us from the *advaitic* and *Jnana yoga* traditions? What is the difference between *self* & Self? The differentiation in the meanings of the two terms - notwithstanding the same word and even the very same pronunciation, being used in both cases - probably alerts us to a rather paradoxical truth. In that, though both may have a mysterious relationship with each other; say, like belonging to the same genus; or, like the *self*, being a peculiar derivative of the Self; or, through being fundamentally inseparable; yet as the world of the *self* and the world of the Self, are so disparate and far-flung from each other, they may well be taken to be akin to the irreconcilable worlds of hell and heaven, which are clearly poles apart.

A number of mature seekers the world over, may have already slaked their spiritual thirst at the springs of Krishnamurti's *self* - Knowing. Nevertheless these seekers may be small in number in comparison with multitudes of seekers who have been walking on the traditional *advaitic* and *Jnana yoga* path of Self - Realization; not only in our own age, but also over the bygone centuries and millennia. The corpus of Krishnamurti's writings, talks and dialogues too, spanning seven significant decades is also very vast, in likeness to a continent. For these reasons, the description, *nascent and virgin* continent of *self* - Knowing, came to mind. *Virgin,* because at this moment, some three decades after the passing away of Krishnamurti, this continent of *self* - Knowing, bears a likeness to the continent of America, the new world, just about a century or so, after Columbus had made a landfall on that continent.

The Dichotomy and Duality between *self* and Self

So, in one way, *self* and Self, may be inseparable and of a kindred kind, yet they are also unmistakably, like polar opposites. If we take this latter kind of a relationship alone of having diametrically opposite properties - where there is a sharp paradoxical contrast - the proper term for that would be a dichotomy. Thus in our thinking, we will be obliged to make allowance for the fact that while there is indeed a dichotomy between *self* and Self, we must not forget that there is also an underlying unity between the contrasting *self* and Self - under certain unusual conditions. The central problem in *moksha* therefore, seems to be, one of intelligently digesting the co-existence of this dichotomy and duality between *self* and Self, on the one hand; with the undeniable unity between the two on the other - under certain conditions. In later chapters, we will be exploring into the conditions under which *self* and Self, lose their dichotomy and duality and come through as the two legitimate faces of an *advaitic* reality.

The *Atma* of the Hindu *Moksha Shastras* is really the Self

The Hindu *Advaita* and *Jnana yoga* traditions, have a special Sanskrit term for the Self, namely, the *Atma*, or the inner Self, the Seeing, Illuminating and Knowing Light. *Though the Atma, has nothing whatever to do with our thoughts and feelings, nevertheless, It constitutes the deepest essence of who we are, not even as Divine souls, no; but rather as the Divine Light Itself.* This *Atma* then, is the Knowing and Seeing Light, which is itself the Self, behind the scenes, as it were.

What then is the *self*?

What however is this *self,* which appears to have received so much of importance in Krishnamurti's life-long work? How is this *self,* formed in the first place? Is it good or bad, for our material and spiritual life? While the spiritual life in *dharma,* often goes on with perfect ignorance of the difference between *self* and Self; that in the farther sphere of *moksha,* demands a clearer understanding of the dichotomy between the two, and the paradoxical unity between them, as well. At the very commencement of the spiritual journey in the terrain of *moksha,* one has the obvious, feeling that one is only the *self;* yet as the journey advances, one ultimately goes on to make the monumental discovery that far from being the *self,* which, one had all along imagined oneself to be; one is, on the contrary, the Self, which is Itself the Seeing Light, the imperishable *Atma.*

In a metaphoric sense, Self, which is the *Atma,* may be likened to the Sun, whereas, the puny *self,* may be taken to be nothing more than the *distorted reflection of this Sun in the troubled waters of man's consciousness.* The more agitated and sorrow-stricken this consciousness, the more 'twisted', even this *self* is going to become; for, after all, it is only an aberrant and distorted reflection and nothing superior with a truth-bearing power. If on the other hand, the waters of man's consciousness were to reach a state of purity and tranquility, then naturally the reflection of the Sun, in those limpid waters is also going to be faithful to the original source, the *Atma.* Under the condition of such tranquility then, the *self* which was formerly an untrustworthy and unfaithful reflection, now begins to faithfully reflect the Divine glories of the *Atmic* Sun.

There is one other rather tragic thing about traditional Self - Realization that comes to mind, which we will do well to discern. If a *mumukshu* or a mature seeker goes after Self - Realization on the traditional path, imagining it to be an achievement, like the other achievements in *artha and kama*; without the *self,* having undergone the actual calming and silencing, there is indeed the grave possibility of this *self,* sooner or later, *revelling in the thought* that it is one with *Brahman* and that it is the *Atma*! Such a grave possibility is not an anticipation, triggered by our fear or criticism of the traditional path; rather, it is an often occurring happening that is certainly not of any salutary value. It occurs, because in the traditional path of Self - Realization, this final truth alone is rammed in, a million times in an idealistic way, even when the *self* is still rather immature and has not brought to a natural finale, it's materialistic pursuits in *artha and kama*. It is a tragedy, because this reveling *self,* still may have its temptations in *artha and kama,* and more often than not, has not crossed the milestone of the *sthitha prajnya.* Its only merit, if we may call it that, is its conceptual understanding of *Atman* and *Brahman.* But we may legitimately ask, of what great use is this conceptual understanding, when the heart and intelligence *(prajnya)* have not been awakened at all?

Though we may not utter one word of criticism against such as idealistic aspiration of the *mumukshu's self,* because, this is quite in tune with how any *mumukshu* ought to progress on this path; what is however, unwholesome and undesirable in *moksha,* is the possibility that when the *mumukshu's self* has not actually fallen silent, this *self*, through the above mentioned idealistic aspiration, may come to revel in the comforting idea that *moksha*, has after all been secured. Such a revelling in the sphere of *moksha*, sustains the *self*, rather than liquidates it.

From the point of view of the *mumukshus* who have been travelling on the austere path of Krishnamurti's *self* - Knowing, this revelling of the *mumukshu's self*, will be patently seen as *self* - deception, rather than Self - Realization. The reason is that, the so-called Self - Realization is possible *only after the self has fallen silent*. If *self* - Knowing had preceded, then the seeking would have ended by itself, and such a thing as even 'seeking Self - Realization' would not even have come into existence in the first place. This possibility of *self* - deception, may convince us at least priovisionally and intellectually, why Krishnamurti's *self* - Knowing is really of paramount importance and *sine qua non* in the terrain of *moksha*.

In passing we may note the rather amusing fact, that much like the *self* and *Self*, which are related to each other through a dichotomy, as well as a paradoxical unity; even the *nascent and virgin self* - Knowing and the *ancient and haloed* Self - Realization, are related to each other through a dichotomy, as well as a paradoxical unity. Both being *moksha shastras*, certainly have common ground, so they enjoy an underlying unity, whereas, as they are also the *alpha* and the *omega* points in *dharma and moksha*, they also are seen to suffer from a concomitant dichotomy. With these preliminary observations, we are now ready to embark on a closer examination of the four Hindu goals of life, which constitute the matrix for this entire work. In later sections, after having adequately grasped *dharma and moksha*, we will be returning to re-examine this dichotomy and duality between *self* and Self, from newer points of view. This will enable us to understand why in the spiritual life, in the terrain of *moksha*, we would be far wiser to begin with the *nascent and virgin self* - Knowing, rather than with the *ancient and haloed* Self - Realization.

Dharma, Artha, Kama, Moksha: Hindu *Purusharthas* (Goals) of Life

As a preparation for understanding the intricacies of the spiritual life in the ancient Hindu world (as well as in our modern world) we are obliged to take a closer look at the four Hindu *purusharthas* (goals of man in life), *dharma, artha, kama and moksha*. One sees in the spiritual life, endless confusion and conflict between our so-called material aspirations on the one hand and the spiritual life of *dharma and moksha* on the other. *Only a clear understanding of these four purusharthas, taken as a whole, may be able to lay at rest the demon of this confusion and conflict.*

There are many nuances of meanings of *dharma*, depending upon the particular connotation we are looking at. In one sense, *dharma* is natural or social justice, social order or even social stability. And this has to be invariably rooted in social virtue. A collective manifestation of virtue in society at large must in turn only stand upon the ground of the moral order or moral virtue in the individual. *In ancient Hindu society, such an individual moral order had an undeniable spiritual foundation of profound depth.* It arose from the individual's thought and feeling, word and behavior, being inspired by an insightful understanding and devotion either to the imperceptible inner Self, the *Atma*, or if this was too intangible, then, at least to an outer manifestation of that *Atma* as a worshipful deity - *which like 'God' is but an objectified form of that self same imperceptible Inner Self, the Atma.*

As a preparation for the actual realization of this *mature form of dharma in later life*; children were initially anchored to a spiritual master *(guru)* and spiritual teachings *(dharma)* and also naturally, to the ethical values that spring from the soil of such teachings. This was achieved through a well thought out humane system of spiritual-education, commencing at the tender age of seven. You may introspect at this stage to find out whether you were fortunate enough to have this foundational basis in *dharma* during your early years of upbringing, or as a compensation for the precious time lost in the early part of life, it was only in later life, that you finally succeeded in finding a *guru* and a *dharma*?

Importantly for the Hindus, *dharma* is also the very first of the four successive goals in human life. Etymologically it means, 'that which holds up or supports' (see glossary), namely, social justice, which in turn has to be supported by the individual moral order as well. The *rishis* (sages) used the effective model of *the metaphoric bull of dharma* to communicate what they had in mind regarding the different orders of social justice and moral stability that become possible in each successive age *(yuga)* of a civilization, as it inevitably succumbed to the natural process of the break-down, decline and fall of that civilization. They realized that this was anyhow bound to happen with the inexorable turning of the *cosmic wheel of time (kala chakra)*. *Kala* is cosmic time and *chakra* being wheel.

The Model of the Bull of *Dharma*

To secure deeper insights into the whole process of break-down, decline and fall of a civilization, they invoked this metaphoric bull in different postures of strength and stability (or of weakness and instability). When it would be strongest and possessing the utmost stability, it would naturally be standing firmly on all four legs. So, they called this *sathya yuga*, the age of *satya* (truth), when *dharma* was also expected to flourish at its maximum strength of 100%. As the civilization begins to break-down, the bull must be expected to develop some weakness, say in just one leg to begin with, so that in this age, characterized by a break-down, it could still be standing though somewhat less firmly, but at least on the remaining three strong legs. They identified this as *treta yuga*, the age characterized by only 75% *dharma* and 25% *adharma* (moral chaos or moral instability).

With the inevitable further aging of the civilization, which happens with the onset of decline, from among the bull's remaining three healthy legs, we may expect a still further weakening, say, again in one of the remaining three healthy legs. However, even in this condition of increased weakness, even if the worst comes to the worst, the bull would still be able to stand with some difficulty, at least on two of the four legs, both of which may be supposed to still possess their full strength. This they called *dwapara yuga*, the age characterized by 50% *dharma*, because the remainder has been eroded by the emergence of *adharma* (moral chaos).

As the process of break-down and decline continues further, the final fall is approached, and the bull may now be imagined to be standing most precariously, on just one leg only (suppose this acrobatic position were actually possible!), as in *kali yuga* the darkest of the four *yugas*, we expect to have only 25% *dharma*, but 75% *adharma*. We may also take note that the four legs of the bull of *dharma*, would correspond to such macroscopic manifestations of *dharma* as, 'law and order', 'natural justice' as dispensed by the small and big courts in that society, 'ethical governance' dispensed by the king or the government, 'ethical values and conduct' of the subjects, etc. In *kali yuga*, most of these pillars of *dharma* are so debilitated that they are close to tottering and falling.

Sri Yukteswar Giri's model for the chronology of *Yugas*, based on the Precessional Cycle of the Equinoxes of roughly 24,000 years [1].		
	Yuga	Extent in Time
Descending Half of the Cycle	*Satya*	11501 BCE to 6701 BCE - 4800 years, inclusive of *sandhis*
	Treta	6701 BCE to 3101 BCE - 3600 years, inclusive of *sandhis*
	Dwapara	3101 BCE to 701 BCE - 2400 years, inclusive of *sandhis*
	Kali	701 BCE to 499 CE - 1200 years, inclusive of *sandhis*
Ascending Half of the Cycle	*Kali*	499 CE to 1699 CE - 1200 years, inclusive of *sandhis*
	Dwapara	1699 CE to 4099 CE - 2400 years, inclusive of *sandhis*
	Treta	4099 CE to 7699 CE - 3600 years, inclusive of *sandhis*
	Satya	7699 CE to 12499 CE - 4800 years, inclusive of *sandhis*

According to Sri Yukteswar Giri, who was not only a fully Self-Realized Hindu master but also a *Vedic* astrologer, we are currently in the ascending cycle of the *dwapara yuga*.[1] See the chronology of the *yugas* as given by him, based on the precessional cycle of about 24, 000 Yrs of the Earth's axis of spin. Considering the timing of India's independence (1947) and the strong spiritual ingredients of *satyagraha*, *ahimsa* and a general Hindu ethos of *dharma* enkindled in the consciousness of all Indians during the freedom struggle by Mahatma Gandhi, and the emergence of so many illustrious Indian spiritual luminaries in the 20th Century, it seems reasonable to suppose that this political and spiritual rebirth of India could have happened, only after she had emerged from the darkest period of *kali yuga*, and entered into the relatively more luminous age of *dwapara yuga*.

In the view of the *rishis*, after the completion of such a *maha yuga*, the cycle was deemed to start afresh all over again, through a cosmic purgation and cleansing of the massive debris of the fallen civilization, through the proverbial 'flood', or cosmic deluge *(pralaya)*. It is important to note that the measure of *dharma* varied from one *yuga* (age) to the next, depending on which *yuga*, i.e., whether *sathya, treta, dwapara* or *kali*, one was actually looking at.

Dharma as the Hindu System of Spiritual Education

Being the very first goal of human life in traditional Hindu society, *dharma* was naturally centered on spiritual education and learning and the understanding of the Self *(Atma)*, the Divine *(Brahman)* and the world on the basis of a *Vedic* and Divinity-centered world-view. In this way, Hindu male children studied for a period of fourteen years (up to their 21st year), at the feet of a competent spiritual master *(guru)* and his consort *(gurupatni)* in order to gain a firm foundation in *dharma*. Such a foundation in spiritual education *(dharma)* was intended to serve as the bedrock for the whole of the future life, which was soon scheduled to unfold, the moment the individual completes this stage of spiritual education and steps headlong into the seemingly irresistible, yet also what will later prove to be the treacherous waters of the mainstream of his adult life.

We may also mention in passing, a *Vedic* astrological insight, which may appear a little disturbing at first sight and which pertains to the question of whether *everyone in life* (at least the males of the species, as Hindus were thinking in the last five hundred years, in their fallen condition in *kali yuga*) *will be fortunate in securing a guru in life?* It is only when an individual has either a strong Jupiter in his birth chart, or a strong IXH (ninth house) or a good *Navamsha* DC (divisional chart) that the *guru* manifests in life *(sutra)*. Sometimes, individuals with abundant blessings in the birth chart (*Rasi Chart* or RC), may also be their own *guru*, or the scriptures may serve the role of a *guru*. In some cases, where the above astrological variables, which point to a *guru* are afflicted, the *guru* may vanish from our life, or relationship with him may be fraught with much pain. In fact the possibilities are too numerous, but *Jyotisha* helps us to see what blessings are in store for us in this matter and what wrath of *Isvara*, we must be prepared to face, as a result of past life *karma*. You are already seeing here the brilliant light *Jyotisha* is beginning to throw on the enigmas and paradoxes of life.

After *Dharma*, came the Goals of *Artha and Kama*

The second and third goals (which always occur as a complementary pair) were called *artha and kama. Artha* was the seeking and subsequent attainment of wealth, status, professional proficiency, *but through compliance with dharma*. Whereas, *kama* was the seeking and subsequent attainment of the aesthetic enjoyment of all aspects of human life, including all the sensory gratifications and even the aesthetic enjoyment of the whole of nature, the arts, music, dance, poetry, theatre, but *again only through the compliance with dharma*.

Artha and Kama vis-à-vis *Dharma and Moksha*

Before we venture to learn something about the esoteric notion of *moksha*, it might be good to begin by taking a bird's eye view of all the *purusharthas* (goals of human life) taken as a whole, namely, *dharma, artha, kama and moksha*. As we know, these represent the four successive goals and aspirations of human life in a traditional Hindu society. Understanding the ramifications of these four goals in that ancient society will give us a definitive advantage, in that it will awaken us to the importance of having to constantly bear in mind the sphere of life - whether *dharma, artha, kama* or *moksha* - in which the individual in question is moving at the time, before any specific question, astrological or otherwise, is being taken up for analysis.

We shall see that these four goals and pursuits, taken together, will give us a highly satisfying and all encompassing picture of human life. In Isvara's (see glossary) beautiful creation, as man is a miraculous synthesis of body, mind and spirit, it was recognized by ancient Hindus that if society had to have stability as well as ample scope for creativity, then the fulfillment of the appetites of body, mind, and spirit had to be provided for. In meeting these requirements, they took on the challenge of satisfying the appetites of body and mind first, and once this was over and done with, they turned to the subtler challenge of fulfilling the appetites of the spirit.

The former appetites constituted the spheres of life called *artha and kama*, whereas the appetites of the spirit were dealt with in the spiritually more advanced spheres of *dharma and moksha*. The ancient Hindus achieved this by blending the worldly aspect of our human nature which was brought to fulfillment and appeasement in the period of youth and middle age (*artha and kama* spheres), with the spiritual aspect of our human nature, which was brought to flower in the afternoon and evening of life (*dharma and moksha* spheres). *For the very reason that they accommodated the worldly as a prelude to the spiritual, ancient Hindu society had built into itself, ab initio, what may appropriately be called 'the completeness and fullness of life'.*

Put differently, *artha and kama* provided for the fulfillment of humanity's physical, emotional, artistic, intellectual and social appetites. They took into account the important fact that humans were social beings who needed to relate to people, and that the seeking of skill, honor, achievement, vocation, status, wealth, property and prestige on the one hand *(artha)*; and spouse, family, pleasure, enjoyment, children, home-life *(kama)* on the other, was but an inevitable aspect of being human, and that unless these appetites on the physical, emotional, intellectual, and social planes were fulfilled, there was not much meaning and purpose in the pursuit of a spiritual life in which there was not going to be room for any of these mundane cravings and satisfactions.

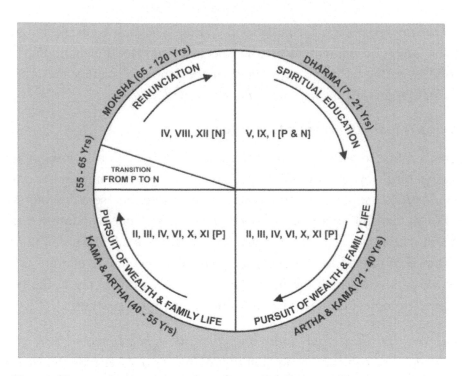

Four Purusharthas [Goals] of Life in Hindu Society

The above figure illustrates the progression of goals in a traditional Hindu society. We must start with the upper right quadrant and move in a clockwise direction to follow the progression of these goals. The first quarter of life (the school going years) was devoted to spiritual learning or *dharma*. *This was to be a spiritual foundation for the whole of the adult life to follow, but was to bear the highest fruit of moksha only in the last quarter of life, which was entirely devoted to the fulfillment of the spiritual life (moksha).* Note that the spiritual goal of *dharma* was the first of the goals of life, whereas the highest spiritual goal of *moksha* was the last of the goals of life. The Roman numerals in the four quadrants of the following two figures refer to the 'houses' or areas of human life in *Vedic* astrology to which these goals or *purusharthas* correspond.

The second and the third quarters of life were devoted to *pravritti* (extroversion or involvement in the worldly spheres of *artha and kama*). *Artha* meant the acquisition of wealth and achievements in life, whereas *kama* meant the graceful surrender to the temptations of life and the aesthetic enjoyment of the same, which marriage and family life provided for. Significantly, *dharma was to be the guiding light even as the individual traversed through these worldly spheres. Artha and kama* are necessarily intertwined and constituted the second and third goals of life.

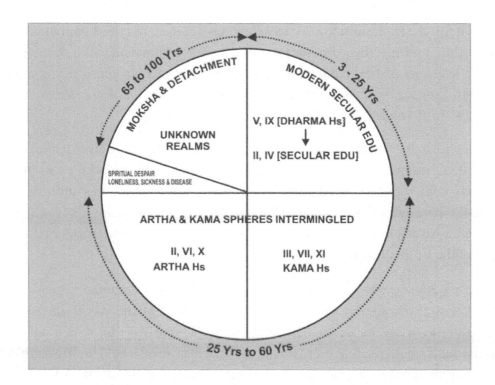

Four Purusharthas [Goals] of Life in Modern Society

Artha and kama were intended to bring about a full blown fulfillment to all desires; at the end of this journey, the individual was spiritually self composed and mature enough to *withdraw from worldly involvement, responsibilities and enjoyments through renunciation (nivritti).* To facilitate this renunciation and to make the transition to a profound spiritual life of solitude and bliss, smooth, ancient Hindus provided for an intermediary third stage of life called *vaanaprastha or withdrawal into the seclusion of a forest hermitage.* This intermediary stage was intended to make a passage to the profound spiritual goal of *moksha* devoid of any sense of shock on account of *withdrawal from the world and its enjoyments.*

Hindu *Purusharthas* Vitiated in Modern Secular Society

The above figure pertains to the goals of life in a modern secular society. In a modern secular society by contrast, the first goal of life, namely *dharma*, undergoes dissociation from its spiritual and religious roots with secular education taking its place. The spiritual and moral foundation for the whole of the adult life is now lost; even the possibility of *moksha* in the last stage of life becomes only remote, if not an impossibility, as this *moksha* cannot come to pass, without the foundation of *dharma* in the first quarter of life.

The essential interconnectedness of *artha and kama* is as valid in a modern secular society as in a traditional Hindu one. Significantly, on account of the fundamental shift that has occurred in the nature of *dharma*, the goals of *artha and kama* must now necessarily be pursued without the moral and the spiritual foundation that *dharma* had provided in a traditional Hindu society.

Worst of all, the aspiration to seek *moksha* does not even manifest, and old age, now bereft of spiritual wisdom and insights, becomes burdened with despondency and despair. Under these conditions, the last goal of life, namely, *moksha* becomes *terra incognito* for us moderns-*unless we seek this through our individual initiative in spite of our modern secular society remaining completely indifferent to our spiritual appetites.*

Once we have grasped the meanings of these four goals in the original context of the ancient society, it will then become possible for us to see what the transformed versions of these four goals are in our own contemporary Hindu society, which, at this hour, has unfortunately already succumbed to the pressure of Westernizing itself at the expense of losing its Hindu heritage. And this misfortune has struck more forcefully in an important section of the creative minority in Hindu society, namely the English educated Hindu intelligentsia.

Narrowing our focus to *moksha* now, we see that throughout human history, whether it was in the very ancient *Vedic* society or in the later civilizations of the world, *moksha* had always remained an esoteric affair, as the highest blessing in the spiritual life, which only a handful of fortunate individuals could receive. For Hindus, *moksha* has always held an irresistible fascination as the fourth and last goal of human life-the *summum bonum* of life itself. And as moderns who are quite out of touch with the spiritual ethos of our ancients we might well wonder what the nature of such an esoteric *moksha* could possibly be.....

At this stage, as a seeker, you may do some stock taking, and see if your life would fit into the model of the modern secular society, in which the Hindu goals of life are vitiated. You are naturally going to ask the legitimate question of whether under these conditions, there is not going to be any hope for building a spiritual life, without the foundation of *dharma*, in the early years of schooling and upbringing. A little reflection will tell you that in the circumstance when society does not by itself offer encouragement and opportunity for the pursuit of spiritual goals, the impetus for the same, will have to come from your own initiative. Thus in the modern setting, you will have to pursue the spiritual life and build it, through your own effort and initiative, and this is the only way in which you may successfully compensate for the absence of a spiritual foundation in our modern secular society. *In fact this compensatory process is already underway, thanks to the numerous spiritual movements at this time offering encouragement and opportunity to attend to our much neglected spiritual flowering.*

Moksha, after Artha and Kama

Moksha is the ending of all our inner sufferings that are rooted in past *karma* and in the egoistic and disorderly functioning of the illusory *self*. This perception of *moksha* may be a little hard in the beginning, but as you ponder over it in the light of your own life experiences, everything will become clear in course of time. In our present disorderly state, the *self* appears intangible to us, only because of our excessive extroversion. For this reason, we are unable to know what it is, even unable to know that it is in fact illusory, notwithstanding being so central to the whole of our life. In fact, it may even appear to be the most real thing so far as we are concerned. However, as we start an introverted observation of *what is*, which is our 'now' state of consciousness, we will be able to acknowledge the disorderly style of functioning of the *self*, and in this way, the *self* will no more appear intangible, and its illusory nature will also come home to us, as the effortless *choiceless awareness of what is* (J. Krishnamurti's sense), just happens to us as a blessing.

Such a blessing of *moksha* can come to pass only when a two-step process of inner purification and transformation attains completion. Firstly, there has to be an insightful meditative understanding of how this *self* functions in a *self*-centered and *self*-perpetuating way. Secondly, in the wake of this insightful meditative understanding there has to occur a *phase transition*, manifesting either as a radical shift in the very style of functioning of this *self*, or the *self* may also palpably fall silent. This is the kind of structural change that physicists would describe as a *disorder-order phase transition*, such as occurs for example, when either the gaseous, the disordered state of steam ('disordered' because of thermal agitation in the gaseous state), undergoes a condensation to the much more orderly and fruitful state of water. Or even better still, when the already fairly ordered state of water undergoes a *phase transition* to the maximally ordered solid-state of ice ('maximally' ordered, because in this solid state, the molecules of ice are arranged in a perfectly ordered crystal lattice).

In actual terms, it results in a more or less, constant and sometimes, even a profound sense of inner well-being, clarity and serenity that is the fruit of liberation from all bondages, sufferings and from all ignorance *(maya)*; all of which, had in the earlier disorderly state, constituted the very stuff of the illusory *self*. Under certain conditions, when the same is also accompanied by mystical experiences of cosmic consciousness, or other esoteric manifestations of an awakened *kundalini*, we may take that to represent the exalted climax, the farther reaches of *moksha*. But it should be noted that these exalted transcient states of cosmic consciousness and awakened *kundalini*, will never endure, they will come and go, lasting for shorter or for longer durations. We should therefore never take these exalted states of cosmic consciousness to be the the hall-mark, the definition, or even the pinnacle of *moksha*. On the other hand, it must be noted that the freedom from all sufferings resulting in a perpetual inner clarity and serenity, is what may be considered to be the primary hall mark of *moksha*. The reason is that many seekers and *mumukshus* who experience these transcendental states for a while, can also, in the wake of these exalted experiences, become extremely confused with the yoke of duality and suffering still heavily resting upon their shoulders, with hardly a clear understanding, as to what the Divine is, and more importantly, who they are, in relation to the Divine?

It is the fourth and final goal of human life in Hindu society since very ancient times. In the *Vedic*-Hindu tradition, the ultimate unmanifest aspect of the Divine is held to be unknowable, beyond all understanding even, so that only the process of a chain of negations of every knowable thing, in an enquiry into the Divine (or into our true nature), along the lines, *neti,*

neti (not this, not this; or neither this, nor that), was held to be the reliable means of 'reaching' the unknowable, which paradoxically was also the imperceptible inner Self *(Atma)*. This kind of an enquiry alone was expected to burn out and terminate *becoming and searching*, and thereby facilitate the abidance in being, which is both, who we are, as well as the portal to the unapproachable, unknowable, unmanifest Divine.

While Hindus were aware of *moksha* since the early years of their upbringing, it was really only after sixty-by which time, they would have become more or less free of the enticing pull of *maya*, and therefore, would have also handed over all their family and social responsibilities to their children - that they could take that final plunge with full dedication as full fledged seekers into the last goal of life, *moksha*.

Moksha as we have seen can also be taken to be that *insightful understanding* of the nature of absolute Reality, the unknowable and an *insightful understanding into the nature of the self, as a prelude*; so that this understanding results in a constant equanimity, clarity and empathy with the whole of life. A constant awareness, fascination and sense of unity with the Divine in all its infinite mystifying manifestations is the wellspring underlying the blessing of *moksha*.

Artha and kama, which were the natural goals of life between 21 yrs of age and 60 yrs of age, were intended for the fulfillment of the *self,* whereas, *moksha* (after 60 yrs of age) was held to be the result of an *insightful understanding of the self*, and consequently, *implied a negation of the self into the Divine, an ending of the self,* so that this was also a total liberation from every conceivable suffering that human beings were heir to (because of the illusory *self*), in the three preceding spheres of *dharma, artha and kama*. The result if attained would naturally be a state of well-being, undistracted attention and equanimity, arising from the unity with the Divine, and even with the whole of life itself, which in the *Vedic* view was after all, only a manifestation of that same Divinity, the source of our life.

The Importance of *Intellectual Conviction* in the Spiritual Life

In our modern times, due to the *perennial solace* provided to seekers in the material spheres of *artha and kama,* by the many contemporary spiritual mass movements as well as by the traditional spiritual institutions of ancient religions; seekers may not clearly recognize to what a great extent, *intellectual conviction*, is necessary for actually moving forward in the spiritual spheres of *dharma and moksha*, and for even undergoing that critical transformation from being mere seekers to *mumukshus* (seekers of *moksha*).

Much of the time, seekers can be seen becoming self-complacent and may therefore not not be in a position to seek *moksha*-because they have found, instead of *salvation (moksha),* at least, the more easily available and more *self*-satisfying *solace* - from all of the spiritual institutions, masters and *gurus*, mentioned above. *The most important reason why seekers do not undergo metamorphosis into mumukshus is the absence of an intellectual conviction in them-about the importance of pursuing moksha.* Thus while there are millions of seekers leisurely walking along in the sphere of *dharma*, very few, manage to graduate into *mumukshus* and thus cross over to the terrain of *moksha*.

If there is no proper understanding of *dharma and moksha*, intellectual conviction and the concrete steps necessary for the pursuit of *moksha* may not be forthcoming, so that *moksha* remains no more than a mere nominal goal.

It is for this reason, we have to go back to the past and see what a perceptive indologist, a brilliant scholar-commentator and an illustrious Hindu master have had to say about the importance of intellectual conviction in this regard. We may also note in passing that such an intellectual conviction, whose importance we seem to have completely missed, also happens to be one of the essential ingredients in every one of the following seven chapters.

Prof M. B. Emeneau in his presidential address delivered to the American oriental society in Toronto (1955), had brought home to us, the full significance of the Hindu predilection for *intellectual conviction.*[2]

"Intellectual thoroughness and an urge towards ratiocination [3], intellection, and learned classification for their own sakes, should surely be recognized as characteristic of the Hindu higher culture. It has often been pointed out that the Hindu is spiritual, i.e. concerned with his soul and its relation to the universe, and that his philosophy is a means of *salvation* whereby his soul may be released from the bonds of the phenomenal and may attain to union with the spiritual element of the universe. *It should be just as often stressed that the Hindu's intellectual urge has not allowed him to be satisfied with the minimum of theological philosophy that might suffice for a conviction of salvation. He must elaborate and refine the intellectual substructure before he will go on to the mystical experience of his salvation that is to be based as firmly as possible on this foundation.* Since, notoriously, philosophers cannot agree, a large number of philosophical substructures have emerged from Indian thinking-monist *(Advaita)*, modified monist *(Visishtadvaita)*, dualist *(Dwaita)*, and pluralist, theist *(Asthika)* and atheist *(Nasthika)*, based on a soul *(Atmavada)* and denying a soul *(Anatmavada)*, concentrating on the substantiation of evidence and relatively neglectful of this. *One suspects often enough that the Hindu enjoys philosophizing for its own sake, even though his warrant for philosophy is that it leads to salvation."* (Sanskrit terms added in parenthesis by me, so too the emphasis through italicizing.)

Adi Sankaracharya on the Importance of *Intellectual Conviction*

We cite below another instance of the same kind of emphasis on the *paramount importance of intellectual conviction* in the spiritual life, sourced in critical commentaries of the illustrious *Adi Sankaracharya* and brought to our notice by a brilliant Western commentator. Trevor Leggett, translator and commentator of '*Sankara on the Yoga Sutra-s*'[4], in his introduction makes the following observations regarding the importance of *intellectual conviction* for the Hindus.

"A Western reader may be surprised to find so much philosophical discussion in a text (the *Yoga Sutras* of *Patanjali*) which claims to be a practical manual. *But the view in India was that, as Adi Sankaracharya explains at the beginning, people will not continue practice which demands their whole life unless they are intellectually satisfied about the goal and the means to it. This view is based on wide experience of human nature.*

"As a Western example, Dr Esdaile in Calcutta (1840) carried out hundreds of operations, including amputations, under hypnosis without pain to the patients, and modern surgeons who read the reports find them impressive; but he could give no account of how it worked, and his medical colleagues gave him no support. Lord Dalhousie, the Governor of Bengal, however, who knew prejudice when he saw it, backed Esdaile and put him in charge of a hospital in Calcutta. But when Dr Esdaile returned to Britain, he was far less successful with the patients in his native Aberdeen. They must have longed to be freed from pain, *but because of their intellectual doubts, could not give the full co-operation required. The Indian patients on the other hand, could do so because there was justification in their own culture for the idea that mind could be separated from the operation of the senses.* Soon after (1846), ether and chloroform were discovered, and the whole subject was dropped with relief. There is still no satisfactory account of hypnosis in Western intellectual terms, and this is undoubtedly a barrier to its further development; *there is a justifiable unease about employing something not properly understood.*

"Adi Sankaracharya stresses that *intellectual conviction is supremely important* in the early stages of *yoga* especially. Before there has been any direct experience, however small, it is all second hand as it were. After the first direct experience (as he explains on pages 148 and 149 here), there is an invigoration of the whole personality, *and doubts no longer trouble the practitioner.*"

In the light of all these observations made by Prof M. B. Emeneau, the illustrious *Adi Sankaracharya* and the brilliant Western commentator, Trevor Leggett, we may now rest satisfied that the inclusion of intellectual conviction in the tenor of this teaching will go a long way in transforming mere seekers of *dharma* into seekers of *moksha (mumukshus)*.

The *self* in the Spheres of *Dharma and Moksha*

Our concern at this point is to sensitize ourselves to the *self* and its ways, and even consider the esoteric theme of the possible silencing of the *self*, for in so far as we are able to see, *moksha*, seems to be just this very subtle blessing, which comes with the calming and silencing of the *self*.

We have seen that *kama* is the goal of the aesthetic enjoyment of all aspects of life, including every kind of sensory gratification and appeasement. This happens through the comforts of a good life, through the eating and drinking of things delicious, through the pampering of the body and the *self* in innumerable ways, through the watching and hearing of delightful artistic creations, even an aesthetic communion with nature, through adventures in the wild, through family life and marital relationship, through sexual enjoyment and progeny.

Then we also surveyed the spiritual goals of *dharma and moksha*. Life began with the first chapter of spiritual education or *dharma* (7 to 20 yrs of age) and culminated in the last chapter called *moksha*, because it brought in the highest spiritual fulfillment, characterized by an imperturbable inner peace and tranquility. Such an almost impossible spiritual fulfillment usually happened either through the dramatic and spontaneous silencing of the *self*, as in the case of a fortunate few, or, through the less dramatic, but certainly, humbler and wiser option of the *conscious renunciation of the self and its ways,* as in the case of the majority. This more deliberate process; though 'still tainted' in the sense that, even this desire to renounce, is but an expression of that very *self*; it is nevertheless, at least a mature means to liberation from the totality of sufferings-which are a natural concomitant of the *self* and its ways. Such liberation *(moksha)* was held to be possible, at any stage between 60 yrs of age and the end of life, depending on the actual level of maturity of the individual, and the structure of his destiny. This is to be contrasted with the full social sanction for pursuing headlong the life of the *self*, with its inevitable share of joys and sorrows in the earlier spheres of *artha and kama,* spheres which covered the more ebullient and energetic years of youth and middle age.

As we are verily this *self* we probably do not know enough about ourselves as the pleasure-seeking, success-seeking, enjoying, brooding and sorrowing *self*, the subject, and this ignorance is especially striking in the earlier spheres of *artha and kama*. This is after all expected, for the spheres of *artha and kama* are by and large devoted to sensory indulgence and gratification, which is possible only with the extroversion and engrossment of the *self* in the pleasure gardens of life. In such an extroverted condition, the *self* has no opportunities at all for getting to know itself truly-for it functions here under the Divinely programmed delusion called *maya*, that it is indeed only the body, or at best, the body and the accompanying sense of *self* in consciousness.

In fact, as long as the *self* is still feeding incessantly on the pastures of *artha and kama*, it is obsessed all the time with one form or the other of, what is truly not the *self*, but rather, the 'other', which is invariably one of the attractive sense objects and the polar opposite of the brooding, seeking and enjoying *self*. The immersion and engrossment of the *self* in the pleasure gardens of *artha and kama* is generally a continuous process, except when the *self* has to face the challenge of a denial of its pleasures-then of course it becomes temporarily despondent as a sorrowing *self*. Because of this, throughout the exciting and pleasurable life of the *self* in the mundane spheres of *artha and kama*, a sustained and compelling opportunity never arises for the *self*, to take stock of its sorrow-breeding activities, to look within, to introspect and go to the end in its search for its true identity. Going to the very end in this ultimate search can possibly happen only with detachment and this can come to pass only with a greater awareness of the impending end of the body - we know too well that this happens, if at all, only in the last sphere of *moksha*.

When we enter into the spiritual sphere of *dharma* during the early years of our discipleship, our attention comes to be temporarily centered on the Self *(Atma)*, for the first time, but this happens only on the superficial, conceptual and intellectual plane, for there is no opportunity as yet, so early in life, to discover the Self, to be that very Self, that seemingly unknowable and imperceptible fulcrum, on which the whole of life and consciousness seems to be so delicately poised. In the mature sphere of *moksha*, the situation is entirely different. Here life-circumstances make it necessary for us to know the *self* (*self* - Knowing) with a greater degree of intimacy through introversion, say, along the lines suggested by either *maharshi Patanjali* in his *Yogasutras* or along the lines suggested by the master Sri J.Krishnamurti, *through a dispassionate watching of our actual state of consciousness i.e., what is, through choiceless awareness.* Without the calming and silencing of the *self*, through *self* - Knowing, there is no possibility of Self - Realization. This will be shocking for people on the path of *advaita and Jnana yoga*, but this is the truth which is generally true, except in the case of extraordinary exceptions like Sri Ramana Maharshi, who secured *moksha* without the slightest seeking.

Knowing Self as *Siva, thinking and feeling self*, as *Sakti*

In the first place, this whole theme of *the self and its ways* and even *its falling silent*, may not make much sense to seekers, in general. There are bound to be vast numbers of seekers, who may still be quite unaware of the *self*. The abode of the *self* is human consciousness-this is where it properly belongs. It arises, changes, suffers and builds itself here, and if at all, it is fated to wind up its mad activity, this desirable ending will also transpire here in its own abode, leaving the residue of the *Atma*, the Self.

We will have to either 'locate' the *self* in the abode of human consciousness or, identify the nature and mechanism of its working in this same abode. As we observe our human consciousness closely, we find that though the *self* is certainly indivisible and integral, yet, it also appears to consist of two rather complementary halves, two kinds of engines, with two distinct styles of functioning. A subtle, almost invisible, imperceptible, quiescent, almost 'non-existent' but nevertheless ever present Witnessing and Knowing Self (if you like, you can call this Self, the Knower, yes, but without the implied individuality). This Knowing Self is aware of and serves to perpetually register two kinds of stimuli or impressions which knock at is's door. (i) The sense impressions streaming in from the outside world. (ii) And all the feelings and the thought perceptions generated by the *thinking and feeling self*, from the inner world.

This *thinking and feeling self* is the other half, and the other dimension of our human consciousness. Thus, we seem to have two facets or aspects of the self, the Witnessing and Knowing Self, and the *thinking and feeling self*. The former is in the background, unchanging and timeless, imperceptible, silent, watchful and passive, the latter is in the foreground, changing, ever wandering between the past memories and the imagined future, perceptible, active, energetic, restless, noisy, selfish, chaotic, stubborn, sorrowing, pleasure-seeking, the source of all the 'chattering', to use Sri J. Krishnamurti's apt description.

As a rule, most of us appear to be unaware of the Witnessing, Knowing Self, while everyone will readily attest to the existence of the *thinking and feeling, noisy and chattering self.*

To go more deeply and create some appreciation for the central role of the *self* in the spiritual spheres, we must bring in some fundamental framework of understanding in which we may cast these two complementary halves. Once we do this, we will have more clarity and can then move on faster down the road.

There is a universal *sutra* available from the Hindu scripture of the Bhagavad Gita, from Ch XIII, as sloka 26.[5] The theme of this chapter is *the differentiation of the Knower from the known*. By 'known' is meant the field observed by the 'Knowing Self'. It is so universal a *sutra* that we can turn to it, to understand a wide variety of phenomena, irrespective of whether it be the foundations of *vastu shastra* or *Vedic* astrology or even our human consciousness.

यावत्संजायते किंचित्सत्त्वं स्थावरजङ्गमम् ।

क्षेत्रक्षेत्रज्ञसंयोगात्तद्विद्धि भरतर्षभ ॥   ॥ १३.२६ ॥

Yāvat sañjāyate kiñcit sattvam sthāvarajaṅgamam I
kṣetrakṣetrajña samyogāt tad viddhi bharatarṣabha II   II 13.26II

Its meaning is this: "Whatever comes into existence, whether a so-called living being or a non-living being, know that, it is the union of the observed field, the 'other'(*Kshetra*, or field of observation) and the observing Knower *(Kshetrajna)*."

Going a step further, we should identify the Observing or the Knowing Self as the Knower *(Kshetrajna)* with the *Siva* aspect of consciousness; whereas, the observed field, in which the activities of the *thinking and feeling self*, transpire, namely, the 'other' *(Kshetra)*, should be identified with the *Sakti* aspect of consciousness *(in the circumstance that we as the Witnessing Self are looking inwards and watching this thinking and feeling self in action)*. Implied in this is the truth that the Knowing Self is indeed the auspicious *Siva*, whereas, the frenetically active *thinking and feeling self* is *Sakti*. Human consciousness has the option of being either dominantly *Siva*, or dominantly *Sakti* or even a balanced harmonization of both. When there is the falling silent of the *self* or the calming and silencing of the *self*, then the *thinking and feeling self* or *Sakti* becomes void, and with it *maya* too becomes void, leaving *Siva* alone to be majestically and serenely present as the *Atma*, the imperceptible inner Self. The other extreme is the so-called 'fallen condition' of humanity, one in which *Sakti* or the *thinking and feeling self* is so frenetically active and so dominant (the *thinking and feeling self* fully under the spell of *maya*) that *Siva* is eclipsed, and goes missing!

This same truth is also reiterated and corroborated by the *Mundaka Upanishad* (III.1, 2, *slokas*) [6]:

द्वा सुपर्णा सयुजा सखाया समानं वृक्षं परिषस्वजाते ।

तयोरन्यः पिप्पलं स्वाद्वत्त्यनश्नन्नन्यो अभिचाकशीति ॥ १ ॥

dvā suparṇā sayujā sakhāyā samānaṁ vṛkṣaṁ pariṣasvajāte |

tayoranyaḥ pippalaṁ svādvattyanaśnannanyo abhicākaśīti || 1||

समाने वृक्षे पुरुषो निमग्नोऽनिशाया शोचति मुह्यमानः ।

जुष्टं यदा पश्यत्यन्यमीशामस्य महिमानमिति वीतशोकः ॥ २ ॥

samāne vṛkṣe puruṣo nimagno'niśāya śocati muhyamānaḥ |

juṣṭaṁ yadā paśyatyanyamīśamasya mahimānamiti vītaśokaḥ || 2||

Their meaning: "Two birds are always together on the same tree (i.e., the body), both with beautiful plumes and similar to each other. One of them eats the sweet fruits; the other simply looks on without eating anything". In terms of our understanding, the bird which eats the sweet fruits is the thinking, enjoying & feeling *self*, fraught with desires as well as disappointments, the *Sakti* aspect, the individual *self;* while the other bird, who is ever vigilant and ever observing, is the Knower, the Knowing and Witnessing Self, the *Siva* aspect.

Again the meaning of the second *sloka*: "The individual *self* is with the Cosmic Self on the same tree (i.e., the body). Because the *individual self* is engrossed, deluded and therefore unaware of its own Divine nature, it is given to sorrowing. However, *when* the *individual self* sees its essential oneness with the Cosmic Self, *then*, it is released from all sorrows." Here the translator has used the expressions, the *individual self* and Cosmic Self, whereas we had coined the more reasonable terms, *thinking and feeling self* and Knowing Self respectively.

In its engrossed and deluded state, the *individual self (thinking self)* cannot possibly know its identity with the *Siva* aspect of consciousness, Cosmic Self (Knowing Self). It is only when its excessive activities subside, Self - Realization becomes possible. This is the reason, the condition, *when* in the *sloka* becomes extremely significant. We have cited the authority of the Hindu scriptures, just to drive home the fact that our present line of analysis, using the terms, the *thinking and feeling self* and the Knowing Self is not by any means speculative and arbitrary, like a modern line of psychological reasoning. On the contrary, it is also in unison with the Hindu sacred texts, rooted in the Self - Realization of countless sages in the ancient tradition.

Krishnamurti's *self* - Knowing is *sine qua non* for *Dharma and Moksha*

Knowing is also seeing, perceiving and understanding, so this faculty of knowing seems to be also the unsuspected, faculty of intelligence. Wondering, pondering, gazing also belong to this knowing. But for these higher potentialities to come into manifestation, it is very necessary for the *thinking and feeling self* to more or less fall silent, to renounce its activities and learn how to make way for the imperceptible, Knowing Self. With its falling silent, there is *awakening of intelligence*, a spiritual happening corroborated by the Bhagavad Gita in Ch. II [7], and repeatedly emphasized by Krishnamurti. [8]

In fact, our knowing is automatic. If we consider this carefully, we will even come to the rather startling conclusion that though the body has been steadily ageing, the faculty of knowing, i.e., *the Knowing Self, alone seems to be practically untouched by time*, and we also feel, we are this 'unknown Knower'. 'Unknown', yes, because while we may feel comfortable with being referred to as the Knower, at a deeper level, we certainly have no clue - wherefrom this mysterious Knower sprang into existence? Did this happen, possibly as a quantum leap in the evolutionary development of hominids, or maybe, even, insects, birds, animals, mountains and rivers, all have this same 'Knowing Self, the *Atma*?

We have to realize that the *thinking and feeling self* is a dynamically active process that is more or less going on all the time, using and retrieving memories, making decisions, creating goals, planning the future, brooding over the past, remembering the hurts, shying away from pain, manipulating, building castles in the air, etc. And all of this dreaming built on the foundation of *maya*: that the *thinking self* is identical with the body, or some *anatma* (false Self) of what the *thinking self*, imagines itself to be.

However in our entirely extroverted state of consciousness, the sense objects we perceive on the one hand and the stuff of the *thinking and feeling self*, on the other 'come upon' the Knowing Self so completely that we, as the Knowing Self, seem to have totally lost awareness (inherent in the Knowing Self) of our true spiritual identity as the same is completely encroached upon, overwritten, eclipsed and swamped not only by the dazzling sense impressions streaming in from the external world, but also by the incessant frenetic activity of day dreaming and worrying, in which the *thinking and feeling self* is engrossed. This is the reason we are total strangers to the *Siva* aspect of our consciousness, and remain puny, with only the limited identity of the *thinking and feeling self*.

We have been emphasizing that in the spheres of *dharma and moksha*, the *self* will be our focus of attention, mainly because in these spheres, we will be concerned with the life of the *self* as a prelude to its falling silent in the last sphere of *moksha*. For J. Krishnamurti, the *self* on which all human civilizations are based, had undergone periodic liquidation, so it was easy for him to question the foundations on which this *thinking and feeling self* rested. In paying attention to his philosophical enquiry into the genesis and activities of the *self*, we will become better equipped to examine both the *self*-perpetuation of the *self*, as well as its falling silent in the farther reaches of *dharma and moksha*.

"How is the psyche, the ego, the *self*, the 'I', the individual, put together? How has this thing come into being and from which arises the concept of the individual, the 'me', separate from all others? How is this momentum set-a-going, this sense of the 'I', the *self*? We will use the word *self* to include the person, the name, the form, the characteristics, the ego. How is this *self* born? Does the *self* come into being with certain characteristics transmitted from the parents? Is the *self* merely a series of reactions? Is the *self* merely the continuity of centuries of tradition? Is the *self* put together by circumstances, through accidents, happenings? Is the *self* the result of an evolution, the gradual process of time, emphasizing, giving importance to the *self*?"[9]

It is obvious that all of J. Krishnamurti's observations and questions pertain only to the *thinking and feeling self, for it is this thinking and feeling self, which weaves maya or the illusion that one is the body, and that one is a separate individual, etc.* Krishnamurti, for some reason is not making any reference at this stage to the Knowing Self, which is the Divine Knowing Light in us, unobtrusive and in the background of our all too noisy, chattering and frenetically active *thinking and feeling self.* So long as the *thinking and feeling self* is not liquidated, even the Knowing Self, will suffer a complete veiling, though this Knowing Self is certainly bereft of all mischief and all calculations. But with the liquidation of the *thinking and feeling self,* even the Knowing Self, may experience itself differently, in that, there may not be a Knower any more in the sense of any individual, though knowing and wondering may continue undiminished.

See further, how Krishnamurti's caution when applied to the *thinking self,* the *seeking self,* in its quest for enlightenment, reveals that this could be an utterly illusory quest:

"The 'me' can never become a better me. It will attempt to, it thinks it can, but the me remains in subtle forms. The *self* hides in many garments, in many structures; it varies from time to time, but there is always this *self,* this separative, *self*-centered activity which imagines that one day it will make itself something which it is not.

"So one sees there is no becoming of the *self.* There is only the ending of selfishness, of anxiety, of pain and sorrow, which are the content of the psyche, of the me. There is only the ending of that, and that ending does not require time. It isn't that it will all end the day after tomorrow. *It will end only when there is the perception of its movement. To perceive not only objectively, without any prejudice, bias, but to perceive without all the accumulations of the past; to witness all this without the watcher.* The watcher is of time, and however much he may want to bring about a mutation in himself, he will always be the watcher. Remembrances, however pleasurable, have no reality; they are things of the past, gone, finished, dead. Only in observing without the observer, who is the past, does one see the nature of time and the ending of time."[10] *(Italics for emphasis)*

Here, the master Sri. J. Krishnamurti is suggesting being aware of the activities of the *thinking and feeling self* even as they are happening, but without the motive to alter what is perceived. According to him, any desire to change what is seen going on, in the *thinking self,* will be futile, because it is bound to add only further momentum to the *thinking self* and this way, desire to change or correct will come in the way of its falling silent. 'Watcher' as he uses the expression is only an aspect of the same *thinking and feeling self*, that aspect, which has taken up its position as the 'reformer' and the 'policeman', in the hope of effecting a radical transformation. The kind of observation he is talking about, totally bereft of all motives is what he calls *dispassionate observation of what is, or the choiceless awareness of what is. For him, choiceless awareness opens the doors to self - Knowing and also to the ending of the activities of the self, as choiceless awareness of what is, brings about a radical transformation of what is, or a silencing of what is. In the sphere of dharma and moksha, this is a never before heard of meditation, unknown to the the ancient and haloed tradition of Atmajnana and* Self - Realization. If a seeker learns this *self* - Knowing, it has the power to deliver the seeker to Self - Realization, provided the seeker also studies the *moksha shastras*, for understanding what has happened to him, as a result of continued dedication to Krishnamurti's *self* - Knowing.

In Krishnamurti's writings, reference is invariably made to the *self* that sustains thinking and feeling and which in turn is itself also thrown up, by the very processes of thinking and feeling, as both thinking and feeling arise in response to challenges of survival. This *self* is invariably only the *anatma* (false Self) that one is the body, or some other *anatma. Much of human thinking and feeling, becomes wasteful and conflict ridden, when centered on the self, as an anatma.*

However, we must not fail to realize that in clear and deep thinking or enquiry into truth (such as we meet with in creative thinkers, artists and scientists), *this self may have no place at all, it may simply be non-functional, during deep enquiry and spurts of clear wondering, contemplation and insightful perception.* In such cases, where lofty thinking and feeling is free of the *self*, thinking and feeling becomes sanctified, truth-bearing and fruitful. Implied in this is the precious converse *sutra* as well: that where thinking and feeling are contaminated and corrupted by the *self*, such thinking and feeling loses the fruitful, truth-bearing potency *(sutra)*. Some of us may have been witnesses to such comical phenomena, seen in the conversations between people.

In the case of Ramana Maharshi, the definite ending of the *thinking self* happened suddenly, through a definitive and irrevocable kind of Knowing, and is best described in the Maharshi's own words. In this remarkable example, it is the Knowing Self which has had the Self - Realization-because, the *thinking and feeling self* seems to have ended more by an abrupt stroke of fate, by the invisible hand of the Divine. A *Vedic* astrological decipherment of this very usual happening constituted the theme of Sri Ramana Maharshi's Moksha.[11]

"It was about six weeks before I left Madurai for good, that the great change in my life took place. It was quite sudden. I was sitting alone in the room on the first floor of my uncle's house. I seldom had any sickness and on that day there was nothing wrong with my health, but a sudden violent fear of death overtook me. There was nothing in my state of health to account for it and I did not try to account for it or to find out whether there was any reason for the fear. I just felt 'I am going to die' and began thinking what to do about it. It did not occur to me to consult a doctor, or my elders or friends; I felt that I had to solve the problem myself, there and then.

Ramana Maharshi's Self - Realization: Abrupt Ending of the *thinking and feeling self*

"The shock of the fear of death drove my mind inwards and I said to myself mentally, without actually framing the words: 'Now death has come; what does it mean? What is it that is dying? The body dies.' And I at once dramatized the occurrence of death. I laid with my limbs stretched out stiff as though *rigor mortis* had set in and imitated a corpse so as to give greater reality to the enquiry. I held my breath and kept my lips tightly closed so that no sound could escape, so that neither the word 'I', nor any other word could be uttered. 'Well then', I said to myself, 'this body is dead. It will be carried stiff to the burning ground and there burnt and reduced to ashes. But with the death of the body, am I dead? Is the body, I? It is silent and inert, but I feel the full force of my personality and even the voice of the 'I' within me, apart from the body. So, I am spirit transcending the body. The body dies, but the spirit that transcends that, cannot be touched by death. That means I am the deathless spirit.' All this was not dull thought, it flashed through me vividly as living truth, which I perceived directly, almost without thought-process. 'I' was something very real, the only real thing about my present state, and all the conscious activity connected with my body was centered on that 'I'. From that moment onwards, the 'I' or Self, focussed attention on itself by a powerful fascination. Fear of death had vanished once and for all. Absorption in the Self continued unbroken from that time on."[12]

The Knowing Self Reflexively Turned Upon Itself (Self - Realization)

It is obvious that by the term, 'I', the Maharshi must be meaning only the Knowing Self, after the *thinking and feeling self* had become void, leaving only the majestic and serene presence of *Siva*, as the Knowing Self. His concluding words sum up the realization, and confirms to us, how his consciousness became *Siva* filled and *Siva*-centric, with hardly any room for *Sakti* or the *thinking self*: 'From that moment onwards, the 'I' or Self, focused attention on itself by a powerful fascination.' In the *Siva-Sakti* drama that is going on in our human consciousness, the Knowing Self as a rule never turns permanently upon itself in a reflexive 'fall-back', for it is ever Knowing only what it perceives as the 'other', namely either the sensory impressions which are streaming in, or Knowing all the goings on in the *Kshetra* (field) of the *thinking and feeling self*. In the case of the Maharshi, the Knowing Self, discovered Itself alone, as the primal Reality, and neither the body nor the sense impressions, nor even the contents of consciousness nor the world, beyond. This was the Maharshi's Self - Realization.

The Importance of paying heed to Ancient Traditions

Though I found the life-time work of the master J. Krishnamurti, as well as the master Nisargadatta Maharaj throwing *brilliant new light* on entirely different aspects of *moksha*, the former on *self* - Knowing and the latter on Self - Realization; nevertheless, there was, one common factor in their teachings, which for me was unsatisfactory. Both had decisively turned their back on the verdict of ancient traditions, rather than being truly open and therefore willing to dialogue with the best of the traditional teachers and learn what they had to say - if that was indeed warranted. It is true that J. Krishnamurti dialogued with leading thinkers from many different walks of life, but where the dialogue turned in the direction of the traditional religious matters, Krishnamurti showed more of an antipathy, rather than a sympathetic understanding of the wisdom inherent in traditional approaches, especially for seekers, who had utmost faith in those approaches. That J. Krishnamurti had a revolutionary new point of view that was entirely unknown to the religious tradions, is undeniable. Notwithstanding his extrodinary sensitivity, intelligence and originality, Krishnamurti, somehow was not vulnerable to important lessons from traditional teachings. For these reasons, notwithstanding having benefitted vastly from both exceptionally original masters, I must say that I lose resonance with both of them, when I see them critically turn their backs on the wisdom of numberless sages and saints - a priceless treasure, which is still available to us, and what can still come alive in our lives, if we will but turn in the direction of the traditional texts and care to study them diligently.

Freedom was certainly J. Krishnamurti's original synonym for *moksha* that *choiceless awareness of what is* was expected to lead to, when the same was pursued relentlessly to its farther reaches. Though both masters were fiercely independent and stood out as courageous lions in opening up their spectacularly original paths to mature seekers and *mumukshus*, their unwillingness to listen deeply to the voice of traditional *moksha shatras*, should not be considered, a meritorious virtue that is beyond questioning, rather it should be considered as a weakness, concomitant with their originality and brilliance as teachers.

Tradition is not just a lack-lustre shroud, for it is the cumulative wisdom of numerous original sages and seers, in the last ten thousand years. So, the brushing aside of the voice of hoary traditions, carries with it the risk of being arrogant and also resistant to the priceless living wisdom of ten thousand sages and seers. Seen in this light, though three decades have passed off since J. Krishnamurti and Nisargadatta Maharaj have shuffled off their mortal coils, at least those whose hearts have been deeply touched by these extraordinary masters, may do well at least now, to critically re-examine the teachings of both masters in the broad flooding light of the ancient Hindu *moksha shastras*.

This is what I have in fact done in the Tat Tvam Asi retreat. While the teachings of many masters have stood out as beacons of light in my own spiritual journey, I have not allowed this to come in the way of a critical reappraisal of the fruitfulness of their life-long work.Both were masters on the *nivritti marga*, that is, in the sphere of *moksha* only. Neither was a scholar, so in that sense it may not have been their lot, i.e., their *swadharma*, to look back at the living wisdom of the past sages, in search of common ground. The search for common ground, usually falls to the lot of scholarly compilers, seekers or *mumukshus*, who are the ones who usually struggle to find common ground in various *moksha shastras*, for gaining that *intellectual conviction*, which undeniably is an advanced milestone in their *sadhana*. In contrast to both these brilliant masters, Sri Ramana Maharshi was an exemplary Self - Realized master, who also wonderfully bridged the gap between his own experience of Self - Realization and the *ancient and haloed* continent of Self - Realization. He diligently studied every *moksha shastra* in the *Saivite* tradition of South India and also translated some of them into Tamil, his mother tongue-for the benefit of *mumukshus,* who came to him in search of this Self - Realization. Further, he encouraged mature seekers and *mumukshus* to study many of these *moksha shastras* diligently and with great devotion.

The Invocation of Ancient Hindu *Moksha Shastras* in this Retreat

Lest, we succumb to a spiritual fall, through *self*-delusion and *self*-deception, as we soar into the dizzying heights of an independent enquiry, I have deliberately kept the doors open, so that the light of the sobering wisdom of the sages and seers, will save us from the dangers of the above pitfall. We will thus periodically apply the traditional yardsticks, the *sutras* from the works of Adi Sankaracharya's Viveka Chudamani, the Bhagavad Gita, Ashtavakra Gita, Upanishads, Kaivalya Navaneetham, Yoga Vasishtam, Advaita Bodha Deepika and Vedanta Panchadasi; to ensure that our spiritual journey in *dharma and moksha* is indeed corroborated and sanctified by the haloed *moksha shastras* of the Hindu tradition.

self - Knowing via-à-vis Self - Realization

In the Hindu *moksha shastras* such as the Upanishads, the works of Adi Sankaracharya and in Ramana Maharshi's and Nisargadatta Maharaj's teachings, Self - Realization is the goal, for such of those seekers who have flowered into *mumukshus*. Self - Realization is a modern term for the classical term of *moksha* or *Atmajnana*. In this context, by Self (spelt with a capital S), is meant, the universal Self or the *Paramatma*, which is essentially also the same as the *Atma*, the Self, as felt and experienced by *mumukshus,* post Self - Realization.

On the contrary, *self* - Knowing, is *an entirely nascent field* that has been opened up for the very first time in the sphere of *moksha,* through the life-time work of J. Krishnamurti. The ancient Hindu tradition has been obsessed with the *Atma* or the Self, and our realization of that as our essential nature-who we really are. This Self, is naturally the omega point of the spiritual quest of the *mumukshus, their final destination, so to speak.* The, alpha point of the spiritual quest, by contrast is the miserable *self* (italicized and with, 's' in lower case) - *what humans actually feel themselves to be, who they actually consider themselves to be.*

However, from the point of view of the Self - Realized sage, this human *self*, is what may be called a false-Self or an *anatma*. The paradox is that, so long as one is without Self - Realization, this *self*, is the most real thing in any human life, in fact it is the only thing to which humans cling. It is all that humans have, it is the only tangible 'observable', the *mumukshu* has got, namely his own suffering *self*, as he sets out on his solitary quest for permanently annihilating and liquidating this *self (moksha).* In other words, the alpha-point of the spiritual journey is this known *self*, whereas the Self, of which the sages speak is completely intangible, incomprehensible, the unknown, at best only a purely dazzling intellectual idea, the omega point of the final destination.

Preface

The long line of Hindu Self - Realized sages, including the illustrious Adi Sankaracharya and even, the contemporary sages of the last century, Ramana Maharshi and Nisargadatta Maharaj, all of them completely missed coming upon the profound significance of *self* - Knowing, simply because, in the post Self - Realization phase, the *self* appears to be a mirage, an illusory thing, so this *self*, of which they were not even in a position to have direct knowledge, ceased to hold the attention of all these Self - Realized sages.

In the case of the Maharshi, as he had lost the illusion of the *self*, even before he could perceive that to be the real cause of all human sorrow, it was his fortunate lot, never to know anything about *self*, nor about the potency of *self* - Knowing. His *swadharma*, or the calling bestowed on him by the Divine, as we may infer by retrospectively looking at his life, seems to have been to make the ancient and esoteric goal of Self - Realization, once more, a tangible goal for present day *mumukshus*. He was a unique living example of how this Self - Realization would possibly express itself in a given human life, and so, that was more than enough for *mumukshus* to gain a conviction that this esoteric goal was really the *summum bonum* of human life. *When serious seekers, posed the pertinent question to the Maharshi, as to whom his path of Atmavichara (enquiry into the Self) would be ideally suitable; he never minced matters, but straightaway declared that, it was a path for the most mature and the noble-minded.*

Implied in this is the fact that for the vast majority of seekers, who are as yet, nowhere close to graduating into *mumukshus*, his clearly laid out path of *Atmavichara*, would not actually make the slightest sense. As these seekers are not certainly seeking *moksha*, nor even interested in it, the light of *Atmavichara* will necessarily recede and fade away from their spiritual quest, much like the sun going down the horizon at sunset. So, what do we expect such sincere seekers to do, those who are still engrossed in *maya* and in duality, and still travelling in the mundane spheres of *artha and kama*? As the Maharshi's *Atmavichara* and the *moksha shastras* of the Hindu tradition, will sooner of later fail to attract their attention, what are these helpless seekers to do, for undergoing a genuine spiritual transformation, while still young, while still being interested in *artha and kama*, while still under the sway of *maya*?

After the master J. Krishnamurti passed away, after he had, so to speak, completed his *swadharma*, we may infer retrospectively, that the seekers whose years in *artha and kama*, still seem to be unfinished; for them, the appropriate starting point would have to be, the alpha-point, that is, *self* - Knowing. Though Krishnamurti's, seemingly humble beginings in *self* - Knowing, may not appear to be so lofty and sublime, as the direct hit at Self - Realization that Ramana Maharshi had envisioned; it turns out that, it is the commencement of the serious spiritual journey at the alpha-point, or *self* - Knowing, that is the more appropriate for seekers still travelling in the *artha and kama* terrain. The unbelievably thing is that, this path of *self* - Knowing, imperceptibly flows into the omega-point of Self - Realization. This may appear hard to believe in the beginning, but for sincere seekers who actually embark on this inner spiritual pilgrimage, this will be borne out by their own experience, as it was in my own case.

Unlike Ramana Maharshi and a few other gifted mystics and exceptional cases, humanity suffers enormously (and paradoxically also intensely enjoys), because of the *self*. From this arises the paramount importance of *self* - Knowing. Thus, J. Krishnamurti's *self* - Knowing, opens an entirely new door to *moksha*, a door, even the existence of which was, entirely missed in the ten thousand year long tradition of Self - Realization.

In the Tat Tvam Asi retreats, it is *self* - Knowing, that takes us all the way to the farther milestone of the calming and silencing of the *self*. At that farther milestone, the goal of Self - Realization begins to emerge on the horizon, naturally and brilliantly, whereas, without the precursor of *self* - Knowing, Self - Realization would have remained *terra incognito* and a utopian ideal that the vast majority of seekers will never ever achieve.

———————————————

Organization of the Retreat

The Origin of this Work

In Feb 2016, I conducted a week-long spiritual retreat, centered on *self* - Knowing and Self - Realization. The twenty six seekers who participated were from six nations. The entire teaching was cast in the form of a PPT (Power Point Presentation), with a pre-recorded audio sound track in English, synchronized with every slide of the PPT. As there were also Spanish speaking seekers, there was a Spanish translation synchronously audible in headsets worn by the Spanish seekers, even as the original teaching in English was streaming in through headsets - to the English speaking participants. As this is not certainly a customary teaching method, some explanation and justification is called for, which I shall try to provide in the following paragraphs. The present work is simply the teachings given at that retreat.

The Teaching was in the form of 'Conversations'

The audio sound track became necessary, as I could not possibly speak 7 or 8 hrs a day, for seven days at a stretch. I had always spoken extempore in all of my previous week-end retreats, taking the cue from the successive slides of the PPT, as the PPT had always provided me the basic framework. However, this former method could not obviously be adopted in the present context of the retreat extending to a full week.

The teaching was therefore in the form of a carefully pre-recorded audio commentary (sound track) in the form of questions (Qs) and answers (As) and in this way an English script emerged quite naturally. This preparatory work was done over an eight month period at our home by my wife, Dr Prema Shanker and myself and this took on a final shape, with an excellent audio quality at a digital recording studio. Thus every slide was synchronized with a sound track that was played, when that particular slide was projected onto the screen, and this was heard by the seekers through good quality headsets.

The Qs raised by Prema, pertained to the content of each slide. She put herself in the shoes of the seekers 'who are keenly listening' and so many of her Qs are from 'the point of view of the seekers'. As she has been keenly watching the gradual unfoldment of the spiritual work ever since 1987, and had also been with me in everyone of the spiritual retreats both in India, as well as in the other countries of North and South America, since 2012; she has imbibed a very clear understanding of the nature and scope of this teaching. To the extent of some 40%, I too suggested other Qs, since I felt those Qs to be also pertinent for almost every one of the topical discussions. I wanted Prema to be critical of my stand as a teacher and to challenge my views as I presented them, rather than be accommodative and adduce justification for my stand through a more deferential and traditional approach.

I had enough time to think over what I was expected to speak. I was aware that what I was going to speak was going to be seriously listened to. In my long years of experience I found that people often do not exactly give utterance to truth, as they felt it in their souls - for fear of offending others, who may hold different views, etc. I had often seen socially and even spiritually eminent leaders doing injustice to themselves and to their listeners by toning down and diluting their own perceptions, just for being socially more acceptable and pleasing to their listeners. I did not want to repeat this age-old blunder to which leaders in every age seem to have succumbed.

Thus, here in these audio files, you will hear me speaking directly from my heart, that is, without making any attempt to soften or dilute my stand. *I made it clear at the very beginning that this path may not suit every kind of seeker. I have always asked seekers to be discriminative in looking for a path which will please them and suit their unique individual temperament.* Following then, this simple and innocent rule of integrity, Prema and myself put together an English script in the form of Qs and As. The idea behind such a script was that, once in the digital studio, both of us will find it easier to read directly from the script. In practice however, as I had many 'second thoughts' during the studio sessions, I resorted to the option of being unpredictably spontaneous and thus came to deviate from the script and ended up speaking 'new and different things' in the last minute. Prema also resorted to this *impromptu* approach though probably to a lesser extent.

You will find the tenor of the retreat to be serious, with absolutely no room for any kind of spiritual entertainment, in a lighter vein. Throughout the retreat, I kept the doors open for questions from the participants - as they spontaneously responded to the pre-recorded audio sound track. Whenever I spoke extempore, answering such *impromptu* Qs, all that I spoke on those occasions was also translated by Ricardo Bravo into Spanish. However, none of the extempore answers provided by me are part of the present sound track-they were something which only the participants in the retreat could possibly give ear to. *Once this work is in your hands, you also have the option of requesting for the audio sound track, which is like an audio version of this book.*

Glossary of Sanskrit terms for English-speaking Seekers

To help seekers become familiar with the special vocabulary, I created a glossary of Sanskrit terms in English, so that at least the English-speaking seekers could understand each Sanskrit term clearly, without any confusion or ambiguity of meaning. Thus, a copy of the glossary was given away in the dosier right at the commencement of the retreat. Unfortunately this glossary could not be translated in good time also into Spanish, before the commencement of the retreat. Nevertheless, as he went along, Ricardo Bravo, because of his deep familiarity with these Sanskrit terms, kept on translating even such terms into Spanish, whenever he felt the need for the same. You will find this Sanskrit glossary appearing at the end of this work.

Spanish Translation by Ricardo Bravo

The retreat was conducted with Ricardo Bravo *synchronously translating into Spanish*. Ricardo, my collaborator and leader of the Spanish speaking group, could do this 'magical and psychic' translation synchronously, as he was deeply familiar with this teaching and the special Sanskrit vocabulary that I use as part of the teaching. Since 2012, he has been translating at all of my week-end retreats in Santiago, Brasilia, Mexico City and Punta Del Este. It was his deep understanding of the teaching that resulted in this 'magical and psychic' character of the translation. He would say that often, he was translating without the interference of conscious thinking on his part. It may be noted at this point that on all former occasions mentioned above, Ricardo did not have any English script on hand - of what I was going to speak, for on all those occasions, I had spoken extempore, directly taking the cue from the slides.

The Use of the English Script for the Spanish Translation

Such an English script in hand was certainly a great aid for Ricardo, *but the script in Ricardo's hand, was not continuously and always helpful.* For, I invited Qs, as soon as each slide's sound track was completed. As I then answered all such Qs, then and there, this also called for an instantaneous Spanish translation. Thus Ricardo's challenge of translation suddenly and unpredictably shot up on many occasions. However, intuitive and psychic as Ricardo was, *he also resorted sometimes to translate directly, without looking at the script in his hands.* As he had a good rapport with me and the teaching, with the many *sutras*, the challenge of having to translate spontaneously could also be easily met by him.

Contemplating on this new teaching method that I had brought into this retreat in the form of a pre-recorded sound track; Ricardo envisioned future retreats to also have an already well translated Spanish script on hand, so that the strain of translation vanishes and in its place Ricardo will have the delightful aesthetic experience of enjoying reading directly the Spanish script, which he would have anyhow produced himself through a direct translation of the original English version.This in fact, became the plan for the next longer ten day retreat in 2017.

Acknowledgements

As always, profound gratitude to the beloved master Sri Sri Bhagavan, for having initiated me into Hindu philosophy and the writings of the beloved master Sri J. Krishnamurti (along with my late beloved mother); at the tender age of fourteen. Profound gratitude to the beloved *Jyotishacharya*, Prof. V. K. Choudhry, for having taught me the Systems Approach (SA), which is an all pervasive research-based understanding of *Vedic* Astrology. Importantly, heart-felt profound gratitude to the late beloved, Dr. N. Sivakamu, an early patron of my work.

I certainly could not have put together this multi-faceted retreat and also this book in the sequel, without the exemplary partnership, constant loving encouragement and excellent suggestions and solutions from my beloved wife, Dr. Prema Shanker. She spontaneously discontinued her Paediatric clinical practice, for two months, so as to be an integral part of this work, before the retreat commenced. I must also thank the rest of my family, my beloved daughter, Gayatri and my beloved son-in-law, Shreenivas, for contributing thoughtfully to the retreat, in several ways, during the many months of preparation.

It goes without saying that I am deeply indebted to the visionary, Dr. C. Rajan Narayanan, the Founder, Exe. Director and the moving spirit, behind the 'Life in Yoga Institute and Foundation', Maryland, USA. Through this institution, he has rendered yeomen service in the field of 'Measured Yoga Therapy' as well as in the establishment of International Standards for Yoga, and in being recognized as the unique Yoga Institution which offers Yoga courses as 'Continuing Medical Education (CME)' for doctors and health practitioners. I am deeply grateful to him for his warm encouragement on many fronts, for his receptivity to my work, and for having consented to write a foreword for this book, at such short notice.

My profound appreciation of the advice given to me, goes to the noble-minded publisher, Sri Gautam Sachdeva of Yogi Impressions, Mumbai. Because of the deep spiritual moorings of his family and his strong spiritual inclinations, it has always been a delightful experience to merely relate to him at a sublime human level, or at the level of the soul. I am also thankful and sincerely appreciate the efficient and meticulous publishing services provided to me by the professional team at Yogi Impressions, which helped bring this work out in an unusually short span of time.

Sri G. P. Venkateswaran and Dr. Chandra Venkateswaran, of the Anugraha Educational and Consultancy Services (Pvt) Ltd, Chennai; were kind and generous in providing me with the excellent pre-publishing services of their DTP professional, Sri. J. Jayakumar. He has done a painstaking, dedicated and very skilled job in bringing the entire manuscript, along with all the illustrations into a beautiful final format, ready for publication. It was a real pleasure to work with him, side by side throughout the whole course of the DTP work. I will always remember him for his commitment and capacity to quickly come up with good solutions.

The keen-eyed, partial editorial service rendered by Dr. Jaya Indus, is also hereby gratefully being acknowledged; especially as she took time off, from her daily schedule of work at the Theosophical publishing house, Adayar, to critically scrutinize, two chapters of the MS, in the last six weeks, before the MS was despatched to the publisher.

In the Context of the 'Tat Tvam Asi' - 'Vedic Flower' International Retreat - Febuary, 2016

We open our hearts to the life coach Ricardo Bravo and to his energetic Spanish speaking participants, who had crossed the high seas to come to this retreat. Their passion for the truth is all too evident. Words fail us, as we attempt to convey our appreciation and gratitude to all of them. Likewise much gratitude goes to Sri S. M. Kumar (USA), Ms Dawn Giel (USA), Dr. Manjusha Coonjan (Mauritius) and all dear Indian participants from different parts of India.

Ms Devika Dorai wonderfully supported the preparation of the English script. Her keen intellect, alacrity and resourcefulness were assets, without which this retreat could not have been so nicely fulfilled on all fronts. She took much of my strain away by asking me to speak extempore in a recording smart phone and later transcribed that speech into script. This could not have been an easy task at all. Devika shouldered enormous responsibility in the overall organization of the whole retreat-from start to finish. She continuously coordinated with the event managers, worked with all participants and gave them the best possible suggestions and deals, looked into every aspect of the event and was perpetually vigilant. Her commitment, sensitivity and awareness will always be gratefully remembered by my wife Prema and myself.

S. M. Kumar offered calming and relaxing *yoga* practices, every morning and this was appreciated by all the participants. This was a loving service he rendered to all participants. Sri Kannan, Sri Kumar and Sri Sambasiva Ramanananda, very thoughtfully organized, paved the way, and also guided the Tiruvannamalai pilgrimage. Likewise both of them (Kannan and Kumar) did a highly dependable job in receiving International participants at the airport upon arrival and travelled with them (Kumar) all the way to Le Pondy.

The homa was generously sponsored by Ramanananda, while, Kannan, Ramanananda and Sri Gokulan did all the thoughtful planning for the same, months ahead of the event. Sri Raja Shastrigal, the priest, and his supporting team conducted the homa in all sincerity and care, leaving the participants in a fulfilled and peaceful state.

Ramanananda offered selfless support throughout the retreat, especially in managing the musical background and the special meditational music. He was continuously available to me, for

Acknowledgements

any help. Likewise, Devika, Kannan, Kumar, Gokulan and Sri Mohan Sarma, extended the utmost co-operation on many fronts.

Smt Uma Mohan aesthetically rendered the *Brahma Tat Tvam Asi* Sanskrit chants, exactly as desired by us and set them to beautiful music. Baba Prasad did a painstaking and skillful job at his digital recording studio, as Prema and myself had demanded his undivided attention for nearly 60 hrs, for creating the complete audio sound track. Much gratitude to both of them.

The event managers of DMC Leisure Pvt Ltd, Sri Kumaran, Sri Shamnad and Sri Shibbu were very sensitive people and their co-operation contributed to the fruitful fulfillment of the pilgrimage and retreat.

Contents

Chapter I

Introduction, First Principles, *Jiva (self)* and *Atma* (Self)

Your Personal Meditative Journey from *what is* to the *Atma*.

Chapter II

By Being the Atma,
You can Identify, Observe and Understand the *Jiva*

Contents

Two 'Tat Tvam Asi' Birds

Understanding the *Jiva (self)* and the *Atma*

Chapter III

By Being the Atma,
Knowing and Taming of the *Jiva, happens*

Chapter IV

By being the *Atma*,
Calming and Silencing of the *Jiva (self)*, happens.

Chapter V

By Being the Atma,
The Awakening of Intelligence *(Prajnya)*, happens

Chapter VI

By Being the Atma,
You Discover *Parabrahma* and His 'All Merciful' Nature

Contents

Chapter VII

By Being the Atma,
You discover a two-way intimate bond with *Parabrahma*.
Through this devotional bond, you will discover 'Tat Tvam Asi'.

_____

Chapters I – IV of the Book : Part I

Chapter I: Introduction, First Principles:
Jiva (self) & *Paramatma* (Self)

Part I:

Chapter II: *By Being the Atma*,
Identify, Observe & Understand the *Jiva (self)*

Chapter III: *By Being the Atma*,
Knowing & Taming the *Jiva (self)*

Chapter IV: *By Being the Atma*,
Calming & Silencing the *Jiva (self)*

Chapters V – VII of the Book : Part II

Chapter V: *By Being the Atma,*
the Awakening of Intelligence *(Prajnya) happens*

Chapter VI: *By Being the Atma,*
you discover *Parabrahma* (the unmanifest Divine),
and His 'All Merciful' Nature (He is 'Karunakara')

Chapter VII: *By Being the Atma,*
you discover an invisible two-way intimate bond with *Parabrahma,*
like that between you and your loving Father or Mother
This is the essence of 'Tat Tvam Asi'

Chapter I

Introduction, First Principles, *Jiva and Atma*

Introduction
Topics 1 - 16

The Two 'Tat Tvam Asi' Birds: *Jiva (self) and Atma*
Topics 17 - 33

Your Personal Meditative Journey from
your *what is* to the *Atma*
Topics 34 - 44

Q : *Are we to suppose that the seven chapters represent the day-wise progression of the retreat, one chapter per day?*

A : Yes, indeed.

Q : *After chapter I is completed on the first day, we find that chapters II, III and IV are lumped together and you have called this Part I. So are these three chapters, namely Part I, devoted only to the understanding of the Jiva (self)?*

A : Yes, indeed. And chapter I is introduction, which is quite important, because in the introduction, you learn the first principles, and the nature of the *Jiva (self)*, and *Atma* (Self). All these are recurring themes, which are central to this retreat, and which in turn are also needed to absorb the retreat in its totality and depth.

Chapters II, III and IV go together, so, I have called this Part I.

Q : *Are you hinting that the knowing, taming, calming and silencing of the Jiva (self) is an absolute prerequisite for graduating into the next block of three chapters, which constitute Part II?*

A : Yes. This is the great secret of *moksha*. In fact, the calming and silencing of the *self* is the master key to *moksha*. Part II deals with the discovery of the unmanifest Divine, called *Parabrahma*, and strangely, we will find the unmanifest Divine to be the deepest part of ourselves.

Q : *What is the new term you have introduced: prajnya? How does this tantamount to the awakening of intelligence?*

A : *Prajnya* is a Sanskrit term, it means awareness that is also intelligence. Awareness is also *Atma*, so this intelligence is *Atmic*. When the *Atma*, which has got entangled in the field of the body and consciousness, *is rolled back, withdrawn, and comes to rest within itself*, then this intelligence called *prajnya* will come into manifestation, provided, this is not blocked or veiled by the activities of the *self*.

So, when the *self* has been calmed and silenced, by the withdrawal of the *Atma*, *prajnya* becomes active and will express itself. Otherwise it is dormant in all.

Q : *Are you implying then that if we do not successfully graduate through chapters: II, III and IV, that is, through Part I, then intelligence or prajnya will only be dormant and not awakened?*

A : Yes of course, that is the whole idea that without the silencing of the *Jiva (self)*, which happens as an end result of a whole long process, *prajnya* is not awakened. The process consists of identifying, observing and understanding the *self* and then subsequently, knowing that *self*, and being compassionate to that *self* and as a result, the *self* undergoing taming. Otherwise the *self* is like a wild beast and then the mature form of the *self* in the form of a calmed and silenced *self* never manifests. Once that happens, then the Source which is behind the *self* and which is behind the *manas*, which is behind the scenes as it were, that Source comes into relief. So unless the veiling comes to an end by the calming and silencing of the *self*, there is no hope whatsoever for us to access the *intelligence* which is part of the *Atma*, the imperceptible inner Self.

Q : *In chapters VI and VII, you are using the term 'discovery' of the unmanifest Divine - would this 'discovery' also mean the 'discovery' of the Self (with a capital 'S'), which is another term for the Paramatma?*

A : Man has seemingly got two selves. He has got an active, dynamic *self* in time and which in the scriptures is called *Jiva* or *Sakti* and in that *Jiva (Sakti)* there is a complex web which is called the *ahamkara*. Sometimes this *ahamkara* is also called the *Jiva* and sometimes it is also called *self*. Apart from this *Jiva* or *Sakti*, which is the *self* of man in time, there is the Self of man which is *timeless*, which is the all perceiving *awareness*, which does not age, which was not born and which will therefore not die and which is altogether outside space and time. And the traditional name for that is *Siva or chit or Atma or awareness*. And if the calming of the *Jiva* does not happen, i.e., if we do not cross the milestone of being the *sthitha prajnya* (one in whom the intelligence which is awakened has been stabilized or *sthitha*), then obviously we have no chance at all to discover that *we are one with the Divine*, one with the *Atma* and that the *Atma* is the very core of who we are. We have no chance! *This is not a thing to be believed, this is not a thing to have faith in, but this is a thing which has to be actually meditatively discovered and understood. Like scientists discover black holes, electrons or quarks, in the same way this has to be discovered.* The only way to make this discovery is by crossing the milestone of the *sthitha prajnya*.

Q : *The word, 'discovery' would refer to 'an external object', like the discovery of America by Columbus or the discovery of 'Penicillin' by Alexander Fleming. So now, in the expression 'discovery' of the Divine, is it implied that the Divine is external to us, and separate from us?*

A : This is actually a good question. Probably discovery is not the right term at all to use in this context, because this is at best an *inner discovery*. And the Self which we indicate with capital '*S*', that refers to the *Atma, or Siva,* the Source that is very deeply buried in the consciousness of man, and when we hit that ground as it were, then we know absolutely there is nothing, there are no labels, no names, no properties by means of which the ground can be identified. So the scriptures describe this ground as *nirakara, nirguna, nischala Parabrahma*. It is nameless, formless, qualityless, and propertyless - so it is impossible to actually discover it like how anyone would discover a sensory object, so probably discovery is not the right term.

It being subtle, being an entity which is subtler than the subtlest, somehow we have got to figure this out and the figuring of this has to be done by the seeker-who is paradoxically that very Source, and that very intelligence (prajnya)-which alone is capable of making this inner discovery. Once the seeker has figured it out, then he will assert it with supreme clarity and certainty. Because he knows that this is the ground of all existence, he will be able to say how to 'get there', by just abiding within oneself. But all people may not be able to 'get there' because this is only for seekers who are prepared to make that journey all the way till the end. Such seekers certainly will be able to 'get there', provided they are tenacious in this quest. Thus, it is an inward discovery or it is the going within yourself until you hit the very ground on which the whole of consciousness and the whole of the cosmos stands. That ground is just your pure being.

Q : *Would this 'discovery' process also imply a lot of 'following the trail', and research and investigation on our part? And would it also mean that without this research, the 'discovery' will not happen?*

A : It is quite clear from the examples of the saints and sages, the way their lives went, that there are no short cuts to this discovery. And because this discovery is not a matter of belief nor faith; it is not a thing which you can accept blindly so that you can take security in it, you can kind of anchor to it or cling on to it. Belief, faith and anchorage will no doubt give some superficial solace in hard times, nothing more. Whereas, this is an authentic discovery which everyone has to make for himself, by walking on a solitary path. And this discovery cannot be done without research, without deeply considering, without deeply dedicating oneself to this inward journey if we may call it that. So, without undertaking that solitary quest, we are certainly not getting there. But there are rare freaks in the history of humanity, freaks who are born and for whom it has been almost self evident or a thing of atmost ease to discover the ground on which the whole of life, whole of cosmos stands. They are probably very fortunate and the rest of humanity is not in their shoes. So the rest of humanity has to undertake the journey themselves, just the same way in which we undertake a journey to a foreign country. We have to take the pains, we have to make the enquiries, we have to apply for a visa and then make the journey. So it is a similar kind of process.

Q : *You have used a rather provocative term, 'awakening of intelligence', are you presupposing that the whole of humanity is bereft of intelligence? What about all the Nobel prize winning discoveries in the sciences and humanities, and great creative works in arts-do you mean to say that in all of these great works happening outside the spiritual spheres of life, there is no evidence of intelligence?*

A : Wow, this is a fantastic question and I seem to be floored! The question is very legitimate and intelligence is neither equitably distributed, nor is it uniformly dormant in the whole of humanity. Astrologers and psychologists have got independent methods of ascertaining what the measure of intelligence is in any given human being, in any given consciousness and in any given life. And it's more like whether one has a certain skill or one does not have it. One person has a certain propensity for mathematics or one does not have it. It is a thing like that. It is a variable which varies from person to person and surely every human being has got a certain kind of intelligence. That is why people are making astonishing inventions & discoveries.

And the source of this intelligence is actually the *Divine* or the *Atma* itself. So in what way is the *intelligence, prajnya* which is a special kind of *intelligence* which I'm talking about, differ from the *intelligence,* the creative artists have, which the creative poets have and the creative scientists, engineers, lawyers and doctors, all of them have.

What is this intelligence? Now the intelligence of the artist or the doctor or the scientist or the poet, that intelligence is invariably outward directed. It is keen on observing certain aspects of nature or it is observing art forms or it is observing patterns in physical laws and the behavior of celestial bodies, or the behavior of atoms or certain mathematical equations and so on. So that intelligence is focussed on happenings in nature or happenings in the outer world which the senses are perceiving.

Now there is a special name for that intelligence which makes a different kind of exploration or discovery, which tries to seek the source of life and the source of man's consciousness. Where from does it arise? And what is this consciousness? That intelligence has a different name in the scriptures of India it is called *prajnya*. And Ramana Maharshi calls *prajnya*, the *intelligence of the enlightened* and in the spiritual *sadhana* or the spiritual journey that the spiritual seekers have to undertake, one has to cross this very important milestone.

That milestone of the *sthitha prajnya* is the milestone when this intelligence is awakened and is no more flickering and becomes very steady. And what does this intelligence do? What is its function? Is it going to discover another planet in the solar system or is it going to discover another elementary particle or is it going to discover another economic system or another political system or is it going to discover some other new antibiotic?

No! This intelligence turns inward and this intelligence alone can search for the source of life or the creator or God, if you will. Now God is a very loaded term, so this intelligence goes backwards, it does not move forward. It goes back, it hunts for the source of life, hunts for the mystery of life and it has to be awakened for the search to begin at all. And that intelligence, *prajnya* is capable of fathoming, the otherwise impossible to fathom, Divine.

Nobody knows who the Divine is, what the Divine is, where the Divine is. So long as consciousness is outward turned these questions will never be answered. But *prajnya* can resolve this mystery. *Prajnya* will find answers to the three questions. *Prajnya* cannot even communicate this to another human being unless that human being undertakes the journey himself or herself.

Q : *In the last and VIIth chapter, you have spoken of an invisible two-way bond between a human and the unmanifest Divine, and you seem to be laying great emphasis on the All Merciful nature of Parabrahma. Is this, Tat Tvam Asi, then the climax of the inward journey?*

A : Yes, to give you a direct answer, Tat Tvam Asi is the important destination in this inward journey, which happens when the *Atma*, pulls out, retreats, and rolls back from the field of the body, senses and consciousness, in which it was formerly interested and engrossed. The *sthitha prajnya* is one who abides in the *Atma*, the one who has surrendered to the Divine, or to the *what is*, and such a one, can easily discover the truth of Tat Tvam Asi. It has to be understood that the journey back home, i.e., the *Atma* rolling back, can happen to every one of us, as every one of us, will have misfortunes at some time or the other in life and such misfortunes are gold mines, which offer the best opportunity for discovering, who we are, and where our home really is.

Q : *Belief, faith, discovery, understanding, and scriptural corroboration - is this then the road, the path of understanding, that is central to this Tat Tvam Asi retreat?*

A : Yes, this is the way it ought to go.

Q : *I see that, from chapter II to VII of this retreat, that crucial clause, 'By Being the Atma', recurs so significantly. This perhaps means that, when we are not the Atma, the chapters II to VII, fail to move forward, but fall on their face-is this what you are implying?*

A : Yes, the discovery that we are the *Atma*, is the essence of it all. The whole retreat constantly addresses this one important central theme.

Usually, teachers keep the last step as the last, namely the *Atma*. I have chosen to start with the ultimate destination, first. The master J. Krishnamurti has said, "Somehow in all this, you must begin from the other shore, from the other end, and not always be concerned about this shore or how to cross the river", and this is what I have done in my own journey, and also now for the retreat. Sri Nisargadatta Maharaj also says, "We are already in the final destination" (because we are the *Atma*), so I started with this final destination, which is our true Self or *Atma*.

Q : *As the clause, 'By Being the Atma', is so foundational, for the retreat, can you briefly say, what this Atma is and how it differs from the Jiva (self), with which the retreat starts?*

A : I am glad you have raised this important question. *Atma* is the true Self of man, but it is imperceptible, being the subject. It is the knower of all objects, and all objects exist in its 'field'. It cannot be reduced, to further smaller essential parts, since it has no parts, no sub-systems. The *self* is the *ahamkara*, so may be considered to be the *ahamkara* of the *Jiva*, or it is not wrong to consider the self to be the same as the Jiva also. It is simply the reflection of the marvelous *Atma*, in the mirror of the body and consciousness. The *self* is changeful, whereas the *Atma* is changeless, timeless and spaceless. The *self* does have some 'fragrances' of the Source, the *Atma*, *self* gives pleasure and pain, *Atma* gives bliss. *Atma* is the same in all humans in all creatures, in every particle of matter, etc.

Q : *You are stressing the unmanifest Divine, or Parabrahma, rather than the manifest Divine- is this distinction significant and important for all of us?*

A : Yes, extremely important. The unmanifest Divine is the true Divine, all that is manifested is the 'lower nature' of the unmanifest Divine. The important point to note is that the inner Self, the Pure 'I' or *Atma*, is one with this unmanifest Divine. It is this

Source which is worshipped in innumerable forms, in innumerable ways, in all the temples, churches, and mosques.

----

1. For Whom is this Intended?

1. For *mumukshus* (true seekers of *moksha*).

2. For spiritual seekers (seekers in *dharma*).

3. For *yoga* teachers, Hindu and non-Hindu spiritual teachers.

4. For healers, for better understanding the source of their healing energies.

5. For those in misfortunes, and searching for peace, grace and the ending of their sufferings.

6. For those who love the spiritual wealth of India.

Q : *You have divided all the likely and eligible participants into 6 categories. So, do we as participants here, have to identify which category we belong to? So will such identification, be the very beginning of our meditative journey?*

A : Actually, my idea in introducing this topic was to remind seekers who may be drawn to this retreat, to check out to which category they belong - this is of course only their outer disposition. And this clarity - which is actually one kind of *self* - knowledge - will actually go a long way in being able to ascertain one's true path. In truth, each seeker is already the *Atma*, at the deepest inner level - this is the inner disposition, which is the same for all seekers. However, each seeker is also unique, his/her destiny is also unique, so, it follows that the path of each seeker must also be unique. One's motivation or outer disposition is the starting point of such a unique path, so one better be aware of what this disposition or starting point is.

Q : *We get the feeling that the first three categories: mumukshus; spiritual seekers in dharma; yoga teachers, Hindu and non-Hindu spiritual teachers; are all generally spiritual people-am I right?*

A : Yes, your surmise is correct, everyone in these three categories is truly spiritual-otherwise they may not have got into those kinds of calling at all.

Q : *You have called spiritual seekers as seekers in dharma. Will you explain what you mean by dharma, because your statement is a little confusing.*

A : Yes, by *dharma* is meant, that which upholds or supports moral order, and this is invariably moral or ethical law that is inherent in the whole of creation. At least the more spiritually aware people are expected to recognize and adhere to this cosmic moral law (namely *dharma*) - for their own happiness and well being, as also for the well being of society as a whole. There are a wide variety of spiritual teachings in the world (these are also called *dharma*). They are in a higher sense, the same one truth about the moral order, about ethical living, but at the same time, they are also different teachings, because, each teaching is emphasizing a different aspect of the spiritual life, a different aspect of *dharma*. So there are many kinds of spiritual seekers following different kinds of teachings (different *dharmas*). People in the spiritual sphere of *dharma*, seek truth, integrity, honesty, self-purification and try and practice goodness in action. *However they need to mature more to become mumukshus.* Thus seekers in the sphere of *dharma*, have to be distinguished from *mumukshus,* who are seekers of *moksha. Moksha* means liberation from, ignorance, from all illusions, from suffering, from a sense of division and separation, from the *self or Jiva.*

Q : *In the third category of yoga teachers and Hindu spiritual teachers, you have also encompassed non-Hindu spiritual teachers. Firstly why have you chosen yoga teachers?*

A : The goal of *yoga* in the *Vedic* tradition, is not just to have a healthy body and a calm mind, it is not even merely for discerning the Divine and being devoted to It. Rather the goal of all *yoga* is to attain union with the Divine *(moksha).* For many *yoga* practitioners, even this may not be the vision - they may have come to *yoga* for more mundane reasons: for maintaining better health through the practice of various *asanas*, for overcoming pain, for learning to breathe more intelligently, or for living a more vital and energetic life, etc. In truth however, Self - Realization *(moksha)* is the ultimate goal of *yoga*. So, I expect all the serious *yoga* teachers to be intensely aware of this and such seekers are likely to be consciously or unconsciously, also seeking *moksha,* or liberation from

10

the human condition of pain and limitation. This retreat is about Self - Realization, so *yoga* teachers have a natural place here.

Q : *Why have you also brought in non-Hindu spiritual teachers, side by side with Hindu spiritual teachers?*

A : There are many religions and many faiths in the world, and we know that there are very many serious seekers from the other nations and other cultures. Among people of non-Hindu religions, there are also seekers who have gone deeply into one or more Hindu teachings. Not only many of these non-Hindu seekers have made living the Hindu *dharma* part of their daily life, but they are also good teachers of the Hindu teachings. So, non-Hindu spiritual teachers may be on par with Hindu teachers. Truth is truth, and it would be narrow on our part to say that what was historically, Hindu or *Vedic* should only belong to Hindus. Thus, we must also recognize non-Hindu teachers of Hindu teachings, whenever they have gone deeply into these teachings and surely, because of their openness, they too will benefit from this retreat.

Q : *I would like to take all healers as already deep into the spiritual life - is this also your perception? Then, may be, the next two categories of participants (5 & 6) will not strictly qualify to be spiritual seekers, perhaps they are on the threshold of the spiritual life? Would you agree with me and go with me?*

A : Firstly, healers are indeed spiritual people, because of their empathy and the kind of work they do. Coming to your next question, we have got to bear in mind that, often it is misfortunes which trigger the onset of the spiritual life. Also art and cultural historians, indologists, philosophers and mythologists, may have a deep interest in *self* - Knowing and Self - Realization, but they may not yet be *mumukshus* or even spiritual seekers. But who is to tell, what will happen in the future in any given life - what begins as an innocent interest in India's art and cultural heritage, may well deepen and eventually make them enter into the sphere of *moksha*.

----

2. Human Nature and the Hidden Divine Nature

Humans have an obvious human nature (as the *Jiva*) and also a 'hidden' Divine nature (as the *Atma*). The human nature arises from being the *Jiva*, with pain & pleasure; conflict & sorrow; fear & guilt; love & hate; anger & jealousy; cruelty & violence; self-centeredness & perversity- as hallmarks.

This meditative journey is from our tragic human nature as a *Jiva* to our 'little known' Divine nature, as the *Atma*. 'Little known' because only on rare occasions we approach life from this Divine nature with selflessness and therefore with the highest virtue.

Q : *What is the relevance of first principles in this introduction?*

A : First principles define the world-view, which is everything. Being entrenched in a wrong world-view, you cannot hope to come upon the truth, or if you do manage to come upon the truth, it will immediately call for a throwing away of your wrong world-view, or you may reject the truth even. So before, the realization destroys the wrong world-view, it may be wiser for us to throw away the wrong world-view and start using the right world-view which will be consistent with the truth of the Divine. Hence the emphasis on first principles, which define the world-view, even at this initial stage.

Q : *You have contrasted our human nature with the Divine nature of humanity, but as you say, the Divine nature is hidden and also perhaps unknown. If our Divine nature is hidden, we may have to seek it out, but if it is unknown, then what is the use of pursuing it?*

A : Whatever the human consciousness pursues belongs to the field of the known, the past or the imaginative future. The Divine can never be brought into the realm of the known,

It will always belong to the realm of the *unknowable,* yet without the Divine, man's life will also be incomplete, tasteless, and bereft of mystery and sacredness. So we also need to take the plunge into this quest, into the unknown for sanctifying and ennobling our lives and for knowing the hidden Divine side of our nature.

3. The *Atma's* Earthly Sojourn as *Jiva*

1. You are in truth the birthless and deathless *Atma.* The body was however born and will die, but not the *Atma.*

2. You, as the *Atma* arc one with Godhead *(Parabrahma* or *Brahma*n*).* This is the highest Truth ('Tat Tvam Asi').

3. This *Atma* is veiled and masked by *maya* and ignorance. *Atma* 'veiled' is *Jivatma* or *Jiva* for short. So, as the *Jiva* you are veiled and 'blinded' by *maya* and ignorance.

Q : *How do we come to know that we are deathless beings, and that we were not also born?*

A : We have been told millions of times that we are the body, so we have come to accept this programming, this brain washing as the truth. Then after 40 years of this conditioning and wrong programming, we hear in a retreat like this or when we read the Gita and find out that we are deathless beings. Our first exposure to this shocking truth, is the beginning of the journey back home. In accepting the words of truth, we open ourselves to the possibility of actually discovering this truth, so that it is unnecessary for us to believe in it anymore. *Depending on the intensity of our discontent, we will come upon this truth sooner or later in our life, or not at all, if we are very very lazy!*

Q : *So, when we are convinced that we are the body, that we are so and so, is all this conviction as to who we are, itself maya?*

A : Yes, this is *maya*. But by my affirming that it is *maya*, I'll not be able to make an iota of an impression on you, until you become ready for this discovery. A day will come, when there will be profound disturbance, your cherished world and all your concepts will crumble into the dust, then you may be open to this truth. It is said in the Hindu tradition that when the disciple is ready and ripe, the master will manifest in his life. Like the seed growing into the sapling and becoming a tree, this spiritual flowering will also happen. Some are more sensitive to their inner life and know that the life of the *Jiva* is full of misery and contradiction - this perception is the beginning of the new life.

4. *Jiva's* 'Curse' and *Jiva's* Blessing

1. However this *Atma* is veiled and masked by *maya* and ignorance. This veiled *Atma* is called *Jivatma* or *Jiva* for short. So, the *Jiva* is 'blinded' by ignorance.

2. *Jiva* is the experiencer of *punya karma* (gives joy) and *papa karma* (gives sorrow). *Karma* is 'collective'.

3. *Jiva* unmasked is *Atma*, so *Jiva* has *Atma sakti* as it's birth right. Using *Atma sakti, Jiva* can create 'heaven' or 'hell', during it's earthly sojourn.

Q : *What does paapa and punya mean?*

A : *Paapa* means sinful, that which inevitably breeds sorrow, while *punya* is that which is auspicious, and this invariably produces joy and well being. In each human life both *paapa karma* and *punya karma* exist.

Q : *So as a Jiva, in spite of having paapa karma as our curse, we also seem to enjoy the blessing of Atma Sakti. Is this the reason, man is so proud and arrogant-because of this Atma Sakti?*

A : The *Atma Sakti,* is not certainly by itself a corrupting influence, what is proud and arrogant is the *self,* the *ahamkara.* We will learn about its presence in the life of the *Jiva.* It is this *ahamkara,* which is proud and conceited.

5. 'You must Somehow Begin from the Other Shore...'

"In all this movement you must somehow begin from the other end, from the other shore, and not always be concerned with this shore or how to cross the river.

"You must take a plunge into the water, not knowing how to swim. And the beauty of meditation is that you never know where you are, where you are going, what the end is."

- J. Krishnamurti in 'Meditations' [13]

Q : *In this beautiful meditation from Krishnamurti, we must realize that most of us suffer from the fear of the unknown, so how would you expect us to take the plunge, as it were and reach out to the other shore?*

A : We have two dimensions, a human dimension, to which all your logic applies, the fear, etc. However, we are also a timeless being, a witness, with infinite Divine possibilities. Because, we are always with a swarm of thoughts and feelings, we are never able to know ourselves, as we are - without these thoughts and feelings. This witness is our deeper nature, and this whole retreat is devoted to the discovery of this hidden nature called the *Atma. Atma* is the realm of infinite possibilities.

Q : *So, is it like pressing the 'emergency button', which may be always there, but which we are unaware of?*

A : Yes, we are unconscious of the mechanism of how some of our difficult problems get resolved. We call that Grace, result of prayer, blessing, etc. However, this Divine Source is also our very Self. We do not know this, we cannot be aware of it as we can be aware of the sun and the moon and the trees. This retreat is intended to help us to get at this treasure, which we are already. It is not a new treasure or a new blessing which will come to you from the outside world, from another source.

Q : *Why does Krishnamurti say the, "the beauty of meditation is that, you never know where you are, where you are going, what the end is?"*

A : Our limited human nature makes us everlastingly seek security, we need to be constantly assured that we will find some great treasure, if not now, at least in the future, etc. However, when our Divine nature comes into play, as it surely does in these meditations, then we are naturally going to be fearless, rather than afraid. *In fact all creative minds have this enormous courage and spirit of adventure-without this, they would never have discovered, all the wonderful things they discovered. Theirs was a journey into the unknown.* So, Krishnamurti says, this is the nature of these meditative journeys, they are mysterious journeys into the bosom of truth, into the unknown, without any guarantee of security.

----

6. 'Self-Realization is only Realization of One's Own Nature'

- Your thought: "All these masters are Self-Realized, they are in possession of a priceless wealth, call it *Atma* or Self. **I do not have this wealth, I am trying!**"

- This is utterly wrong, this thought is your enemy, since you are at the core, only the *Atma*.

- "As the Self of a person, who tries to attain Self-Realization is not different from him and as there is nothing other than or superior to him to be attained by him, Self-Realization is only the realization of one's own nature."

- Sri Ramana Maharshi[14]

Q : *I think what you are trying to convey is this: That the Self - Realized person, may find the whole business and effort of running after Self - Realization to be absurd, from the point of view of his state. However, as there will always be seekers in the world, the journey has to start by seeking, isn't it?*

A : Yes, it is absurd, from the point of view of the one who has settled within himself. The seeker begins his seeking. It must also end, and when it ends, he comes to abide in himself, then he will find his erstwhile seeking absurd.

My idea of making you remember Sri Ramana Maharshi's words in this context is this: All seekers are intimidated by Self - Realized masters and carry the unconscious thought that the masters have something 'great' which they do not have and which they have come there to acquire. I want to dispel this unconscious thinking in all seekers. The Self of the master is the same as the Self of the seeker, as there is only one Self for the whole world. The *Atma* has rolled back from the field of the master's body, senses and consciousness, whereas the seeker's *Atma* is still engrossed in the field of the body, senses and consciousness. If a seeker takes this in, he will vastly benefit from this.

7. Firstly, Words, Metaphors and Pictures. Then, Insight and Understanding

We need apt words, metaphors, concepts and mythic pictures, **only as tools and means** to get to the final insight and understanding (direct perception). Let us always remember this. The insight and understanding, sourced in intelligence will bring liberation.

However we must also be wary of words, concepts and mythic pictures, for they are only pointers and can mislead and deceive us. If we are unaware, we may become slaves of words and concepts. If we are aware, then there is never going to be any enslavement to words and concepts.

Q : *Are you saying that in every topic that we are going to be looking at, we have to be so vigilant that we continually ask ourselves, whether we have grasped the inner philosophical and spiritual meaning - so is this what you want us to do, for every topic-be aware and introspective?*

A : Yes, in a way that is what is expected of us. Because for communication unfortunately we have to use words, however sometimes we may also communicate through silence. Such silent communication is very rare. So when we use words there is always a scope and possibility of misunderstanding. In using a particular word in a specific sense and you understanding the same in a totally different way, which was not meant by me, confusion will arise. So a lot of pictures, metaphors and concepts, mythological themes are used in this teaching. And we have to always pause and have to see if we have *assimilated the inner meaning* which is behind those words and those analogies, behind those metaphors or those ideas. Because that is the important thing. Ultimate clarity is based on insight and understanding. So we have got to get to that destination, and the means to that are these words, mythic pictures, these *sutras* or principles and so on.

8. What is the Meaning of 'Meditation' ?

To meditate means: To listen deeply, to feel, to understand, to empathize, to be aware, to contemplate deeply, **to move away from past and future, to be still within, to be empty**, to abide in the 'I am ness' *(Atma)*, the witness consciousness, the 'I' consciousness.

So, one can meditate on the Divine *(Brahman)*, or on pain, on jealousy, on fear, on goodness, on the impermanence of life, or on death....

These meditations will stand on silence, which is the *Atma*-existence-awareness-bliss *(Sat-Chit-Ananda)*.

Q : *This meaning of meditation is so different from what we have been taught. We were taught to sit still in a certain comfortable posture, close the eyes, think of our deity, or repeat a mantra 108 times, or watch the breath, or control our thoughts. And you are saying, both past and future should become empty! Is this going to happen at all?*

A : This may not happen so easily in the beginning. And first of all there are a large number of philosophical schools in India and likewise philosophical and theological schools in other religions as well. And every religious *darsana* or philosophy has its own approach to meditation. So, it is never a universal thing which will be the same for one and all. And there are widely different methods as well and this is a certain approach towards meditation and therefore it is my responsibility to qualify what I mean by the often used term meditation. So I say that it entails deep listening and deep feeling and that it entails disassociation from the past and future mentally and to have the capacity to be still within and to be empty and at the same time also to enquire from that stillness and from that calmness and from that seeming emptiness, to be the 'I', the conscious presence, without any associations. To be with *what is,* is also meditation. So all of this is meant by the term meditation.

Meditation here does not mean repeating a *mantra*. This is a particular path of *Jnana yoga* or the *path of understanding*. Not the path of knowledge, but, it will be a *path of understanding* the *Atma,* of who we are. And it may be good for us to remember at this stage that the entire movement of science is a movement in understanding, based on first principles. So the same thing we are doing, but we are doing in the field of the religious life, in our inner life. That is what we do here.

Q : *You are asking us to meditate on jealousy, violence, fear, death, and these are things that we keep a safe distance from in our daily life. Are you saying that, these so-called negative things are so much part of our human life that it is high time we start thinking deeply about these realities?*

A : That is the whole idea. Think of the traditional form of meditation, where there is jealousy and fear, where there is a reality of impermanence and the reality of death and you never touch any of these with a barge pole and then you sit and close your eyes and you repeat a *mantra*. This method belongs to a different system of meditation, the traditional system of meditation called *mantra sadhana. And that will certainly work under certain conditions when the individual is free of any disturbance in consciousness.* That is, when the *sadhaka* or seeker is in a condition where consciousness has already become calm and pacified. But when, we are dealing with individuals who may be plagued by fear or jealousy, or with seekers, who may not have sufficiently come to terms with the impermanence of life and death and who may not have assimilated the reality of death – then, we have got to have a different approach to meditation. So we prepare the ground slowly and we study jealousy, fear and anger - all within ourselves. Unless we do this and we prepare the ground, in my view, we do not have the qualification to meditate at all. So one has to kind of get ready in order to qualify to meditate. So we have got to do all these things which normally people will not touch with a barge pole. Here the approach is different.

Q : *Do we then reach the silence by constant practice, tenacity of purpose, sincerity, devotion to the goal, etc?*

A : Yes, that is the ultimate destination, the *Atma,* if you can put it that way. But you see, the use of the will has very little place in Self - Realization. Because will belongs to the *self* and you cannot undertake a journey whose destination is the ending of the *self* using will power. Because will power makes the *self* stronger, empowers it and builds the life of the *self*. So this is a meditation where we have to negate the *self*, because we are enquiring to find if there is life beyond this little *self*. To get there we cannot use will power and we cannot ignore all the problems that play in us like fear, jealousy, lust and a constant divisiveness in our thinking between ourselves and others. Instead we have to start paying attention to all these things. And when we do pay attention to all these things, probably we will gain in maturity and we will become equipoised in consciousness and then the whole exploration of this *meditation* will acquire greater depth and intensity.

9. 'Tat Tvam Asi' [Thou Art That]

Q : *What are you trying to convey through this ocean-wave metaphor?*

A : One is trying to make plain the meaning of Tat Tvam Asi and how we are to approach it, necessarily intellectually in the beginning, through analogies and through metaphors. Now the ocean represents 'That', the Infinite Beingness which the mind cannot reach and which words cannot describe. That Infinite Ineffable Being who has given birth to this world and who is the Father and Mother of this world - the ocean represents 'That'.

When the ocean becomes active, then the ocean breaks into waves. And a wavelet can be formed on the ocean's surface and the wavelet can arise above the ocean's surface and can experience a sense of separation and then the wave can think (if it is a sentient being) that it has got an individual existence of its own. And it may be in a complete state of unawareness that its own life is but the life of the ocean, now, in a particular manifestation and so it will live its separative existence for a while under the delusion (mistaken impression) that it is a separate living entity. That movement or that breaking away from the Father and the Mother is shown by the arrow in black color. This is the ocean becoming the wave. And this is creation.

Then there is a returning wave, the *nivritti* which is the opposite of *pravritti* or the outer movement, which is the going back home. That is the white arrow which is shown in the picture. The wave doing its home work and realizing through devotion, clear thinking, clear understanding and clear realization that it has no individuality what so ever and that all the life in itself, of which it is so proud, is but the ocean in a certain miniscule form - this is liberation or *moksha*. So when it has the realization that tantamounts to the loss of its separative existence, the loss of the illusion that it is a separate entity and a separate organism, that realization tantamounts to going back home. This is *moksha*.

Q : *Why has the out going process shown in black('red' in the original PPT), and the reversing of this out going process, shown in white('yellow' in the original PPT)?*

A : I have actually anticipated this question and have already answered this. As mentioned earlier the color red (black in the book) stands for *rajas* in the Hindu world view, it is an out ward going movement. Yellow (white in the book) is the color of Jupiter energy which is *sattvic* and which is a sign of intelligence and which is always sourced in the Divine. So yellow (white in the book) has been chosen to go back home and red (black in the book) has been chosen to break away from home.

----

10. The Ocean-Wave Metaphor

- Wave, a temporary excitation of the Ocean surface is **the individuality, the separative existence. Two aspects of man as an individual and as the whole are *Jiva (self)* and *Atma*.**

- The Ocean *(Paramatma)*, from which the *self* arises is 'That', the *Paramatma* (The Divine, the Source).

- The *self* is unique, the *Atma* is the same in all.
  Billion waves, only one Ocean.

Q : *The self always thinks of itself as a permanent independent entity, and here the metaphor challenges this view and shows that the self is just a transient and temporary excitation, arising from, an eternal ground. Is this the reason, why this metaphor is being brought in here, because it challenges our firmly held belief about ourselves as separate independent entities?*

A : Yes. In this retreat so many metaphors will be invoked and so many metaphors will be presented to every *mumukshu* and every *seeker* in order to kind of create a new perspective, a perspective which is contrary to the unconsciously held impression that individuality is very natural and true to us. So the metaphor is very simple and therefore it is easily intelligible. But one has to internalize it and make it one's own, by contemplation, thinking deeply and by being silent till such time as it becomes your own realization. That is the idea.

Q : *If we keep on contemplating and remembering this metaphor, would we then realize that the self, is just a temporary formation, never having a separate existence, but is only a part of something much vaster?*

A : Yes, so this alternative view point is presented to you and one of the important things in this spiritual life as one does some kind of *sadhana* or the other is to remember the truth even though we may not have realized it. The truth will be given to you in the form of a mythic image or in the form of a *sutra*, say from the Bhagavad Gita or some other scripture. Or it can be given to you as a pithy statement and you have got to memorize that. A good seeker or a good student will memorize the *sutra* and will dwell on that *sutra* till such time as that *sutra* kind of explodes and you realize the truth yourself. So in this case this is one of the metaphors which you will have to memorize as a picture and often think of. Then suddenly a day will come in your life, when the whole thing becomes absolutely self evident without an iota of doubt. That indeed is the idea.

Q : *One does understand that the ocean is the same for all the waves, that may arise from the ground of that ocean, and coming to think of it, even every wave which arises, has to have its individual uniqueness, and you seem to be emphasizing the uniqueness of the self, because in this metaphor, the wave seems to represent the individual who is coming into manifestation?*

A : Applying the mythic model, to every human life, it is easy to see that each human life, and human *self* is unique, because each human life arises because of a unique combination of the cosmic benefic and cosmic malefic life energies. This uniqueness of the *self*, and the human being has far reaching consequences, for the spiritual paths of individuals. We will go into this in a later topic.

----

11. Two Hands: Heart *(Siva)* and Head *(Sakti)*

The right hand represents your thinking capacity *(Sakti)*, while the left hand represents intelligence, deep feelings, insights *(Siva)*.

Therefore receive this retreat with both hands.

Q : *Which hand is associated with which faculty? What are in fact the two faculties that all humans have?*

A : All humans have two faculties. The faculty of rational thinking for which the left brain is the center and the faculty for intuitive perception for which the right brain is the center. And the right hand goes along with the left brain and the left hand goes along with the right brain. Also, the right eye is connected to the Sun and the left eye to the Moon. And so the right hemisphere is the feeling part, is the emotional intelligence, the spiritual intelligence and the left hemisphere is for the logical thinking and is for rational and analytical thinking.

Now in being in this retreat and absorbing and assimilating everything which is presented to you and taking time to internalize it, you have to approach it with both faculties. You have to think about it very clearly, absorbing it analytically, without any confusion and then if you do that and yet you are not able to feel the truth of it at all, there is no feeling dimension to it. Then that is only a kind of a partial understanding or partial absorption.

On the other hand if you feel deeply about what every topic is revealing to you and at the same time you have no analytical and intellectual clarity into that, then that also is some kind of handicap. So you have got to use kind of both hands to receive this truth and the left hand is intelligence, feeling and insights which is *Siva* and the right hand is a logical thinking and so on, *Sakti.* So one has to be aware of whether one is just approaching it emotionally and with deep feeling with no analytical clarity or whether one is approaching it with analytical clarity and understands everything clearly and perfectly and yet the heart is dry, you have no feeling towards all these things then that is also pretty worthless. So there has to be a very delicate balance between feeling and thinking and both have to kind of walk hand in hand to completely absorb, assimilate and internalize this truth.

Q : *Do you mean to say that all of us have two independent faculties, and that in this retreat, we are not supposed to use one faculty, more dominantly over the other faculty, but rather use both in a balanced way?*

A : Clearly if we study, if you ask a good psychologist then he will be able to tell us that some people are more of the thinking type and some people are more of the feeling type. And both are very powerful faculties and both are actually complimentary to each other. So the thinking types may have a natural tendency to approach any problem in life through the capacity of thinking and the feeling people may have a tendency to approach any problem in life through feeling. And thinking is masculine and feeling is feminine and both have advantages and both are distinct capacities, but the point we are emphasizing is that, whatever be our disposition, whether we have the feminine intelligence or the masculine intelligence in the form of thinking or intelligence in the form of feeling, we should be aware that in this retreat maximal absorption of the retreat will happen if we can but kind of press both faculties into service and receive everything that is being said with both faculties, that is the idea.

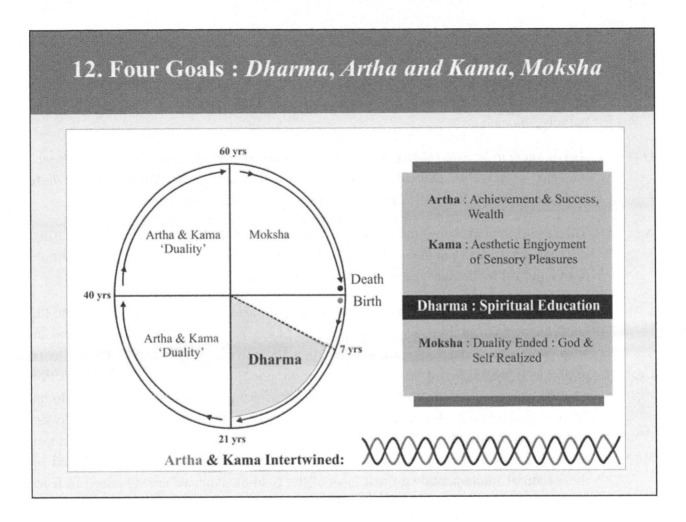

12. Four Goals : *Dharma, Artha and Kama, Moksha*

Q : *In the first quadrant, from birth to 21 yrs of age, you have divided it into two parts, why have you done this?*

A : This is very simple. Children can be weaned away from their parents not before they are 5 years old and it is good for them to be bonded to their parents, especially the mother, because the mother is a very important teacher for every child. The child is at home with the father and the mother and at 7 years the child is independent enough to be put on a learning path. At that stage in ancient Hindu society, children were sent to the home of a teacher and his spouse, life partner, and they were called *guru* and *gurupatni* and there they lived with the teacher and his wife for at least 14 years. They served the *guru* and *gurupatni* and they learnt everything they had to learn about the Divine and about the Self, about the life purposes of man and about all the skills that their particular temperament was inclined to learn. Whether it was architecture, martial arts or medicine or whether it was some other skill like *ayurveda*, anything they learnt from these teachers and so that by the time they were 21, they were fully equipped for facing the adult life.

They went to this *gurukula ashrama*, the home of the *guru* and the *gurupatni* only at 7, hence you have the first quarter of life falling into two distinct sectors. One sector - life with the parents and another sector - life with the *guru* and the *gurupatni* and during this period of 14 yrs they learnt the spiritual and ethical foundations necessary for humans, namely, *dharma*.

Q : *As you seem to be using Sanskrit terms, will you please give the etymology for the terms, dharma, artha, kama and moksha, so that all of us who are not at all familiar with these technical Sanskrit terms, will also get a good understanding of the basics?*

A : Thank you for reminding me to introduce these 4 terms. There are 4 important terms: *dharma, artha, kama and moksha.* Actually their meanings are very simple. We should not be put off by the fact that these are Sanskrit terms.

Dharma is moral law which follows from laws of *karma. Karma* means action and the consequences of action. So the universe is like a *karma* machine. If you send an auspicious action that does good to others then the universe very naturally has a way of giving us a feedback and bringing us something good. If you sow a seed of bad action into the cosmos, then the cosmos has got a way of bringing the bad harvest back to us. So it is like a feedback machine. *Dharma* is based on the recognition of the *Divine*, which is central to the spiritual life and recognition of the law of *karma*, the recognition of the law of oneness of all life. So *dharma* is virtue and moral foundation based on these natural fundamental spiritual laws of the cosmos. And we are supposed to learn the principles of *dharma* which is the moral law, the foundation of any good human life, between the ages 7 and 21.

Artha and kama mean something entirely different. *Dharma* is spiritual. If you want to put it that way, *artha and kama* are, kind of materialistic quests. And the Hindus realized that the so called materialistic quest was not wrong. Because the materialistic quest had its basis in the perception of our individuality and so long as we perceive ourselves and others as individuals then *artha and kama* become inevitable and natural.

Artha arises from the out pouring of desire as a quest for economic stability, survival in terms of professional excellence, achievement, success and fulfillment. And *kama* as an aesthetic enjoyment of life, which is the natural result of the senses and sense objects. Senses and the sense objects are created by the *Divine*, they are not the creation of - 'Saturn' or some evil force. And because they are created by the *Divine* in human life, they have a legitimate place in life. Therefore sensory enjoyment and fulfillment is part of the human drama in the Hindu perception of life. It is not to be eschewed, it is not to be spat out, it is not to be suppressed because the spiritual life is all important. No! Unlike Buddhism and Jainism which speak too little about *artha and kama*, Hinduism is eloquent about *artha and kama*. It has a natural place in life and we have to pursue *artha*, we have to seek achievement, wealth, excellence and success and we have to enjoy what the senses give us. And that whole journey of *artha and kama* lasts for 40 years and it is a very important part of the human drama from 20 to 60. And after that the body becomes weak, the senses tired and feeble and then man asks more philosophical and more existential questions. Like, is there truly a Divine? And if there is a Divine why don't I see the Divine? And if there is a Divine how do I seek the Divine for greater happiness? So, those are *moksha* questions and they sprout naturally in our life after 60 or 65, provided *artha and kama* are perfectly fulfilled for us. If the goals *artha and kama* are not fulfilled then probably even after 60, we will be still creatures of pleasure and we will be still behaving like young people, though we have become old and we will still be in search of money, in search of enjoyment. Then of course, *moksha* does not even happen. But if we are fulfilled in *artha and kama*, then we come to the 4th goal of life which is *moksha*. *Moksha* means liberation. Liberation from what? Liberation from sorrow, liberation from the idea that we are individuals, liberation from pain and liberation from attachment which is the source of pain. So that entire quest starts around 60 or 65 and it will complete itself before we are dead, if we are serious seekers at all. If we are not tenacious or serious seekers, then the quest for *moksha* may be naturally left incomplete.

So the 4 goals of life are:

Dharma, between 7 and 21 years of age.

Artha and kama, between 21 to 60 years of age.

Moksha, the last goal of life from 60 till the time we say good bye to the planet.

Q : *Do you mean to say that between the ages one to seven yrs, the parents of the child do not inculcate any dharmic values, and that all dharma comes only after the age of seven?*

A : No, that is not so. The parents have enormous responsibility right from the moment of conception, till they put their child at the feet of a *guru and gurupatni.* They give values to the child and the mother especially has a whole lot to contribute to upbringing and right action, right thinking, right feeling, right behavior and that is a very important contribution because many people believe that by the time the child is 5, actually the blue print and the foundation for the life is already laid. So the parents do their jobs. But the job which has to be done after the age of 7 is too technical in nature, so it calls for knowledge of the sciences and the arts which the parents are ill equipped to teach. So they definitely have to send their children to some school, which in ancient Hindu society was a private school at the home of the teacher and his wife. So they sent their children to these private *gurukula ashrams* which were essentially schools of spiritual education, but which were not averse to teaching secular subjects like medicine, *ayurveda* or sculpture or house building, *sthapatya veda* and so on. And everything was learned, so that by the time the child was 21 he had a good and sound knowledge in a subject with which he could earn a livelihood and with some spiritual knowledge with which he could face up to the challenges of life.

Q : *Most of us have not had (in modern India, but also in other countries of the world) any system of dharma or morality taught to us between the ages 7 to 21? Does this mean that we are ill-equipped to meet the challenges in adult life?*

A : I know that you are going to feel little bad or you may become upset when I tell you that the lack of a *dharma* education or a spiritual education is certainly a handicap in so far as a higher spiritual life, adult life, especially in the later part of life is concerned. We may become more competent technologically, as adepts in science and technology, but in so far as our humanitarian outlook and spiritual outlook in life is concerned, the absence of a *dharma* education and an absence of a *dharmic* foundation in the earlier life, in the first quarter of life, is certainly going to take its toll as we make the pilgrimage in *artha and kama* for the next 40 years. But fortunately as we get our blows we wake up and we will start learning and we will pick up fragments of *dharma*, fragments of humane and virtuous life from various teachings of *gurus* and masters as we go on this *artha and kama* pilgrimage for 40 years. So that is a kind of saving grace for us.

Q : *By equating dharma with spiritual education, are you then saying that this refers to our school education, whether we go to a Christian missionary school, or a Hindu mission school, or a modern secular public school?*

A : In ancient society the foundational education of 14 years from 7 - 21 was essentially *dharmic* and they were taught a great deal about the spiritual truths of life, about the Divine, about the *Atma* and as to *what right action is* and *what wrong action is* and what is *karma*, what are the consequences of *karma* and how to relate to parents and so on. In modern times, by contrast, we do not have this sound spiritual education anymore. In our schools and colleges we have an intense focus and exposure to mathematics, sciences like physics, chemistry, etc., so at 21 we are quite proficient in so far as scientific knowledge and academic knowledge is concerned and we are probably spiritually under equipped, spiritually under prepared for meeting the challenges of life. Since the modern civilization is predominantly a technological civilization, nobody recognizes that the lack of spiritual education has any serious deficiency, unless we are hit by the deficiency very hard in the next 40 years of our life.

We will know the significance of this spiritual education as we get knocks in our life for the next 40 yrs and then as a result of these knocks we are of course going to seek the spiritual knowledge/wealth which was not given to us in the first quarter of life and as we get that and as we internalize that, probably our inner happiness will be restored

Q : *Why have you made artha and kama as two continuous quadrants-beginning from 21 yrs of age and going all the way to 60 yrs of age?*

A : You will notice that properly speaking, each quadrant roughly occupies about 25 years, as *artha and kama* are two powerful goals, commencing around 20 years, together, they will certainly span another 40 to 45 years; hence it is only at 60 or even a little later, that, *artha and kama*, may have their first chance, to come to an end.

Q : *What is the plaited and intertwined figure at the bottom of the diagram?*

A : That shows that the fountain of desires that are welling up in us, the moment we cross the milestone of 21 years, that is *kama* and the fulfillment for this fountain of desire which is *artha,* they go hand in hand. Without having economic means and money power in your hands none of your desires can be fulfilled. So in order to have sensory fulfillment and sensory gratification which is a very natural part of the human drama, it is important for us to be standing on an economically sound footing. So we have to earn the money that we need and we may earn this money by practicing one of the systems of the knowledge we have learnt for 14 years. Through the practice of the knowledge and skills we earn money and with that money we get an aesthetic enjoyment of life which is *kama*.

Artha and kama are an inseparable conjugate pair and so they have to go together. So in the figure you see the plaited, intertwining strings represent the fact that *artha and kama* are intertwined and the Hindus did not eschew desire from the totality of life. They never said that all people must become *sannyasis*, they never said that. Desire and its fulfillment has a natural place in life. They also gave you an extremely long span from 21 – 60, some 40 years to have that fulfillment. You need to have the fulfillment and if you have the fulfillment perfectly which is the *artha and kama* phase, during the 40 years of period between 20 - 60, which was meant for that; then at the end of it after 60 you are supposed to be so mature that you will turn your back on the game of desire fulfillment and you will naturally start asking philosophical and existential questions like the great philosophers asked at an earlier age. So you will ask: 'Is there a Divine'? 'What is the purpose of life'? 'Can we become completely free of sorrow'? And then you will start making enquiries into all these things. And that journey is called *moksha*.

Q : *What is moksha to you and to us, in our day to day life?*

A : This question seems to me to be premature, in so far as *moksha* for you is concerned. What it means to me, this is the retreat itself. Because, so long as we are traversing the terrain of *artha and kama* we know nothing of *moksha and* we don't need to know anything of *moksha, if we have not 'had a calling' from that sphere*. We need to be learning all the time, learning from all the knocks, from all the experiences, learning about the *self* and learning about the Divine, in piece-meal fashion of course. We need to keep doing this as far as it is necessary for our inner and outer well being and happiness. And then after 60, the mysterious *moksha* will call us and then we will awaken to the call of *moksha* and then the goal becomes very real to us. It does not become real generally before 60, while the fire of *artha and kama* are still strong.

Q : *Is moksha the fourth and the last stage and goal of human life in traditional Hindu society?*

A : Yes, indeed.

Q : *Do you think, this idealistic model which you say was operational in traditional Hindu society, thousands of years ago, is also relevant in our modern society?*

A : It is a little absurd to talk about the relevance of this model in our modern society. Because we lost this model and parents no longer send their children to schools where the primary focus is on the life of the spirit. Academic learning has become far more important than learning of the humanities, learning of religion and the spiritual life. So we have lost this model. And the Hindu sages who created this model had a very deep understanding of the totality of man's life. So they created a model which satisfied all of the appetites of man, the mundane appetites, side by side with the spiritual appetites. And they ensured that the satisfaction of the material appetites happened, before the final satisfaction of the greatest appetite of the spirit which is *moksha*. So, this model is now lost to us. We have another model now, where *dharma* is missing and instead of *dharma*, we have only secular education in the form of mathematics, physics and chemistry and so on, with the Divine all together gone from our life.

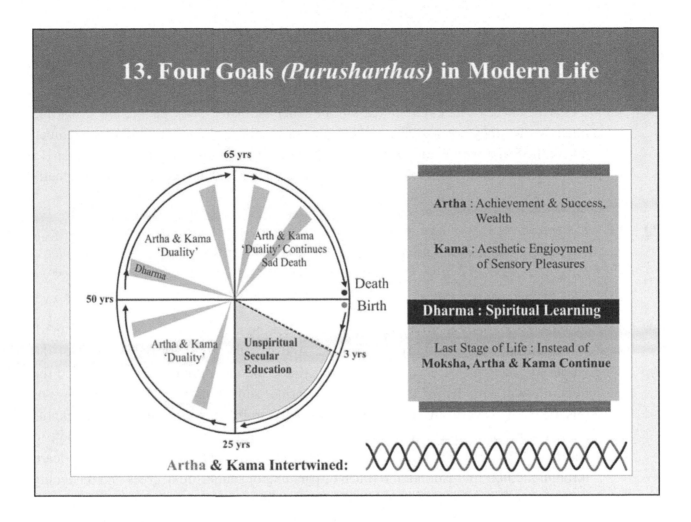

13. Four Goals *(Purusharthas)* in Modern Life

Q : *In this picture, the period of childhood and parental care, has been shortened to 3 yrs - whereas it was 7 yrs in the earlier model. What is the reason for this difference?*

A : You know the answer to this question very well. In modern times man is struggling too hard, he does not observe nature, not only are adults more unhappy because they are under enormous pressure to perform and excel in their professional work. Even children have become very unhappy, because they have lost the freedom to be playful, they have lost the freedom to observe nature and to use the senses more aesthetically and more pleasingly. Instead of being free till about 6 or 7 years, they are rushed off and packed off to the so called lower kinder garden (LKG), by the time they are three years old. At three they are still infants, but they are packed off to school. So this is a disgraceful situation, but we justify it, saying that we need this in order to make our children more competent in their later adult life. So that is the reason there is a shift from 7 years to 3 years in this picture

Q : *The end of the first quadrant has now increased to 25 yrs, previously it terminated at the age of 21.Is this because we are all spending many more years in our university education?*

A : Yes, I would say that even 25 years is an under estimate, many people are struggling much harder, they are studying at their universities till they are 25, or 30 or even much later till 35 and they even get married when they are 40 and they have lost about 15 years of their youthful life. So this is an absurd situation and the second diagram actually tries to remind you of this ugly fact.

Q : *Do you mean to say that a few centuries ago or even thousand years ago, diligent physicians, mathematicians, astrologers, astronomers and musicians, had all completed their scholastic education by the time they were 21? I do not think this could ever be true, even in ancient times. What have you to say about this?*

A : In ancient times and in all ancient societies education may not have been so structured, so organized and so brutally competitive. And it is the competitive character of the modern education that is very disgraceful, where the individual is actually denied the freedom to dream, denied the freedom to consider something very deeply. Because of this, he or she is very suffocated and he or she has to find the relief in pleasures. So his pleasures become much more important. In ancient times by contrast, men took to learning. Probably because of true interest in learning, they continued to learn throughout their life. But not too much of parading of scholastic degrees and university decorations and so on. Certainly learning was a lifelong passion for all the gifted people in ancient times and here we are doing it much more for bread and butter, than it is for the aesthetic enjoyment of life.

Q : *Looking at this diagram, the 2ⁿᵈ, 3ʳᵈ and even the 4ᵗʰ quadrants are all only in the materialistic spheres of artha and kama. This is shocking, where then is the goal of moksha in modern society?*

A : Modern society has placed a greater emphasis on the materialistic spheres of life called *artha and kama*. This is much to the detriment of the last stage of life which ought to have been dedicated to *moksha*. In ancient societies we can see that there was no emphasis on *artha and kama* - if we compare the structure of modern society with the structure of ancient society in which *moksha* had a natural place. And what repercussions does this have? Now, the repercussion is that even though people pass 60 or 65 years of age they are still seeking pleasure, like how people in the youth seek pleasure. They are still suffering from attachment and they are still leading a life which is giving more importance to sensory gratification. Therefore philosophically they become under developed and spiritually they become under developed, which is the consequence of extreme emphasis in modern society on the spheres of *artha and kama.*

Q : *What are all those grey colored sectors, distributed throughout artha and kama?*

A : These are kind of substitutes for the spiritual growth which happened in the 14 year period of childhood and adolescence at the feet of a *guru* and *gurupatni* and that learning had a very strong tilt towards the religious life, i.e., towards the life of the spirit. And in modern times because we no longer have the benefit of spiritual learning in childhood and in early adolescence, we step on to the threshold of adult life very much bereft of a spiritual back ground, so we are naturally going to find life in *artha and kama* difficult to cope with. So whenever we face problems which we are unable to solve, then we seek a solution to these problems by going to many masters and by attending many retreats and by taking to *yoga* and self-improvement workshops. So, all the grey patches are the piece-meal kind of spiritual learning, *dharmic* learning and *yoga* which offer substitutes for the complete loss of spiritual life in early childhood, in our high school years, up to adolescence and up to 20 years of age.

Q : *Do you mean to say this piece-meal kind of solution to the dilemmas and crises in life in the artha and kama spheres is sufficient to restore our inner peace and tranquility?*

A : Nobody knows to what extent it is adequate and will prove to be sufficient. People who are born with a spiritual aptitude and spiritual inclinations, may not even need these grey patches of spiritual solace and spiritual understanding. They may get it from their innate spiritual nature. But there may be a large number of people who are not born spiritually gifted and who do not have an innate sense of what *dharma* is, and what is morally correct. For them certainly these piece-meal solutions are indispensable and they are very necessary for finding a balance. Otherwise we may slip and fall on the floor of *artha and kama* too often and we may in fact become kind of intellectually, emotionally and morally crippled. So that the life journey in *artha and kama* cannot move forward.

Q : *Concerning the last stage of life, is it reasonable to expect everyone to be able to seek moksha? Or could it be that while a few alone seek in a whole-souled fashion, the majority may only be making half-hearted attempts?*

A : In modern society, because *artha and kama* have been kind of put on a pedestal and put into relief to the detriment of *moksha,* it is very doubtful even, if in the afternoon or in the evening of life, if people will really become *mumukshus.* Because society is not going to offer us any encouragement and any invitation to cultivate the spiritual life in the later years of our life. So, if at all we become *mumukshus,* it has to be at our own insistence and our own calling. So we have got to see whether what society is offering us is adequate for the satisfaction of our soul and if this is not adequate for our inner joy and inner fulfillment, then we have got to take additional pains to seek this path, which society is not readily offering and then we have got to build the spiritual life and lead it up to *moksha*. And not everyone will succeed in this endeavor, because society kind of turns a blind eye to this need for spiritual growth and development in modern times. So, we have got to kind of take that call ourselves at a personal level.

Q : *This also raises the question: Is it wrong if someone does not feel inclined to seek moksha in the last stage of life?*

A : I would say it is unfortunate if someone does not seek *moksha* in the last stage of life. Because that is rather akin to a tree which in its biological development starts out from the seed form, becomes a sapling in the early stages of its development and then it goes into flowering, finally it goes into a kind of fruiting or it may not go into fruiting and much less ripening of the fruit. So a kind of stasis has set in, in the biological development of the tree, whereby the fruits do not appear in the tree and the flowers just fall off when a strong wind blows or something like that. So the tree does not grow to its full potential. So man not flowering in the sphere of *moksha* would tantamount to a healthy tree not giving us its ripe and delicious fruits.

----

14. Looking at our Intentions *(Samkalpas)*

1. What are you seeking through this retreat?

2. Have your natural aspirations been fulfilled:

   (i.e., in *artha and kama*) ?

3. Are you *a mumukshu* (seeker of *moksha*), or are you just gathering deeper and wider experiences?

4. What is your path till now, do you have a *guru*? Conflict?

5. Do you take responsibility for your spiritual life?

6. Are you prepared to eventually be your own teacher?

7. Faith, devotion, humility, sincerity, priority are necessary for coming home to the *Atma* (Divine).

Q : *Why are you suddenly asking all these Qs-what is your intention in asking these searching Qs?*

A : We are about to board a long flight, so this must be considered to be some sort of a 'security check', before participants board the correct flight. Just ensuring that the destination is already fixed, etc. It is my responsibility to raise all these Qs, for the welfare of the participants.

Q : *In point two, you are making an enquiry to see if the so-called normal human desires have been fulfilled. Many of us may not have achieved it yet, does it mean then that we do not qualify for the rest of the retreat?*

A : If one is to be honest, then one has to say that either you come to this retreat with a sense of fulfillment in *artha and kama* so that the question naturally occurs to you as to, 'what next is there in life? What does life have to offer after we have beautifully brought *artha and kama* to a finale?' So you have to either be in that position or if you are not in that position your journey in *artha and kama* could itself be so frustrating and so stifling that you are calling to question many of the fundamental things that you took for granted in life. And you took for granted, that pleasure was the most important thing in life and that questing for pleasure was the most important thing. And now that pleasure has brought in an immense amount of pain in the wake of that pleasure, you are asking the question, 'what the hell is all this about? Is there nothing more serene and nothing more deeply peaceful, than this pleasure seeking and all the inevitable pain?' So if you are in that kind of a quandary also, then you qualify to be present at this retreat. Then you are going to understand many of the further questions which we are going to raise.

Q : *This is regarding your point 3, many seekers may be seeking 'something', they may not know what it is. Nevertheless, they get drawn to various teachers, satsangs, retreats, books and in this process they are all learning something, so why are you sounding so challenging, when you call to question, their search for deeper and wider experiences?*

A : I guess if we have a sincere teacher who intends to take his flock in a certain direction, he will naturally be strict. It is because he knows that if he is lenient and very lax in setting the milestones and the standards, then his flock may just wander away. So he has to make it absolutely clear where we are all headed. And if you have gone to various teachers, *satsangs,* retreats and started reading books, then there is nothing better than that. Because all that is a preparation for fulfillment in *dharma and moksha.* So that does not come in any kind of deviation from the spiritual path. It comes in as a solid blessing, which means you have done a lot of thinking, so that is going to help us further in this week long retreat.

Q : *In point six, you are saying that we will have to be our own teachers. Is this possible?*

A : This is where many of us may ask ourselves, 'can I really be my own teacher?

The truth is, if there is to be true learning, we can depend on a teacher, follow that teacher and learn a lot from the teacher, in the initial stages; but if we have to be absolutely authentic and absolutely true to ourselves, then sooner or later we have got to do a great deal of thinking and soul searching within ourselves. Because if you are not going to do that soul searching, if we are not going to be terribly and absolutely honest with ourselves, then we may just be stepping into a lot of illusions and a lot of placebos. Since nobody wants to meet that sad state at the end, one has to take the responsibility to learn diligently and be one's own teacher and to discern one's own mistakes. And that is the high road on which all of us will have to travel. We may not like this, because this means a lot of hard work and we think that we can go to a retreat, can read a book or be with a teacher and suddenly we become illumined! The fact is nothing can be more idiotic than that. So there is no getting away from the fact that we have to be our own teachers sooner or later. Paradoxically, we all have been our own teachers in *artha and kama.*

Q : *In point seven, are you not setting very high standards for the spiritual life leading to moksha?*

A : Point seven is faith, devotion, humility, sincerity and priority. These are very important for coming home to the Divine.

Now, if you are very worldly and you are very engrossed in your materialistic pursuits and are excessively pleasure seeking and you live a life of self-gratification - then these things may look like deterrents. They may look like impossible qualities to have in a spiritual seeker. But as a teacher in this context, just as you have the responsibility to me, I too have a responsibility to you. The question arises, 'should I be actually pampering you? And telling all of you that you are wonderful souls, you are noble people, you have already advanced 75% in the path', when in fact, the truth may be that you do not know how far you have travelled on the path. Or, rather, should I be honest with you and say that these are the qualities that I expect from you and this is how you must progress and that I will be checking this out as we go along. And in my own personal opinion, I think I will be doing a great deal of disservice if I were not honest with you and if I did not tell you what this spiritual journey is all about. If I gave you a kind of soporific illusion that you can lead your life in any way you like and still you will reach home to the Divine, that would be my dishonesty. So, I can't do that! That will also be the height of disservice. So, I have got to tell you what is what, as it is, namely, that faith, devotion, humility, sincerity and priority of the spiritual life are all necessary for coming home to *moksha*.

Now you don't have to feel scared that you do not have all these blessings at this juncture or at this point of time. They will come in due course as you become more and more sincere in your quest. That is all that matters. Sincerity is all that matters, then the rest of it will just fall into place.

----

15. The Path of *Sakti*, The Path of *Siva*

In Life up to 60 or 65 yrs *(artha and kama)*, you have to generally walk on the path of *Sakti* (path of desire and its gratification). This is so because *maya* will be strong during the *artha and kama* journey. Note however this is the average pattern and exceptions will not fall under this average pattern.

After 60 or 65 *(dharma and moksha)*, you have to shift from the path of *Sakti* to the path of *Siva*. **This shift is a natural process of growth and maturation. This is the general pattern (seed, sapling, flower, fruit).**

Q : *What is the new terminology that you are suddenly introducing? Your earlier model for the goals of life, pertaining to traditional Hindu society and also then modern society (world-wide), was quite clear. We understood the goals of artha and kama and also dharma and moksha in both the diagrams. But now, you have equated the journey in artha and kama with the path of Sakti and the journey in dharma and moksha, with the path of Siva. What is the justification for this?*

A : You will see the justification as we go along. *Siva and Sakti*, they are two complimentary aspects of the Divine. The *Sakti* aspect of the Divine pertains to the world and the life of the senses, desires and the search for the gratification which is obviously a very important part of the human drama. So we can't throw a blanket over it and pretend that that part of our life does not exist. And that 'only the Divine exists' and that we are all saints and we have to go running behind the Divine. That just is not true. And of course Divine is *Siva per se*. And *Siva* is *being* and *Sakti* is *becoming*. And the fact is the greater part of the human life is in the terrain of *becoming*, of seeking something, of getting something and a feeling of a sense of getting satisfaction in our earthly life. And all these constitute *artha and kama*.

Artha means the pursuit of a goal and *kama* is the fulfillment of aspiration, fulfillment of desire and the aesthetic enjoyment of life. So life begins with the quest for *artha and kama*, which is the path of *Sakti*. But after 60 or 65 the senses tire and the body tires, then a different kind of seeking takes birth and the journey begins to move *towards* the inner plane and that is the path of *Siva*. That is a season when we have to get back home to *Siva* before our body goes into the dust. So, these are very different paths. The path of *Sakti* which pertains to the worldly life and the path of *Siva* which pertains to our spiritual and our religious life. So we should not be afraid to distinguish between the two paths and say that one path is till 60 and another path is after 60 when we have lost the fascination for the world.

Q : *Is it also possible that people remain only in artha and kama, and never graduate to dharma and moksha?*

A : This is a good question. We have seen in one of the earlier topics, that in modern society, the maturation of man from mundane life and mundane perceptions to a spiritual outlook on life does not happen so easily, because there is an over emphasis on *artha and kama* to the detriment of *moksha*. So this has had the result that people in the evening of their lives are still behaving like young people. They are still pleasure seekers. For them still consciousness has not calmed down to such an extent that they have come to enquire about the meaning and purpose of life, about the Divine. They have not yet started their inner journey or sought answers to very pertinent questions like, 'Where actually is the Divine? What is the Divine? Who is the Divine? And how to seek union with this Divine?' Instead, they are still engrossed in materialistic existence.

Because of the over emphasis on *artha and kama*, the sphere of spiritual life, i.e., the sphere of *moksha* is likely to suffer. And you see this, as you observe life closely you will see that many people in their old age are attached to their children, attached more to their grand children even. They keep interfering in the lives of their children, and their children don't actually like this, but what to do, the elders are not sensitive enough to perceive this. They are still caught in the life of the senses and they neglect their inner spiritual life and the spiritual journey to *moksha*. At that stage in life, when they have to pursue *moksha*, their life is unfortunately arrested in the spheres of *artha and kama*, through a prolonged continuity in these materialistic spheres, when that should never have been the case.

Q : *By the same token, is it also possible that in the younger years, seekers could have been in dharma and moksha, and in later years, they settle down to a householder's life?*

A : This is actually an amazing question. Because the patterns we have seen in the two diagrams, the pattern pertaining to ancient Hindu society and the subsequent pattern pertaining to modern secular society, they are kind of a statistical mean of the life of humanity. So, all this means that if you kind of draw a graph, such as what you will see in many of the science journals, then you will find that most of the points get clustered as a pattern and take their positions very close to the curve (the graph), but, you will notice that some of the points are *off the main curve of the graph* and these are called statistical fluctuations and they represent the life of individuals who do not strictly conform to the regular/ simplistic patterns shown, corresponding to the models of ancient Hindu society and modern secular society. So, it may happen that sometimes the spiritual life transpires till you are 40 or 50 and after 50, your worldly life could well commence. It is a kind of topsy turvy kind of situation.

However, since you have lived a spiritual life for 40 - 50 years, then even if you kind of open a new chapter in your materialistic life and start living a life of sensory gratification, you are not going to get engrossed in it to such an extent that you are thrown off balance. In this scenario you go through life with a great deal of stability and a great deal of balance. And that can indeed happen, as a statistical fluctuation. That is the main point and it is not that it is impossible.

It can happen in a few exceptional cases and at the other end of the spectrum we also have cases like Ramana Maharishi for whom there was not the *artha and kama* chapter at all, in the entirety of his life. Because at the age of 16, the Divine just swallowed him up and there was only *moksha* from the age of 16 till the age of 70. And he attained immortality at the age of 16, but the body perished at the age of 70. Thus the materialistic spheres of *artha and kama* did not exist in his life. He led a life of renunciation and he was a sage from the age of 16. Not that the wisdom of the sage was maturing progressively in stages, not that at all. In his case, it was a full blown maturity at the age of 16 and that maturity is the climax which is called *moksha* which is undiminished and it went on and on till finally his body perished at the age of 70. So, all kinds of pattern can happen, but they are exceptions. And the two models presented here represent the statistical mean.

----

16. You *(Jiva)* and Your Path are Unique

1. Our *Atma* (our true Self), is masked by *Jiva (self)'s maya.*

2. However, you as *Jiva* are unique, so your destiny is also unique.

3. *Your (Jiva's) path to the discovery of the Atma is unique.*

4. *You (Jiva) have to cut your own path and this path begins with misfortunes. However, sages and saints will be very helpful.*

5. *Appears hard, but will be easy for honest sincere seekers.*

Q : *In point one, you have said, we are the Atma, before birth and after death, are we not the Atma in the interim period, between life and death?*

A : Of course we have to be the *Atma* after birth and before death as well. But the point is that humanity finds it hard to make the discovery that this is our true identity - that we are the *Atma.* And that is what makes the religious or spiritual life very hard. Because there are illusions which hinder the discovery of this truth of the *Atma.*

Q : *So, this mystery of our true identity - will never be known, unless, each of us begins this quest earnestly and is deeply interested in the resolution of the mystery, isn't it?*

A : Yes, though we are the *Atma,* we are born with the veiling of the truth of the *Atma* - a thing which in Hindu scriptures is called *maya* or illusion. And in Christianity it is called the *original sin,* where by, the original truth is hidden from us. And therefore unless and until we actually undertake the task of deciphering this mystery and of searching for our true identity we may never know who we really are. So we will continue to have the superficial definition of ourselves that we are the body, we are so and so, the president of an organization, the head of a family, the husband or wife of somebody, the father of somebody and so on. And life goes on like this for the vast majority of human beings and so in a retreat like this, it is important that either we continue the enquiry and the quest which we probably started earlier or we could also begin the quest during this retreat to find out for ourselves what our true identity is. To crack this mystery and go deeper into it. That is the purpose.

Q : *Looking at point two, I get the feeling that the cosmic benefic and malefic life energies are all throwing a veil on our true identity, making it difficult for us to know ourselves - am I right?*

A : Yes, this veiling power is called *maya*. And we have got to get round this power. And in the *Gita* it is said by Krishna, who is the teacher in that scripture that if we take refuge in him and if we have faith in him, then it will be easy to surmount this obstacle of *maya*, which is a kind of deluding power in our consciousness and our perception and if we are not able to take refuge in him, then probably the enquiry becomes somewhat harder. The key thing here is that we are unique, because the *Atma* is unique. There is only one *Atma* for 10 billion people. The *Antaratma* (inner *Atma* or Self) is unique and we are that *Atma*. So every time a human being incarnates, it is the *Atma*, the Divine, which is incarnating. And now this is not to be a belief for us. It has to become a personal discovery and a personal truth. And we are here to make the discovery and to go into the truth.

Q : *Looking at points one and two again, a great deal of emphasis is being placed on our uniqueness, what is your reason for doing this - because this emphasis on uniqueness must be rather new to every one of us?*

A : Normally human beings think that they are unique: they are unique as personalities, they are unique in their physical features and psychological makeup, in the way they talk, the way they think, they think they are unique. But that is hardly important here, because that uniqueness sooner or later goes into the dust. Your personality goes into the dust, your body goes into the dust, so none of that is the everlasting truth. So here we are talking of something else. Here we are saying that at the very core of your being you are unique and you are unique even in the constitution of your personality and even your destiny is unique. *So what works for one of us will never work for another of us and therefore each of us will have to find out a different path to reach the Divine.* Because we are each unique. So we have got to understand our uniqueness. We need to stop comparing ourselves with our friends and family members and feeling good about it or feeling bad about it. So none of these things is going to help. So we have to feel it in our gut that we are unique and because we are unique we have to find a path that works for us. And there are no short cuts here. We can't blindly follow a path which is supposed to be laid out by a great *avatar* or by a great saint or a great sage or a great *rishi*. Then we are not going to reach home. And that is not the way it works. And this is bad news for lazy spiritual people who are looking for easy spiritual solutions, because this is the truth.

Q : *We have been brought up on the gratifying thought that the sages and saints have all worked hard to get the paths ready for us and you are coming and telling us something, which nobody would like to hear about, namely, that we have to cut our own path, since our path is unique and valid only for ourselves. We are all likely to heave a despondent sigh, when we hear this kind of a thing, which robs us of our cherished and soothing beliefs!*

A : Yes, in a retreat like this would you not agree with me that we will have to shed our wrong beliefs, our wrong conclusions and our prejudices, which we have. Because if we retain our wrong beliefs, wrong thinking and wrong prejudices and thought process we are not going to make any progress in the spiritual life. Therefore we have got to know that we are doing a lot of wishful thinking. We think that somebody has actually worked hard to make the path for us and all we have got to do is just walk on that path. *Now nothing can be more foolish than this.* Because the obstacles and misfortunes we have in our life are unique to us. They are not there in the life of anybody else. So we have to learn our own lessons and chalk out our path to go through these misfortunes, to absorb the misfortunes and to resolve the mystery till we reach home. And that is the hard truth and we have got to digest that truth. The good news actually is, if you are sensitive, that we are unique and not in a sort of a superficial sense that each of us have a unique nose, unique eyes. But the way we are structured and the way we think is unique and because we are unique we have to work with this uniqueness in order to find the path which makes absolute sense for us. That is the way we are going to get hope into our lives.

First Day (Chapter - I), 1st 'Tat Tvam Asi' Meditation

Understanding and Intellectual Conviction:

1. *Artha, Kama, Dharma, Moksha*, 2. Wave & Ocean, 3. Your Uniqueness,
4. Paths of *Sakti & Siva*, 5. Head and Heart, 6. Your Intentions and 7. Seven Stages.

17. The Two 'Tat Tvam Asi' Birds

Self *(Atma)*, Awareness, 'Conscious Presence', Witness, 'I am ness'.

Jiva (with *maya & self*)

Q : *Now this topic speaks of two Tat Tvam Asi birds of the Mundaka Upanishad. As a Hindu, I am somewhat aware that the Upanishads are part of the Vedas, the deepest scriptures of the Hindus. However when this retreat is offered to Western seekers, how would people understand these Sanskrit terms, and even the meaning of 'Upanishads' and 'Mundaka'. Should you not be giving us the meanings of these terms, so that even Hindus like us, may have an even clearer understanding?*

A : It will be good if seekers do understand the meanings, especially the etymological meaning of these Sanskrit terms, Upanishads and *Mundaka*. But this is actually not so necessary for our present purposes of *self* - Knowing and Self - Realization. Nevertheless, for the sake of completeness, let us go into this.

The term Upanishad:

Upa is composed of two parts which is U + Pa - meaning '*Near the feet*'. And '*nishad*' means sitting beneath the feet-implied that these are the feet of the master.

It is suggestive of a disciple or a seeker or a *mumukshu* sitting at the feet of a Self - Realized master, having humbled himself and having the very essential quality of humility. So sitting at the feet of a master, is symbolic of the extremely humble posture, for without this humility no learning is possible. It is a teaching which is received and centered on the *Atma* and on *Brahman*. *Atman* is the hidden deeper aspect of consciousness and *Brahman* is the Divine. So the Upanishads teach us about *Atman and Brahma*n, i.e.; *Atma vidya (knowledge or learning about the Atma)* and *Brahma vidya (knowledge or learning about Brahman or the Divine)*.

In India the *Vedas* are the ancient spiritual corpus of the Hindus. And Upanishads are considered to be the *Veda siras* - the crown of the *Vedas* or *Vedanta*- the highest peak of the *Vedas,* which is naturally centered on Self-Realization.

Coming to the Adjective *Mundaka:*

The word means 'shaven off'. Why is this adjective used here? It is probably used because to shave off the head, which is what the *sannyasis* do in India, is symbolic of renunciation of the ego, the *self.* Renunciation of the idea that one is the body, that one is the *self* and shaving off of the head or tonsure is symbolic and a ritualistic act, signifying, 'the casting away of the *self',* or individuality, or the notion that 'we are the physical body'.

So, *Mundaka* Upanishad will probably indicate an emphasis which is based on detachment from the body, detachment from the *self,* without which this teaching may not get internalized and come home to us. So detachment and renunciation of the idea that we are the body, that we are the *self,* are central to this Upanishad. And this is a teaching given by a particular sage, and every Upanishad is a teaching by a particular sage. The key thing here is that no two teachings actually are the same, because every sage speaks from his own realization. So that is the reason there are so many Upanishads. There are more than 100 or 200 Upanishads and each of them has equally legitimate insights, which that particular sage had in his life and which he is presenting to us in the form of teachings and these teachings will be helpful to us in our own pursuit and discovery of the truth of the *Atma* and *Parabrahma.*

Q : *Are the two Tat Tvam Asi birds seen in this picture, metaphors for some teaching in this Upanishad? If so, what exactly do they represent? Most importantly, why are you describing these birds as Tat Tvam Asi birds?*

A : At the outset, I wish to emphasize that every one of us will benefit by memorizing this mythic picture or this metaphoric representation of the truth, which is an analogical understanding of the truth. Yes, indeed it is a metaphor. You will see one bird is very engrossed in the act of eating, which is symbolic of sensory-gratification and the pursuit of pleasure, something which is such an integral part of the human life and the human drama. The other bird is not involved and not engrossed in the act of the pursuit of pleasure, instead it seems to be detached and only witnessing the whole act of the pursuit of pleasure, the search for sensory gratification, the search for survival, emotional and economic security. This other bird is a complete outsider to this whole drama and is only a witness and probably has got the capacity to learn, the capacity to negate the life of the lower bird. If we like we may call the bird which is engrossed in the pleasure seeking and search for security as *Sakti* and the other wise bird which is just watching everything, as *Siva*. And I have given the particular name Tat Tvam Asi birds because in truth there are not two birds. There is just one bird, capable of being in both states, so we are both the birds.

This is one of the most important principles in this retreat - that we have a body and mind centered *self* (our human nature), and another Self, the *Atma,* that is imperishable, unborn, deathless, timeless, pointing to our Divine nature. So we will have to commit this picture to memory, like we recommended committing to memory, the ocean-wave metaphor. The ocean-wave metaphor is also a Tat Tvam Asi metaphor, likewise these two birds are also a Tat Tvam Asi metaphor.

The eating bird represents the *Jiva* (*self*) which enjoys and suffers, the witnessing bird represents the timeless awareness *(chit),* the *Atma,* a higher spiritual potential we all have, and which we use far too inadequately. So it is, if we may use these terms, a powerful faculty, which is unrecognized and used unconsciously and insufficiently. Every human being has two dimensions or two aspects, a very manifest human aspect, and a hidden Divine aspect. The witnessing bird represents the hidden Divine aspect of every human being, and the pleasure-seeking and eating bird represents the very human nature of every human being. In topic 2, we have already dealt with the human nature vis-à-vis the Divine nature of every human being. 'Tat' refers to our mysterious, unknowable Divine nature, 'Tvam' refers to the core of your so-called human nature, and 'Asi' means 'are', so 'Tat Tvam Asi', the Upanishadic *sutra* says, the very essence of each one of us is the Divine Itself. *The two birds are thus different aspects of ourselves, the eating bird, the mask, the self, and the witnessing bird, the hidden Divine nature, the Atma or the witness consciousness. Thus we are both birds, simultaneously, this is a paradox. Hence the adjective Tat Tvam Asi is quite appropriate.*

Q : *So, this is yet another way of driving home the same point of Tat Tvam Asi, that we are the Divine - not as the body, but as the root of our consciousness?*

A : Right, that is the hint that is being given by this particular metaphor- that we are both. We are the pleasure seeking entity and we are the entity seeking survival, security perpetually and feeling insecure in this whole endless process. That is the *Sakti* bird. But we also have to discover and realize that we are also the witnessing bird, we are intelligence which is now buried. So the teaching will help us to know that we are both the things. When we understand the teaching deeply, then the seeming contradiction between the *Sakti* bird and the *Siva* bird will completely disappear and we will know/ realize that there are no contradictions and that we are both aspects of consciousness, hence the truth of Tat Tvam Asi.

18. A Model of the *Jiva* with *Maya:* Metaphor

Man's body = *Atma,* Sticking algae = *maya, self,* memories, experiences, attachments, fears, *anatmas.*

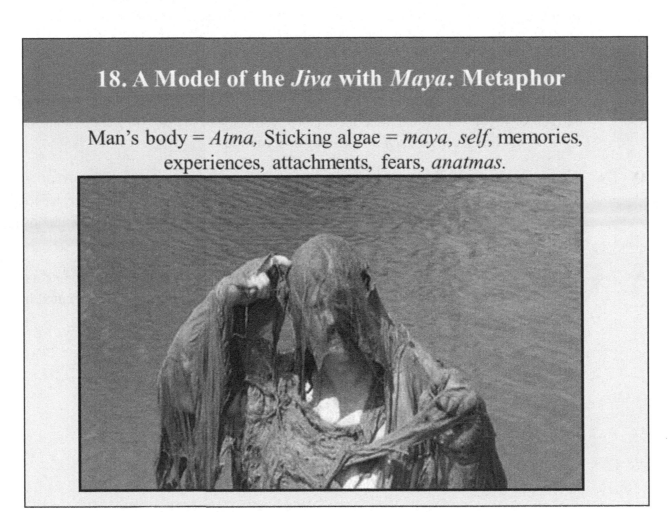

Q : *What is the inner meaning of this metaphorical picture?*

A : We have to go slowly here, for this metaphor has two different meanings. The man's body here represents the *Atma,* the true Self, which is hidden and the algae represents the multiple false selves, shrouding the *Atma. This is one interpretation so that we may all get the intellectual conviction of the importance of purification.* The same metaphor can also mean the following. The man's body represents the erroneous thinking of the *Jiva* that, it is the body. And the algae represent all the mischief and illusions and other false selves of the *Jiva.* In the usage of this metaphor in this way, there is no room for the *Atma*, but the metaphor brings into relief the root illusion which is the *Jiva's* thinking that it is the body.

Q : *You have again brought in the word self and referred to it as the sticking algae. Will you explain how this self is different from the so-called Jiva, if it is different at all?*

A : *Jiva* is a term found in the *advaitic* literature of India. Ages ago Adi Sankaracharya has said, *Jivo Brahmaiva na paraha,* this means that the *Jiva* only is *Brahman* or the Absolute Truth, not anything other than this. When is this true? Only when the *Jiva* is purified, for then alone, all the algae is stripped clean and the *Atma* shines. In the literature of J. Krishnamurti, the term *Jiva* is not used, but *self* is used. In truth *Jiva* is the *self* or if you want to be more meticulous, you can call the *self* the very essence of the *Jiva.* So it is the *Jiva's self,* in one way of speaking.

Q : *Honestly speaking, this seems a most wonderful metaphor, coming to think of it. However, you have referred to the body of this man as the Atma, whereas, everywhere else, you are saying, that the very identity of the Jiva that it is the body is the curse on mankind. Are these usages not contradictory?*

A : These usages are not contradictory because they are mentioned in different contexts. We always have to look at the inner meaning of the metaphor and also at the context in which it is being used.

----

19. Water Contaminated by Algae : Metaphor

Clear Water = *Atma* = 'I', Algae *(Jiva's maya)* = Thoughts, feelings, beliefs, fears, desires, memories, hopes, experiences of pleasure, pain.

Q : *The contamination conveyed by this metaphor is very shocking. Is the extent of this contamination different in different people?*

A : Of course! The more ignorant you are more the contamination and the more lucid you are, less the contamination.

Q : *More the contamination, more the pain in life?*

A : More pleasure to begin with. And this more and more pleasure will invariably end in a tragedy, which is the impossibility of continuing the pleasure, which is pain. So more the contamination, more the pleasure and consequently, more the pain.

Q : *After the cleansing of consciousness, through choiceless awareness, and learning about the Jiva (self), do you think, Jiva becomes calmer and more silent?*

A : Think of the man with the algae enmeshing him (topic 18). We had said that his body represents the *Atma* and the enveloping algae was the *maya* and the ignorance. So now the *Jiva* is the man with all the algae. The *Jiva* attempts to observe itself. This is possible

51

because the *Atma* is at the heart of the *Jiva*. As the *Jiva* observes itself, awareness comes into play and learning happens and if one has the desire (*Jiva* has the desire) to achieve some end through this choiceless observation, then the learning will be unfruitful. But if there is intense interest and no surging desire, then the *Jiva* will be calmed and silenced.

Q : *How does the Jiva get into maya?*

A : This is a Divine doing and the tragicomedy is that as the *Atma* is the Divine itself in creation, it is the Divine which has got entangled, but of course as a human being. The moment the Divine creates the world, this *maya* and entanglement comes along. It is very sweet and delicious, but soon turns bitter, so in the end you have to spit it out.

Q : *One understands that hurts and pain are contrary to Atma's blissful nature, so these are contaminations all right. But how are aspirations and ambitions also contaminations?*

A : Many people are not going to like this answer, because every aspiration and ambition is fundamentally *self*-centered. So it implies a blindness as to who we are and this ambition invariably will lead to stepping on other people's toes and causing them great pain and importantly being so obsessed and pre-occupied with the ambitions and aspirations that one necessarily has to lose all peace and all intelligence. This lesson is usually learnt only after a fall, never while the game is actually going on.

----

20. Water without Contamination by Algae

Q : *Looking at this absolutely clear pond, can such an ideal state be reached?*

A : When there is integrity for the *Jiva*, and the *Jiva* has no private and secret agenda of its own and has *nirguna bhakti* (the seventh or highest *bhakti*) to *Parabrahma*, then the pond will be blemishless like this. Integrity, that is the perfect alignment of thought, word and deed and detachment are essential for the pond to be blemishless and remain blemishless.

----

21. *Jivatma* Purified is the *Paramatma*. *Jivatma's* Impurities: *Maya*, Associations, *self*

Human nature is typified by the *Jivatma*.

Jivatma's limitations are two fold:

(i) Attachments and associations with body, people, status, sensory objects; likes and dislikes; this has lead to the *Jivatma* losing knowledge of its true nature.

(ii) The *self (Jiva)*, which has arisen for survival reasons, is the second serious obstacle to *moksha*.

Q : *As we do not seem to know anything outside of ourselves, how are we supposed to know, that which lies beyond us?*

A : By turning away from the mess we have accumulated as memories, attachments, likes and dislikes and by negating all of this, which man has held dearly, we come upon peace and another dimension of life.

Q : *Do we take the self of the Jiva, to be the 'motor' of all it's self-defensive mechanisms?*

A : Indeed, that is right. Either we can use *self* and *Jiva* interchangeably, or we can take *self* to be the 'motor' of the *Jiva*, both perceptions are valid.

Q : *So, bereft of all its impurities and coatings, is that the Paramatma?*

A : From the metaphor of the man and the enshrouding algae, you already know that this is true, though you may be uncomfortable with this idea-because you have such low self-esteem that, you can never consider yourself to be the Divine. If the impurities are removed, then your thinking will also change and you will become comfortable with the idea that you are the Divine, that, all is the Divine, in fact.

22.'Tat Tvam Asi' Birds: Their Relationship

"Just as a brahmin (i.e., a saintly person) who is drunk, behaves strangely when intoxicated by liquor, so too the Self, though *Sat-Chit-Ananda* and timeless, associated with the body and 'consciousness', appears changed as the *Jiva (self)*, wallowing in *samsara*. Hence the *Jivatma* to know itself, as it is, must disassociate, withdraw from its involvement with 'consciousness'."

- Advaita Bodha Deepika[15]

Q : *This seems to be a beautiful analogy to drive home the, 'impossible to believe' truth that man is the Divine only. So, it is maya, and the associated ignorance, which has lead the Divine astray, and made it materialistic?*

A : The Advaita Bodha Deepika [15], an ancient text on *Advaita* is throwing this light and the text says, 'yes'. All of this will make sense, only for a seeker, who has become hungry and restless for the truth. If, *mumukshutvam*, or the desire for *moksha* (unity with the Divine) does not arise in a seeker, then none of these beautiful teachings will make any sense. So, this ancient text is saying that the Divine *in its fallen condition* is the *Jiva*. Nobody is responsible for this, the Divine is itself the cause and also the effect.

----

23. Awareness vis-à-vis Consciousness

"Awareness is primordial, it is the original state, beginning less, endless, uncaused, unsupported, without parts, without change. Consciousness is on contact, a reflection against a surface, a state of duality. There can be no consciousness without awareness, but there can be awareness without consciousness, as in deep sleep. Awareness is Absolute, consciousness is relative to its content. Consciousness is always of something. Consciousness is partial and changeful. Awareness is total, changeless, calm and silent. And it is the common matrix of every experience."

- Sri Nisargadatta Maharaj[16]

Q : *As the title itself suggests, Maharaj's statement seems to be, exactly the truth of the two Tat Tvam Asi birds, cast into the form of words. Where, awareness would refer to the witnessing bird or the Atma and consciousness would refer to the eating bird, the Jiva?*

A : Exactly. I would like to make one additional point. All *sutras*, whether from Ramana Maharshi, Nisargadatta Maharaj, Krishnamurti, Bhagavad Gita, Ashtavakra Gita, Kaivalya Navaneetham - I would like sincere seekers to commit these *sutras* to memory and then churn them in their consciousness. For example, Maharaj's *sutra* on awareness and consciousness, may be mapped on to the two Tat Tvam Asi birds, in order to enliven them even more.

----

24. 'Tat Tvam Asi' Birds-Common Ground
(The 'I' is the same in both Birds)

Witness Bird (Self)
- Self=*Sat-Chit-Ananda*
- Mute, only Witnesses
- Intelligence *(Prajnya)*
- Awareness *(Chit)*
- *Ananda* (Causeless Joy)
- In Freedom, Immortal
- Constant, Timeless
- Sense of Oneness, Innocent.

Eating Bird *(Jivatma)*
- 'I' am the body, mind
- Chattering nature *(Jiva)*
- *Jiva* suffers, enjoys, changing
- *Jiva* thinks & feels mostly about body & experiences
- *Jiva's* thinking /actions-cunning, survival based, very lonely
- Fear of disease, old age, death
- *Jiva* has a troublesome *self*
- *Jiva* limited by attachments, *maya*, confused.

Q : *This is a question about your nomenclature, the way you are using certain words and certain symbols, to point to the truth. You use Self, with a Capital S, to denote the Atma or the witness bird, whereas, you are using self, in italics, to point to the eating bird?*

A : That is right, so that, all can see the difference between the two. The *self* is the reflection of the *Atma*, but often it turns out to be a caricature of the *Atma*.

Q : *The 'I' in the witness bird, is the pure 'I', without any contamination. Whereas the 'I' in the eating bird, is camouflaged, by all the coatings, which are the thoughts, hopes, fears, memories, and attachments. This was dramatized by portraying all this as the algae. Is the camouflage the real reason, for the feeling of the 'I' being the same in the eating bird, as well as in the witness bird?*

A : Yes, we just have to remember the coatings of the algae. Let us also remember what Sri Ramana Maharshi has said about a situation such as this: *"The 'I' casts off the illusion of the 'I' and yet remains as 'I'. This appears to be a paradox to you, it is not so to the Jnani."*

Q : *Looking at the sharp contrast of the qualities of the two birds, it looks like, the 'I', is completely 'lost' in the eating bird, whereas, it is resplendent in the witness bird. Is this because of its disassociation with the body and the senses and manas, right?*

A : You are correct, this is what it is, exactly.

---

25. What Solution does the *Jiva* Aspire for?

1. As a *Jiva*, you have hundred desires, hundred problems, endless suffering.

2. Somebody has to tell you that your problems will continue to exist, so long as you retain your *Jivahood*, they are an integral part of being a *Jiva*. **Your problems arise from the way you receive and react to various events in life.**

3. If however, you renounce your *Jivahood* and accept the *Atmahood*, you will not have a single sorrow, single problem. Life will be delicious and mysterious, everyday!

Q : *When we have problems, we seek an answer to them, either by reading some self-help books, talking to elders, going to satsangs, seeking advice from masters and gurus, and now you are telling us that our problems will not go way in spite of all this effort. Isn't this too pessimistic and too fatalistic?*

A : The *Jiva* can be very easily fooled, because it is susceptible to appeasement, becomes temporarily calm when the carrot of hope is dangled before it and ever wants to believe that it will succeed always in all it's endeavors. Such grandiose aspirations it has, only because of its Divine *Atmic* nature, which is deeply buried. It is like a beggar going out begging and kind people who are ignorant and lacking in clarity, always dropping a coin or two, a piece of bread or a banana in his bowl and this is done, just to appease his clamouring. What if I told you that he has a ton of gold under his cot?It is much more important to make him stop begging and send him back home, to unearth the treasure under his cot, than to give him a small measure of hope and happiness, to suit his small befooled mind. I am trying to make people stop begging, because to me it is very clear that all beggars are kings, with abundant treasure deep within themselves. Is this too pessimistic and too fatalistic, because I am speaking the truth?

Q : *So, is this retreat meant to bring home the lesson to us that we ought to renounce the Jivahood in favor of the Atmahood?*

A : Yes, this is the goal, as already mentioned at the very beginning.

Q : *Is it easy to identify such people?*

A : No, it is not, there are no outer signs. People mistake good looking people to be good or spiritual people. But a good looking person, can have a very foul heart. Even if I brought before you, ten such people who have crossed over to *Atmahood*, your polluted minds, will find it hard to see the truth, because you will go on judging. So, what is important is the purification of the *Jiva,* when all things will become clear and the judgments will fall away.

----

26. Activating the 'Atrophied' *Atma*

You have two faculties, a human and a Divine one, *Jiva* and *Atma*. *Jiva,* you know so well, it is who you have been with endless problems. *Atma* is an unused 'faculty', because it is always, 'behind the scenes' and is not a sense object for you to perceive, but the very core of your being, even as a *Jiva.* You may initially, struggle to find the centre of your own being, this *Atma*, because it is very subtle: It is calmness, awareness, causeless joy *(ananda)*, this is you. It is the silent source, where problems cannot be formed.

Q : *You have used the adjective, 'atrophied' for the Atma. Is it because, the Atma is never used?*

A : Never used directly, but indirectly, nothing will work without the *Atma*. The *Atma* is the source of life itself, it moves the *chitta, manas, buddhi* and even *ahamkara*. However, these 'faculties' in the human consciousness, which have their life and sustenance in the *Atma,* somehow, they have become far more important and the 'mother' of all these faculties has been totally forgotten. When the *Jiva* is purified, or when the *Atma* is recognized and allowed to shine forth, then we may say, the *Atma* begins to have a place in human life, which humans badly need. So, because we live life, not from the *Atma*, but mainly from consciousness, I am saying the *Atma* is unfelt and unused. Hence the term atrophy.

----

27. *Jiva* is the *Atma's* Reflection, in the 'mirror' of the body-mind

1. If the 'mirror' is perfect, the 'reflection'*(Jiva)* may be faithful to the original (i.e., *Atma*).

2. If the 'mirror' is defective/imperfect, or broken or shaking, then the 'reflection' *(Jiva)* will be a greatly impoverished version of the original *(Atma)*.

3. If the 'mirror' is rectified through *yoga*, etc., then the 'reflection' *(Jiva)* may not be 'so bad a copy' of the original *(Atma)*.

Q : *Where is the mirror, which you are talking of?*

A : Usually in using the metaphor of the mirror, we should have three things, the subject, which is the source, the mirror and the object which is the reflection of the subject in the mirror. Here, the subject is the *Atma*, the mirror is the 'field' of the body, along with the consciousness. The *self,* is the reflection or the object which arises, when the *Atma* develops this association with the 'field' of the body and consciousness.

Even 'reflection', may be somewhat inappropriate. Think of sugar, which is the *Atma*, and when that intensely sweet sugar, is introduced into a cup of muddy water (that is the body and the associated consciousness), the entire cup of muddy water becomes sweet, but this weak sweetness is nothing compared to the sweetness of the original lump of sugar, which is the *Atma.*

So, we should probably say, the *self,* is the presence of the *Atma,* in the muddy waters of the body and consciousness, or the transformed version of the *Atma,* as it 'falls' into the muddy waters of the body and the associated consciousness.

28. You are not the body, but The Conscious Presence of 'I am ness'

"You know that 'you are'. That you have your 'I - consciousness' (I am ness). At present, you wrongly identity yourself as the body. Body is given a certain name; you consider that to be yourself. But I say, in this body, consciousness is present, or the conscious presence of 'I am', as I call it. You should identify yourself with this conscious presence, 'I am'. That's all."

- Sri Nisargadatta Maharaj[17]

Q : *So, does this presuppose that each of us, must have a pretty clear idea of that 'I' consciousness, which is supposed to be always there, and which we are supposed to be?*

A : Yes, this may be the first and the last step in the journey inwards.

As this 'I' consciousness, which Maharaj is referring to as the, 'I am ness' does not abide in itself, as being, but instead, is 'drawn out' as becoming, the activity of thought must subside to a certain extent, for each of us to succeed in getting hold of ourselves, as the 'I' consciousness. Once you have discovered the essence of your being as this, 'I' consciousness, many things will fall into place. This, 'I' consciousness is the core of all of our inner goings on.

Q : *We are not even aware that we (that is, the 'I' consciousness) have made the wrong identification with the body. So, should we not be, first of all, aware of this wrong identification?*

A : Fortunately, for us, as we are the 'I' consciousness, we have the possibility of watching how we function in our inner life and outer life as well. The body association for the

'I' consciousness must be watched and studied first. As Nisargadatta Maharaj says, *this is our only capital* and we have to be this, to commence the inner life. This, 'I' consciousness is a mystery. How did it come about? When was it created? We have to explore into this. This 'I' is the root vibration of the Divine, as our consciousness. Getting hold of this 'I' consciousness, the very root of our being may be the first as well as the last step.

Q : *Why is the I, the first person, pronoun, always in capitals, irrespective of where it comes in a sentence?*

A : I do not know the answer to this Q, but I have a feeling that someone who has studied the philosophy of the English language, may have an insight into this reason. In Sanskrit, *aham* is the first person pronoun, it consists of 'aa' plus 'ha', which are the first and last alphabets of the Sanskrit language, thus the fact that 'I' supports everything, from alpha to omega, the universal nature of this 'I', is built into the Sanskrit understanding and language. All ancient cultures were spiritual, in those times, this truth might have had a universal and well recognized identity. This could be the basis and the answer to your good question.

----

29. 'I' with body-mind association= *Jiva**
'I' without body-mind association= *Atma*

"Whenever man limits his consciousness to body and mind, he is called *Jiva, or Jivatma,* otherwise, he is absolutely independent of these two-which are always acting or reacting. Unconditioned consciousness or awareness *which expresses itself in various shapes and forms is all One, whether it be an insect, a big boar, a big man, there is no difference whatever.*"

- Sri Nisargadatta Maharaj[18]

*with the attendant maya, essence of the self.

Q　:　*So, in our present condition of having come under maya, we are the Jiva, and not the Atma, right?*

A　:　Correct, we are the *Jiva* only.

Q　:　*So, in every stone, every insect, the very same essence, the primordial, 'I' is there as the life essence?*

A　:　Right, you have to digest this truth, then we will have greater unity with the whole of life, the whole of this mysterious nature.

----

30. Loneliness vis-à-vis Aloneness

1. 'The lonely bird', 'the bird of aloneness'.

2. Many people are lonely in life, especially in Western societies, which are more individual centered, rather than family centered.

3. The solution for such loneliness is the shifting of our consciousness from 'The lonely bird' to 'The bird of aloneness'.

4. Difference between loneliness and aloneness.

Sankara: "It is so sad to observe that human beings, whether they are young or old, married or unmarried, with friends or bereft of them, are so utterly lonely. Many of us, may have observed this sad phenomenon, but may not have lingered to ponder over the universality of this human malaise. Why is this so, are we going crazy as a species? Or, is this age, a particularly desolate one, in so far as as our inner life is concerned? Or, is all this morbid thinking? Some of you may even be developing this cynical disposition-seeing the universality of the human condition of loneliness. I maintain that most of us will be able to gain freedom from such loneliness-if we will but pay more attention to this problem and if we will be patient to study it further, along the lines shown by the master Sri J. Krishnamurti. In this Tat Tvam Asi retreat we deeply go into this univerasal malaise, and if we are sincere, we may well gain a liberating insight and freedom from such loneliness, once and for all. Having been surviving on sensory stimulations, our basic problem may well be traced to limitless and excessive extroversion, much to the detriment of our inner life. If we will but find peace within ourselves, we may be rid of loneliness, once and for all. *But the question is, are we serious enough to seek and find that inner peace and contentent?* In this retreat, there will be opportunities for finding that lasting peace within ourselves."

31. 'Tat Tvam Asi' Birds in the *Mundaka Upanishad* (1)

Dvā suparṇā sayujā sakhāyā
samānaṁ vṛkṣaṁ pariṣasvajāte |
tayoranyaḥ pippalaṁ svādvattya-
naśnannanyo abhicākaśīti || |

'Two birds' = Individual *self (Jiva)*, Cosmic Self *(Atma)*.
Sayujā=closely related, *Sakhāyā*=very much alike,
anaśnan=refrains from eating. *Abhicākaśīti* = watches like a
detached spectator=*Sākṣhī*.

Sankara: "Prema will rely on the commentary of Swami Lokeswarananda of the Ramakrishna mission, as he explains the sloka of this *Mundaka Upanishad* in such a simple way that all will understand."[6]:

"The two birds are always together on the same tree, which is the body. Both birds have beautiful plumes and are similar to each other. One of them eats the sweet as well as bitter fruits; the other simply looks on without eating anything. The Upanishad is again explaining, how the individual *self* and the cosmic Self, the *Atma*, are relating to each other. One bird is engrossed, eating different fruits, sometimes happy and sometimes suffering, but the other bird simply watches, uninvolved. In the same way, the cosmic Self, the *Atma*, is always calm, and self-composed. It is merely a witness. The individual *self* however is restless. It is at the mercy of the desires and is happy or unhappy, according to its experiences. Subject to the conditions in which it lives, it is tossed between pleasure and pain, thus, it is always changing. *The paradox is that these two are not different. They behave and function differently, but in fact, they are one and the same."* **(Prema)**

32. 'Tat Tvam Asi' Birds in the *Mundaka Up* (2)

Samāne vṛkṣe puruṣo nimagno'
nīśayā śocati muhyamānaḥ |
juṣṭaṁ yadā paśyatyanyamīśa
masya mahimānamiti vītaśokaḥ ||

The *Jiva (self)* is on the same tree (body), as the cosmic Self. It is steeped in ignorance and is overcome by a sense of helplessness and is unhappy. However, when this *Jiva (self)*, falls silent, the cosmic Self, bereft of attributes, emerges in place of this *Jiva* and goes beyond all sorrow and realizes Itself as the majestic cosmic Self.

"The individual *self* is with the cosmic Self, the *Atma,* on the same tree, which is obviously the body. Yet, so long as it is engrossed in pleasure seeking and brooding, it is ignorant of its Divine nature. That is why it suffers from sorrow, but this same *self*, becomes free of sorrow, when its pleasure seeking and senses centered activities subside - then the cosmic Self, the *Atma*, the conscious presence, arises and is another dimension of the individual *self*. The cosmic Self has no sorrow, but is full of clarity, peace, joy and unity with all life." (**Prema**)

In the retreat, there was the chanting of both the Upanishadic *slokas – 'Dwa suparna and Samane Vrkshe'* (Audio File S32A.wav).

Q   :   *Looking closely at the topic 32, wherein you have given the second sloka pertaining to the two Tat Tvam Asi birds, - my question is, why is the watching bird referred to as the Self with a capital S, and the active seeking bird spelt with the small italicized self? Can you throw some more light on this distinction?*

A : The italicized, *self*, stands for the thinking and feeling *self*. The Self which is used with capital S, stands for the cosmic Self, the *Atma*, or the Knowing Self, this Knowing Self is completely outside time, whereas the individual *self*, is in time.

---

33. The Masters on the 'Tat Tvam Asi' Birds

One Bird (Self- 'I'-sense, awareness) only watches every happening in consciousness. It can also watch the *Jiva (self)* (the other miserable bird), suffering and enjoying. Out of this watching arises *self* - Knowing.

(*Pākā āmi* = 'Witnessing bird' ('ripe' I), *Kāñcā āmi* = 'Eating bird' ('unripe' I) in Bengali, Sri Ramakrishna Paramahamsa)

Adi Sankaracharya: Witnessing Bird = '*Parameshwara*' = '*nitya, shuddha, buddha, mukta, swabhavaha*' (Divine nature)

Q : *We see in this topic that two illustrious masters are throwing light on the two birds of the Mundaka Up, so is this Upanishadic metaphor thousands of years old?*

A : You are right, it is very ancient. The Upanishads are by themselves thousands of years old. And these masters, they give meaning to the *sutras*, the principles and metaphors in the Upanishads.

Q : *When the master Sri Ramakrishna Paramahamsa uses the metaphor of the fruit, for the immature self and the mature Self, can we interpret this as the ripe fruit, falling off from the tree, implying complete detachment, and freedom from all bondages?*

A : Actually what you have anticipated is incorporated in the *mrtyunjaya mantra* where liberation is the focal theme and they talk of the vegetable cucumber, dangling from a creeper. And then when it ripens fully, it just breaks off from the creeper and naturally falls to the ground. And that tantamounts to liberation in good time when the thing ripens and yes, therefore the analogy is very apt that there is a time for the ripening and the emphasis that this time is after 60, gains more credence from the point of view of Ramakrishna Paramahamsa's interpretation.

Q : *Then, we do understand the beautiful and appropriate metaphor of Ramakrishna Paramahamsa of the ripe and unripe 'I'. However when we come to that illustrious master Adi Sankararacharya, his interpretation is astounding. How would you now proceed to convince us that Adi Sankararacharya's interpretation of the witnessing bird is as lofty as he presents it to be?*

A : You see, each of us will have to do our own enquiry and our own *sadhana*. If we don't do this, we will just be blind second hand believers and second hand followers. Now, when Adi Sankaracharya, describes the witnessing bird as *Parameswara*, as the Supreme Being having the adjectives of *nitya, shuddha, buddha, mukta, swabhavaha*, we have to work this out in our own mind as a result of our *sadhana*. If we do not do this, it will remain as a mere belief for us-which may be a good thing provisionally, but that cannot be the final form of our understanding of what Adi Sankaracharya is saying.

Nitya - means eternal, that is, its position is outside of time. Therefore nothing ever happens to that witnessing bird.

Shuddha - It is *vimala* - It is completely stainless. Because it is outside of time

It is *buddha* - that means, it is awakened, illumined.

It is *mukta* - that means, it is liberated from every tyrannical sorrow.

Swabhavahah - that is his real nature.

That is, it is *nitya, shudha, buddha and mukta* - that is the real nature of the witnessing bird. *Swabhava* of the bird, nature of that bird.

We have to work and contemplate and we have to work this out which is why we are here in a retreat like this. So, we have the time to do this kind of deep thinking and introspection.

Your Personal Meditative Journey from your *what is* to the *Atma*

Example: When your *what is*, is 'loneliness'.
Journey from 'loneliness' to aloneness *(Atma)*.

34. Krishnamurti's Meditations

"The soil in which the meditative mind can begin is the soil of everyday life, the strife, the pain and the fleeting joy. It must begin there, and bring order, and from there move endlessly. But if you are concerned only with making order, then that very order will bring about its own limitation and the mind will be its prisoner."

- J. Krishnamurti in 'Meditations' [19]

Q : *This beautiful and moving piece of Krishnamurti's writing seems to imply, that he places far more emphasis on our daily life, on self - Knowing, rather than on God, Atma, or on Brahman, or on the scriptures. He seems to be an original philosopher, or thinker, than a religious teacher. Is this right?*

A : You are right, he never spoke from the position of a Hindu or religious teacher. He was original and radical, you may even say, he was a revolutionary teacher, who challenged spiritual progress when the same was claimed along rigid traditional lines. His was the way of dispassionate inner enquiry, *self*-critical *self* - Knowing, awareness, what he had called, *choiceless awareness of what is.*

Q : *And is it your suggestion that, we should concentrate on the problems in our daily life, start learning by study and enquiry and also not make the mistake of being obsessed with success, where the resolution of the problem is concerned?*

A : Right, this precisely, is my idea and I go more deeply into this, later in the retreat.

35. Real Security is the *Atma*, *Jiva* is full of insecurity

- The *Jiva* (human nature) is the ever busy other bird, eating all the bitter and sweet fruits in the tree (body). In *artha and kama* spheres, *Jiva* suffers and enjoys, whereas, Self (Divine nature) is 'missing', dormant, too much behind the scenes.

- The 'seeking bird' *(Jiva)* is full of insecurity, whereas as soon as the *Jiva* falls silent, the identity shifts to the *Atma* ('witness bird'), you become detached and grounded on the shore of 'rock-like security'. *Jiva* is attached. Self is detached.

Q : *So, just to get things straight, it seems, when the activity of the Jiva (self) subsides, the background, the Atma, which was eclipsed by the incessant frenetic activity of the Jiva, comes into relief and the Jiva, discovers who he is, in reality. Is this what is actually happening?*

A : Yes, this is what is happening, thus the two Tat Tvam Asi birds, are in truth, the mature *(Atma)* and immature versions *(self)* of the same consciousness of the *Jiva*.

----

36. The Abode of the *Jiva* - 'Memory Lane'

Throughout life the *Jiva* keeps on wandering up and down that single 'memory lane' - of its memories, pleasurable and painful experiences. This journey is very limited, stifling, suffocating. The body may travel to all the seven continents, but the *Jiva* never gives up this one 'street'. Can the *Jiva*, get out of his rut?

Q   :   *This is the picture of a solitary woman walking in a narrow lonely street-what are you trying to convey?*

A   :   As the text accompanying this picture explains, by and large, humans seem to be trapped in their memory lane, all the time, making a solitary walk from one event to another, things which already happened and obviously, this is very tiresome and boring, which is the reason we are perpetually seeking escapes from this monotonous walk. We want to get out of this rut-we do this through our escapes, etc.

Q   :   *Can I now say that creative people, whether in the arts or in the sciences, are the ones, who are no more imprisoned and wandering in this one street of their past, but have disconnected themselves and are now on an endless voyage of discovery?*

A   :   You are absolutely right, all the intelligent people and the creative people are not perpetually walking in this memory lane, they are all out of it and have abundant energy, for examining, learning about a hundred new things. Probably, barring these people, the rest of humanity may be in this prison of the memory lane.....

37. The *Jiva* as a Lonely Wanderer in the 'Memory Lane'

Q : *Is this a picture to drive home the same point?*

A : Absolutely, and also we must see if we are that solitary walker!

Q : *Now that you have given, such a beautiful metaphor of this lonely street. Endlessly walking up and down this silly street-is this not the root cause of boredom?*

A : Exactly, boredom arises, from perpetually walking up and down this dull and uninteresting street. Some houses are pleasurable, some are very painful. You can visit these houses, once in a way, but can't be walking up and down all your life!

----

38. *Jiva* Experiences Emptiness and Loneliness

1. *Jiva* first perceives an inner emptiness, inner loneliness, which is the bitter fruit of its *self* centered activities. This is frightening for the *Jiva*. It is afraid of being that, so flees from it into various outer activities. Through these activities, *Jiva* tries to find an escape from this emptiness and loneliness.

2. *Jiva* feels lonely, because *Jiva* is separated from life. Actually *Jiva* is that loneliness only, so might as well be that. Wave is lonely, small and separated, not the Ocean, which is full, complete and infinite.

Q : *Most people feel that they are a 'nobody' in life, yes this is true. But, are you suggesting that there are moments of acute perception, when the self, perceives this emptiness, this loneliness?*

A : Yes, I am saying that while many may have the haunting feeling that comes on and off, that they are a 'nobody', sometimes, such a perception also becomes very acute, that the *self* is utterly empty, utterly lonely. We must concentrate on these acute perceptions only, as and when they actually occur. These are generally fleeting, but painful inner experiences.

To give greater meaning and reality to what we are examining, we also need to understand that these acute perceptions that the *self* has, need not always pertain to that emptiness or loneliness. In the particularly striking example, we have taken *what is*, to be, a certain, burning context in consciousness, it is this, emptiness and loneliness, that is all. This *what is*, which is always very difficult for the *self* to handle, could also be some other problem, like, fear, or jealousy, or anger, or lust, or hate, or revenge, or the fact of perpetual lying, or gluttony, etc.

Going back, my point is that, the *self* being unable to face this loneliness, this emptiness, now tries to fill this emptiness with various respectable activities, so that the *self,* feels secure once again.

Q : *Why should they always be respectable activities, after all many people make themselves happy just by going to clubs, movies, etc., and some of them may be doing this just to fill their void. Others of course, may be seeking this pleasure for the sheer enjoyment of it (I hope nothing is 'wrong' with this kind of an enjoyment!).*

A : Yes, you are right. It is not always that the despondent *self* seeks respectability. Sometimes, it can flee from its own emptiness, by indulging in various other activities, in which the *self* is absent, so to speak. Children are most happy when they are playing, for example, because the *self* is absent at such times.

Q : *It appears that the self, by its very nature is separative, self-enclosing, self-isolating, as all these seem to be its innate tendencies. And respite from the consequence of all this, which is loneliness, may come only when the activities of the self themselves subside?*

A : Yes, the answer to loneliness is the cessation of the activity of the *self.* There is a lot for us to learn here, this is a very fertile field in which *self* – Knowing can bloom.

----

39. How can the *Jiva* free itself of this Emptiness, Loneliness?

1. Without solving this persistent problem of loneliness and emptiness, we have no foundation for right relationship with anybody.

2. J. Krishnamurti has thrown the greatest light on this problem of how the *Jiva* may tackle this loneliness and emptiness. He calls the *Jiva*, 'observer', 'thinker' and 'experiencer'. Note the terminology.

3. We will next go directly to what the master J. Krishnamurti has to say.

Q : *Regarding first point, many of us, may not even be aware that we have to set things right within ourselves, in order to qualify for harmonious relationships.*

A : Absolutely right, we have *to put our house in order*, as Krishnamurti would say. This creates the basis for being related to the world, otherwise our consciousness will never be whole and integral.

Q : *It can also happen that people use each other, to fill their own inner void. For example, this can happen between a husband and wife or between two friends, where the company of the 'other' is so interesting and exciting, because it gives a release from the inner loneliness, inner boredom and inner emptiness.*

A : Wonderfully put. This is surely another example of how the *self* flees from its boredom and loneliness. This is the phenomenon in consciousness that we are now looking at. *Though it is a widespread phenomenon, it is so little observed and therefore so little studied, so little understood.*

Q : *So are you going to present a radical solution for the widespread problem of human loneliness and emptiness?*

A : That is why we are gathered here, so, let us look at the solution, which now follows. We have to pay very close attention here. Importantly, the *self* can free itself of this mess, only when the dimension of awareness, comes into play and resolves the conflict, between the *self*, as the 'observer' and the *self* as the 'observed'. This is extremely subtle, so we have to be extremely attentive.

Q : *You have introduced some new terms that Krishnamurti uses and this calls for some clarification, because his usage and the meaning which he attributes to certain terms like, 'observer', 'thinker', 'experiencer' should coincide with our special vocabulary, introduced so far and not be different from the way these terms are used by us. For, if there is a difference, there is going to be conflict and confusion in our thinking and understanding. So we need to sort this out at the very beginning. Let us take Krishnamurti's term, 'observer'. All of us, may suppose that, by the term, 'observer', Krishnamurti, may be referring to the witness bird. Is this true?*

A : No, not at all. By the term, 'observer', Krishnamurti does not point to the witness consciousness, or the awareness. At this stage, the dimension of awareness has not yet come into the picture in this particular sequence of themes, concerning emptiness and loneliness.

By the term, 'observer' this master, is still referring only to what we would call the *self*, in our vocabulary. The witness consciousness has various names in the spiritual literature of India. Nisargadatta Maharaj, and the Hindu scriptures, use the expressions, awareness, *chit*, witness consciousness, *sakshi*, etc. Ramana Maharshi uses, for the most part, only Self *(Atma)*. Krishnamurti, never uses the phrase, witness consciousness, or *Atma*, he always sticks only to awareness.

So, here in this context, Krishnamurti is referring to the self, which has arisen like a sudden wave or sudden surge in the matrix of chitta, in the likeness of a 'policemen', to chastise and reform, the sudden wave or sudden surge of emptiness and loneliness, which manifested, just one fleeting instant before. This is an utterly futile chastisement, futile reformation, because the self as this 'observer', was, just one fleeting moment before, itself the 'observed', which in this instance is emptiness or loneliness. Both are sequential bubbles, bulges or surges, one following the other in quick succession in time in that matrix of the chitta.

In terms of our very rewarding metaphor of the Tat Tvam Asi birds, this will be an instance of the eating bird, taking up the role of the reformer, 'policeman', as the 'observer', in response, to a surge in *chitta*, which happened just one fleeting moment ago, a surge, which is the 'observed'. We are talking of a context, in which the *self*, is struggling with reality in consciousness, in *chitta*, it is the 'observer', and it is unable to deal with the 'observed', which may be emptiness, loneliness, fear, boredom, lust, anger, etc. The dimension of awareness, the witnessing bird, has not yet come into the picture, in this Krishnamurti's meditation.

---

40. The *Jiva* has to cease being an observer of this loneliness

These are the words of the master J. Krishnamurti:

1. "So far we have approached it as the observer. Now the observer himself is empty, alone, is lonely. Can he do anything about it? Obviously he cannot.

2. "Then his relationship to it is entirely different than that of the relationship of the observer. He has that aloneness. He is in that state in which there is no verbalization that 'I am empty'.

Sankara: We will understand what Krishnamurti is talking about, if we apply the algae-man metaphor of the *Jiva*. The *Jiva* is shrouded in *maya* and duality, having lived a *self*-centered and body-centered life, it sees everything as a polarization or duality or battle or separation between itself (as the body, as the *self*) and various kinds of 'adversaries'- in the form of people, situations, it's own anger, etc. We must remember that witness consciousness or awareness *(Atma)* is very much here in all this going on, but 'buried' as the *Jiva* is the *Atma*, covered over by *maya* (algae). In spite of the implicit presence of the *Atma*, within the *Jiva*, yet, the Jiva, operates in life, as the body-centered *self* only, so, sees, duality here too as the 'observer', after having momentarily experienced, loneliness and emptiness. This experience of emptiness and loneliness does not last, so fades away quite soon. But, immediately, in the wake of this, arises, another kind of experience. What is this? In this experience, the *Jiva*, in a moment of unawareness, forgetting that, it had that experience of emptiness and loneliness, now, takes on the role of the 'observer' of this loneliness and emptiness, *objectifying it fully, as though, the Jiva, had no share in that former experience of loneliness.* Yet, the *Jiva*, exclaims, 'I am empty', 'I do not want to be this', etc. This perception is due to *self*-deception, which is a happening process in consciousness. The liberation from this quandary, will come, only when the *Atma*, buried within the *Jiva,* is pressed into service, as awareness. With awareness, made to function, for the first time, the *Atma*, will realize, it was that emptiness, that loneliness, *and so the externalization and 'objectification' of that original feeling, will be recognized to be a subjective feeling*, from which the *Jiva*, will now have no justification to stand apart from that former experience of loneliness.

----

41. *Jiva* has to Settle in the Pit of Loneliness and Emptiness

3. "The moment he* verbalizes or externalizes it, he* is different from that. So, when the verbalization ceases, when the experience ceases as experiencing loneliness, when he* ceases to run away, when he* is entirely lonely, his* relationship is itself loneliness, he* is himself, that. When he* realizes that fully, surely, that emptiness, loneliness, ceases to be."

- J. Krishnamurti[20]

*Jiva

Sankara: The *self* arose in the matrix of *chitta*, it was a *fleeting happening* in that flowing movement of *chitta*, like a sudden wave bulging locally in a moving river. The *self,* arose, in response to another *happening, which was also fleeting*, namely *that* *momentary feeling of emptiness, that momentary feeling of loneliness.This momentary feeling is the result of excessive self-centred activity, excessive extroversion.*

The *Atma* which is beyond *chitta* and the *self,* is nevertheless, just, behind the scenes, in the background, as it were, watching and knowing. As the *Atma* rolls back and stands back, the drama in *chitta,* so too, the drama of the *self,* greatly subsides. So long as the *Atma,* docs not stand back and roll back, as the witness, the limited *self,* as the 'observer', as the 'thinker', as the 'experiencer' tries to solve all his problems 'himself'. Of course he fails, we all know this. *The answer to his problems lies in the cessation of the activities of the self and this beautifully happens, when the Atma, rolls back.*

----

42. Loneliness vis-à-vis Aloneness

4. "But loneliness is entirely different from Aloneness. That loneliness must be passed, to be alone. Loneliness is not comparable with Aloneness. The man who knows loneliness, can never know that which is Alone. Are you in that state of Aloneness? *Our minds are not integrated to be Alone. The very process of the mind is separative and that which separates, knows loneliness.*"

- J. Krishnamurti[20]

Sankara: This specific meditation of *facing loneliness, sinking into this loneliness, without the desire to be free of loneliness,* is something which is new, as a way of meditation. Nevertheless, though it may appear hard in the beginning, sincere seekers, after some initial failures, will indeed be able to be that very loneliness, from which they as the *self*, have separated themselves (as though they are different from that loneliness) and are then 'searching' for a solution for their 'loneliness'.

In this Krishnamurti meditation, which we have called *amanaska yoga*, the seeker, by contemplation, has to digest and understand that desire to be free of that loneliness or even the desire to be that loneliness, is the greatest obstacle to be that loneliness-without any verbalization. *Amanaska yoga* is another name for *choiceless awareness of what is*. In the present example, *what is*, is loneliness. In this so-called *choiceless awareness of what is*, it is implied that, we have become free of the desire nature, for only when we are free of our desire to achieve any result, can we indeed be choiceless.

The thing to be discovered is this: That, the loneliness, from which we have separated ourselves is not different from us and that in fact we are precisely that very loneliness. *This insightful discovery can happen, only when desire and verbalization do not come in the way of the observation of that loneliness, the experiencing of that loneliness.* Then, as we sink into that loneliness and abide in that, we would know, what it is to be alone, having nothing to do with any thing which is going on in consciousness. Once this happens, because the *self*, stops struggling, we will have a strange calmness and silence; for by then, we would have landed on the ground of aloneness, which is the ground of inner wellness.

Thereafter, loneliness can never again be experienced by us, because in experiencing loneliness, as it is, the separative movement of the *self*, which is the root cause of loneliness, is discovered and it suffers suspension, through the mere experiencing of this *what is*. It is then that we become integrated, whole, without the *self*, working in a cunning way, for its own imagined permanence and security.

----

43. From Loneliness to Aloneness

5. "Aloneness is never separative. However the *Jiva*, the 'thinker', the 'observer', the 'experiencer' while being utterly lonely, in that loneliness, without any separation from that loneliness, without running away from it, comes to lose that loneliness for ever and comes to abide in Aloneness". (Witnessing bird, *Atma*).

- J. Krishnamurti[20]

Sankara: By abiding in loneliness, which is the *what is,* rather than by observing and verbalizing this loneliness, duality between the *self* and the observed loneliness, comes to an end and we move from a fragmented consciousness (the eating bird), to a whole, well integrated consciousness and settle as the *Atma,* because of this wholeness, bereft of all conflict. The entire meditation, namely the *choiceless awareness of what is*, results in the silencing of the *self*, and the consequent awakening that we are the witnessing awareness. As a witnessing awareness, we are alone, serene, because the activity in duality, in which the *self* was caught, comes to a halt through this meditation. *Desirelessness and absence of verbalization, are necessary, for loneliness to undergo this metamorphosis into aloneness.*

---

44. Similarly, a Transformation from 'Duality' To 'Wholeness'

- From fear to fearlessness

- From guilt, conflict, lust, jealousy, lying, to facing and accepting the presence of demonic energies in yourself and forgiving yourself.

- From anger, violence, hatred, conflict, fights in relationship to seeing the 'other' as the '*self*'.

- From depression, self-deprecation to contentment, equanimity, inner wholeness.

Sankara: For each human being at a certain time, there may be a certain contentious *what is*, so one has to identify that first. The method of coming to grips with this *what is*, is the same as what we followed when *what is*, was loneliness. The same kind of meditation, namely, *choiceless awareness of what is*, accompanied by *the giving up of all verbalization*, will lead to *the ending of separation between* what was observed and the *self*, as the observer. It was this very observing and experiencing *self*, which was one fleeting moment before, the thing that was observed. Because of the swiftness of these happenings in consciousness, the right relationship between the *self* as the 'observer and experiencer', and what it observed and verbalized could not be discovered and understood. Consequently, the *self*, befooled by this process called *maya*, succumbed to the delusion and the belief that it is an independent 'observer' and 'experiencer', which would like a mastery over what it observed, whereas, the truth of the matter is that what was observed and experienced is pushed away, as though it is wholly different from the same *self, which has now taken on the more secure mantle of the observer and experiencer.*

This meditation is the monumental contribution of Sri J. Krishnamurti.

First Day (Chapter - I), 2nd 'Tat Tvam Asi' Meditation

Meditative Journey in *self* - Knowing from Loneliness to Aloneness

----

Chapter II

By Being the Atma,
you can
Identify, Observe and Understand the *Jiva*

Identifying the *Jiva (self)*
Topics 1 to 19

Two 'Tat Tvam Asi' Birds
Topics 20 to 22

Understanding the *Jiva (self)* and the *Atma*
Topics 23 to 49

Q : *I am tempted to take a second look at the titles in Ch II: identifying, observing, and understanding the self. In this topic, I feel, I am in a science laboratory, where I identify an object of study, like let us say a living cell or amoeba, then I go on to observe it, and then understand it. So, here, obviously the object of study is the self (whatever this may be), so how do I find this object called self?*

A : I will have to say, this *self* is actually not an object of study, for this is the essence of even the observing subject, the observer, the *Atmic* light which is observing, the complex web of goings on in one's consciousness…

Q : *Does this mean that I am the subject and also the object? If so, this is new and extremely paradoxical, for the subject and object are always considered to be different. What do you have to say to this confusion?*

A : In our common sense world, the subject and object are separate and unconnected, but whenever we go very deeply into the workings of nature, like observation at the level of the atomic world, then the subject and object influence each other- as in quantum mechanics, for example, where the very observation colors the thing observed and modifies the observed object, but we cannot go more deeply into this at this stage at least, maybe we can go into this more deeply during one of the separate group discussions.

Q : *Let me suppose that I am standing in front of a mirror. Then my physical form, the body, is the subject, and the object becomes the reflection of the body in the mirror. Is this reflection not the same self, which is standing in front of the mirror? If that is so, what do I learn by looking at myself?*

A : Your question presupposes that, you already know yourself well enough, and so by looking at the mirror image, you automatically recognize yourself, so you probably mean to say that identifying the *self* is not a serious problem at all.

However, it is never as simple as this physical analogy makes us believe, because physical things like the body can be easily perceived by the eyes, but things happening in consciousness are not easy to observe and perceive. For example, you may be a very vain person, having a strong desire to be physically attractive, and this desire to be beautiful and attractive can be so strong that it will never actually give you a chance to discover that something could be amiss with, your face, say, your nose could be crooked. So, unless you actually take an impartial view of yourself, as you are in your thinking and feeling; you are never going to discover, what you actually are in reality - *because how you look in reality, will always be different from how you wish to appear to others.So, this identification of the self has to be carefully done, without desire dominating us.*

Secondly we looking at our *self* in the mirror is too gross an example of looking at the *self.* We will go into this more deeply with each passing topic. I hope I am making myself clear.

Q : *Yes, you are. Regarding, observing the self, when we observe ourselves, we find that there are some, not so nice things about ourselves, so do you want us to observe even these 'not so nice things'? On the contrary, when we observe ourselves, and find these 'not so nice things' about ourselves, we would like to improve ourselves, better ourselves and feel good about it. So, my question is, what should we be doing in such cases, when we are deluding ourselves with ideals which are a far cry from our reality?*

A : Yes, obviously we have to observe all the things, irrespective of what opinion society may have about that particular thing, which may be disturbing to us. Realize that, that so called 'bad thing' came into existence, and it could not come into existence, without the will of the Divine, mandating it, so we may as well be compassionate to those so-called dark things and accept even that as part of ourselves, namely the *self.*

Q : *The very word, 'observation' reminds us of scientists, looking through microscopes or telescopes, and minuteness of observation is implied. Are you then meaning that we too should be observing ourselves so very carefully, so as to pick up all the subtle nuances of the self?*

A : Indeed, minute observation, but without effort, because effort will distort what we observe. There should be an attitude of seeing things as they are, not as we wish them to be.

Q : *After dwelling on identification and observation of the self, you have moved on to the third level of understanding the self. What is going to come out of this understanding of the self? Are you implying that something good is going to happen to us, that is, to the self, which we are - as a result of this understanding?*

A : By understanding this *self*, you will come to know that, this is not what you are, even though, you imagined, that you were this only. This *self*, will never give you a durable sense of *self*.

Q : *You have now put the self, under a microscope and I find that the self is full of negative manifestations, like anger, jealousy, selfishness, greed, lust, dishonesty. You mean to say that the human self has nothing positive about it?*

A : Oh no, there are obviously, also positive things, like consideration, empathy, because the *Atma* has flowed into the field of the body-consciousness. But do not make the mistake of identifying yourself with this *self*, this is at best a 'non-*self*'. You are the *Atma* only, and this *self* is but a temporary passing show, a shadow of the *Atma*, in the troubled waters of the agitated body-mind.

Q : *Why are you giving so much importance to the self? In fact, I find that in India and maybe even the world over, the emphasis is mostly on the guru and/or on God, and their endless virtues and excellences. Why then are you making such a pole shift in the emphasis from God the great to self the mean?*

A : This is a very perceptive question, which takes us to the difference between religion in its populist form and religion in its esoteric and pristine aspect. Religions like Christianity, Judaism, Hinduism, Sikhism, Islam have mostly taken populist forms, which always have a mass appeal. This does not go against the fact that, even in the Christian, Islamic, Hindu and Judaic faiths, there are esoteric aspects, which mostly refer to the inner life of the devotees, rather than the externalized forms of *guru* and God. When it comes to Buddhism, Jainism and the inner essence of Hinduism, the emphasis is entirely on the *self* to begin with and then going on to the Self *(Atma)*, as the imperceptible inner aspect of the Divine. *In the populist versions of most religions, 'God' or the Divine has been externalized, and this goes against the inner Divine nature of man. Here in this retreat, we are reminding seekers that instead of* *beginning with guru and God, it will be much better for us to begin with the seeker and his self-for this is much closer to the Source.*

---

1. 'You must somehow begin from the... the other shore'

"In all this movement, you must somehow begin from the other end, from the other shore, and not always be concerned with this shore or how to cross the river.

"You must take a plunge into the water, not knowing how to swim. And the beauty of meditation is that you never know where you are, where you are going, what the end is."

- J. Krishnamurti in 'Meditations' [13]

Q : *In this meditation from Krishnamurti, we must realize that most of us suffer from the fear of the unknown, so how would you expect us to take the plunge, as it were and reach out to the other shore?*

A : We have two dimensions, a human dimension, to which all your logic applies, the fear, etc. However, we are also a timeless being, a witness, with infinite Divine possibilities. Because, we are always with a swarm of thoughts and feelings, we are never able to know ourselves, as we are. This witness is our deeper nature, and this whole retreat is devoted to the discovery of this inner essence, called the *Atma* or the 'I am'. It is the realm of infinite possibilities, but never clearly recognized.

Q : *So, is it like pressing the emergency button, which may be always there, but which we are unaware of?*

A : Right, we are unconscious of the mechanism of how some of our difficult problems get resolved. We call that grace, result of prayer, blessing, etc. However, this Divine source is also our very Self. We do not know this, we cannot be aware of it as we can be aware of the sun, the moon and the trees. This retreat is intended to help us to get at this treasure, which we are already. It is not a new treasure or a new blessing which will come to you from the outside world, from another source.

Q : *Why does Krishnamurti say the, "the beauty of meditation is that, you never know where you are, where you are going, what the end is?"*

A : Our limited human nature makes us seek security, everlastingly, we need to be constantly assured that we will find some great treasure, if not now, at least in the future. However, when our Divine nature comes into play, as it surely does in these meditations, then we are naturally fearless, rather than afraid. In fact all creative minds have this enormous courage and spirit of adventure-without this, they would never have discovered, all the wonderful things they discovered. Theirs was a journey into the unknown. So, Krishnamurti says, this is the nature of these meditative journeys, they are mysterious journeys into the bosom of truth, into the unknown, without any guarantee of security.

----

2. 'Is Gold Itself Crooked?'

"Is Gold Itself crooked? But when you make an ornament out of it - that is, you give Gold a form and name, it becomes distorted and crooked!

"Just by giving yourself a name, you became crooked! Gold as such is not stupid! Gold means the Self without name and form. But when this Gold was transformed into an ornament, and given a name, the distortion and stupidity started!"

- Sri Nisargadatta Maharaj[21]

Q : *Is the analogy of gold, referring to the Atma?*

A : Yes, indeed. It also refers to the witnessing bird, the ocean, in the metaphors, we have been discussing.

Q : *The adverbs and adjectives used by Maharaj, do they refer then to the little self?*

A : Correct, the little *self,* the *Jiva* is being referred to, and it is sometimes stupid, because of its limitations and attachments.

This *sutra* from Maharaj, may be memorized and remembered, because it portrays our true Self, the *Atma*, in very graphic terms and how the *Jiva* is a crooked caricature of the *Atma*.

----

3. Meditational Methods for Parts I & II

Part I (Knowing the *Jiva (self)*):
Krishnamurti's Choiceless Awareness of *what is*, which leads to the calming of consciousness (silencing of the *Jiva (self)*)

Part II (Self-Realization):
Sravana, Manana, Nidhidhyasana
(Listening, Reflection, Abidance in the *Atma*)

Q : *So, if I remember right, you had defined Part I as chapters II, III, and IV, and Part II as chapters V, VI, and VII. Am I right?*

A : Yes, I had defined these two Parts that way only.

Q : *In this topic, you have adopted one kind of meditational method for Part I, and an entirely different meditational method for Part II. Why is this so?*

A : Every genuine teacher, in the farther reaches of the spiritual life, namely, *moksha* has a different approach and methodology.

The essential nature of my approach is its systematic character.

This systematic analytical method is in fact a hall-mark of several Hindu scriptures. In my case, this probably comes from having been a researcher in theoretical physics in my formative younger years, for a full decade. Let me explain how I approach the whole quest for *moksha*.

There are two Parts in this quest, Part I and Part II. Part I is concerned with bringing *order* in the realm of the *self*, and this *order* arises, the moment the *self* is calmed and silenced. Part II is the discovery of the Divine, understanding, who is the Divine? where is the Divine? what in fact, is the Divine?

Q : *I understand this, but is there a necessity for the difference in your meditational methods for Part I and Part II? And is this what we have got to understand?*

A : So, let me get on with what I was saying. If the *self* is not calmed and silenced, the *self* is not truly qualified to approach the Divine through the path of understanding. The reason is that without the calming and silencing of the *self*, the spiritual and *Atmic* intelligence *(prajnya)* that is necessary for fathoming the Divine, may not become available to us, even though that special intelligence *(prajnya)* is always and ever with us, but in some dormant unavailable form. In other words, Part I must be completed, before Part II can bloom.

Please note that often in life, the *self*, even when it is not calmed and silenced, is still seen to be approaching the Divine, *not on the path of understanding, but rather on the path of devotion and faith.* You see this happening all around you. *Such approaches to the Divine, through devotion and faith (though basically only because of fear and desire), are not on par with the approach to the Divine through the path of understanding, which is our present path.*

In Part I, we rely on J. Krishnamurti's *choiceless awareness of what is* and of the ways of the *self*, as it is more efficacious than the traditional methods for calming and silencing the *self* - this has been my own experience. The traditional methods are poorer, because in them there is no *self* - Knowing, and where there is no real *self* - Knowing, there is every possibility of self-deception.

Just as an experimental scientist working in a laboratory is also required to go to the library and read some research journals, after he has completed his experiments, for better understanding his own findings in the laboratory; in the same way, the *mumukshu* too has to read the scriptures or the writings of the sages, as this is necessary for giving him that full blown understanding, bereft of all doubts, contradictions and confusions. So, in Part II, one has to study the scriptures and check, to see if our experiences tally with what the scriptures are saying.

Q : *I want to recapitulate the real meanings and significances of the two terms what is, and choiceless awareness, as these are J. Krishnamurti's special vocabulary and you seem to use them frequently in this retreat.*

A : We have already seen that the *self* comes into existence in the context of a certain life situation, say one, triggering anger, lying, or jealousy, etc. That troublesome life situation, that difficult moment which we are never able to handle, is: *what is*, meaning *what really is there, at that moment.* Importantly, this *what is*, is ever changing, never fixed, and this change happens both within our consciousness as also out there in the world at large. It was mentioned earlier that only in the context of *what is*, can we study the *self.*

Choiceless awareness is always there, in the background, this is who we are, but because we are constantly extroverted, we have lost sight of who we are, so in this extroversion, we take ourselves to be the body, or 'someone', 'some big guy', we think ourselves to be, etc. The *self* has likes and dislikes, so would like to make choices in all its activities, but *choiceless awareness*, which is the witnessing bird, in our Tat Tvam, Asi metaphor, is always shining brilliantly without any choice. It was described in sloka 22 in Ch. XIII of the Bhagavad Gita, where we understood it to be the Sovereign Supreme, the Unconcerned Witness, the Sanctioner, the Enjoyer, the Protector, the *Paramatma*, and being beyond the *self.*

----

4. Exploratory Approach of Trial & Error - 1

Throughout history, man discovered the natural laws only through an exploratory approach of trial & error.

Ex: Wheel, fire, aero planes, wave-particle duality. You learnt to talk, walk, sing, drive, only this way-by trial and error.

So even here we must rely on the same exploratory approach finally resulting in insights and understanding. By following, obeying and by having faith alone, you will not be able to go into the farther reaches of *dharma and moksha*.

Q : *All the discoveries in the life sciences or physical sciences or inventions in technology were presumably made by creative men and women, who had fiery imaginations and who were presumably relentlessly seeking and searching.*

However, when we come to the spiritual field, are you not implying that we will reach the goal of moksha only through this same kind of relentless search, this quest, this journey into the unknown, this creativity? Is this not what you are implying, when you say, go on an exploratory 'trial and error' path?

A : Right, I say that unless, you actively and vigorously seek this knowledge, this understanding, this clarity and realization, it will not come to you. If you remain a gullible believer, or a person of faith, then you will not get this in a first hand way.

The example which I have given may seem to create a block for you. From the history of the sciences, we know that behind all discoveries and inventions, there were creative and passionate people, so you may think, *only a chosen few* can get this-this is likely to be your block. The seeker's stumbling block may be his very perception, that

96

'I am not so creative, I am not so intelligent, so how can a mediocre person like me, get at this ultimate truth?'

This very thought and perception will be inimical to the discovery of the *Atma*. One has to be aware of this perception and consciously put it aside-because I am asking you to do this.

Importantly, though your outer personality may be intelligent or stupid, the *Atma*, which is your imperishable nature, being the essence of intelligence or *prajnya*, your whole objection that this quest for *moksha* maybe only for creative people, falls on it's face. You are already 'That', it is just that by the force of *maya*, you do not know this.

So, contrary to your fear and belief that this is 'difficult', it is in fact, meant for all, and especially after 60, the quest will become furious, and then when the seeking suddenly ends, you will know that the quest was after all not futile, because you have always only been 'That'.

Q : *Insights and understanding would only come after deep introspection and soul-searching?*

A : Yes, surely. The important thing is to get interested, make this a goal. While this being a goal after 60, is valid for all, it is only during the younger years, that it is less common to have this goal. The older you are the more qualified you are to pursue this. Once you start devoting time, start reflecting, then insights will pour in and astound you. Every insight is a sudden flash of understanding.

Q : *So what about the large number of people who are just on a path of belief or faith, and who do not ever question the truth of what the scriptures are saying?*

A : This seems to be an important question. Belief, faith are important qualifications for being on a path of *dharma*, on the path of some religion, but they are not of much use when it comes to the pursuit of *moksha* or liberation from all sorrow and pain. In the sphere of *moksha*, it is enquiry and understanding and the reading of the scriptures that will help. There are spiritual teachers on the plane of *dharma* and spiritual teachers on the plane of *moksha*. Masters on the plane of *dharma* will not say anything very significant, in so far as *moksha* is concerned. Whereas, masters and spiritual teachers in the sphere of *moksha* are not likely to say anything of value, for the sphere of *dharma*. So, you as a *mumukshu* or seeker must clearly understand that *dharma and moksha* are distinct in their own way.

Q : *There are surely a lot of people who may be thinking that it is very wrong and sacrilegious to question what is given by the religions, such people may have fear coming in the way of their original discovery of the truth of the Divine? Is there no true 'coming home' for them?*

A : So long as fear hems in a seeker, he can only go so far as his fear permits him to explore. So, one has to start by being aware of all of one's fears. Fear will cripple exploration and produce either stagnation or a condition of drifting, postponing-all of which will lead to a colossal wastage of time.

Q : *Coming back to the above topic, we learnt to talk, walk and drive only by falling and hurting ourselves, till we mastered the art; so are you implying that even in this quest for moksha, we will meet with many unexpected failures, before we actually succeed?*

A : I am so glad you raised this point. Many people in the *artha and kama* spheres, are so worldly that 'success' is their main goal, not even what means is adopted to become successful. A true seeker, will never think in terms of success and failure, he just goes behind the truth. In the whole movement of life, success and failure are bound to come in alternating cycles, this is the very nature of life itself, so 'falling down' is part of the journey. But the important question should be, are we learning anything at all because of our failures? Such falling down is often a blessing, because we become wiser, after the fall.

----

5. Exploratory Approach of Trial & Error - 2

Sankara : "Have you observed how you are cunning and a researcher, when it comes to matters of survival, matters in which the *Jiva* is deeply interested? You followed an exploratory approach of trial and error in these matters.

"When you search for a life partner, for a boy friend or girl friend, when you are buying a house, car, land, or when you go shopping, or select a profession, you followed this method only! How come in the spiritual life, you are so very passive and content to follow? Is it because, your heart is not actually in this quest?"

Q : *Yes, what you are saying - that we are so dedicated and committed when it comes to our goals in artha and kama, but that we lack the same kind of fire, when it comes to the pursuit of moksha, is totally correct, and we will have to accept this. Is it due to destiny that there are not many seekers of moksha?*

A : We have covered this kind of a question in topics 12 and 13, yesterday (chapter I), when we went into the four goals of life, *artha, kama, dharma* and *moksha*. Strictly speaking the last quarter of life has to be devoted to *moksha*, though not the earlier years. As a preparation for the last quarter of life, don't you think, each of us must strive to seek *moksha*, in at least a lukewarm way during our younger years?

Q : *Now that you present things so convincingly, yes, each of us must exert ourselves more in this direction, as it is this alone and not any other worldly quest which will give us lasting peace, especially during the last quarter of our life.*

In this context, the question arises, if something can be done by all spiritual teachers on the one hand and by all seekers of moksha on the other, to bring about a more satisfying spiritual growth in the spheres of dharma and moksha?

A : As I said, we are not dealing here with the sphere of *dharma* at all, we deal only with *moksha*. The teachers of *dharma* are different from the teachers of *moksha*. Seekers must look out for good teachers of *moksha* and start learning from them, so that eventually the seekers become their own teachers. But before this maturity comes about, usually, seekers will have to go to many kinds of teachers, and see which teacher suits them better and so on.

6. 'Understanding is the only Direct means to Liberation'

1. Each one of us is the true Self *(Atma)*, but in creation, we are obliged to wear the mask of an individual *Jiva* (unique personality, with 'I').

2. Feel free to ask Qs, and 'feel' the *sutras*.

3. "Of all the means to liberation, understanding is the only direct one-as essential as fire to cooking; without it liberation cannot be gained."

- Adi Sankaracharya in 'Atma Bodha' [31]

Q : *You have emphasized the path of understanding. First of all, is this your own spiritual path?*

A : Yes, this has been my path, and this is what I am teaching.

Q : *There seem to be so many spiritual paths, suited to people of different temperaments, and are you saying that in this path of understanding, feeling deeply our daily human experience, and the importance of contemplation, learning and enquiry into the Divine constitute important sadhana?*

A : There are basically two kinds of *sadhana* I am recommending.

In Part I, which is devoted to *self* - Knowing, I recommend, observation of *what is*. Sri J. Krishnamurti calls this *choiceless awareness of what is*. This *sadhana* is fundamental to Part I. In Part II, which is devoted to Self - Realization, *sravana, manana and nidhidhyasana* are the methods of *sadhana*.

Q : *What can you say in general terms about the importance of asking Qs, seriously in the spiritual realm, because you seem to repeatedly emphasize this?*

A : I like this question. Broadly there are three kinds of seekers. The more contented, stable and *tamasic* seekers may not ask any Qs at all. The *rajasic* seekers, may trouble their teachers with too many impatient Qs. The *sattvik* seekers, after realizing that the most sensible thing to do, will be to put the Q to oneself and wait-incubate on their own Q, till they receive an insight, they will not only ask deep Qs, he or she will also put that question to themselves. I maintain that, without proper and serious enquiry, we will never reach the goal. The fruit of our *sadhana* will not fall into our lap, without proper human effort of the right kind.

Q : *What do you actually mean by feeling the sutras? Can you throw some light on this?*

A : On the first day, we had seen how it is important to receive all these *sutras* or teachings, with both hands, with the head and also with the heart. To feel the *sutras*, is to develop an emotional bond with the truth they convey. To approach the *sutras* through the head is to logically work them out and make them perfectly self-consistent. Many *jnanis* and *bhaktas* weep, while reading the works of great masters-this is a regular experience for me too, this happens when the *sutras* just fall into the heart and you feel strongly about the truth they convey.

----

7. By Being the *Atma*, Identify the *Jiva*

Identifying,

Observing,   } the *Jiva (self)*

Understanding

Identifying the *Jiva (self)*:

The *self* is full of secrecy, hurts, divisiveness, hypocrisy, self- protection, self-seeking, self-improvement, fear, lying, vanity, violence in words, in actions, jealousy, lust, ambition, anger, domination and servility, surviving, pleasure seeking, ...ever-lasting seeking of pleasure and security.

Q : *As we have the task of identifying the self, now that you have given us abundant cues, as to the kind of situations, where the self may be lurking, is it understood then that, whenever we meet with the above conditions in life; namely, secrecy, sense of being hurt, divisiveness in thinking, self-protective moves, self-seeking, self-improvement, fear, hypocrisy, lying, vanity, violence in words and actions, deceptions, jealousy, hatred, excessive lust, ambition and greed, anger, domination and servility, pleasure-seeking, searching for security and a cosy future - we are to infer that these are sure abodes of the self?*

A : Yes, this is how the meditative journey has to commence. It has to commence by firstly identifying the *self*, and then going on to observe it carefully. This is the only way by which we can come on a path of *self* - Knowing. Those seekers living in a spiritual utopia and dreaming their idealistic dreams, may never look within their own hearts and minds, so they may react sharply to this wholly different approach of turning inwards and looking at the *self* and its activities, for they will not be able to see any connection between the condition of the *self* on the one hand and the mysterious Divine on the other. Even in the spiritual traditions of Hindu India and also in the other religions, great emphasis has been placed on *chitta shuddi*, which means purity of inner consciousness, though only few teachers may be actually able to give clear guidelines, as to how to achieve this inner purity and inner integrity. *In my view, this inner purity and integrity is in fact the master key to moksha.*

---

8. Consciousness and the *Jiva*

1. *Manas* = Faculty of feeling (blue water in topic 9).
    Emotional ingredient of consciousness.
    Responsible for attachments.

2. *Buddhi* = Faculty of thinking (not intelligence), reason.

3. *Ahankara* = *self* or the 'maker' of the *self*, or individuality of the *Jiva*. *Aham* = *self, Kara* = maker.

    ('Will' belongs to: *Ahankara*). Creates ambition, cravings.

4. *Chitta* = 'The stream of thoughts / feelings' (Time), the matrix, on which the drama of consciousness happens.

Q : *I presume that we are still getting hold of the self, that is, trying to identify it-for the self seems to be in 'the field of consciousness', among some other 'functions and faculties' of consciousness.*

A : You are correct, this is what we are trying to do. However, I do not want to do this in a common sense kind of way, for our common sense definition of the *self* could well be wrong. So, here I am relying on the Hindu scriptures which are throwing light on the structure and function of consciousness.

The sages say, man has four inner organs (*antah karana,* is the name in Sanskrit). By this they mean, the four faculties and functions in consciousness, namely: firstly, *manas* (the faculty of feeling and knowing), secondly, *buddhi* (the faculty of thinking, but not the faculty of intelligence), thirdly, *ahankara* (the complex of the ego or the *self*) and fourthly and lastly, *chitta* (the totality of the individual and collective consciousness, including memory, all sub-conscious contents like *samskaras*, dreams, our urges and that movement of collective consciousness). This *chitta,* may be compared to an infinite reservoir or a vast river in movement.

These four faculties are dynamically changing and they are subject to time, or rather by their inherent movement, the thing called, time, comes into existence. Time will stop for us, only if the subtle movement of consciousness stops. My point is that, the *self* which is the mischief maker in man's life, to use   J.Krishnamurti's vocabulary, and the cause of sorrow, is the *ahankara,* or the *self,* as defined in the scriptures.

Q   :   *Would the ahankara be referring to the ego - since we know that the ego is the mischief maker in man's life?*

A   :   In one sense yes, what you are saying is true, but I wish to clarify further. One of the admirable hall marks of the Sanskrit language is that the etymology of every Sanskrit word is clear and transparent. That is, the etymology, invariably throws a lot of light on the meaning and significance of each word. Having said this, I would like to go a bit further, are you ready for this next step?

Q   :   *Yes, please go on.*

A   :   Pardon me for saying this, but the word 'ego' is not rich enough etymologically, even though as you correctly point out, we all know that it is the ego, our sense of individuality, which is the cause of sorrow and which is the mischief maker in our life. Coming to the Sanskrit word, *ahankara,* its etymology says, it is the *kara* or the 'maker' of the sense of *self (aham).* Think of the spider and the web, which it creates- all for what? Often, but not always, for trapping and catching its prey. So the spider's web is much like the network of manipulations and machinations of the *self,* for its own continued survival. Thus, *ahankara* gives much more insight than the word ego, it shows that the *self* far from being a static thing is in fact a dynamical process, and *the whole complex process in thinking, is what makes for the self.* Though *ahankara* is a noun, it stands for as dynamical process.

Q   :   *If you say that ahankara is the self which is the mischief maker, will this ahankara, leave the manas, the buddhi, and chitta, uncorrupted and uninfluenced by it?*

A   :   This is a very deep question. Actually, the *ahankara,* does make use of *buddhi* and *manas,* for its own convenience, even though, *manas* and *buddhi* are powerful independent faculties in consciousness. Likewise, *self,* can also make use of *chitta,* the movement of consciousness, for safeguarding its own continued survival.

Q : *Why is the ahankara so very powerful, that it is easy for it to lord over the buddhi, manas and chitta? What is the source of this power?*

A : The *ahankara*, is actually, like the other three faculties and functions in consciousness, powered by the *Atma*, and is in fact a distorted and very limited reflection of the *Atma*, in the troubled waters of the consciousness and the body, naturally. As the *Atma* is all powerful and sovereign, its sense of Self, is seen and reflected in the *ahankara*, but with the important difference that this little *self*, operates within the highly limited domain of the body and our human consciousness, whereas the *Atma* holds the whole cosmos. In other words, if the *Atma* is the soul, its projection or display is this splendorous cosmos.

Q : *Why is the ahankara not so strong in all individuals?*

A : The human *self* is unique, meaning that each human *self* is a particular unique combination of the *cosmic benefic and cosmic malefic life energies*, and we already know from the *mythic model* (see Ch. III. topic 16), that these *benefic and malefic life energies*, are sourced in the Divine. Then again the *Siva* essence is the same in all human beings, whereas the *Sakti* essence varies, depending on the details of the combination of the *cosmic benefic and cosmic malefic life energies*. Whenever the *Sakti* essence is strong, then the *ahankara* will be strong and also likely to be aggressive, whereas when the *Sakti* essence is weak, the *ahankara* is likely to be weak and amicable.

Q : *So, have we now completed at least identifying the self?*

A : To a certain extent only, we have done this. Next we must start observing this *self* at work. Actually, as the *self* is different from one individual to another, one cannot do the work for another, even your *guru* will not be able to do your work, though he will certainly bless you for doing your own work. Each has to look within and each has to do his home work-this is the only way to *moksha*.

Q : *Can we now take these ingredients of manas, buddhi, ahankara, and chitta, as giving us a good anatomical understanding of consciousness?*

A : Yes, in general terms only, as the details will vary from one individual to another. As it is the details which prove to be problematic, a great deal of work remains to be done, to which only the individual must address himself. He will have to walk on this road alone.

----

9. Manas, Buddhi, Ahankara (self), Chitta

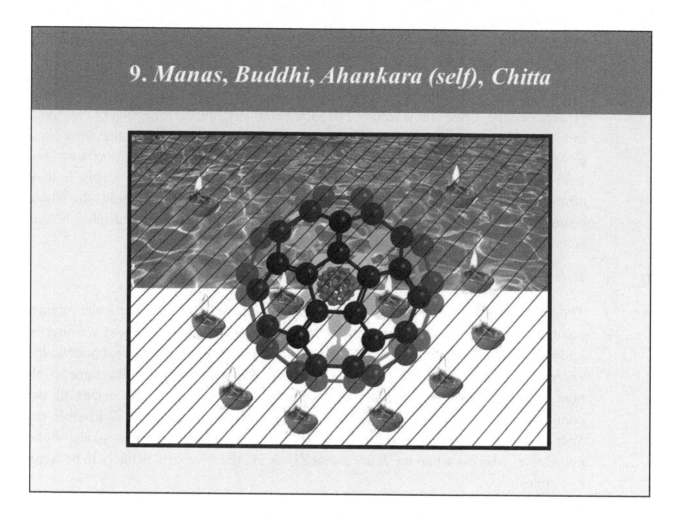

Q : *Can you explain this topic, telling us what the various entities therein are?*

A : Till now we have introduced four kinds of 'functions and faculties' of consciousness: (i) *manas*, the faculty of feeling, (ii) *buddhi*, the faculty of thinking, (iii) *ahankara*, the mechanism of the *self*, (iv) *chitta*-the whole flowing movement of consciousness. The picture shows this truth graphically, that is all. The central molecular structure is the *self* or *ahankara*, it is a formation of many thoughts, memories, feelings, all coming together suddenly, in order to defend 'something'. The blue water (shown in dark gray color here) with ripples is the *manas*. The small lamps denote the flashes of intellectual understanding *(buddhi)*, the white background is the flowing movement of *chitta*, which creates the reality of time. So this simple picture illustrates the 'faculties and functions' of consciousness.

Q : *You are saying that manas is the feeling nature or the feeling aspect of the 'I'. Is this what you call feeling from the heart?*

A : Yes, this can be taken to be the heart, it is the emotional centre of your being, your 'being' nature. In astrology, it corresponds to the IVH and the Moon.

Q : *You have said that buddhi is represented by the lamps. Would you say, these are the flashes of understanding that the intellect often gives us?*

A : Right. Either these insights or results of correct logical thinking, can come from the store house of past memories and your data bank, or these flashes of insights can also come from the *Atma*, the Source.

Q : *Is chitta, the movement of feelings and thoughts in our consciousness? Are you saying then that this is exactly like a motion picture? And that this movement is inherent in consciousness? If it is inherent, then are we to suppose that the very functioning of consciousness, as this flowing movement is the cause of time?*

A : Yes, you got it all, it is exactly like a motion picture and this indeed is the cause of time. But as we are the *Atma*, in reality, the timeless witness, time is only a passing show before us, who are timeless beings.

Q : *Why is the self or the ahankara, shown like a molecular structure, with many bonds? And what is the dense red thing at the centre of this structure?*

A : The word, *ahankara*, means, the thing that does the function of the ego or the *aham*, the sense of *self*. Unless, a chain of thoughts, so to speak, come together in succession, or in an orchestrated manner, the feeling or sense of *self*, may not arise at all. Thus, both the speed of thoughts and a variety of them, arising from memory, cause, this thing, called *ahankara*, it is indeed, like a temporary molecular formation, because, as the witnessing awareness, we can testify that only sometimes, this formation happens, at other times, we do not have a strong sense of *self*. I think, you will all agree with me. So, I have used a molecule, with a very large number of atoms, called Buckminster Fullerene, to signify the *self*, in a schematic way.

The red dense structure (in dark gray) at the centre is the *self* of the *sthitha prajnya*, more orderly, more stable and unresponsive to the usual human and sensory provocations. Unlike the 'flighty electrons', the *sthitha prajnya's self* is portrayed as a nuclear centre, 'grave, self-composed and silent'.

Q : *Why have you used the black color to depict the structure of the self?*

A : As *self*, by definition, seeks survival and security, fear is an integral part of its defense mechanism. Everybody will agree that fear is negative energy, rather than positive energy. Fear implies a division between *self* and 'other', so the black color, which stands for *tamas*, or darkness, has been used as appropriate.

Q : *What is that in the centre, a very dense dark grey tight structure-more like a nucleus?*

A   :   As I have tried to explain, this is a more *self*-composed, grave, and silent *self*, practically calm, practically mute and silent-namely like that of the *sthitha prajnya*. In other words, it is the calmed and silenced *self* of the *sthitha prajnya.*

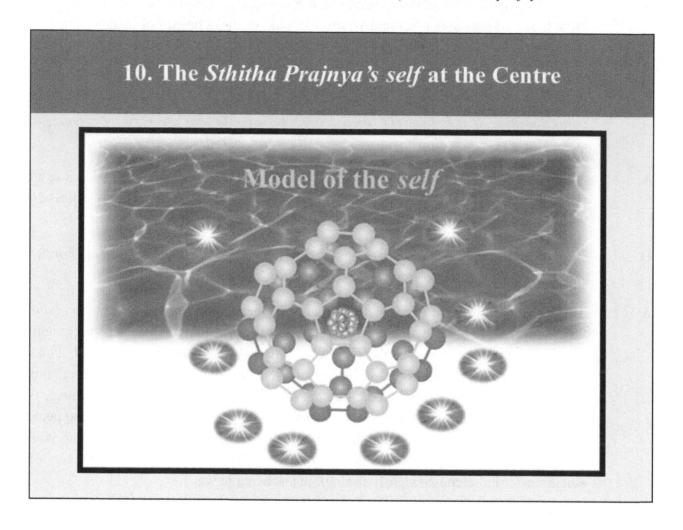

10. The *Sthitha Prajnya's self* at the Centre

Model of the *self*

Q   :   *This model of the self is more luminous, I see more light everywhere. Even the flashes of white light coming from the 'lights' of the buddhi are more luminous-does this mean that the intellect is more awake and more active? Would this be an appropriate model of a more spiritual person?*

A   :   Yes, this is what I had in mind. The senses and consciousness are very awake in a *sthitha prajnya*, and because *prajnya* or *Atmic* intelligence is awakened, the flashes of insights will also be more luminous and many more in number. The *sthitha prajnya's* consciousness is well connected to the *Atma*, bereft of conflict and there is constant joy-this picture tries to convey all this info.

Q   :   *The molecular structure also has less black color. So are we to take it that this consciousness is more fiery (because of the greater presence of the light)?*

A : Indeed, the red color of the renunciants, the *sannyasis*-has to do with the fire element, *aruna,* the red of *Jnanagni* (the fire of illumination).

Q : *You have now embedded an Aum symbol on the collapsed inner core, which you said represented the calmed and silent self of the sthitha prajnya. Does the Aum signify that the sthitha prajnya is connected to the Divine? And what do you mean by sthitha prajnya?*

A : Firstly I'll say something about *Aum.* Then about *sthitha prajnya.*

Aum, the *Vedic* symbol stands for the Divine, *Parabrahma,* the unmanifest aspect of the Divine. *Aum* also stands for *Ganesha* and the *Atma. Sthitha prajnya* is one in whom the *Atmic* intelligence called *prajnya* is operational. *Sthitha,* because the *prajnya* which has been kindled is not erratic, but steady and stable *(sthitha).*

11. *Jiva's self* has come into Existence for Survival

Sankara : "In every relationship, even in the most intimate relationships-between husband and wife; two lovers, parents and children; brother and sister; even between *guru* and disciple, there is no honesty, innocence and openness, but only lying, deception, hypocrisy, a twist in thought.

"Have you observed this? Don't you find this rather tragic and unfortunate? What would happen, if these 'twists' are straightened out, so that consciousness becomes whole and full of integrity-totally bereft of any games?"

Q : *Many people are playing games on a daily basis, to use your parlance, and may consider it to be very necessary for basic survival. But these very people are very quick to perceive that someone else is playing a game too, yet, what amazes us is their* *total blindness to their own game playing or machinations. Is this lying and game-playing what you would call human nature?*

A : Indeed. As we know the light of consciousness has the default setting of *outward perception*, and therefore, *inward perception* can happen only by changing and modifying this default setting which comes with the human birth, our conditioning, society's pressure on us to compete and survive, blinds us to truth. *Inward perception* is necessary for us to be able to look at ourselves, and this is, as we all know, more of an exception than the rule. And this *condition of being fixated in the outward perception* may be understood to be, certainly not our best human nature, rather, it may be considered to be a lower aspect of our human nature - this rank inability to look at oneself, this meanness, this self-defensive nature.

Q : *Now you have used a term, lower human nature for the first time. Till now, you had only mentioned the human nature vis-à-vis the Divine nature. What would then be our higher human nature?*

A : You all know the answer yourselves, why do you want me to spell this out?

Q : *You have reflected the question back to me. Higher human nature is perhaps, the most selfless human behavior, in thought and feeling, in words and actions?*

A : Yes, this is it, and we know this higher human nature in ourselves and in others, co-existing side by side with our lower human nature-this is fairly obvious, would you agree?

Q : *Yes, certainly, this is quite obvious, as we think about it. But the next question immediately arises, how then do we look at ourselves?*

A : As I just said, by modifying and reversing the default setting of our consciousness. And the reversing of this default setting is through the meditations that we have in mind. This retreat is for learning how to effect this reversing of the *fixated outward perception*.

----

12. Body-Centered *self*, 'I am the body'. But, this is an *anatma* (non-Self) of the *Jiva*

Q : *Why have you have given the adjective, body-centered, to the self? The self is the ahankara and is obviously not a physical thing, it is rather only a web-like structure in consciousness-we have already gone into this a few topics earlier, so why are you associating the physical body with this self?*

A : If we are so perceptive that we are already fairly clear that our essential nature, namely, our *self,* is only a process in consciousness and not really anything connected with the body; then we would have already come a long way and much of the illusion would have been taken away from us!

In truth, though the *self,* which is a network in thought and feeling, is not physical, the whole of humanity has the feeling that we are the body, so the body is our primary identity and our primary concern and this physical body is central to the image making process in consciousness. Probably, most human beings think of themselves as the body - they are hardly even aware that they are in fact, not the body, but the web of the *self* in consciousness. This is the reason, I am stressing that for every human, the physical body is the definition and reference for the *self.* If we were to take an opinion poll, then 99.9% of humanity would vote for their identity as the body, only .1% may

111

even recognize that there is that web-like structure in consciousness called *ahankara* or *self* - which is their essential nature, and not their bodies.

13. *Jiva* says, 'this is my 'wife', my 'husband'. This too is an *anatma* (non-Self) of the *Jiva*

Q : *In the earlier topic, we had only one man, so it was a case of, 'I, me, myself', shall we say. And in this picture, we have two people, a couple, so are you then meaning that the narrowest, circle of 'I, me, myself' has now expanded to include at least one another person, the spouse?*

A : It is important to observe that earlier the individual man only loved himself. Everything else in the world, including his parents, brothers and sisters, was something other than the *self*. As the *self* is of the nature of love, where we meet with a boundary of the *self*, there love will also stop and it will not go any further. In the case of the couple, it must be noted that the man loves his wife and the wife loves her husband, because *self* is love, and it follows that both of them, while they love each other, they do not love anybody else - that is how small their world is! I want seekers to apply this understanding in their day to day life and see how limited and shallow our life is.

If, another human being falls outside the boundary of the *self,* then we do not care for that person, because he is not part of our definition of the *self.*

Q : *Now I understand that the circumscribing thick circle is extremely significant, it draws our attention to the boundary of the self, and says, anything falling outside the circular boundary, does not get our love, because it is not part of self. Right?*

A : Absolutely.

**14. *Jiva* says: 'This is my family'.
Alas! This too is the *Jiva's anatma* (non-Self)**

Q : *Here the thick circle has expanded, so we are able to love more people, and we will also naturally be happier for it. So here again, can I say, anyone outside the boundary of the self, does not get our love?*

A : Yes, this is the truth, but each must come to this disturbing discovery, by their own enquiry and inner perception, and they have to be objective in this. If they have the ideal that, 'I should love all', because such an ideal may be foisted on us by the religions, then that ideal, will block the discovery that in fact, our love, stops at the boundary of the *self.* I hope, I am making sense.

Q : *Then we will have to be true to ourselves and say that we are unable to love everyone, is this right?*

A : That is correct, we have to come to this discovery. Having an ideal of love and trying to love, is *entirely different* from being able to love and being in love. As the *self* is love or *ananda,* anything which falls outside the *self,* will not give us *ananda,* and we will not be able to dissolve the gap between ourselves and that object of our love, which we are presumably trying to love, because of our idealism.

15. *Jiva:* 'My friends, I love them!'
These attachments make the *Jiva* limited

Q : *So, this is then the same old story of the self?*

A : Rightly so, but in differing social contexts. If friends define the *self,* rather than the family, then friends will be loved more than the family, for example. All this must be applied to our daily life till we get insights into where the defining boundry of the *self* stops in our particular individual life.

16. *Jiva* defined through Language, Society: 'I am a Tamilian'

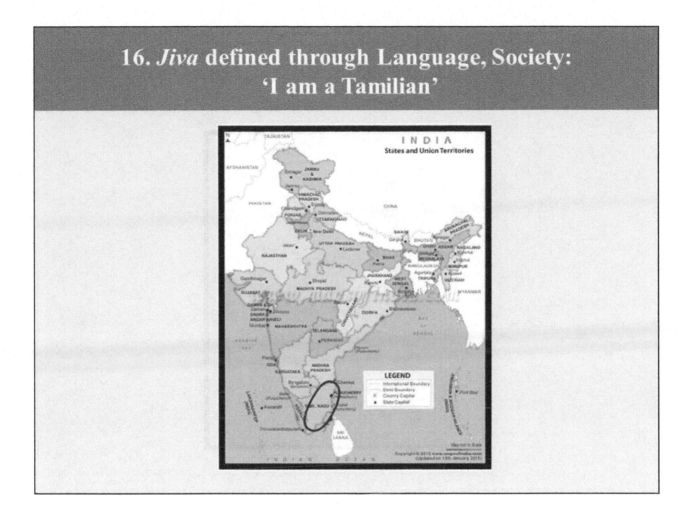

Q : *Here in this next topic the thick circle, the boundary of the self envelops a certain state, a certain language, a certain people. If this is the way the self is defined, then what happens to the family, friends, wife and husband, will we stop loving them, don't they also belong to the self?*

A : Please understand clearly that real and authentic love goes only as far as the *self* goes. In a societal context, we may identify our *self* with a language, a region, a country. This means we will love those people as 'my people'. The family and friends will also be loved naturally, because the *self* also encompasses them-we have already covered this aspect of the *self*.

All this is a consequence of being human, identifying with something or the other, so we are not levelling a charge on the *self*, just trying to understand the manner in which that human *self* functions.

----

17. *Jiva*: 'I am an Indian'
Another 'respectable' *anatma* (non-Self)

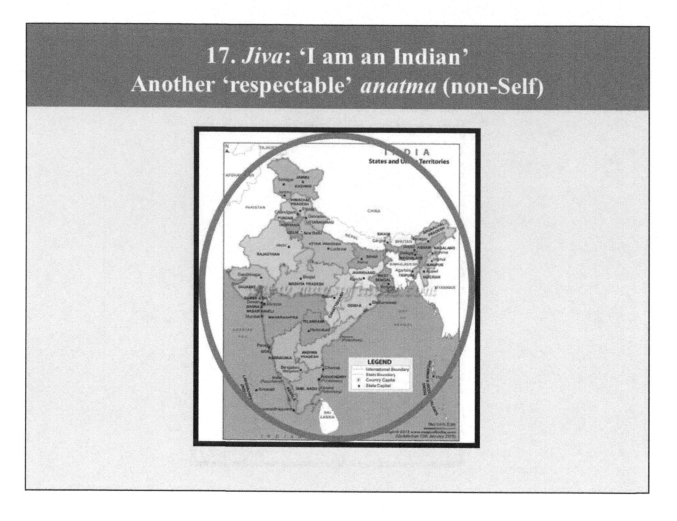

Q : *Is it wrong then to have a patriotic self?*

A : Certainly not. We are not passing value judgments here, not criticizing any body, even a nation, all we are saying is that in the human experience, you see the *self*, taking all these forms. In every one of these associations and identifications, there will be conflict between *self* and the other, and this conflict, which is the essence of duality will go only when through *self*-Knowing, the *self*, falls silent, so that the *Atma* has a chance to make its presence felt in human life. *Once this happens, the feeling of being separate from everything else, which is a tell-tale sign of the self will fade away.*

On a practical level, no one can deny that we belong culturally and politically only to one nation, be it India, Chile, Brazil, US, and any other nation. This cannot and need not be changed. What can however be changed and should be changed is our inner identity, this should become as vast as possible, encompassing the whole world, as we hear it said in the *Vedic* ideal: The whole world is one family - *vasudaiva kutumbakam.* We are in truth the *Atma,* and in the Hindu world, to know this deeply and without an iota of doubt is the last of the four goals of life.

18. 'The Soil in which the meditative mind can begin....'

"The soil in which the meditative mind can begin is the soil of everyday life, the strife, the pain and the fleeting joy. It must begin there, and bring order, and from there move endlessly. But if you are concerned only with making order, then that very order will bring about its own limitation and the mind will be its prisoner."

- J. Krishnamurti in 'Meditations'[13]

Q : *This beautiful and moving piece of Krishnamurti's writing seems to imply, that he places far more emphasis on our daily living, on self-Knowing, rather than on God, Atma, or on Brahman, or on the scriptures. He seems to be an original philosopher, or original thinker, rather than a religious teacher. Is this right?*

A : You are right, he never spoke from the position of a Hindu or a religious teacher. He was original and radical, you may even say, he was a revolutionary teacher, who challenged spiritual progress when the same was claimed along rigid traditional lines. He pointed out that much of tradition is lifeless, *tamasic*, without the important seeds of *self*-Knowing. His was the way of inner enquiry, self-critical *self*-Knowing, through *choiceless awareness of what is*.

Q : *And is it your suggestion that, we should concentrate on the problems in our daily life, start learning by study and enquiry and also not make the mistake of being obsessed with success, where the resolution of the problem is concerned?*

A : Yes, this precisely, is my idea and I go more deeply into this, later in the retreat.

117

19. By Being the *Atma*, Observe the *Jiva (self)*

To observe the *Jiva (self)*

- We (as the *Atma*), must observe (what is.)
  (As J. Krishnamurti used this term).

- What is this (what is?)

- (What is) 'The context in consciousness' in which the *Jiva (self)* has revealed itself: anger, hurt, jealousy, lying, manipulation, cheating, etc.

Q : *You are now introducing a new term, what is, and you are also saying, this is part of the master J. Krishnamurti's special vocabulary. My obvious question now is, what did Krishnamurti, actually mean by this term what is?*

A : *What is*, as the words imply, is the actual state of our life or our consciousness, at any given moment. Usually, if life is going smoothly, without any inner and outer pain, nobody pays any attention to *what is*. It is when we have to face misfortunes, like death or a major illness, or a marital life falling apart through divorce, or when dishonor and disgrace are staring us in the face; that, *what is*, becomes disturbing and painful enough to demand out attention. *What is*, for example, can be our angry, dishonest, jealous or lusty nature that has suddenly come into existence, it is any challenging or nagging life-situation that calls for attention. The spiritual life commences by our paying attention to such a challenging and nagging *what is*.

Q : *How is this what is, related to manas, our feeling nature; buddhi, our intellect; ahankara, our self; and chitta, the whole flowing movement of consciousness? I feel* *that my question is very pertinent, because, what is, seems to be a condition or a happening in consciousness?*

A : Quite correct, *what is*, is a crisis situation in consciousness, or it may also have a counter-part in our outer life. When there is an inner crisis, then *what is*, is that very crisis, then we lose our peace of mind, become very disturbed, have a lot of conflict, and our sense of *self*, may also be threatened. When this is the case, the *manas*, *buddhi*, *ahankara*, *chitta* - all are disturbed profoundly from their equilibrium positions, resulting in inner confusion and sorrow.

Q : *You also seem to imply that to observe the self, it becomes necessary to observe first of all, the matrix or the context, in which the self suddenly comes into existence. For example, the self may arise only during an argument between myself and another - so are you saying that there has to be, first of all an observation of the context of the argument, which is, the what is, for the self seems to arise only in this context?*

A : Yes, the *self* arises in such difficult contexts only. The 'show' of the *self*, is not perpetually going on, for us to run and take a look at this 'show', whenever we have the time to look, or whenever we are free to look, so to speak.

Q : *Looking at your examples of the contexts, in which the self may suddenly spring into existence, I wish to ask, if these contexts are always negative? Why have you chosen only negative contexts?*

A : When the contexts are happy or pleasant ones, they do not call for attention. We do not seek medical help when we are healthy, but only when we are sick.

Q : *This whole business of observing the self, and observing what is, the context in which the self arises, seems to be entirely different from what we have been taught in childhood. Nobody ever told us to observe the self at work, we were always told to control our anger, hold our tongue, control our jealousy, control our desires, and so the question arises, whether what we have been taught earlier is wrong or an inferior moral teaching?*

A : Bringing up children is enormously hard, and in doing this, we destroy their natural intelligence, by making them conform to societal norms, which cannot be considered to be salutary for the moral, spiritual, emotional and intellectual welfare of children. The function of the parents or educators is actually to preserve the natural intelligence, the *prajnya*. By making us conform, this *prajnya* is suffocated and often, many foolish and harsh methods are used by both parents as well as educators, for making children obedient and well-behaved-without the slightest regard to the inner life of children.

Naturally the superior method will be one, which is much more sensitive, along the lines which blossom in this retreat. The home schooling in the West, Krishnamurti, Aurobindo, Montessori, Rabindranath Tagore, Rudolf Steiner, all of them were attempting to uplift a system, which by design was survival oriented, rather than for the purpose of the emotional, intellectual and spiritual flowering of children.

Second Day (Chapter - II), 1st 'Tat Tvam Asi' Meditation

Do you have a difficult *what is?*
Identify the *what is* and abide in it.

Distinguish between *Jiva* and *Atma.*

The *Jiva*, 'borrowing' the *Atmic* Light, 'saw' the world. Now, we must Identify, Observe and Understand the *Jiva's self*, by Being the *Atma.*

20. Two 'Tat Tvam Asi' Birds : A Recurring Metaphor

Self (*Atma*), awareness, 'conscious presence', witness, 'I am ness'.

Jiva, mired in *maya* and suffering thro' *self*

Sankara: We have already learnt about the two 'Tat Tvam Asi' birds (Ch. I, topic 17). Nevertheless, let us study this metaphor again, so that we have another opportunity to internalize it fully, so the content of topic 17 of Ch. I, is reproduced here.

Q : *Now this topic speaks of two Tat Tvam Asi birds of the Mundaka Upanishad. As a Hindu, I am somewhat aware that the Upanishads are part of the Vedas, the most ancient scriptures of the Hindus. However when this retreat is offered to Western seekers, how would people understand these Sanskrit terms, and even the meaning of 'Upanishads' and 'Mundaka'. Should you not be giving us the meanings of these terms, so that even Hindus like us, may have an even clearer understanding?*

A : It will be good if seekers do understand the meanings, especially the etymological meaning of these Sanskrit terms, *Upanishads* and *Mundaka*. But this is actually not so necessary for our present purposes of *self* - Knowing and Self - Realization. Nevertheless, for the sake of completeness, let us go into this.

The term *Upanishad*:

Upa is composed of two parts which is U + Pa - meaning *'Near the feet'*. And *'nishad'* means sitting beneath the feet-implied that these are the feet of the master.

It is suggestive of a disciple or a *mumukshu* sitting at the feet of a Self-Realized master, having humbled himself and having the very essential quality of humility. So sitting at the feet of a master, is symbolic of the extremely humble posture, for without this humility no learning is possible. It is a teaching which is received and centered on the *Atma* and on *Brahman*. *Atman* is the 'I am ness' of consciousness and *Brahman* is the Divine, especially as the totality of manifestation. So the *Upanishads* teach us about *Atman and Brahman, Atmavidya (knowledge or learning about the Atma)* and *Brahmavidya (knowledge or learning about Brahman or the Divine)*.

In India the *Vedas* are the ancient spiritual corpus of the Hindus. And *Upanishads* are considered to be the *'Veda siras'*- the crown of the *Vedas* or *Vedanta*- the highest peak of the *Vedas,* which is naturally centered on Self - Realization.

Coming to the Adjective *Mundaka:*

The word means 'shaven off'. Why is this adjective used here? It is probably used because to shave off the head, which is what the *sannyasis* do in India, is symbolic of renunciation of the ego, the *self.* Renunciation of the idea that one is the body, that one is the *self* and shaving off of the head or tonsure is symbolic and ritualistic act, signifying, 'the casting away of the *self',* or individuality, or the notion that 'we are the physical body'.

So, *Mundaka Upanishad* will probably indicate an emphasis which is based on detachment from the body, detachment from the *self,* without which this teaching may not get internalized and come home to us. So detachment and renunciation of the idea that we are the body, that we are the *self,* are central to this *Upanishad.* And this is a teaching given by a particular sage, and every *Upanishad* is a teaching by a particular sage. The key thing here is that no two teachings actually are the same, because every sage speaks from his own realization. So that is the reason there are so many *Upanishads.* There are more than 100 or 200 *Upanishads* and each of them has equally legitimate insights, which that particular sage had in his life and which he is presenting to us in the form of teachings and these teachings will be helpful to us in our own pursuit and discovery of the truth of the *Atma, Parabrahma.*

Q : *Are the two Tat Tvam Asi birds seen in this picture, metaphors for some teaching in this Upanishad? If so, what exactly do they represent? Most importantly, why are you describing these birds as Tat Tvam Asi birds?*

A : At the outset, I wish to emphasize that everyone of us will benefit by memorizing this mythic picture or this metaphoric representation of the truth, which is an analogical understanding of the truth. Yes, indeed it is a metaphor. You will see one bird is very engrossed in the act of eating which is symbolic of sensory-gratification and the pursuit of pleasure which is such an integral part of the human life and human drama. The other bird is not involved and not engrossed in the act of the pursuit of pleasure, instead it seems to be detached and only witnessing the whole act of the pursuit of pleasure, the search for sensory gratification, the search for survival and the search for emotional, economic security. This other bird is a complete outsider to this whole drama and is only a witness and probably has got the capacity to learn and even the capacity to negate the life of the lower bird. If we like, we may call the bird which is engrossed in the pleasure seeking and search for security as *Sakti* and the other wise bird which is just watching everything, as *Siva*. I have given the particular name Tat Tvam Asi birds because in truth there are not two birds. There is just one bird, capable of being in both states, so we are both the birds.

This is one of the most important principles in this retreat - that we have a body and mind centered *self* (our human nature), and another Self, the *Atma*, that is imperishable, unborn, deathless, and timeless, pointing to our Divine nature. So we will have to commit this picture to memory, like we recommended committing to memory, the ocean-wave metaphor. That is also a Tat Tvam Asi metaphor, just as these two birds are also a Tat Tvam Asi metaphor.

The eating bird represents the *Jiva (self)* which enjoys and suffers, the witnessing bird represents the timeless awareness *(chit)*, the *Atma*, a core spiritual being, we all are and which we use far too inadequately. So it is, if we may use these terms, a powerful faculty, which is unrecognized and used unconsciously and insufficiently. Every human being has two dimensions or two aspects, a very manifest human aspect, and an inner Divine essence. The witnessing bird represents the veiled Divine aspect and the pleasure-seeking and eating bird represents the very human nature of every human being. In topic 2, Ch. I, we had already dealt with the human nature vis-à-vis the Divine nature. 'Tat' refers to our mysterious, unknowable Divine nature, 'Tvam' refers to the core of your so-called human nature, and 'Asi' means 'are', so 'Tat Tvam Asi', the *upanishadic sutra* says, the very essence of each one of us is the Divine itself. *The two birds are thus different aspects of ourselves, the eating bird, the mask, the self, and the witnessing bird, the inner slightly buried Divine nature, the Atma or the witness consciousness. Thus we are both birds, simultaneously, this is a paradox. Hence the adjective Tat Tvam Asi is quite appropriate.*

Q : *So, this is yet another way of driving home the same point of Tat Tvam Asi, that we are the Divine - not as the body, but as the root of our consciousness?*

A : Right, that is the hint that is being given by this particular metaphor- that we are both. We are the pleasure seeking entity and we are the entity seeking survival and security perpetually and feeling insecure in this whole endless process. That is the *Sakti* bird. But we have to discover and realize that we are also the witnessing bird, we are intelligence which is now buried. So the teaching will help us to know that we are both the things. When we understand the teaching deeply, then the seeming contradiction between the *Sakti* bird and the *Siva* bird will completely disappear and we will realize that there are no contradictions and that we are both aspects of consciousness, hence the truth of Tat Tvam Asi will prevail.

---

21. 'Awareness is the Common Matrix of Every Experience'

"Awareness is primordial, it is the original state, beginningless, endless, uncaused, unsupported, without parts, without change. Consciousness is on contact, a reflection against a surface, a state of duality. There can be no consciousness without awareness, but there can be awareness without consciousness, as in deep sleep. Awareness is absolute, consciousness is relative to its content. Consciousness is always of something. Consciousness is partial and changeful. Awareness is total, changeless, calm and silent. And it is the common matrix of every experience."

- Sri Nisargadatta Maharaj[16]

Q : *Going back to the previous topic of the two Tat Tvam Asi birds, Maharaj's present statement seems to be, in complete correspondence with the metaphor of the two Tat Tvam Asi birds, except that, Maharaj's statement has taken the form of words. Would awareness refer to the witnessing bird or the Atma and consciousness would refer to the eating bird, the self?*

A : Exactly. I would like to make one additional point. All *sutras*, whether from Ramana Maharshi, Nisargadatta Maharaj, Krishnamurti, Bhagavad Gita, Ashtavakra Gita, Kaivalya Navaneetham - would like sincere seekers to commit these *sutras* to memory and then churn them in their consciousness. For example, Maharaj's *sutra* on awareness and consciousness, may be mapped on to the two Tat Tvam Asi birds, in order to enliven them even more.

----

22. Relationship between the 'Two Birds'

1. *Jiva* is concerned only about survival of the body, food, pleasure, security in relationships, and security in 'ownership', name and fame.

2. *Jiva (self)* is the 'reflection' of the Self, in the troubled waters of the body and consciousness.

3. Self is Infinite and Perfect, *Jiva* is limited, imperfect, and insecure.

4. Can the *Jiva* ever reflect the glory of the Self?

Q : *Looking at the above topic; to recapitulate, the eating bird is the small self, isn't it? This bird seems to be eating the sweet as well as the bitter fruits - so it thereby enjoys and also suffers- and are you saying that this eating bird is the reflection of the watching bird which is the Self, the Atma, the cosmic Self?*

A : Your question is quite right. You are *actually disturbed* by what appears in the topic - namely that the individual *self* is a reflection of the cosmic Self, are you not?

Q : *Yes, I am disturbed, simply because the individual self is very limited, because it enjoys and suffers, whereas the cosmic Self as shown in the picture is just watching. These two functions of eating and being involved on the one hand and being detached and watching on the other - seem to be poles apart - then how do you say that the eating bird is the reflection of the watching bird?*

A : It is true that the picture of the two birds, while it does justice to the eating bird, it does not do justice to the watching bird -simply because it is impossible to convey in a picture, the cosmic or the Divine dimension of the watching bird. So, when we actually remember that the watching bird has this infinite or Divine dimension - which

126

the eating bird does not at all have - one will naturally be shocked, as to how the eating bird could be a faithful reflection of the watching bird. This seems to be your problem?

Q : *Yes, this is where it is confusing.*

A : We have to think of faithful reflections and distorted reflections. A faithful reflection will always do justice to the original, whereas it is not so with a distorted reflection. Having said this, we must now add that the individual *self* is not a faithful reflection of the cosmic Self to begin with. But if we address ourselves to the challenge of *calming and silencing this individual self,* then this reflection becomes faithful, rather than distorted, provided, we also make allowance for the fact that the cosmic Self has chosen the limited human body, as its temporary vehicle.

Q : *For any reflection to be faithful, like the example of a reflection in a mirror, obviously the mirror must be free of distortions and defects. And you seem to imply that it is the calming and silencing of the self, which makes the mirror distortion-free. Would you say then, the calmed and silenced self, alone can reflect the glory of the cosmic Self?*

A : Yes, only under the conditions mentioned by you, the glory of the cosmic Self appears in the human being.

Understanding the *Jiva (self)* and the *Atma*

23. Understanding the *Jiva (self)*

"Understanding of the *self (Jiva)* requires a great deal of intelligence, a great deal of watchfulness, alertness, watching ceaselessly, so that it does not slip away."...

"The whole process of that, namely, competition and every form of desire is the *self* and we know when we are faced with it that it is an evil thing. I am using the word, 'evil' intentionally, because the *self* is dividing: the *self* is self-enclosing: its activities, however noble, are separative and isolating."

- J. Krishnamurti in 'The First & Last Freedom'[32]

Q : *If, too little of the witness bird, or awareness, or the Atmic presence is present in the Jiva, then this understanding of the self, will not even start isn't it?*

A : Yes, that is what will happen, but remembering the metaphor of the man covered by the algae, we know that there is always the *Atmic* presence in the *Jiva*, though the encasing *maya*, may be more or may be less. As the unused faculty of the *Atma* or awareness is indeed there, though in a buried condition, it can be accessed and brought into relief, even when it was totally submerged in *maya* to begin with. So, in no case, need we become despondent.

Q : *Another thing emphasized by Krishnamurti is the dedication and persistence in observation, in watching. Does this not mean, that we have to give this task the highest priority?*

A : Indeed, if we are already intelligent, already perceptive, already fortunate, we will do just this. If we are lazy, we may hear of this and say to ourselves, 'this is hard, so let me come back to it at a later time', that of course, would be a cunning trick of the *self*, to continue its self-enclosing existence. This is an investment, one has to make, and one obviously will not make it, because a promise has not been given that by making this investment, one is going to secure some grand reward, for the material life as well as for the spiritual life. If one is lucky and fortunate, one will do this home work, or at any rate at least make a sincere beginning and from there, learning will continue, depending on how much of pain, we have in life and how helpless we become.

Q : *Don't you think, Krishnamurti, when he calls the self, an evil thing, he is striking some fear in us?*

A : You are already so full of fear and desire that you can never see *what is,* nor anything objectively.By following closely what is being said here, you will be free of fear, once and for all. You know that fear is a very bad thing, because it is the breeding ground for a whole host of negative thinking. This is the truth that all great teachers have spoken, and in your wreched condition, as truth, threatens the very existence of the *self,* you are getting scared.

For example, a kindred teaching of the master Jesus comes to mind. This is from the gospel of St. Thomas: 'If you bring forth what is within you, what you bring forth will save you.If you do not bring forth what is within you, what you do not bring forth, will destroy you.' In this the master was obviously referring to the *self.* And the profound teaching of the master Krishnamurti is this, that this *self,* cannot be eradicated, by fighting with it, rather we have to understand it completely, when perhaps, the same *self* will probably start working in an entirely different way and this time, even in an auspicious way.

----

24. *Asmita*: Nucleus of *Jiva* when mind-body centered

1. I am ness = *asmita* = Nucleus of *Jiva* - when mind-body centered.

2. Nucleus of *Jiva* - essence of separative *self*.

    In the first few years of childhood, this *asmita* came upon the Absolute *(Parabrahma)* in association with the body. Prior to that, the child had no individual consciousness that was a separate entity, centered around the body.

3. Conscious presence is awareness or *Atma*.

    Observe *what is* from conscious presence *(Atma)*.

Q : *We have heard that in the Yoga sutras of Patanjali, the asmita is taken to be the essence of the individuality. How does it differ from the ego?*

A : '*Asmi*' means 'am', so the feeling that you exist as a separate entity, as the body and as a separate *self*, this is *asmita*. In one sense, it is the irreducible, sense of *self*. It is not an *anatma*, a false sense of *self*, but the core feeling that you exist separately.

In the *Yoga sutras*, *asmita* is one of the taints that blocks Self - Realization.

Q : *Does this asmita then not be responsible for the divisive and mischief making mechanism of the self?*

A : Yes, this *asmita* is not the mischief maker, but it is the ground, on which stand all other activities of the *self*.

Q : *So this root of the self, is formed in infancy, because of constantly telling the infant, that he is so and so?*

A : That is how it got formed, that is the origin of the wrong identification with the body.

25. 'Awareness expresses Itself in various Shapes and Forms'

"Whenever man limits his consciousness to body and mind, he is called *Jiva, or Jivatma,* otherwise, he is absolutely independent of these two-which are always acting or reacting. Awareness which expresses itself in various shapes and forms is all one, whether it be an insect, a big boar, a big man, there is no difference whatever."

- Sri Nisargadatta Maharaj[18]

Q : *We seem to have the intellectual challenge of stomaching the rather unbelievable idea that the essence of any form, be it a mountain, an insect, a goat, a stone, a river, a man, or a woman, a galaxy, is the self-same Atma. Don't you think, in a retreat such as this, notwithstanding the revolutionary nature of this idea and its implication, some of the meditations at least must be devoted to the challenge of intellectually digesting the idea, that behind the varying and multiple forms of the animate and inanimate things, there is the same, life of our life, etc.?*

A : There is nothing, extra revolutionary in the ingredients of this retreat, that are not already there, as the essence of the Hindu realizations, in the Upanishads, the *Puranas,* the Bhagavad Gita, etc. We do not study enough of the scriptures, and even if we do study, we do not study them with adequate attention. Rather, we study them at best with some faith and this is not good enough. You are not able to go deeply into your scriptures, because there is not enough social pressure on you to do so. Because of your attachments to your position, your salary, your family, you never have enough energy to go deeper into this study. You are creatures of conditioning, conditioned by materialistic values, by body-centered thinking, etc. Thus, your so called common sense, materialistic perceptions and thinking, becomes for you the truth, whereas, religions will tell you that the appearances shown to us by our senses are false and illusory.

So, to return to your question, indeed we need to be thinking in terms of the new paradigms, given to us by all the masters and the great timeless texts, and make that our world view. We are doing this to some extent in this retreat, but this is not enough, we have to do this on a daily basis, so that, our conditioning, which is due to sensory knowledge, may be overwritten. In that vein, the essence of each one of us, is not different from that of another, even here in this seminar room. Each of us, is also the other.

Q : *If each of us is the other, then where is the uniqueness that you spoke of earlier on?*

A : Our bodies and the way our minds work are so different, where is the doubt in this? This difference, makes our paths different, so this is where the uniqueness comes in. However, here, we are looking not at the way our bodies and destinies and consciousness work, but rather, we are looking at the underlying one common essence. In this one common essence, we are all the same, we are one. So, at different levels, we see differently.

Q : *So, awareness or Atma is the one common essence?*

A : Yes, that indeed is the one common essence.

----

26. Only the *Jiva* is present!

Q : *We are seeing here only the eating bird. You have blanked out the watching bird. Are you trying to say then that we as the eating bird are so engrossed in our pursuit of pleasure, that we are not at all aware of another dimension of ourselves-as the witness or as the awareness, or even as what we call, the conscience?*

A : Right, most of humanity may be living only as the eating bird, in complete obliviousness of the timeless awareness, which is our veiled Divine nature. This topic also conveys the very limited world-view of the atheists and the agnostics, who are kind of trapped in their limited existence as the eating bird.

Q : *This picture of the eating bird obviously is not to be taken literally like a human body eating. Rather, the metaphor of eating, seems to point to an activity of pleasure-seeking and security-seeking which is going on all the time in our consciousness. Am I right in this perception?*

A : Indeed, this eating is not to be taken literally. The eating is really an activity in consciousness, whereby the *self* or *ahankara* is seeking pleasure, for the sake of bodily enjoyment and for the sake of self-gratification. It goes on uninterruptedly throughout life, even in old age, with probably momentary brief spells of rest for the eating bird.

Q : *Does this mean that when the eating bird is fully satiated, the activity of eating, that is of pleasure seeking and of self-gratification, will indeed come to a stop?*

A : Many things can happen. Brief spells of rest for the eating bird are not uncommon, but they lose significance, because they resume and continue again in an endless way. The question of whether there can be a satiation is legitimate. In fact, suddenly, right in the midst of very mundane activity, when the inner eating bird is still busy, a radical shift can happen, whereby the whole activity of the eating bird can cease, even without the eating bird seeking this out. This is what happened to Sri the Ramana Maharshi as well, when he was just 16. We will certainly have occasion to deal with this later in the retreat, when we pay closer attention to this dawn of Self-Realization and the consequent falling silent of the *self* in Ramana Maharshi's own words.

27. Who is Identifying, Observing and Understanding this *Jivatma*?

1. 'That somebody' has to be the 'Knower' ?

2. If only the *Jivatma* is there by itself (as some may think!), then does it mean that in those people, there is no 'Knower' at all ?

3. As those people will at times admit that they lied, they had lust, they cheated, surely the 'Knower' exists in them (in the *Jivatma* itself).

4. *Atma* is the 'Knower'.

Q : *How do we ever recognize that somebody or some power, is there as a knowing power to take note of all the activities of the eating bird?*

A : This is very simple, but very subtle, so we have to pay close attention to what happens to us in our inner life. All of us say to ourselves and even to our friends and family, that 'I was greedy', 'I lied', 'Oh my God, I was so angry, so foul', etc.

Does this not imply that we have within us, a power of knowing or a knowing power - which discerns all things which are going on within consciousness and also outside consciousness?

Q : *Yes, I can see that this power of knowing is always with us, though we are not at all aware of it. And, yes, it must exactly be just this power of knowing, which makes us acknowledge what we are, and cognize what is going on within us.*

A : Now that we are in fact thinking of our consciousness as present in the form of two Tat Tvam Asi birds, my next question to you is this: Does this knowing power reside in the eating bird or in the witnessing bird?

Q : *The knowing power is obviously, always resident in the witnessing bird, but because, the witnessing bird is so subtle and entirely free of thoughts and feelings, very unlike the eating bird, which is completely wrapped up in thoughts and feelings; we will not be able to come upon this witnessing bird, if we do not make an effort to track it down, in one sense of speaking-because we are also that very witnessing bird, when we have fallen silent.*

This brings up the question-whether we can through some meditative process, come to a clear unmistakable recognition that, we are in truth, the witnessing bird only?

A : Yes, you are both the Tat Tvam Asi birds. When you start thinking and feeling, you get masked by coils of thoughts and feelings, and because of this wrapping around and coiling, we imagine we are the body interacting with so many other bodies and so on. When we distance ourselves from all thought and feeling, then we can be the witnessing bird, which is entirely outside the world of our thoughts and feelings. So, to return to your question, it is the calming and silencing of the *self*, which will enable us to be the witnessing bird, so the meditative process, you asked after is the calming and silencing of the *self*.

Q : *Is this knowingness, which is deep within our consciousness, really something so subtle and intangible - is this what the scriptures describe as Atma?*

A : Indeed, this *Atma*, has nothing to do with the goings on in the world of thought and feeling, and it is the *Atma*, which has the knowingness, and this is our true nature, but to get here, we have to turn our back on worldly things and enjoyments, we need a great deal of detachment to know that we are the *Atma*. So long as we are engrossed in the world of thought and feeling, knowing that we are the *Atma*, may be impossible.

At least during retreats like these, we should be able to abide as the *Atma,* for short moments and thereby make a discovery of our *Atmic* nature.

---

28. In the 'eating bird' *(Jiva)* is there no Knowing?

1. The activity of the 'eating bird' is the activity of it's *self* - right?

2. Does not this 'eating bird' *(Jiva)* Know things, which it experiences, like food, pleasures, cars, opposite sex, music, sunset?

3. Does the *Jiva* Know itself - like we Know sense-objects, namely, apples, ice-cream, opposite sex, moon?

4. (Answer = No, not as yet!)

Q : *We still are concerned about the same problem of knowing what is going on in the life of the eating bird, isn't it?*

A : Yes, we have now realized that side by side with the eating bird, there is a knowingness, which we placed in the witnessing bird. Having covered this ground, what would anyone seek to know further?

Q : *Let me go to the three points in the content of this topic. The first point is obvious, so we will leave that.*

Coming to the second point, I feel that there is a trap here in this very question, because the question, is almost suggesting that the eating bird, has also the faculty of knowing, which seems to be a part of it? Is this true at all?

A : You are right in your skepticism-this faculty of knowing, which seems to be present and bound up in all activities of the eating bird, is actually what we have thus far identified as the witnessing bird, however because of the inseparable nature of the two birds, we as the eating bird, feel that that knowing is also part of us - am I making sense?

Please take note at this stage that the *Mundaka Upanishad*, uses for the two birds, the two very significant words, *sayuja*, which means closely related, and also *sakhaya*, which means very much alike. Because of this inseparability, we must realise that the eating bird also has the *Atmic* faculty of knowing side by side with all of its pleasure seeking activities. The metaphor of the man covered over the algae illustrates this excellently.

Q : *Looking at the second point again, we see that the eating bird per se, is not the agency for knowing what is going on in its life and experiences. Rather this faculty of knowing is outside of the eating bird, correct?*

A : No! The eating bird also has the *Atmic* presence, so it has the faculty of knowing too. The metaphor of the man covered by algae, makes this truth abundantly clear.

Q : *Now taking up the last and third point, the first thing that comes to mind is that all the sensory objects mentioned, like ice-cream, apples, opposite sex, moon, etc., are all external. The question of whether the eating bird can know itself per se, like it knows all external objects; like the taste of apples, the taste of ice-cream, the appearance of the moon, etc., is a startlingly new kind of question-never heard this before! So what are we to do in this new situation? How do we proceed?*

A : Yes, you are right, this is a new question, and it naturally takes us into the beginnings of *self* - Knowing. We have already realized that the faculty of knowing is not really external to the eating bird. Rather, it is inseparable from the eating bird and this inseparability is what makes the whole business of *self* - Knowing more subtle and tricky.

The faculty of knowing and seeing which has been kind of unconsciously and automatically working, in all the activities of the eating bird, will now have to be skillfully turned in a different direction, namely upon the working of the *self* itself.

This is clearly possible, because the faculty surely exists in our life, but the new thing is that, we are going to very consciously use it not to taste and enjoy ice-creams and apples, but to observe the *self* at work. Apples and ice-cream are gross external sensory objects, whereas the *self* is a subtle, inner phenomenon. Nevertheless it will be a perceived object in this observation by the faculty of seeing and knowing.

Q : *I see that you have started using seeing, as though it were the same thing as knowing. Why have you suddenly brought in this new terminology?*

A : All the sages of India, who taught this *Jnana yoga* of Self - Realization and the lesser known *self* - Knowing have used seeing, and the scriptures also use that term, because it is more natural, as this seeing is going on all the time. In fact, more of seeing is used, and less of knowing. In truth, both are the same, and it is the *Atma* which is capable of both seeing and knowing.

29. The 'Enjoyer' *(Bhokta)* - Who is He?

Upadraṣṭā'numantā ca bhartā bhoktā Mah'eśvaraḥ |
Param'ātm'eti c'āpyukto dehe'smin puruṣaḥ paraḥ ||

- Bhagavad Gita : XIII.22 [26]

In this body, beyond the *Jiva*, there is also the Supreme Spirit, who is described as the Supreme Self *(Paramatma)* and Sovereign Lord *(Maheshwara)*; the unconcerned Witness *(Upadrashta)*; the Sanctioner *(Anumanta)*; the Supporter *(Bharta)*; and the Enjoyer *(Bhokta)*.

Q : *In the previous topic, we deciphered the mystery of knowing and seeing and discovered that they were sourced in the Atma, or the witnessing bird. Now you are talking of the faculty of enjoying, and are you trying to decipher the mystery of the enjoyer?*

A : Yes, I am trying to do just this. I am taking the support of the Hindu scripture of the Bhagavad Gita, Chapter XIII, which deals with the field of experience and the knower of this field. From that Chapter, I have selected this one sloka, because it throws special light on the witnessing bird [25].

Please note that the metaphor of the two birds is not from the Bhagavad Gita, but from many of the Upanishads. The *sloka* 22, gives a stunning description of the transcendent faculties which we know to be vested in the *Atma* or the witnessing bird.

Q   :   *What is the content of this potent sloka 22?*

A   :   The content is this:

"In this body, there is beyond the *self,* the Supreme Spirit, who is described as the Supreme Self *(Paramatma)* and Sovereign Lord *(Maheshwara),* the unconcerned Witness *(Upadrashta),* the Sanctioner *(Anumanta),* the Supporter *(Bharta),* and the Enjoyer *(Bhokta)."*

From this *sloka,* we will have to intelligently infer that the the Supreme Spirit, which is beyond the *self,* is the *Atma,* or the *Paramatma.*

Very significantly, it has many faculties, all of which are transcendent. Namely, the faculty of lordship and sovereignty *(Maheshwara)*; the faculty of *Sakshi* or *unconcerned witness from close quarters (Upadrashta)*; the faculty of sanctioning *(Anumanta)*; the faculty of supporting or bearing *(Bharta)*; and most importantly the faculty of enjoying *(Bhokta).*

Q   :   *I thought the poor eating bird was the one who was enjoying! Now, you have even robbed the eating bird of the enjoyership. I hope by degrees, you are not going to rob the eating bird of all its powers and faculties, so that in the end, it just becomes very weak, and has to fall down and die!*

A   :   You will be surprised to know that this is in fact my intention to lay a death trap for the eating bird, and unless I do this, the witnessing bird will not majestically rise on the horizon of your life. In truth the eating bird is shining in borrowed feathers, as it has misappropriated all the powers of the *Atma* and so when we reclaim these misappropriated powers, the eating bird will naturally come to an end. Are you with me in this?

Q   :   *Yes I do agree, this is shocking, but seems to have the ring of truth. However, I think we have digressed and moved away from my original question of why the eating bird is not the enjoyer?*

A   :   This whole business of enjoying life, enjoying good food, enjoying a bath, enjoying a conversation, enjoying sex, in fact every sensory delight, centered in the body, is so human an experience that we will have to look at it more closely.

Q : *In that case, let us go into that.*

A : The senses belong to the body, and whenever the senses of the *Jiva* feed on sense objects, there is sensory gratification, and the *Jiva is the experiencer*, because he has identified himself with the body. This delight is intimately tied up with the body, and as the eating bird or the *self* is wholly identified with the body, the eating bird naturally becomes a partaker of all the enjoyments of the body, but as the experiencer. The *sthitha prajnya's* senses also become engrossed in the sense objects, so while there is experiencing and enjoying, there is no experiencer as such. It is for this reason, we *Jivas* feel that we are the enjoyers, experiencers.

Q : *Why are we humans craving for enjoyment all the time?*

A : You are very correct in the observation that humans are craving for enjoyment all the time. We have already mentioned that the eating bird is just an unfaithful reflection of the *Atma* in the troubled waters of our consciousness and naturally also the body. The *Atma* is of the very nature of bliss-this is not 'our second nature', on the contrary, we are all bliss beings. Being bliss beings, and having lost that bliss in our earthly existence, we crave for every form of sensory delight which will come close to that natural bliss. This is a great secret, which sages and saints know so well.

Q : *Let us go back to the sloka 22 of Ch. XIII. There we saw many glories of the witnessing bird. Do these glories constitute our hidden Divine nature? You had said we have two natures, a human nature and a hidden Divine nature.*

A : These glories actually point to our Divine nature, and to come upon this Divine nature, which mostly lies hidden, because of the frenetic activity of the eating bird, the *self*, has to be calmed and silenced, thereafter nothing more needs to be done, the hidden Divine nature will manifest spontaneously and by itself.

Q : *If we are indeed the witnessing bird, then don't you think, we must be in a position to validate and vouch for every one of the glories mentioned?*

A : Technically yes, but there can be a catch here, because the moment the eating bird or the *self*, hears of these glories, its instinctive reaction will be to crave for the same and come into the possession of these glories. Now these glories cannot be pursued, cannot be sought, cannot be the reasons for beginning the spiritual life-in this sense, it may even be wise to veil these glories from the eating bird and the *self*, lest they give a wrong impression of the spiritual life. Rather, when the *self* has been calmed and silenced, because of detachment and awakening to sorrow in life, these glories will be in evidence, but no true saint and no true sage may even speak about them.

----

30. The *Atma* is the 'Close Witness, Sanctioner',...

The *Paramatma*, who is beyond the *Jiva*, is also called the:

1. Close Witness *(Upadrashta)*,

2. Sanctioner *(Anumanta)*,

3. Supporter *(Bharta)*,

4. Enjoyer *(Bhokta)*,

5. Sovereign Lord *(Maheswara)* and

6. Supreme Self *(Purushaha Paraha)*.

– Bhagavad Gita : XIII. 22[26]

Q : *Are we then sometimes, functioning also as the sanctioner, the close witness, the supporter, the enjoyer, the Sovereign Lord, the Supreme Self?*

A : Yes, sometimes, when it is our good fortune to fall silent and be just a witness. However, as we have not read the scriptures, we do not know that this seat of witness, comes with so many other powers and potencies, and we have not experimented enough being a close witness, so we know very little of what this can do as a protector and source of blessing.

Q : *Sovereign Lord means, no other Lord who is above this witness?*

A : Exactly, no other Lord. We need not even call this, witness, instead this is what Ramana Maharshi called, 'I', the Self. And what Nisargadatta Maharaj called, 'conscious presence'.

----

31. Two 'Tat Tvam Asi' Birds in the Mundaka Up.

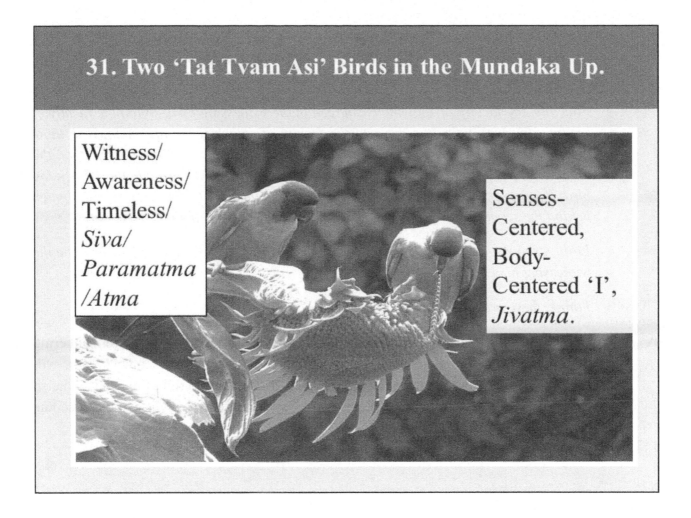

Witness/ Awareness/ Timeless/ *Siva/ Paramatma /Atma*

Senses-Centered, Body-Centered 'I', *Jivatma*.

Q : *Can we say that the intention of this topic is to bring together, all the insights into the two Tat Tvam Asi birds, that we have had up till this point?*

A : Yes, this is the idea. And I want you to recapitulate all the insights.

Q : *So, I'll then gather together all the insights, point wise.*

Firstly, the self is represented by the eating bird. It is body-centered, senses-centered. The self ever dwells in the past experiences (remember the solitary man, and the solitary woman, wandering in the street), or day dreams about the future. Thus the self is limited, lonely, sorrowful and totally incapable of solving any of the problems of life.

Secondly, I would say that the self, which is represented by the eating bird, is our human nature, and quite apart from this human nature all of us also have the Divine nature, which is in the background and which is represented by the witnessing bird.

Thirdly, my understanding of these meditations is that they will help us to discover that we are also indeed the witnessing bird. Thus we are in fact, both the birds, and therefore the words Tat Tvam Asi, for the birds is apt.

Fourthly, the faculty of knowing is sourced in the witnessing bird, so too the faculty of seeing. However, when we come to the faculty of enjoying, we are inclined to think that the eating bird is the enjoyer. After further enquiry, we discovered that the ultimate experiencing, enjoying happens, behind the body, through the witnessing bird. Because, knowing is an integral part of being human, the witnessing bird, though behind the scenes, is very much part of the human drama, as a silent spectator.

Fifthly, so long as the eating bird is ever busy, there is never a chance for us to be the witnessing bird.

I think, these are all the insights we have had till now.

A   :   Good, everything has been summed up cogently. Just like to add, remembering Sri Nisargadatta Maharaj's words that liberation-whether it will come or not, will depend upon whether we are able to remember the truth at the right time and so on, so this tells us that we will have to internalize, everyone of these insights, so they become our breath, our blood, our bones!

32. *Atma* **(Water) without the contamination by** *Maya* **(Algae)**

Q : *Looking at this absolutely clear pond, can such an ideal state be reached?*

A : When there is integrity for the *Jiva*, and the *Jiva* has no private and secret agenda of its own and has *nirguna bhakti* (the seventh or highest *bhakti*) to *Parabrahma*, then the pond will be blemishless like this.

----

33. 'Watching Bird' is the Awareness *(Chit)*

Q : *Is it to drive home the point that the witnessing bird is not really any bird (How could it be?), or any formful, identifiable object-that you have replaced the witnessing bird by the brilliant light?*

A : Indeed, precisely for this very reason. We can never go on an expedition of discovery, searching for the witnessing bird, simply because we are that very witnessing bird. Life does not exist if that witnessing bird, the awareness is not there.

----

34. The '*Paramatma*' Bird is the 'Witness'

Q : *Again emphasizing the witnessing bird, which though seemingly non-existent, yet it is the sustainer and source of all life and the cosmos?*

A : Yes.

Q : *What is the idea in showing the witness bird as light?*

A : Just to drive home the point that it is the light by which we see and we are also this light which sees. Later, you will discover for yourself that, there is no seer, but seeing only, because of this light.

----

35. A Timeless Self *(Atma)* and a 'time-bound' *Jiva*.

1. The timeless *Atma* just 'illuminates', 'seeing' all time-based happenings within consciousness.

2. *Jiva* enjoys and suffers. *Jiva* is a limited, imperfect and distorted image of the *Atma* in the field of the body and consciousness.

3. *Jiva's self* and attachments/cravings must drop out, only then, *Jiva* will discover that it is the 'I', in pure form. Before, it had the coatings of attachments /ambitions and it's horrible *self.*

Q : *This looks like a recurring theme, the two selves of man, which you have already portrayed as the two Tat Tvam Asi birds of the Mundaka Upanishad, and you have also stressed at the very beginning that man has an all too human nature and then also a hidden nature, which is Divine. Am I right in supposing that, you are doing this, with the intention to make this go home to us-because realization may be just this deep understanding and nothing more? Am I making myself clear?*

A : Yes, every good teacher has to go on repeating the same truth from different points of view-I am also doing just this. The Bhagavad Gita, in chapter XIII, stresses that true wisdom is the ability to distinguish between the knower, who is the *Atma*, and consciousness and the body which is the field or *kshetra* [26]. If you ask me whether, this clear intellectual understanding is all there is to it, all there is to realization, then I have something more to add to all this. Detachment, and the calming and silencing of the *self* is a prerequisite to this realization, and this detachment means lessening of desires, lessening of sensory life, lessening of worldly responsibilities-and it is because of all these ingredients that the Hindu sages, said, after 60 or 65, one is a better qualified candidate for *moksha*.

36. '*Siva*' as our True Self *(Atma)*

Sankara : "Something in you has not changed at all, from the time you were a small child. Your body has changed and become old, your thoughts and goals have changed, even your personality has changed. Discover and know that changeless bedrock upon which the drama of consciousness is happening. This timeless bedrock is yourself, at your roots: As Truth *(Sat)*, Intelligence *(Chit)* and Peace *(Ananda)*."

Sankara: The sensory world, the star-studded night sky, the mountains and trees, the mighty rivers, all are so stupendous to behold that, reeling under the spell of this sensory 'invasion', we practically lose sight of the very simple fact that without a human observer, the marvelous spectacle of the universe with its spiralling galaxies and solar system, will not be there! After all, this wonderful spectacle happens to the consciousness of man, not only because of the sophistication of his biological organism, but also because of the awareness in him, the 'I am' (the *Atma*). This awareness is very subtle, in fact almost 'imperceptible', because we are that awareness, so we cannot even perceive it, we can only be that. Yet, notwithstanding this subtle and intangible nature, it is indeed the 'canvas', on which the living world appears. This canvas exists and is the truth, it is *Sat*. This canvas is awareness *(Chit)* and intelligence too. It is also 'wellness', feeling of inner peace *(Ananda)*. The ancient Hindu sages called this 'canvas', *Atma*.

---

37. The Self, the *Atma*

"This Self is 'That' which has been described as, 'Not this', 'Not this' *(Neti, Neti)*. It is Imperceptible."

- Brihadaaranyaka Upanishad [IV.22].

Q : *Is the emphasis on two words, 'That' and then, 'This'?*

A : Yes, the Self is assigned to 'That', which means it is far away from all knowable objects, all recognizable objects, from all perceptible objects, eventhough we are It.

Q : *Does, 'This' refers to all recognizable, knowable sensory objects?*

A : Yes, precisely.

Q : *Does, 'Not This', 'Not This' refer to our systematic putting aside or negation of all perceivable objects, all objects which the senses can detect?*

A : Yes, the idea of *'Neti, Neti'* (Not this, Not this), is to make the seeker, shift his attention from the world of sensory objects to the subject, who is always imperceptible and unknowable-himself. Yet the strange thing is that we are the subject, and we can never know ourselves as any object.

Q : *What is the meaning of this long name, Brihadaranyaka, can you give a simple insight?*

A : '*Brihad*' means vast, *aranyaka* means forest. So this *Upanishad* probably took birth, as a teaching given in some big forest.

38. The Greatest Wonder: The *Atma*

Āścarya-vat paśyati kaścid enam
     āścarya-vad vadati tathaiva cānyaḥ |
Āścarya-vac cainam anyaḥ śṛṇoti
     Śrutvāpy enaṁ veda na caiva kaścit||

- **Bhagavad Gita : II.29[7]**

"Some see the *Atma* as a great marvel,

Some speak of the *Atma* as a great wonder,

Some hear of the *Atma* as a great marvel.

Yet, none understands the *Atma* at all!"

Q : *So, if I understand correctly, taking Arjuna's despondency on the battle field into account, even for ordinary people like us, when there is a horrendous crisis in life, when all things fail to resolve our conflict, do we need the strongest and the ultimate medicine, the truth of the Atma, to free us from the madness of maya?*

A : Indeed, all of us need this strongest medicine, at a critical time, when all other supporting illusions would have collapsed and given way. Then the truth alone will bring in order, if we are fortunate enough to have faith and an open mind. Here the ultimate medicine, is the truth about the Divine and the *Atma*, our true Self.

Q : *Why is it that we do not feel the mystery and wonder of the Atma, is it because we are too much in maya?*

A : In truth, we are blinded by so many attachments and we are therefore not empty. To really see a wonderful thing, we must be empty. In this case, *maya* is our entire attachments to the world, to people, to money to status. And all of these attachments, including the attachment to the body, comes as a veil between us and the truth of what we see. To see the wonder and mystery of the *Atma*, you must be an outsider in this world. As Krishnamurti would say, a respectable man can never come anywhere near this infinite power.

39. Your Two Keys: *Sakti* - Key, *Siva* - Key

Q   : *You have shown two different locks and each has got its own key along with a duplicate. One lock has Saraswati's figure embossed (Sarasawati is the Hindu deity of learning and knowledge) and the other lock has the figure of Ganesha, which stands for spiritual knowledge, Siva and the Atma. So, are you saying that we have to choose that key, which will unlock that particular problem in our life?*

A   : Your understanding is quite correct, but let me say something more about the locks and the keys. In life, there are many problems we have to face, but broadly all problems can be put into two boxes. In one box, we will have all the problems which can be solved by dedicated thinking-these are the problems the scientists, the technologists, doctors, lawyers and even ordinary people are trying to solve. So, in this case, the problem is represented by the *Saraswati* lock, and the key to open it is by skillful thinking. But even in these, spheres in the process of resolving the mystry of life, sometimes the *Ganesha / Siva* key may have to be resorted to.

Then there are other problems which also exist in our human life, *where thinking will never solve that problem.* For example, death happens and the person who died is our beloved-any amount of skillful thinking will not take away the pain, due to the loss by death.

Or take another, more common example - a person, man or woman has been divorced, then that individual is emotionally very hurt and thoughts and feelings do not stop, but they keep raging like a cyclone, day after day, week after week, month after month, and the solution has to be one in which thought stops, not one in which thought will skillfully solve some problem. So in such cases, the whole machinery of thought has to be shut down, and silence must be pressed into service-this is the *yogic* method of negating thought, for only by such negation, the lock can be opened-so this key is different. For the discovery of the Divine, after working with thought for some time, thought must be shut down-this is what we are implying-only then realization can happen. This latter key is the *Ganesha* key.

----

40. 'You' are the 'Master Key'*(Atma)*. The *Guru* points to the Key, shows you how to use It skillfully

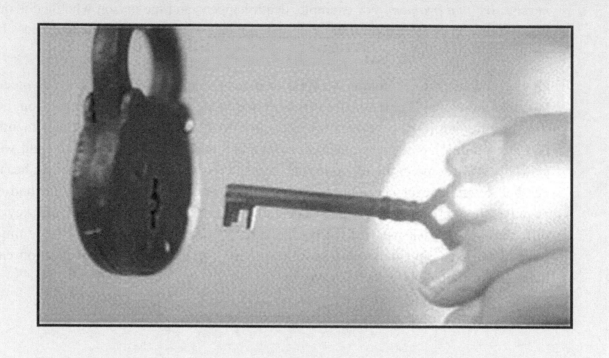

Q : *You have said, 'You, yourself are the master key'. So in other words, if we are silent within ourselves, then, you would perhaps say, the master key is the witnessing bird? Correct?*

A : Yes, absolutely, the witnessing bird is the master key and the key becomes available to us only when we are intelligent enough to negate thought and its activity, so that the witnessing bird has a chance to become functional.

The *guru* is the one who will help you to discover that, you, have this key or he will correct wrong thinking that some *guru* or the other has this key. In the sphere of *moksha*, it is the highest form of ignorance to think that the *guru* has the key and some deity has the key, but that, that key is not with you. Here in Self - Realization, the *Atma* is the lock as well as the key, and this is obviously a paradox.

Q : *At this point, the question arises, whether all gurus, now in the present stage of the world, or in the past, have done this-to point out that one is oneself the master key?*

A : This is a very disturbing question which I'll answer in the following way. Among all the *gurus* of the present and of the past, there are many functions that they are performing. Sometimes they throw light on problems in the two material spheres of *artha and kama*, sometimes, they may throw light on what is *dharma*, or how to inculcate *dharma* in life, and sometimes they may address questions, only belonging to the sphere of *moksha*. So there are various kinds of *gurus*, defined by the domain of their *dharma*, the particular sphere in which they have mastery.

Adi Sankaracharya, Sri. Ramana Maharshi, Sri. J. Krishnamurti, Sri. Nisargadatta Maharaj - all are excellent illustrations of *gurus* who address questions *only in the sphere of moksha, and all these four masters emphatically told you that you were yourself the master key, the Atma.*

When the *gurus* are addressing problems in the spheres of *artha, kama,* and *dharma,* then, they may not reveal this ultimate secret that you are yourself the master key. Because the ignorance and *maya* in the lives of the seekers in those realms may be so thick that the master key may make no sense. In the Bhagavad Gita and in all the Upanishads, the emphasis is on the truth of the master key only.

So I hope with this clarification, it is understood that different masters and *gurus* of the present age or the bygone ages have been working according to their *swadharma*, which is also according to the Divine mandate. Each master or *guru* is fulfilling the collective human need for a certain kind of solace or salvation. Sometimes a *guru* also addresses the human need for fulfillment in all four *purusharthas* of life.

----

41. It is Important to Observe Inner Suffering

1. Outer Suffering………

2. All Outer Suffering Implies Inner Suffering.

Q : *By outer suffering, are you referring to physical things like, a disease, a heart attack, cancer, thefts, loss by floods, dishonor and disgrace in society, enmity, death and accident, law suits, etc. - you mean all of these?*

A : Yes, indeed, every one of these outer forms.

Q : *And by inner suffering, are you referring to how the self, experiences all these outer sufferings - to put it very briefly?*

A : Precisely, for corresponding to every outer form of suffering, there is also an inner form-how the *self* experiences that loss, that disease, that enmity, that disgrace, etc. All that is inner suffering. We have to become extremely sensitive to this inner drama and experience, all that was meant for the *self* to experience, but which the *self*, very cleverly and cunningly, puts under the carpet.

Q : *Why does the self not want to accept its lot of losses in one form or the other?*

A : We have gone into this before, but let us remember the ground we had covered earlier. This *self*, mischievous and ridiculous though it may be - because of the constant *self-*

156

deceptions it is undergoing, it is nevertheless, an image of the imperishable *Atma*, our Divine nature. As the *Atma* is untouched by time, so the *self* too wishes to be imperishable. This is seen in the simple fact of life, nobody wants to die even in old age. So, because the *self,* has the *samskara* of timelessness, it does not want its *ananda* to diminish in any way, even in this perishable human existence-so it tries very unsuccessfully of course, to flee from reality.

42. Some Questions open the door to *self* - Knowing

1. Do *you* live by comparison with others?

2. Do *you* have unbearable grief?

3. Do *you* have a great sense of loss?

4. Are *you* perpetually fighting with yourself?

5. Are *you* bored and restless, directionless?

6. Are *you* constantly looking for excitement?

7. Do *you* suffer from jealousy, dishonesty, greed, hatred, revenge, lust, anger, guilt, fear, pride, addictions?

8. Do *you* think too poorly of yourself?

Q : *This is in essence, the human condition isn't it?*

A : This is so.

Q : *We are all certainly part of this human condition - in answer to your question as to what our condition is. In fact, most of us, may be all of these conditions. So what is the purpose of your question?*

A : While each condition may be true for a certain individual, clearly no one can be happy to be in any one of these conditions. Will you agree?

Q : *Yes, every condition is naturally painful. Are you trying to put us all in a state of self - Knowing, so that we may come to grips with our actual conditions?*

A : This is the idea, to make ourselves *self* - Knowing, because *self* - Knowing is the first step in ending the pain, and in winding up the human drama, winding up the whole painful way in which we have been living.

Q : *Should we take up these conditions, say one or two, which are particularly applicable to us and which still have sufficient emotional charge, almost ready to explode, so to speak?*

A : Yes, you have to identify the *self,* observe the *self,* and as we said, the *self* is always present in a certain context, what we called *what is* and having identified this *what is,* which could be one of these eight conditions, you have to become intimate with this *what is* and this intimacy will give you knowledge of the *self* for the very first time in your life. You never had an opportunity to look at yourself, you were always looking outside, at the world, at others, here for the very first time, you are meeting yourself, your pain-all this is *self* - Knowing. I maintain that without this *self* - Knowing, there can be no spiritual life-all spiritual life becomes a humbug and a non-starter.

----

43. Understanding the Suffering *Jiva*

1. *Who* is suffering? Why does suffering arise?

2. If the *Jiva* stops suffering (by magic, say), then will the outer suffering be experienced in the same way or differently?

3. To end the suffering of the *Jiva*. The *Jiva* must be known, understood, pacified-then it stops suffering. The *Jiva (self)* can and must fall silent.

Q : *In reply to your provocative question, who is suffering, isn't it obvious that the self is suffering?*

A : You got it right, indeed who else can suffer, only a 'centre' can suffer that and that centre is the *self*. But the important point to note is that without the imperishable *Atma*, there can be no *self*, either. Is this clear?

Q : *Yes, this is clear, because you have been reiterating that the mischievous, ridiculous self, is an impoverished reflection of the Atma, isn't it?*

A : Right. So I am glad, it is understood that it is the *self* which suffers. We have to pause and take note at this juncture that, *when we suffer* we are intensely aware and the intensity of the feeling is so deep that, when we pause to think of it, we may not be convinced to relegate this suffering to the *self* only and put the *Atma*, far far away, as though it had no share at all in this suffering. Am I making sense?

Q : *Yes, are you trying to say that the Atma is also suffering, because of an invisible bond with the little self and which the little self is not aware of at all?*

A : Yes, more or less this is what I am saying. In the scripture of the Bhagavad Gita, it is mentioned that the *Atma* is also the *bhokta*, the enjoyer. Now the *Atma* is the *bhokta*, because the nature of the *Atma* is *ananda*, or causeless joy. So the embodied *Atma*, is always delighted when it meets in experience, anything which has a semblance to its true nature. This *Atma* is also pure feeling which is love.

Q : *Another question arises now-if the Atma is ananda, pure feeling, love, how does this Atma ever manage to get into suffering?*

A : It is the *self* which suffers, because the *self*, by definition is limited, and there are only two kinds of experiences for the *self*, one kind which pleases the *self*, another kind which displeases the *self*. You have to notice the fact that everyone likes to be happy, no one likes to suffer, and after all, we are all the time, trying to avoid suffering, are we not? This is so, because our, that is the *Atma's*, root nature is *ananda*, but note that without the *Atma*, there is no little *self*. So the *Atma* implicitly suffers, while the *self*, explicitly suffers. It is much like a child suffering, and immediately the mother also naturally suffering, the mother is the *Atma* in this example, the child is the *self*.

----

44. How Do Humans Get Hurt?

Sankara : "That which is solidly peaceful, the total, unborn, the indefinable, the deathless, the *Atma*, the witness, the timeless awareness, cannot ever get hurt (because for it, the sense of peace and contentment is so deep that nothing can possibly ruffle it). Only that which is limited, fragile like glass, can be hurt/broken. The pure 'I' cannot be hurt.

"Two eating birds can certainly and will get hurt. But two witnessing birds can only have a beautiful, harmonious relationship. One witnessing bird will have no difficulty in relating to any eating bird (in spite of all its weaknesses)."

Sankara: "Let us consider astrological light on getting hurt and freedom from hurts. Astrologically, the IVH lord and the Moon signify inner contentment and peace. When these variables are strong in the rasi chart (RC) and in the div chart (DC) of the IVH (fourth house), we have the condition of equanimity in the *self*. The Su is also a significator of the IVH of the *Atma,* so when the IVH is strong, one has good inner contentment and inner equanimity. People who have a very weak IVH, weak Mo, and weak Su, will be more emotionally insecure, and will get hurt more easily. All this is astrological light on the human phenomenon of getting hurt."

----

45. Who got hurt? The *Atma* cannot get hurt!

Sankara : "The feeling of getting hurt is very real, painful and unmistakable. The *Atma*, being infinite cannot be hurt. It is only the 'investment' of the *Atma*, in the human consciousness as the *Jiva*, which must be getting hurt. When the *Atma* is rolled back, retreats and withdraws Itself from the field of human consciousness, one becomes innocent, and cannot then be hurt. The master J. Krishnamurti has said, 'Innocence is incapability of getting hurt.'"

Sankara: Whereever the *self* has developed attachment to something; say, a philosophy, an individual, a belief, the family, religion, personal God, all of these attachments, make the *self* at once, vulnerable to getting hurt. Why is this so? Only because, there are other selves in the world, who may challenge, threaten, or even take away, what the *self*, dearly holds, as its own possessions. Then the *self*, suffering loss of one of its cherished possessions, comes to grieve. On the other hand, if the *self*, were to be aloof, knowing the 'danger' of attachment; that too, may surprisingly put the *self* at the risk of pain and suffering. Because, rather than loving the world, which is the most natural thing to do; the *self*, has isolated itself, has gone into a secure shell of protection, and, as such a disposition has not become natural for that *self*, but rather, it has only taken that stance, in the fond hope of keeping suffering out of its life; even this way is seen to invite suffering, sooner or later. Thus avoiding the world, and moving away from the world too is no solution at all. By yielding to sorrow in life, and drinking the concomitant pain, which is its lot, the *self*, may come to renounce its ways, and in this way alone, humbling itself, it may diligently arrive at its own peace, with the unexpected glory of *prajnya* (*Atmic* intelligence) as a blessing.

162

46. Two 'Eating Birds' are 'blind', so are prone to pain in relationship

Q : *We are all the time looking for some simple spiritual medicines, like yoga, some special meditation, some practice, which we hope will for ever free us from hurts and also enable us to never get hurt again. What is the way, you are suggesting?*

A : Unless the *Jiva* falls silent, there is no hope for the *Jiva*. We are under the greatly mistaken idea that, if the *Jiva* falls silent, it is as good as death, and so we dread this silence of the *Jiva*. Little do we realize that, this silence of the *Jiva*, is the beginning of life, which means, in spite of all the frenetic activity of the *self*, we are dead with boredom, dead with conflict, dead with insensitivity.

The solution is the ending of the life of the *Jiva* and this is not something to be frightened of, as I said, it marks a new life, full of wonder, full of humility, and grace coming unexpectedly, without praying, without asking.

----

47. A Model of the *Jiva (Atma* with *Maya)*

Man's body = *Atma,* sticking algae = *maya* (illusions), *self,* mass of memories, ambitions, experiences, attachments, hurts.

Q : *Is this just a reiteration of the idea of maya and illusion like in the pond water contaminated by algae.*

A : We have to go slowly here, for this metaphor has two different meanings. The body represents the *Atma,* the true Self, which is hidden and the algae represents the multiple false selves, covering and blinding the *Atma.* This is one interpretation so that we may all get the intellectual conviction of the importance of purification. The same metaphor can also mean the following. The body represents the erroneous thinking of the *Jiva* that it is the body. And the algae represent all the mischief and illusions and false selves of the *Jiva.* In the usage of this metaphor in this way, there is no room for the *Atma,* but the metaphor brings into life the root illusion which is the *Jiva's* thinking that it is the body.

Q : *You have again brought in the word self and referred to it as the sticking algae. Will you explain how this self is different from the Jiva, if it is different at all?*

A : *Jiva* is a term found in the *advaitic* literature of India. For example, a very long time ago, Adi Sankaracharya has said *Jivo brahmaiva na paraha.* This means that the *Jiva* only is *Brahman* or the Absolute, not anything other than this. When is this true? Only when the *Jiva* is purified, for then all the algae is stripped clean and the *Atma* shines (invoking the algae-man metaphor, already familiar to us). In the literature of Krishnamurti, the term *Jiva* is not used, but *self* is used. In truth *Jiva* is the *self* or if you want to be more meticulous, you can call the *self* the very essence of the *Jiva*. So it is the *Jiva's self*.

Q : *Honestly speaking, this seems a most wonderful metaphor, coming to think of it. However, you have referred to the body of this man as the Atma, whereas, everywhere else, you are saying, that the very identity of the Jiva that it is the body is the curse on mankind. Are these usages not contradictory?*

A : These usages are not contradictory because they are mentioned in different contexts. We always have to look at the inner meaning as well as the context of the metaphor.

48. 'When the Heart enters into the Mind, the Mind has quite a Different Quality.....'

"Meditation is not an intellectual affair, but when the heart enters into the mind, the mind has quite a different quality; it is really, then, limitless, not only in its capacity to think, to act efficiently, but also in its sense of living in a vast space where you are part of everything."

- J. Krishnamurti in 'Meditations'[13]

Q : *What Krishnamurti says: 'When the heart enters into the mind, the mind has quite a different quality'-is he here referring to the heart being awakened? Does that mean that we are no longer in that limited cage, defined by our memories and experiences?*

A : Heart entering into the mind is the *self* falling silent, rather than being incessantly active. The *Atma* is the heart. With the silencing of the *self*, automatically the *Atma* comes into relief.

Q : *Does it also mean that our faculties are more heightened?*

A : Yes, the senses are then fully awake.

Q : *If I were to interpret differently, the heart entering into the mind-does it mean the little self, resonating with the Self? What would this resonance mean operationally?*

A : Resonance would mean, the *self* has fallen silent. Once it falls silent, it has wound up its mad activity, its wandering attention, and its movements in insecurity, then it is in resonance with the witnessing bird. Then the new life dawns.

----

49. The danger of pursuing order excessively....

"The soil in which the meditative mind can begin is the soil of everyday life, the strife, the pain and the fleeting joy. It must begin there, and bring order, and from there move endlessly. But if you are concerned only with making order, then that very order will bring about its own limitation and the mind will be its prisoner."

- J. Krishnamurti in 'Meditations'[13]

Q : *In this meditation from Krishnamurti, we must realize that most of us suffer from the fear of the unknown, so how would you expect us to take the plunge, as it were and reach out to the other shore?*

A : We have two dimensions, a human dimension, to which all your logic applies, the fear, etc. However, we are also a timeless being, a witness, with infinite Divine possibilities. Because, we are always with a swarm of thoughts and feelings, we are never able to know ourselves, as we are, without these thoughts and feelings. This witness is our deeper nature and this whole retreat is devoted to the discovery of this concealed inner nature called the *Atma*. This is the realm of all possibilities.

Q : *So, is it like pressing the emergency button, which may be always there, but which we are unaware of?*

A : Yes, we are unconscious of the mechanism of how some of our difficult problems get resolved. We call that grace, result of prayer, blessing, etc. However, this Divine Source is also our very Self. We do not know this, we cannot be aware of it as we can be aware of the Sun and the Mo and the trees. This retreat is intended to help us to get

167

at this treasure, which we are already. It is not a new treasure or a new blessing which will come to you from the outside world, from another source.

Q : *Why does Krishnamurti say, "And the beauty of meditation is that, you never know where you are, where you are going, what the end is?"*

A : Our limited human nature makes us everlastingly seek security, we need to be constantly assured that we will find some great treasure, if not now, at least in the future, etc. However, when we see ourselves as the *Atma*, as it surely happens in these meditations, then we are naturally going to be fearless, rather than afraid. In fact all creative minds have this enormous courage and spirit of adventure-without this, they would never have discovered, all the wonderful things they discovered. Theirs was a journey into the unknown. So, Krishnamurti says, this is the nature of these meditative journeys, they are mysterious journeys into the bosom of truth, into the unknown.

Second Day (Chapter - II), 2ⁿᵈ 'Tat Tvam Asi' Meditation

Do you have a difficult *what is?*
Identify the *what is* and abide in it.

By Being the *Atma*, Identify, Observe, and Understand the *Jiva*,
within the context of *what is.*

Chapter III

By Being the Atma,
Knowing and Taming of the *Jiva, happens*

Accept and understand the *Jiva*

Be with the *Jiva* and be the *Jiva*

Purify the *Jiva* (end conflict, develop integrity)

Be the *Jiva* at times, be also at other times beyond the *Jiva,* as *Siva* (Self, *Atma*)

1. 'You must take a plunge into the water, not knowing how to swim.'

"In all this movement you must somehow begin from the other end, from the other shore, and not always be concerned with this shore or how to cross the river.

"You must take a plunge into the water, not knowing how to swim. And the beauty of meditation is that you never know where you are, where you are going, what the end is."

- J. Krishnamurti in 'Meditations'[13]

Q : *This meditation from Krishnamurti presupposes the situation or context of a seeker standing on one bank of a river and wishing to go over to the other bank. What are the two banks Krishnamurti is talking about?*

A : To begin with, we have to realize that we are the *Jiva*, standing on 'this bank', which is the 'consciousness country'. Life on this bank is full of duality, conflict and sorrow. All sourced in the separation between the *self* and the other, and obviously, the *self* is the *Jiva*. The yonder bank is '*Atma* country or awareness country' - there, there is no separation between *self* and another. We may note that Krishnamurti never used the terms *Jiva* and *Atma*. One understands this very well, because he was not a traditionalist, but rather an original mystic. In his parlance, the other bank is awareness country, or to use another term of Krishnamurti, the country one is in, when thought has ended, thought meaning calculation and divisiveness in thinking.

Q : *That means, the metaphor of the two banks and the seeker crossing from one to the other is inapplicable here in this retreat?*

A : Quite so, because, as I shall presently explain, somehow the *Jiva*, notwithstanding its entanglement in duality and *maya*, paradoxically also does have a foothold on the other bank. Now how can we understand this paradox? Let us go back to the model of the algae man. In that model, you will admit that, notwithstanding the *Jiva* being mired in a lot of illusions, the *Jiva* does also have the *Atmic* presence, at the very core of his being. Now there are people who can acknowledge this *Atmic* presence readily and probably there are also a large number of people, who may not be able to straightaway concede that there is indeed an *Atmic* presence in them. Either way, because of that *Atmic* presence, one may say, the *Jiva* is just an infinitesimal distance away from the other bank of the *Atmic* country. So, one must be wary of rational thought and analogies, such as 'this bank and that bank', for such commonsense metaphors may not reflect reality precisely. Thus, there is the risk of being fooled by the way we use language and common sense metaphors, so one must be very vigilant.

Q : *Krishnamurti's words of taking a plunge into the water, not knowing how to swim-what does it mean in terms of the life and acts of the seeker?*

A : As children, our parents told us what to do in any given difficult situation, so on all those occasions, we never had to think for ourselves. However, in later adult life, it often happens that we have to face some challenge or the other, but we will find, if we are honest and a little introspective that in an impasse, we invariably *do not know, how to proceed.* At such times, we have to pose the question to ourselves and wait for the insight and once the insight flashes from within, we surely know, how to make the next move. So, in kindred fashion, when facing any challenge in our inner or outer life, we have to start facing the unknown and make a foray into the unknown in an intelligent way, by waiting and being fully aware that we do not know how to proceed. By admitting that we do not know and by embracing the unknown, we will get the insight, which will show the way and open doors.

Q : *Why does Krishnamurti say, "And the beauty of meditation is that, you never know where you are, where you are going, what the end is?"*

A : Our limited human nature makes us everlastingly seek security, we need to be constantly assured that we will find some great treasure, if not now, at least in the future, etc. However, when our *Atmic* nature comes into play, as it surely does in these meditations, then we are naturally going to be fearless, rather than afraid. In fact all creative minds have this enormous courage and spirit of adventure-without this, they would never have discovered, all the wonderful things they discovered. Theirs was a journey into the unknown. So, Krishnamurti says, this is the nature of these meditative journeys, they are mysterious journeys into the bosom of truth, into the unknown.

----

2. 'Is Gold Itself Crooked?' - Revisited

"Is Gold Itself crooked? But when you make an ornament out of it-that is, you give Gold a form and name, it becomes distorted and crooked!

"Just by giving yourself a name, you became crooked! Gold as such is not stupid! Gold means the Self without name and form. But when this Gold was transformed into an ornament, and given a name, the distortion and stupidity started!"

- Sri Nisargadatta Maharaj[21]

Q : *Is the analogy of gold, referring to the Atma?*

A : Yes, indeed. It also refers to the witnessing bird and the ocean, in the metaphors we have been discussing.

Q : *The adverbs and adjectives used by Maharaj, do they refer then to the little self?*

A : Surely, the little *self,* the *Jiva* is being referred to, and it is sometimes stupid, because of its limitations and attachments.

This *sutra* from Maharaj, must be memorized and remembered, because it portrays our true Self, the *Atma,* in very graphic terms.

Q : *Why does Maharaj say gold becomes distorted and crooked?*

A : O, I see your difficulty. We have to understand the difficulty of a master, who lives and functions in the *Atmic* country. Though he lives in the *Atmic* country, he is being listened to only by inhabitants *(Jivas)* of the consciousness country. Strictly speaking what the master says will be intelligible only in the *Atmic* country, but somehow he has to make it intelligible to *Jivas*, living in the consciousness country. In the consciousness country, gold is the most valued thing, something all *Jivas* crave for and go after. So, he is making an analogy between what we as *Jivas*, treasure and love to have as the most prized possession, namely gold and *Atma*, the mother matrix of the *Jiva*. So this gold is the *Atma*, and what is carved out of this infinite source, the *Atma*, is the relatively petty *Jiva*, which would then naturally correspond to some small piece of jewelry carved out of that source, gold *(Atma)*. As inhabitants of the consciousness country, we would be attaching quite some importance to a piece of jewelry, but from the point of view of Maharaj, this piece of jewelry, the *Jiva*, is a trifling creation of the *Atma*, so it is full of imperfections and bereft of glory. Unless, we get into his shoes and see how he perceives a piece of trifling jewelry, i.e., the *Jiva*, we may not be able to appreciate the wonderful humor inherent in this metaphor. The adjectives, distorted and crooked, will be self-evident in the *Atmic* country, but unacceptable to you in the consciousness country!

----

3. *By Being the Atma,* to know all aspects (open and hidden) of the *Jiva*

Accept and understand the *Jiva*.

Be with the *Jiva* and be the *Jiva*.

Purify the *Jiva* (end conflict, develop Integrity).

Be the *Jiva* at times. Be also at other times beyond the *Jiva, as Siva* (Self, *Atma*).

Q : *By 'open' are you referring to the self, as the world knows this self, namely its outer appearance in society, in the family - as a 'nice person', a doctor or politician, or very rich and very beautiful, etc.?*

A : Indeed, this is the outer appearance of the *self,* which is visible to the family, to society, to friends, etc. It may be very different from what that individual actually is.

Q : *So, 'hidden' would then refer to the self, that you alone know- your deep dark secrets, your secret ambitions, your anger, your jealousy, your strategies, your enmities, your sorrows, your hurts, all your cunning planning in thought?*

A : Perfect, the hidden part is known only to ourselves. But to say, it is even 'known' to us is quite wrong, because we know the darker side of the *self,* the inner agony, the sleepless nights, the deep emotional hurts, *only superficially,* for society does not encourage us to meet this painful side of ourselves, it is not a part of the mainstream culture of humanity, so man carries this burden all through his life, so in the end death is invariably not a happy leave-taking, instead we depart with an unfinished agenda, full of sorrow.

Q : *Coming to the second point of accepting and understanding the self, is it that the emphasis here is on accepting the hidden part-which is a bitter pill to swallow?*

A : It is indeed bitter pill no doubt, but we have really no option but to swallow it. The alternative would be *to postpone swallowing it*, to postpone even meeting with it-this is what a greater part of humanity is doing (consciously or unconsciously)-again only because humanity may still be only in infancy. Hopefully, as humanity matures, it will become part of the mainstream culture and then our newspapers, our entertainment industry, our parents, our consumer society will induce us to swallow this pill-then it will be a lot easier. It has not become mainstream culture as of now, only because people think that this inner growth and maturation threatens, goes completely against the spirit of a brutally competitive society, based on greed and survival. The challenge for any seeker is to step out of this main stream culture which is to a large extent driven by fear - as to whether one will physically, psychologically and socially survive.

Q : *How does one 'purify' the self?*

A : This is a very pertinent question and very important in the spiritual life - because in India in all the *ashrams*, they are talking of *chitta shuddhi* or inner integrity, inner purity and inner cleanliness - so what can this mean?

Integrity is purity in one sense - this is the first kind of purity. After we have looked at this first kind of purity, we can look at the second and third kind of purity. This means, thought, word and deed have to be aligned in a single unified direction and must not be contradictory to each other. This means, we must not make wild promises to people, and what we promise, we must act according to the words we have spoken. And the words we speak must also reflect exactly what we feel within-this implies that all diplomacy has to be renounced, all sweet talk has to be renounced, you must speak only what you feel within yourself. Obviously, this calls for courage, and becomes possible only with the dissolution of our ulterior motives. Even being silent, when one knows the truth and when one ought to speak it, destroys integrity. So, behavior, thought and word must have no mutual contradiction. This is integrity and this is purity - this is where we have to get. And our starting point could well be the opposite, namely hypocrisy, games, manipulations and so long as hypocrisy, clever talk, ulterior motives, lying, games are going on, there is absolutely no integrity, and no purity. *You have to be your own policeman, since you are also the thief.*

A higher kind of purity comes about, after purity of integrity has been established and this is the purity that comes from negation of the *self*, negation of thought. And even beyond this second purity is the third kind of purity that arises from the calmed and silenced *self.*

Q : *'Being the self at times'-to use your own words-would this mean, being the impure person that one is, say being a liar or being a dishonest deceiver, just continuing your old rotten life, but now never fighting with yourself, but instead just being compassionately aware of that impurity?*

A : Right, this is what has to be achieved in our meditations and in our daily life. We have to be 100% compassionate with ourselves. This is the journey. And the strange thing we will find is that much as we may desire to turn a new leaf, or to reform ourselves, we may find to our dismay that the old habits in thought and action do not come to an end so easily. This means, we may have to be compassionate with ourselves, usually for some years, before the transformation will come about and the new life blossoms of its own accord, fully.

----

4. The Two 'Tat Tvam Asi' Birds - Revisited

Atma, Self, witness, 'conscious presence', 'I am ness'

Atma, in disguise as the *Jiva-* limited and body-mind centered

Q : *The two birds have again come back into focus-is it because you are asking us to remember time and again and probably always, that we have an Atmic nature, and that we will all do well to discover this Atmic nature - through these meditations?*

A : Yes, this is the idea, and the importance of remembering the right *sutras* and the right teachings and of memorizing many *sutras* is underestimated - this point has been reiterated by Sri Nisargadatta Maharaj. Because, remembering a principle, a truth would amount to charging our awareness and Maharaj has said often that it is this which will pave the way for Self - Realization.

----

5. A Model of the *Jiva* with *Maya*: Revisited

Man's body = *Atma*, sticking algae = *maya* (illusions), *self*, memories, hurts, pleasures and pains, ambitions, hopes, attachments.

Sankara: The idea or metaphor of the algae man is here before us. The extent of the algae corresponds to the extent of *maya*, the extent of spiritual ignorance, the extent of sensory engrossment. Thus this veil of *maya* will be thin for spiritually mature people and mature seekers and will be thick for people who are more deeply into *maya*, into addictions to sensory gratifications and in people whose ambitions and selfishness is extreme.

The etymology of *maya* is very interesting. *Ya* means that, *ma* means not. So *maya* is actually what you are not, or what that is not, all that which you are not; it is a veil, a false appearance, which we are not. Just as, Self - Realization stresses on the fact that, 'you are That' (Tat Tvam Asi) where by 'That' we mean the Divine in the unmanifest aspect. Likewise *maya* stresses on the fact that you are not all of the worldly things which you mistake yourself to be. You are not the husband, nor the wife, nor father, neither a man, nor a woman nor anything which you suppose yourself to be, not certainly the body.

----

6. The Fragmentation of Consciousness

Consciousness (represented by the ten heads) as *Sakti* is fragmented. This is represented by the 10 heads of Ravana, each head in conflict with the other heads. When *Sakti* returns to *Siva*, consciousness becomes whole and blessed.

Sankara: When consciousness is broken up or fragmented, then there is no connection to the Divine. It is only when consciousness is whole that consciousness becomes yoked to the Divine, especially after it has undergone calming and silencing. So long as we are surviving, playing our hypocritical games, so long as we are lying and are dishonest and have a divisive approach to life and are divisive in our thinking, our consciousness will never be whole, which means, it cannot be yoked to the Divine. The ten heads in the above demonic form is a schematic and mythic representation of one of the demon kings, Ravana, in the Hindu epic, Ramayana. In a single relationship, when we are lying, for example, being one thing, but putting on an act of being someone else, we have undergone, the most basic kind of fragmentation (Jekyll and Hyde). When our life is filled with dishonesty all around, in all relationships, then that fact of fragmentation, that demonic nature, can only be shown by multiple heads.

When fragmented consciousness, undergoes a transformation through the *choiceless awareness of what is*, then that consciousness, which was previously bereft of integrity and harmony, now becomes whole. In this state, consciousness, which was previously, 'wild and roaming', without any anchorage to the Divine, develops greater integrity and wholeness. In this condition, it gets yoked to the Divine, and life then becomes serene.

Q : *The contamination conveyed by this metaphor is very shocking. Will the extent of this contamination be different in different people?*

A : Of course! The more ignorant you are more the contamination and the more lucid you are less the contamination.

Q : *More the contamination, more the pain in life?*

A : More pleasure to begin with. And this more and more pleasure will invariably end in a tragedy, which is the impossibility of continuing that pleasure, which is pain. So more the contamination, more the pleasure and more the concomitant pain.

Q : *After the cleaning of consciousness, through choiceless awareness and learning about the Jiva (self), do you think, Jiva becomes calmer and more silent?*

A   :   Think of the man with the algae enmeshing him (Chapter I, topic 18). We had said that his body represents the *Atma* and the enveloping algae was the *maya* and the ignorance. So now the *Jiva* is the man with all the algae. The *Jiva* attempts to observe itself. This is possible because the *Atma* is at the heart of the *Jiva*. As the *Jiva* observes itself, awareness comes into play and learning happens and if one has the desire *(Jiva has the desire)* to achieve some end through this choiceless observation, then the learning will be unfruitful. But if there is intense interest and no surging desire, then the *Jiva* will be calmed and silenced.

Q   :   *How does the Jiva get into maya?*

A   :   This is a Divine doing and the tragicomedy is that as the *Atma* is the Divine itself in creation, it is the Divine which has got entangled, but of course as a human being. The moment the Divine creates the world, this *maya* and entanglement comes along. It is very sweet and delicious in the beginning, but soon turns bitter so that you have to spit it out in the end.

Q   :   *One understands that hurts and pain are contrary to Atma's blissful nature, so these are contaminations all right. But how are aspirations and ambitions also contaminations?*

A   :   Many people are not going to like this answer, because every aspiration and ambition is fundamentally *self*-centered. So it implies a blindness as to who we are and this ambition invariably will lead to stepping on other people's toes and causing them great pain and importantly being so obsessed and pre-occupied with the ambitions and aspirations, that one necessarily has to lose all peace and all intelligence. This lesson is learnt after a fall, never while the game is still going on. This ambition will boost you to dizzy heights, then will come the inevitable fall. The fall may cause introspection and the much needed turning inwards.

8. Water *(Atma)* without Algae *(Maya)* – More Learning

Q : *Looking at this absolutely clear pond, can such an ideal state be reached?*

A : When there is integrity for the *Jiva,* and the *Jiva* has no private and secret agenda of its own and has *nirguna bhakti* (the seventh or highest *bhakti*) to *Parabrahma*, then the pond will be blemishless like this. The *Jiva* has a poor sense of *self.* In fact in every aspect of life in the consciousness country, the 'other' which is usually a sense object, will be more real than the *self* of the *Jiva*. In this condition, the *Jiva* may feel terrified by this purity.

----

9. Consciousness is not Awareness - Revisited

"Awareness is primordial, it is the original state, beginning less, endless, uncaused, unsupported, without parts, without change. Consciousness is on contact, a reflection against a surface, a state of duality. There can be no consciousness without Awareness, but there can be awareness without consciousness, as in deep sleep. Awareness is Absolute, consciousness is relative to its content. Consciousness is always of something. Consciousness is partial and changeful. Awareness is total, changeless, calm and silent. And it is the common matrix of every experience."

- Sri Nisargadatta Maharaj[16]

Q : *As the title itself suggests, Maharaj's statement seems to beautifully tally, with the two Tat Tvam Asi birds' picture, cast in the form of words, where, awareness would refer to the witnessing bird or the Atma and consciousness would refer to the 'eating bird'(self)?*

A : Exactly. I would like to place emphasis on one additional point. All *sutras*, whether from Sri Ramana Maharshi, Sri Nisargadatta Maharaj, Sri Krishnamurti; or from the Bhagavad Gita, Ashtavakra Gita, Kaivalya Navaneetham - may be committed to memory by sincere seekers, so that they may later on churn them in their hearts. For example, Maharaj's *sutra* on awareness and consciousness may be mapped on to the two Tat Tvam Asi birds, in order to enliven them even more.

The *Jiva* is a living entity in the field of consciousness. Here the *Jiva*, unaware of its *Atmic* presence, is obsessed all the time with the 'other'. This, 'other' is invariably some sense object. Only when the *Atmic* presence, which is its default setting (which is infused in the *Jiva*); is rolled back, withdrawn and separated from the *Jiva*, does a strong sense of Self, emerge. This is the *Atma*. Once this withdrawal has happened from the consciousness country, only then awareness comes into relief. In the

183

consciousness country, awareness is certainly present, but in a rather drowned, imperceptible and submerged condition.

10. The Dance of *Siva & Sakti*

Acknowledgement : Harish Johari's 'Chakras' and 'Tools for Tantra'. Inner Traditions, India.

Q   : *Here Siva & Sakti are shown as two gods, but in human form. Now I would think that the eternal truth or the Divine source, is not a human form at all, so is this mythological representation only an artist's representation of a truth, which our minds may never be able to grasp?*

A   : That is right. All Self - Realized teachers have emphasized that the eternal truth cannot be captured by the mind and by words. *'Avang-manasa gochara'*, meaning 'not reached by words, by speech *(vak)* and by feelings *(manas)* even. The prefix, 'a' in Sanskrit, serves to negate words, speech, mind and feelings.

Human beings have an innate urge to communicate their discoveries, and this is usually done through speech or song, or writing, through the careful and skillful use of words and sometimes, the eternal truth can also be communicated through dance form and through various art forms, through these mythic pictures even.

In India, art has always been a kind of 'hand-maiden' of religion, whose concern is always with the eternal truth. All the classical art in India has been religious in spirit and in intention. And art can take a great variety of forms of expression. Painting, singing, dancing, drama, writing-all are forms of art only. Indian classical music and classical dance are religious in spirit. The *sapta swaras* [Sa, Ri, Ga, Ma, Pa, Da, Ni] are bound up with the five manifestations of *Siva*.

When a lot has been sung, spoken, and written about the eternal truth, some illumined teachers have also chosen silence as a language, way of living itself, also as a language in which to communicate the eternal truth. *Dakshinamurti* is that manifestation of *Siva* as the silent teacher. Sri Ramana Maharshi also generally spoke very little in life.

Mythology (in the *puranas*) actually has been an independent vehicle for conveying the eternal truth. This anthropomorphic form of *Siva & Sakti* conveys something-not the literal masculine and feminine forms- completely spiritual-so the mythic picture conveys a *sutra*, an eternal principle-of how the Timeless (this, is *Siva*) is the Power Wielder, whereas the changeful, the movement of energy in time and as Time is the Power which our senses see. *Sakti* is this Power. In fact, the Sanskrit word *Sakti* means Energy or Power. And *Siva* is the source, behind the Power, but He is unmanifest, invisible - so we can make the fatal mistake of supposing Him to be non-existent - because He is not a sense object, only *Sakti* is the sense object.

Q : *In this beautiful picture, we see Sakti in the foreground, looking bright and resplendent and dancing with abandon and ecstasy, in freedom. However, in the background, we also see Siva, in a faintly ashen color, but involved with Her in some protective way, just as a mother would be very concerned about her infant. So does this mean that Siva as the Power Wielder, is Her benevolent Master, and because of His benevolence, He has granted freedom to her to do what She likes and goes with Her wherever She wants to go? Is this understanding right?*

A : In fact, *Sakti* is called *Svatantriya Sakti*, meaning independent Power or independent Energy, and She can keep this independence as long as She wishes, till She has the realization that She after all, is shining only in borrowed feathers and so decides to return home to *Siva*, Her beloved Master. So there is an extroverted movement of *Sakti* and then following this there is also an introverted movement of *Sakti*-Her home coming. We may also think of *Siva* as the Sun, and *Sakti* as Sun light.

All our desires, aspirations, cravings, feelings, thinking is the dance of *Sakti*, and in all this, *Siva* is behind the scenes, He is non-interfering and watching as a witness. *So, the dance of Sakti & Siva is happening in our consciousness, within us. It is not a physical romantic or sensual dance.* If *Sakti* is life, *Siva* is life of that life. *Sakti* is becoming, *Siva* is being. *Sakti* is time, *Siva* is timelessness, eternity, death, silence, the beginning and ending of life.

Q : *If this dance of Siva & Sakti is happening in our consciousness, then why is this dance being depicted on a Himalayan terrain?*

A : The floor on which the dance is happening is the Himalayan terrain-this just shows that the dance has transcendental and cosmological origin, mysterious and beyond human comprehension - even though it may be transpiring in the micro-cosmic realm of our limited human consciousness. This dance of *Siva & Sakti* must also be applicable to the cosmos, but in this retreat, we focus on the dance within the human consciousness.

Q : *So, could I conclude that this dance of Siva & Sakti is a metaphor, quite similar to the two birds of the Mundaka Upanishad? Then obviously the watching bird is Siva and the eating bird is Sakti-right?*

A : You have asked two very interesting Qs. Yes, indeed, the dance of *Siva & Sakti* is a metaphor, much like the two Tat Tvam Asi birds. And yes, indeed, it is the witnessing bird that is *Siva*, and the engrossed eating bird is *Sakti*.

Q : *Another intriguing question also comes up. Why do we see so many snakes on Siva's body?*

A : This is a very good question which deserves clarification. The snakes are also metaphors, but not just metaphors too - they represent the mysterious and secret Kundalini energy in the *chakras* and *nadis*, a power which is awakened only as one approaches and comes closer to *Siva*. You will remember that at the Amrit Desai Yoga Institute at Salt Springs, Florida, we had the opportunity to listen to a seeker, who had all these experiences, exactly as seen in this mythic picture of *Siva & Sakti*. In fact, it is such *Kundalini* experiences, which are behind all these mystic art forms of *Siva & Sakti*. Such experiences do befall serious seekers, especially when they are doing sustained *sadhana* in an *ashram*.

However, the emphasis in this retreat is not on *Kundalini* experiences, because in *Jnana yoga*, the path of understanding, there is no place for *Kundalini* experiences, though they may befall some seekers.

----

11. The Mythic Metaphor of *Siva & Sakti*

Mythic 'Picture' of *Siva & Sakti*, the Primal Cosmic Life Energies of *Being and Becoming*.

Being : *Siva* (Self, *Atma*)

Becoming : *Sakti (self, Jiva)*

Acknowledgement : Harish Johari's 'Chakras' and 'Tools for Tantra'. Inner Traditions, India.

Q : *In this second mythic metaphor of Siva & Sakti, are you trying to make us understand that all the natural processes happening around us and also within our own consciousness can be understood through the universal principle of Siva & Sakti?*

A : Indeed, every natural law, or such a mythic metaphor, is but a simple and intuitive understanding of the same natural law, it does just this, it grasps a certain mysterious pattern, deciphers certain patterns in nature, whether in the outside world or within our own consciousness, and in this way, we come to know what is actually happening and what is going on. All mythic metaphors are such intuitive understandings and this *Siva & Sakti* metaphor being such a typical flash of understanding.

Q : *Being and becoming seem to be the two modes of all nature, like potential energy and kinetic energy? Where being would refer to the potential aspect and becoming is the kinetic aspect? And are you identifying these with Siva & Sakti?*

A : More or less. *Siva & Sakti* are actually cosmic patterns or cosmic rhythms, and we can apply this principle to a variety of happenings. *Siva* is naturally being or timelessness, whereas *Sakti* is synonymous with time itself, so *Sakti* is becoming. *Sakti* is certainly

187

kinetic, *Siva* is potential. Look at the Solar system, the Sun is *Siva*, the planetary movements are the *Sakti*. Or, look within an atom, the nucleus is *Siva,* the orbiting electrons are *Sakti*.

Q : *If we were to apply this principle of Siva & Sakti on to our consciousness, we find that some people are so restless and are not able to be at peace with themselves, whereas there are others who are quite unperturbed, but at the same time, because of their tendency to be inactive, they are somehow also more dull and uninteresting. So, isn't it obvious that the restless people seem to have more Sakti nature and the inactive people have more of Siva nature?*

A : Quite right, it is in just this way that we have to go on deepening our understanding of *Siva & Sakti.* Your perception is quite correct that the dynamic people we meet in life, are *Sakti* people while the calm, self-composed or even inactive people are *Siva* people. *However, we have to be careful in understanding the context.* There can also be very unruffled people, *Siva* embodiments, who may be so profoundly silent within themselves*, and who may therefore be mistaken for being dull and inactive on the physical plane, whereas, inwardly they could be in bliss and enjoying a profound insightful understanding and a sense of unity with the whole of life.* In fact, in the last century, Sri Ramana Maharshi was a beautiful illustration of this aspect.

On the other hand, there can be perpetually active people who could be living in an inner hell, and it may be because of this inner restlessness that they are escaping through so much of frenetic activity. So, one has to consider the body and also the inner consciousness. Too much of *Siva*, would tantamount to a peaceful but in a worldly sense, also a 'death-like' state or a 'lifeless' state, whereas too much of *Sakti* would tantamount to madness, inner turmoil, chaos and even sometimes a complete breakdown in the form of insanity.

12. The Two Birds in the *Mundaka Up.*

Witness/ awareness/ timeless/ *Siva/ Paramatma /Atma*

Senses-centered, body-centered 'I', *Jivatma.*

Q : *Are you showing these two Tat Tvam Asi birds to reiterate the previous point of understanding our inner world, in terms of the Siva & Sakti metaphor?*

A : Yes, the intention is to drive home that, whether we use the metaphor of the two Tat Tvam Asi birds or the metaphor of *Siva & Sakti*, we are only pointing to the same eternal and universal principle of being and becoming.

13. 'Watching Bird' is Awareness *(Chit)*

Q : *So in this, Siva is depicted as the brilliant light of awareness, intelligence and peace?*

A : That is right, because *Siva* is formless and propertyless, and the witnessing bird of the *Mundaka Upanishad* was only a mythic representation of *Maheswara* the Supreme Lord. We have already gone into this in quite some length, and here it is being remembered only to emphasize the formless nature of *Siva*.

----

14. Ignorant People do not See the Witnessing Bird

Q : *Why is Siva, or the witnessing bird missing in this topic?*

A : We have already gone into this in the previous two days. There are people in the world who are either atheists or materialists or spiritually ignorant people, who give no importance, or who have not realized the significance of awareness or *chit*, i.e., of themselves, as a conscious presence, so they in their world-view, are totally blind and dead to the reality of *Siva*, of the *Atma*, the Self - this is the point emphasized here. That, the unmanifest form of the Divine, what Hindus call *Parabrahma* and Christians call Father in Heaven, is not part of their world-view-this is being emphasized here.

----

15. Choiceless Awareness and *what is*

1. Do not watch *Sakti* or *Jiva* as a 'pious' ego (an aspect of *Sakti*, after all), but as *Siva*.

2. Are you in *artha and kama* or in *dharma and moksha* ?

3. Identify, *Jiva* (within *Sakti*). How it operates as a 'separative movement', away from the vast flowing river of life.

4. Identify *what is* - shock of death, lust, a crisis, fear.

Q : *Looking at the first point, are you referring to the topic on the devic-asuric energies which you had introduced earlier?*

A : Yes, I have this *devas-asuras* model at the back of my mind, as I place the caution before everyone that, as a good entity, we may be trying to control the bad thoughts and bad feelings which may keep appearing in the theatre of our consciousness from time to time.

Q : *Can we look at that devas-asuras model again, to understand for ourselves what you are getting at?*

Pl see topic 16, which follows the present topic.

A : Yes, let us look at it. Having looked at it, we should come back.

Q : *To recap, is Siva shown as the deity at the top of the pillar?*

A : Yes that is *Siva*, the timeless awareness.

Q : *And the asuras, the dark figures, are the various negative emotions like jealousy, anger, hatred, lust, etc.?*

A : Precisely. They cannot be pushed out, have to be admitted as part of the full spectrum of *devic* (divine) and *asuric* (demonic) energies.

Q : *So what you are trying to say seems to be this - that one of the devic energies, tries to do some policing and controlling of one of the dark and troublesome energies? And you are cautioning us that this is not what you want us to do, because we have been doing this all through our life?*

A : Precisely. Initially, as we commence meditation, this is almost an inadvertent response, almost a reaction, and this is pretty futile. Rather than this kind of a self-control, which is glorified in all religious traditions, we have to watch with detachment, what is transpiring in the theatre of our consciousness- and this watching is actually easy, if we are not greedy and we are not hasty. The awareness which can watch all this, need not even be suddenly turned on, for it has always been on and will always remain switched on only and never switched off. This awareness is *Siva*, and *Siva* who was all along eclipsed by *Sakti*, has to now become functional. His light must pervade our consciousness fully.

Q : *You want us also to figure our clearly where we are in our life journey - whether we are still deeply engrossed in materialistic life, that is in the goals of artha and kama, or whether we have in fact moved out to the terrain of dharma and moksha?*

A : You have to find this out for yourself, not my telling you where you are, and you believing me; rather, you knowing this truth yourself, by examining the direction of your seeking, etc.

Q : *In this third point, you want us to be self - Knowing, before we can have the blessing of this self becoming tamed?*

A : Yes, we have already identified, observed and understood what the *self* is (Chapter II). Now we are in Chapter III, in which *self* - Knowing has to happen-hopefully this will happen in the meditation to which we are now headed. You have to observe the *separative nature* of the movement of the *self.*

Q : *In the last point, you want us to identify the life crisis, which is, what is, for you have been emphasizing that only within the context of that what is, does the self show its ugly face and come into play - right?*

A : Quite right. This identification of the life-crisis is what is expected of you. Some people may be so deadened that they may not realize that their inner life has been like a desert since many years. So, if you have an actual life crisis at this time, you will be the most fortunate one - because that life crisis, which may be a 'misfortune' in so far as worldly life is concerned, may be the very thing which will enable you to secure *self - Knowing. So we must identify that what is, which is the life crisis, be it big or small. And all this is the preparation for meditation.*

16. The Divine *(Siva & Sakti)* govern our Destiny

Devas & Asuras Model

Q : *I find this mythological picture very interesting and puzzling. I see an Ocean in agitation and I see a tug-o'-war going on. On the left side, I am seeing Lord Siva, Lord Brahma and Lord Ganesha and some other gods whom I am not able to identify. My question is, who are these gods fighting against? Are the dark figures, the demonic forces, arrayed against the gods?*

A : What you are referring to as *Siva*, *Brahma* and *Ganesha* are in truth cosmic life energies. Because they have the same eternal life, as all humans, they have been shown here in anthropomorphic form. They are life energies, which are fully alive. They bring into our life, the blessings of the Divine, in the form of all those things, which eventually please the *self* and makes the *self* happy - like a family, a career, a spouse, children, name and fame in society, success and economic well being and good health. The dark energies stand for the wrath of the Divine, wrath because of *karmic* nemesis. Good *karma* begets the blessings of the Divine and bad *karma*, begets, suffering, which is usually attributed to the wrath of the Divine. Both kind of life energies are present in our life.

Q : *If Lord Siva, Lord Ganesha and Lord Brahma are there on one side, where indeed is Lord Vishnu, who is integral to the Hindu trinity?*

A : First of all, the Hindu trinity is not composed of 'three' different gods. There are certainly 'three' distinct functions: creation, preservation and destruction, and to highlight these three distinct functions, for conceptual convenience, usually we are told that there are 'three' gods. By this really we are to understand three distinct functions, but never three distinct gods. The Divine is really one Supreme Source. We should not also take these forms at their face value, basically they are benevolent and malevolent life energies. As this is a *Vaishnavite* world view, *Vishnu* is seen perched right at the top of the central axial pillar, which is the *Atma*. The deity at the top is *Mahavishnu* (the unmanifest form of the Divine).

Q : *In a tug-o'-war we usually have a strong rope-why are we having a snake here? Obviously the snake stands for something-what is it?*

A : This is a mythic picture from the *Bhagavata Purana* [45]. The snake portrayed therein is not obviously a real physical snake, rather it stands for some life-force, so what could it be? It has a name. It is called *kala sarpa*, meaning it is the serpent *(sarpa)* of time *(kala)*. We should pause and enquire, why time is portrayed as such a vicious serpent at all? In many ways, time is not at all in our hands, rather we are at the mercy of time. Krishnamurti refers to time, very aptly as the 'mischief maker'. Time can make kings into beggars and beggars into kings, likewise saints can become sinners and sinners can also be transformed into saints with the passage of time. So, time is indeed vicious, from the human point of view, hence portraying it as a very frightening serpent seems quite appropriate. Put differently, this is a mythologist's version of a time machine, as it drives the ebb and flow of human fate.

Q : *Is there any significance in the multiple heads of the snake being on the side of the dark forces?*

A : You have observed very well. There is a fundamental difference between the *devic* life energies and the *asuric* ones. The *devic* energies are benefic, gentle and sensitive, they bring into any human life the blessings of the Divine, whereas the *asuric* life energies are malefic, rugged and harsh. In the discipline of *Vedic* astrology we know this difference only too well.The *devic* energies are the functional benefic life energies, while the *asuric* energies are the functional malefic ones. As the malefic life energies are harsh and rugged, they have the inherent capacity of the warrior to go into battle and engage with opposing forces. Therefore, on the head side of the serpent, the end from which the serpent will expectorate venom, only harsh and rugged life energies, the malefics, can be. On the other hand, on the tail side, the gentle *devic* energies can easily gain control over that more amenable part of the powerful serpent of time.

Q : *The Ocean is shown to be agitated, why? What does this Ocean represent in our individual life?*

A : The Ocean represents our human life. Life is like a voyage on the high seas, in the small boat of our individual life. Naturally we are at the mercy of the unpredictably tumultuous waters. So the turbulence shows the uncertainty and unpredictable nature of our life in the consciousness country. In this consciousness country life is full of conflict, uncertainty and even our acquisitions and successes may well be taken away from us, simply because, this is the very nature of human existence. It is all a passing show, happy one moment, plunged in grief, in the next and so on. Thus, the turbulence represents the storms, the tidal waves and hurricanes in our outer and more importantly, in our inner life. The Hindus call this, *samsara sagara* (the Ocean of life), implying a perilous voyage on the high seas.

Q : *Who is the figure in the pivotal axis in this tug-o'-war holding an urn? He looks like a god, who is he? What does the urn in his hand signify?*

A : The figure in the pivotal axis is called *Dhanvantari*, the Ayurvedic god or deity of health and well being. You will agree with me when I tell you, that it is not just enough to know 'who is who' in this complex mythic picture, for that would be only factual and superficial information, which is of very little value, in so far as a deeper understanding is concerned. How did this Ayurvedic god, *Dhanvantari* come into this picture? This is what we have to understand.

As the cosmic benefic life energies *(devas)* and cosmic malefic life energies *(asuras)*, which are the gears and wheels of the time machine, churn the waters of our human life and destiny; much like the churning of buttermilk which results in the precipitation of butter; from time to time, benefic as well as malefic events, start manifesting and precipitating in our life. If the events are of a benefic kind, we are joyous, if they are of the maklefic kind, we naturally become sorrowful. Eventually, however, the last fruit of the churning, which must be the *summum bonum* of life, called *moksha* by the Hindus, will be thrown up. This is the greatest blessing that can befall a human, during earthly existence, namely this *moksha*. But what precisely is this *moksha*?

It naturally has to be a perfect understanding (which is usually called realization) of who and what is man, who and what is the Divine and what is the connection between the two? The understanding and clarity has to be so perfect, that it would be in the nature of an irrevocable conviction, or illumination, so that there is absolutely so scope for any further Qs and any further doubts. So, the ultimate fruit of churning is the god *Dhanvantari*, who is bringing to us the urn with *amrit* or the drink of immortality, all brimming over. That *amrit* is the crystal clear understanding we are talking about. Once that *amrit* is drunk, then we become strangers to sorrow and have no more questions - in other words, we have been blessed with *moksha*, the *summum bonum* of life, and this is *Atmic* country, entirely different from consciousness country, where we live and suffer. We must note here that *moksha* is what perfects and sanctifies 'health and well being', so the Ayurvedic god has come into the picture to give us this final fulfillment.

Q : *What is the central axis, around which the life drama seems to be happening, and around which the snake is encircled?*

A : The central axis is obviously not in time at all, for everything which happens, does not affect this axial pillar, which is the *Atma*, our Divine nature, the core of our being. We can become free of the ups and downs of life (due to the churding of the Ocean by the *devas & asuras*), only if we move out of the consciousness country and settle in the *Atmic* country. The central pillar is the *Atmic* country, where there is no time and no pain. This ground of being, the *Atma* is always one with Godhead, *Parabrahma*. He, the Supreme Source is always behind the scenes, shown here perched atop the *Atmic* pillar.The difficulty in discovering the Divine, comes from the unmanifest nature of Godhead, *Parabrahma*. Instead of *Parabrahma*, sometimes in *Vedanta* literature, *Brahman* is mentioned. By this they mean, the totality of the manifestation, as well as the unmanifest aspect, which is correctly described as *Parabrahma*.

Q : *Who is the female deity just below the God-head (Parabrahma) on top? Is She His consort, the Divine Mother, corresponding to the Divine Father, Parabrahma?*

A : You are actually beautifully anticipating the answers. We will see on the sixth or the last seventh day of the retreat, as to how the mysterious Unmanifest Divine, namely *Parabrahma*, is also the home of the Divine mother. She is an independent energy, *Svatantriya Sakti*, hidden and abiding in *Siva*, but when the mysterious time comes for something to manifest; this energy of the Divine mother, which is usually dormant, suddenly flashes out into the manifest world in a wondorous way. She is called in the scriptures, *Adi Parasakti*, meaning, She is the Supreme primal energy. This Divine energy also weaves the illusion of *maya*. She may come into manifestation, to do some miracles, to create something, which was asked for by humans and even all the *devas & asuras* are Her emanations only. So the female deity is *Adi Parasakti*, verily the Divine mother and consort of *Parabrahma*.

Q : *I remember reading in the Bhagavata Purana, the churning of the milk Ocean by the devas & asuras. There in that context, it struck me as a cosmic life drama - not referring to the life of an individual. Here, are you applying that puranic mythic model, to the individual human life? [45]*

A : That is correct, the *Puranas* mention this in a macroscopic context and we are applying it to the microscopic context of the life of an individual. We have the macrocosm on the one hand and the microcosm on the other. The principles *(sutras)* of Divine creation, whether the creation is operational in the realm of the macrocosm or in that of the microcosm, are the same, namely the principles of being and becoming, *Siva & Sakti* and the principle *(sutra)* of the polarization of the energy of the Divine mother into *devas & asuras*. It is true that here, for the purposes of this retreat, we are applying these *sutras* in the microcosmic context of the life of an individual only.

Q : *Should we not remember at this stage the inner meaning of this mythic picture-as this might help in the meditation?*

A : Yes. The picture is definitely a reminder that the drama going on in our consciousness, is not orchestrated by us as the *Jiva*, but rather by the unseen Divine who is behind the scenes. He is symbolically shown perched atop the central axial pillar, around which the conflicting drama between the *devas & asuras* transpires. Every human thought-feeling has to be either a *devic* energy or an *asuric* energy and these are shown in anthropomorphic forms. Watching the drama would mean, not taking sides either with the *devas* or the *asuras*, but being aligned with the Divine, who is the witness of this drama. The central pillar is the timeless *Atma*, the witness and the *Atma* is sourced in the unmanifest Divine.

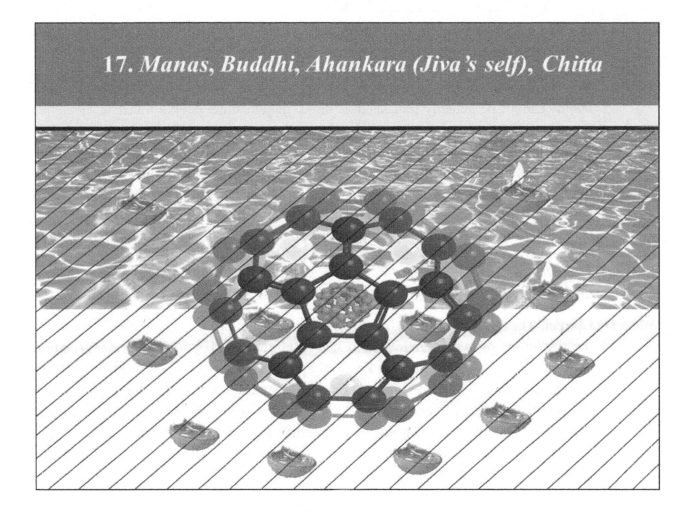

17. *Manas, Buddhi, Ahankara (Jiva's self), Chitta*

In Chapter II, topics 9 and 10, introduced the same themes of *manas, buddhi, chitta, ahankara*. So, let us recapitulate these two topics first:

Q : *Can you explain this picture, telling us what the various entities therein are?*

A : Till now we have introduced four 'functions and faculties' in consciousness. (i) *manas*, the faculty of feeling, (ii) *buddhi*, the faculty of logical thinking, (iii) *ahankara*, the mechanism of the *self*, (iv) *chitta* - the whole flowing movement of consciousness. The picture shows this truth graphically, that is all. The central molecular structure is the *self* or *ahankara*, it is a formation of many thoughts, memories, feeling, all coming together in order the defend 'something'. Often it is not a permanent structure, but a complex which suddenly forms and then also disappears and becomes non functional. The blue water with ripples is the *manas*. The small lamps denote the flashes of intellectual understanding, the white background is the flowing movement of *chitta*, which creates the reality of time. So this simple picture illustrates the 'faculties and functions' of consciousness.

Q : *You are saying that manas is the feeling nature or the feeling aspect of the 'I'. Is this what you call feeling from the heart?*

A : Yes, You could say this. The important point is that this is an independent faculty and *manas* cannot be actually translated as mind, though some people translate *manas* as mind, and that is not right. It signifies the feeling aspect and this faculty of feeling is related to our emotional nature. If we trace it further, it will go to it's root, the *Atma*. And this emotional faculty is a very important faculty which is different from the intellectual and rational faculty of *buddhi.* We may note in passing that in the Hindu spiritual literature, this word, *buddhi* is sometimes used as intelligence and sometimes as intellect, the rational faculty, so one has to be very vigilant and go by the context.

Q : *You have said that buddhi is represented by the lamps. Would you say, these are the flashes of understanding that the intellect often gives us?*

A : Correct. The *buddhi* is like a CPU (central processing unit) in a computer system. It is the machinery of logical, rational and analytical thinking. If you give any information or pose a question to the intellect i.e., to the *buddhi*, then the *buddhi* starts processing, making use of all available information and knowledge and it will come up with an answer that is logically correct. This is the faculty of logical, mechanical, serial and analytical thinking. However, this is not intelligence and it is important for us to make a distinction between the faculty of intelligence and this faculty of rational thought/ intellect which the scriptures sometimes refer to as *buddhi.*

Q : *Is chitta, the movement of feelings and thoughts in our consciousness? Are you saying then that this is exactly like a motion picture? And that this movement is inherent in consciousness? If it is inherent, then are we to suppose that the very functioning of consciousness, as this flowing movement is the cause of time?*

A : You are correct. By repeated watching of this flowing movement of consciousness, it will be easy for us to infer that it is only by the flowing movement of consciousness that time is created. It is the flowing movement of these images and memories much like a train that rattles past a railway station as we stand on the platform; that gives us the feeling of time. So *chitta* is this swiftly flowing river of consciousness. There is actually a deeper aspect to this *chitta*. This is related to the collective consciousness of the whole of humanity, what we normally call the unconscious. So it is just that this collective consciousness is flowing within a certain limited framework of the individual life and memories. If the top layer of this *chitta* is silenced, something which can happen in meditation, then strange thoughts and feelings will be seen to emerge into the individual consciousness and this is proof of the collective dimension.

Q : *Why is the self or the ahankara, shown like a molecular structure, with many bonds? And what is the dense red thing at the centre of this structure?*

A : The *ahankara* as we saw earlier is far from something which is static. It is actually a dynamic formation and is a kind of a dynamical conglomeration of many thoughts, feelings and memories and a bit of will power, forming and sissolving. All coming together and forming a complex, a 'vortex', in order to defend the sense of *self*. All the thoughts and the feelings together, they work for 'somebody'. Now, that 'somebody' for whom these thoughts and the feelings together are working, is in truth an imaginary non-existent personality. It is only a concept which is being created by sensory impressions and images, with the intellect processing these sensory images and then postulating an imaginary 'individual' or an imaginary body-centered *self.*

And the center of this structure, the 'nucleus' of this structure refers to *sthitha prajnya* state of consciousness, where there is complete integrity and very tight bonding between every thought and feeling, without any contradiction. Without any hypocrisy or variation between thought, feeling and action. So, when the whole activity of thought kind of collapses and thought becomes minimally active, then we should imagine that, that state is represented by the central red colored nucleus where the minimal activity of thought and feeling goes on to deal with the mundane activities of day to day living. So the central red core, would refer to the *sthitha prajnya* state of consciousness where there is not much of activity and flurry of thought, but on the contrary, self-composure, peace and awakened intelligence.

Q : *Why have you used the black color to depict the structure of the self?*

A : The black color is used to emphasize that if the *self* had much more of *sattvaguna*, i.e., intelligence, then the *self* is not very good as a warrior. And the *self* is very sensitive, gentle, compassionate, extremely understanding and in that circumstance, it is very doubtful that the *self* is even properly formed - so as to be *self*-defensive. The *self* is formed, only if there is sufficient amount of *self*-defensive ingredients. A kind of divisive nature to mark the boundary between *self* and another. To have such divisive aspect in one's thinking, the guna *rajas* and the guna *tamas* have to be present. I have used black color to denote the guna *tamas*, i.e., the extremely stubborn and willful nature *rajas,* would stand for extremely aggressive nature.

And if the *self* became completely stainless after it is understood, calmed, pacified in silence, then that *self* we should imagine, would have a white colored cloak. Because it is then, more or less very *sattvic*, very serene, highly intelligent, very peaceful. But when it is active and rebellious and is having a strong sense of division between itself and the world, then the red color and the black color would be a more suitable indicator of the activity of the *self*. That is why black color has been chosen in the depiction.

Q : *I presume that we are still 'getting hold' of the self, that is, trying to identify it-for the self seems to be in the field of consciousness, among some other functions and faculties of consciousness.*

A : You are correct, this is what we are trying to do. However, I do not want to do this in a common-sense kind of way, for our common-sense definition of the *self* could well be wrong. So, here I am relying on the Hindu scriptures which are throwing light on the structure and function of consciousness.

The sages say that man has four internal organs in consciousness (*antahkarana,* as it is called in Sanskrit). By this they mean, the four faculties and functions in consciousness, namely: firstly, *manas* (the faculty of feeling and knowing), secondly, *buddhi* (the faculty of analytical and logical thinking, but not the faculty of intelligence), thirdly, *ahankara* (the complex of the ego or the *self*) and fourthly and lastly, *chitta* (the totality of the individual and collective consciousness, including memory, sub-conscious contents like *samskaras*, dreams, urges., and that whole flowing movement of consciousness). This *chitta,* may be compared to an infinite reservoir or a vast river in movement.

These four faculties are dynamically changing and they are subject to time, or rather by their inherent movement, the thing called *time*, comes into existence. Time will stop for us, only if the subtle movement of consciousness stops. My point is that, the *self* which is the mischief maker in man's life (to use, J. Krishnamurti's vocabulary) and the cause of sorrow, is the *ahankara*, or the *self,* as defined in the scriptures.

Q : *Would the ahankara be referring to the ego-since we know that the ego is the mischief maker in man's life?*

A : In one sense yes, what you are saying is true, but I wish to clarify further. One of the admirable hall marks of the Sanskrit language is that the etymology of every Sanskrit word is clear and transparent. That is, the etymology, invariably throws a lot of light on the meaning and significance of each word. Having said this, I would like to go a bit further, are you ready for this next step?

Q : *Yes, please go on.*

A : Pardon me for saying this, but the word ego is not rich enough etymologically, even though as you correctly point out, we all know that it is the ego, our sense of individuality, which is the cause of sorrow and which is the mischief maker in our life. Coming to the Sanskrit word, *ahankara*, its etymology says, it is the *kara* or the 'maker' of the sense of *self (aham)*. Think of the spider and the web, which it creates-all for what? Often, but not always, for trapping and catching its prey. So the spider's web is much like the network of manipulations and machinations of the *self*, for its own continued survival. Thus, *ahankara* gives much more insight than the word ego, it shows that the *self* far from being a static thing is in fact a dynamical formation, and the whole complex process in thinking is what makes for the *self*.

Q : *If you say that ahankara is the self which is the mischief maker, will this ahankara, leave the manas, the buddhi, and chitta, uncorrupted and uninfluenced by it?*

A : This is a very deep question. Actually, the *ahankara*, does make use of *buddhi* and *manas*, for its own convenience, even though, *manas* and *buddhi* are powerful independent faculties in consciousness. Likewise, *self*, can also make use of *chitta*, the movement of consciousness, for safeguarding its own continued survival.

Q : *Why is the ahankara so very powerful, that it is easy for it to lord over the buddhi, manas and chitta? What is the source of this power?*

A : The *ahankara*, is actually, like the other three faculties and functions in consciousness, powered by the *Atma*, and is in fact a distorted and very limited reflection of the *Atma*, in the troubled waters of the consciousness and the body, naturally. As the *Atma* is all powerful and sovereign, its sense of Self, is seen and reflected in the *ahankara*, but with the important difference that this little *self*, operates within the highly limited domain of the body and our human consciousness, whereas the *Atma* encompasses the whole cosmos.

Q : *Why is the ahankara not so strong in all individuals?*

A : The human *self* is unique, meaning that each human *self* is a particular unique combination of the cosmic benefic and cosmic malefic life energies, and we already know from the mythic model that these benefic and malefic life energies, are sourced in the Divine. Then again the *Siva* essence is the same in all human beings, whereas the *Sakti* essence varies, depending on the details of the combination of the cosmic benefic and cosmic malefic life energies. Whenever the *Sakti* essence is strong, then the *ahankara* will be strong and also likely to be aggressive, whereas when the *Sakti* essence is weak, the *ahankara* is likely to be weak and timid.

Q : *So, have we now completed at least identifying the self?*

A : Yes, to a certain extent we have already done this. Next we must start observing this *self* at work. Actually, as the *self* is different from one individual to another, one cannot do the work for another, even your *guru* will not be able to do your work, though he will certainly bless you for doing your own work. Each has to look within and each has to do his home work - this is the only way to *moksha*.

Q : *Can we now take these ingredients of manas, buddhi, ahankara, and chitta, as giving us a good anatomical understanding of consciousness?*

A : Yes, in general terms only, as the details will vary from one individual to another. As it is the details which prove to be problematic, a great deal of work remains to be done, to which only the individual must address himself. He will have to walk on this road alone.

18. Identify the nature of *what is*

Guilt(hidden)

Low self-esteem(h)

Lust & Lying (h)

Jealousy & Comparison(h)

Hatred, Violence(h)

Hurt, Anger(h)

Fear, Cheating(h)

Confusion(h)

Ignorance(h)

Disease(outer)

Poverty(outer)

These are examples of *what is*. See which one of these is actually fitting your life.

Or what was your problem, last month, last year? The old problem may not have gone away.

It may still be nagging you from time to time. You still do not know how to deal with it. You are still suffering from an inability to face it, assimilate it and go beyond it.

Q : *When you say, what is, are you referring to some difficult situation in our inner or outer life at any given present moment? Or, are you referring to a psychological problem, which is continuing for many many years?*

A : Every system of spiritual or religious education has its own special 'vocabulary' and in this particular kind of *Jnana yoga* or the path of understanding, I have chosen to use

Sri J. Krishnamurti's very effective term *what is*. This special term, *what is*, actually refers to *what actually is*, at any given moment or in any given life. For example, at a given moment there can be a surge of anger or a surge of jealousy and then that would constitute a momentary *what is*, in the sense that, that is exactly what is happening at that given moment. On the other hand if we take a human life, which is running on for decades, then anger or let us say lust or hatred could be a predominant feature of that life and one has to discern that this has been a basic feature. In that case if you are looking at an entire life stretched over many decades, then the term *what is*, would refer to a pattern which characterizes the entire life. So *what is*, can be used in two different ways, either *locally* in time, pertaining to a given moment or *globally* in time, pertaining to an entire human life.

Q : *What did the master J. Krishnamurti mean by what is? Are you referring to it in the same way, or are you giving it a different meaning?*

A : The master J. Krishnamurti introduced the special term *what is*, in order to rivet our attention to a certain challenging situation that has come alive either suddenly for the first time, or in a recurrent fashion, because only the present moment can serve as the matrix in which any such problem can erupt and any significant happening can take place. For example, somebody gets emotionally hurt, grievously hurt, and that always happens in the now. It does not happen in the past, nor in the future. But happens at a particular moment. *So that moment is the matrix for that what is, when a challenging situation has suddenly taken birth in consciousness, that is, in our inner life, or that challenging situation can also come into existence in the outer circumstances of life.* Such a, *what is*, invariably signifies a challenging situation which has taken birth at that moment and I am using the term *what is*, in the very same sense in which the master Sri J. Krishnamurti used the term.

His intention was to make us look at ourselves both at our outer life-circumstances and also more importantly at our inner life, at a particular contentious thing. And both in our outer life and in our inner life, we could have a certain pattern of the *what is*. Let us look at another example in outer life. We could have a pattern in which, the boss in the office always dominates us or our life partner whether it is the husband or the wife, always dominates us. And we suffer the domination and we did not have the courage to remonstrate against that domination. And that would constitute an example of a contentious *what is*. Or having a certain desire but never able to speak about the desire and to ask for the fulfillment of the desire and to go about searching for the fulfillment of the desire instead just nursing the desire in a very passive, in a very luke warm and half hearted manner. So that could be another good example of *what is*. So typically if there are a million people then *what is* typically takes a million different forms and million different shapes. And we have got to identify *what is*, the particular *what is*, that has been a challenge in our life. And sometimes as we live many decades of our life there could be many problematic '*what is*' situations which we would have ignored and which we have to finally face in a retreat like this.

Q : *Each one of us will have to then identify, what this burning problem, what is, is, either throughout life, or at any given point in time?*

A : Yes, we have got to find out if in our past memories and experiences whether there is a wound which was a *what is,* which we left unattented because nobody in society - neither our parents, nor our spiritual teachers, nor our well wishers, our friends and family members – none of them told us it was important to pay attention to that *what is. So* we just did not know what to do with that *what is.* We just struggled on with that *what is,* like how people learn to live with chronic migraine or backache for decades. And such an unresolved *what is,* is bound to now and then disturb us. Now and then probably we are pained, so we show a little bit of attention and then that *what is,* is not getting resolved and then it continues to disturb us at a later time. This goes on and on. So this kind of a thing could have happened to us.

And then there can also be a long range pattern in life. Fear could be such a pattern of *what is* in our life, walking and following us like a shadow, and never for a moment without fear. It could be confusion or it could be intense jealousy. In a day we may become jealous 4 or 5 times. Or it could be an intense rapacious lust for the opposite sex. Every day getting 10 times a lusty thought. Some such pattern. And nobody, but ourselves can pay attention to this *what is.* Because this *what is* is the moment of truth. And if you are not going to pay attention to this, then probably there will not be a new dawn in your life and we will be slaves of the past and we will be slaves of day dreaming.

Q : *All of us cannot possibly have one problem all the time, isn't it? The problems would keep changing at various stages in our life, so are we supposed to identify, what were the many painful unresolved 'what is' situations, when we were young, when we were married, when we were professional people or spiritual seekers, etc.?*

A : Yes, there could be many wounds. For example, think of a body which sustained many injuries and many wounds like a sore which never heals. A bone that is broken and to which we did not pay attention. So similarly in consciousness, there can be grievous emotional hurts. And because we did not know how to heal these wounds which always happen to human beings in the process of living, they remain unresolved and continue to sap our energies. These wounds if left unattended, come back and nag us. And if you are not sufficiently attentive to their nagging in our waking hours then probably they will come and trouble us in dreams. So in one way or the other an unresolved *what is* or a painful *what is,* which is in the nature of a wound in consciousness, when not attended to, would cripple and impair our consciousness. So we have to start paying attention and start welcoming all thoughts and feelings that are emanating from the pain, from that *what is*. And there could be many wounds, many instances of *what is,* which call for attention and healing. So we have to very patiently, take them up one by one. Like a doctor who attends to many different ailments the patient may have. Here the patient is himself the doctor. You are the patient and you are also your own doctor.

Q : *Some of us may be very resistant to identify this painful what is. We could be in denial, which is more often the case. Do we progress at all in this retreat, if we are unable to identity the problematic what is?*

A : Oh, this is a very important question. Because, I have noticed that sometimes a certain participant attends a retreat once and he also subsequently attends the next retreat, the following year. In the first attempt he often misses the discovery of the pertinent *what is*. The significance of that pertinent *what is* - that it is the key to transformation in consciousness, is altogether missed the first time. But he manages to become more sensitive and then becomes intimate with all the wounds in that pertinent *what is,* in the next retreat and only then, he moves forward. So here I think it is of paramount importance that we discover what is our pertinent *what is,* that, which has been very troublesome for us and has been nagging us for many years. This is the well spring of our sorrow and this seems to be a never ending problem in our life. It could be lack of family unity and family harmony. Or it could be a state of being unloved by your spouse or it could be a state of a constant lack of fulfillment in your professional life. One thing or the other. Something is there and we have got to become sensitive to that *what is* and we have got to face up to it. Now if you do not want to face up to it and the sense of *self* and the ego are very strong, then you may not want to look small in the eyes of others and you may know that actually you are a miserable being and you may not want to wear your heart on your sleeve and you may not want to disclose to fellow seekers like yourself in a retreat like this, 'yes, I have this horrible mess' in my life, etc. So if you are on such a path of denial, then even God cannot help you. And because you hold the master key yourself, when you decide you don't want to look at this, then I must be honest with you and tell you that you will not make any progress in this retreat. Because the second, third and fourth step will arise only if you face up to this *what is*.

Now if there is no *what is* in your life, because your life is not very interesting, your life is very flat and routine and without much excitement and without much drama, then probably the *self* is not rich enough and the *self* has not had its highs and lows in life. And in that sense, a *self* which has got highs and lows is probably a better candidate for this kind of a retreat than a *self,* which is extremely mediocre. A *self* which is lifeless, salt less, and without any particular taste. So please turn inwards and try to identify the area of your life which has been calling for attention, but, which attention you have not given it so far.

Q : *What happens to people who never attend retreats or who continue to live in denial?*

A : It is true that there are a lot of people like that. And probably we ourselves were in that situation at some earlier time of our life. Everyone of us including myself - we were in that boat for many years in the past and then came a more fortunate time for us when we could face up to our problematic *what is* and that was a point of deliverance for us. So probably there is a different time for the moment of truth for each one of us. And that moment of truth comes all the earlier if you are more sincere, and open to change. If you are insincere and we are on a path of *self*-denial, then probably the moment of truth gets postponed indefinitely. So let us be attentive to our life and let us use the Divine power in us wisely and with a sense of urgency.

Third Day (Chapter - III), 1ˢᵗ 'Tat Tvam Asi' Meditation

Observing and accepting the *Jiva*.

Learing to be compassionate to the *Jiva*.
Seaparating the what should be from the *what is*.
Driking the pain in relationship.

----

19. Traditional Ways of 'Taming' the *Jiva*

1. *self* - control

2. *self* - denial

3. *self* - torture   Role of will power and

4. Suppression of *self*   conflict in all this.

5. Sublimation of *self*

6. Ignoring the *self*

7. 'Taming' through *yoga*, discipline, meditation

8. Immersion in activities, work, company of people, *karma yoga*, escapes (clubs, games)

Q   : *In this topic, we are talking of the self as the mischief maker, the source of all our sorrows, and as the source of all the unhappiness that we inflict on ourselves and others. Here we may also pause to remember the paradoxical truth that the self is also the source of all the little happinesses in life.*

What is the extent to which all these traditional methods of self-control, self-denial, self-torture, sublimation, suppression and ignoring of the self, have really helped seekers in taming the self? Is there any reliable research on the efficacy of these traditional methods?

A   : The whole idea of this first question and the associated topic, is to put the *understanding of the self* and the *taming of the self* which happens consequent to understanding, in proper historical perspective.

Now there have been other methods in the history of the various religions and the history of the spiritual life of man, of how people in the past attempted to bring the *self* under control. In so far as the spiritual life is concerned, the *self* was deemed to be some kind of a beast with the worldly inclinations like appetite for food and appetite for worldly enjoyments and ambition and so on. So when an individual with these cravings and worldly inclinations enters the spiritual life or even spiritual people start the spiritual life, they find that the *self* is quite out of control. So then, what are the natural methods? The natural methods are probably *self* - control and then denial of the *self*. The *self* asks for a certain desire to be fulfilled, it has that craving and then you say to the *self*, '*I'm not giving you this fulfillment for this craving*', as though you are as the controller, are distinct and different from the *self*. So you take that posture, the posture in which there is an *inherent duality between, you as the controller, and you also as the self, the controlled*.

But clearly, the duality is false and self-contradictory. Nevertheless, you take that posture because the desires of the *self* and the appetites of the *self* are very embarrassing and you want to somehow or the other, do away with them. And if this approach of *self*-denial, does not work, you turn to *self*-torture, which is an even more brutal and even more aggressive method, as much more pain gets inflicted on yourself, in this method.

Or, you resort to *sublimation,* that is, you kind of direct the mundane desire, in an ennobled and divinized form onto a deity or on to an absolutely unattainable Divine human being, and if even this too, does not work for you; then, you try outright *suppression of the self*. If you have too much of *rajas* in your temperament, i.e., you have too much of an active, passionate, impatient and aggressive nature, this is the method you are likely to adopt. Some others, who may not have a fighting spirit, a *rajasic* temperament, may also try *the more passive and less aggressive method of ignoring the self,* because, you may be thinking that ignoring the *self* and putting the *self* on a *fasting diet* will probably kind of put an end to the mad desires of the *self,* and may even end the *self* itself.

So people have been attempting all these things and then comes a century in the history of man, where an original teacher, J. Krishnamurti, says, *let us have a more intelligent approach to the spiritual life, let us try understanding the self as a means to taming the self.*

Now, I do not know if there is any research which has been done and any books which have been published whereby they give the whole historical canvas of what people have tried in the past, in so far as controlling, denying, torturing, suppressing and sublimating, the *self* is concerned. But, one thing is for sure, namely, that all these active or passive methods were adopted in the various religions and that they are all very problematic methods indeed. As *duality and conflict is inbuilt into these methods,* the people who resorted to these methods have to be invariably the *rajasic* kind of people who have a very strong will power, for only such temperamental types will even try out these methods.

So in all the religious traditions, man has tried to direct his will power and has tried to subdue the *self* and then comes the seemingly heterodox master J. Krishnamurti who makes us aware of the history of *self*-control and *self*-denial and who goes on to say, that we must have a radically different approach to this problem. This is the approach of understanding. *So this is the line we are taking here in these Tat Tvam Asi retreats.*

Q   :   *self-control, self-denial, self-torture, suppression of the self - are not all these traditional methods, too harsh, too brutal, too insensitive? And will they not breed a great deal of conflict? And, importantly, do they not call for an excessive use of will power? So, how will they work for people who are weak willed?*

A   :   You are very correct in suspecting that these brutal methods are based on the use of a very strong will power or, *self*-chastisement. They may not work for people whose will is weak. So it is like you trying to be your own policeman. You are the thief on the one hand and then you also try to be the policeman. So you divide yourself into the thief (one part of yourself) and then you try to be the policeman on the other hand, who is pursuing the thief. And then you say, 'I am observing. I am not the passion, I am not the ambition, I am not the lust, I am not the greed, I am not the dishonest person. So, now I will try to improve myself'. *And you create duality within yourself. And then you try to correct yourself, you try to control yourself, you try to deny yourself.* So these are methods which are *inherently conflict ridden* because they create a division, where there is unity. You are truly, only the *so called thief*, if we may put it that way. You are not the fictitious policeman, this fictitious policemen has come into existence, because of social compulsions, because of the pressures of social respectability - in all of this, pl observe there is no *understanding of the self*, what soever. The policeman is also the thief. But you can pretend that you are a policeman and you are different from what you observe, namely all the undesirable qualities, which are forbidden in the spiritual life.

So you try all these brutal methods of *self-correction, self-denial, of self-torture,* in the blind hope, bereft of any understanding, that these methods sooner or later will kind of *tame the self.* While observing these things we have got to take note of the fact that there may be a different method, a different approach to the *calming of the self and the taming of the self and perhaps, if we understand the self, may be it will calm itself and may be it will also become spontaneously tamed.*

Or, in some cases, perhaps, we should not even attempt any taming of the *self.* We should just allow the *self* to be wild, because that is the way the *self* has been created by the Divine. And maybe we have to live a wild life of the *self* for some years before the destiny becomes more amenable to the transformation of the *self*. So we have to approach this problem in very many new ways, without attempting a universal solution that may work for all. We will do well to remember the historical back ground to this problem, which is full of these brutal methods and full of duality and full of *self* –contradiction and naturally also *self*-deception.

Q : *Let us concentrate on point 8, on which I have a question. Surely, lot of us are in great pain (because of the self) and we do not seem to know how to deal with this source of pain. So, we run away from this pain by seeking pleasure in innumerable ways: through the company of friends, going to clubs, involving ourselves in sports activities, or even in service to an ashram or a guru, and in this way we seem to become free temporarily from the pain of the self.*

If, happiness is all what we are seeking, and if this happiness is coming to us even through all of these avenues, so-called escapes, what is wrong with these escapes and blind solutions, which may be temporary only? Can't we continue as pleasure seekers, in the same vein?

A : Again an extremely legitimate question. *And the answer to this question depends on whether we are discontented with your lot or not.* Now if we are very self-satisfied with the pleasures which are coming our way and there are no obstructions to this pleasure seeking and no challenges to this pleasure seeking, no frustration of any kind, and no denial of the cravings which are part of our life; then probably we do not seek any guidance or any methods to look for *another life*, where the *pleasure* and the *inevitable pain* will not be there.

We will begin to look for another kind of life, *only if the pain which is the concomitant of the pleasure, kind of surpasses the pleasure.* So the pleasure is initially experienced and then more and more of it, because that is the nature of the *self*, to crave for more and more of pleasure, till such time that this pleasure inevitably gives birth to pain. *This is in the nature of pleasure seeking itself.*

Thus when the pain becomes too much, at that critical point we will probably become somewhat introspective and *self*-examining and when we do that *self*-examination, even without somebody telling us, our conscience and inner voice will probably tell us and our intelligence and awareness will tell us, *that something is radically and fundamentally wrong with the way that we are living, that this is not a truly happy state of affairs.*

We thought that it was a very happy life, we thought that it was a wonderful life and then it dawns on us, after the pain has manifested that it is actually not that happy, as we had hoped it to be. And then we start reading something, we go to some spiritual master or to one or more *gurus and then probably we may realize if you are little less worldly, that another life may exist and then we will have to start to cultivate that higher life.Unless we cultivate that higher spiritual life, it will never come through to us very clearly and loudly that for so many years in this life, we have been actually leading a kind of deadened existence.*

Not that it is wrong, there is indeed a natural season for our materialistic aspirations. *But a time will come, when the material existence yields and gives way to a different kind of life, where for the first time, there is the dawning of understanding of the self.*

Q : *Now, moving to point 7, pertaining to yoga, meditation and a disciplined way of life, don't you think these become accessible to us, only when we have seen through the futility of our continuous pleasure seeking and when we have become nauseated with this process?*

A : It generally happens that either because of our innate temperament being spiritual, we develop a strong inclination for *yoga* and an inclination for *self*-discipline, etc. Or, because of an innate inclination to meditate and contemplate, we may read spiritutal works more deeply and thereby turn our back to a lesser or greater extent on our materialistic approach to life. And so, in one way or the other, we may come on a genuine spiritual way of life.

Another road could be that we could have wallowed a lot in material pleasures and because pleasures invariably breed pain and because of the pain we become nauseated by our worldly style of existence and then as a result of it we become perceptive *seekers*. And we ask the question whether there is another kind of life and if you are fortunate to proceed further in this enquiry and if you have a relative freedom from conflict which means we have a whole lot of energy to enquire into this, then we may probably come on a path where we cultivate *yoga*, meditation and a more disciplined way of life with austerity. And then the spiritual life commences in all seriousness and in all earnestness. So, we may come into the spiritual life, from two entirely different directions.

Q : *Would not yoga, meditation, inner and outer discipline, be a means to sublimation of the self? In the sense of purification and refinement of the self?*

A : Now, this is a more difficult question. *Sublimation* has a completely different meaning in chemistry where a solid like camphor does not go through the liquid phase when it is heated, instead, when heated, it straight away goes into the vapor phase. It vaporizes directly from the solid state and that is the meaning of sublimation in Chemistry. All of us are very familiar with this.

But in the spiritual life *sublimation* has got a different kind of meaning. It means usually a kind of transformation of the sexual desire, sexual passion, which is body-centered, and which is considered to be an obstacle to the spiritual life, into some other kind of desire like dedication to an *ashram*, being a *karma yogi* with dedication to the mission of a *guru* in whom we are able to whole heartedly invest our faith and a *guru* who has touched our heart; or dedication to a deep study or dedication to some other vocation which may be very inspiring for us and very consuming. Alternatively, sexual passion which is proving to be uncontrollable, could also perhaps be directed against a sublime and unattainable Divine being or deity - a circumstance, which excludes the physical fulfillment of that desire. However, such an idealistic process of sublimation, is not expected to work for all, but only for some idealistic kind of people, who are blessed with faith in the saints or in the sages.

We choose one of these approaches and one of these spiritual vocations and then we dedicate ourselves completely to it, while turning a blind eye to craving of the *self*. The *self* is persistently calling for attention, it wants the fulfillment of those desires. But we do not yield to the temptation and the craving and instead we direct that energy differently in another direction upwards, and it is this which may be called sublimation - because, we are making that gross desire sublime. So, sublimation may work for noble souls who have more of *sattva guna* and less of *rajas and less of tamas*. *However, if tamas and rajas, the two modes of the life energy are dominant in an individual, then that individual will find sublimation and dedication to a higher cause very difficult.*

And if we attempt such sublimation, a huge amount of conflict may be pressed into service and the person may become even more frustrated. Instead of that, for persons with that kind of temperament, where there is more *rajas* and more *tamas*, it may be *better to yield to the self gracefully* and allow the *self* to go on its materialistic path till such time the *self* becomes satiated and it by itself is willing to walk out of that kind of life. *So that is how it should go & that is the path it should take.*

Q : *Most of us have already benefitted by these traditional methods of yoga, meditation and discipline in our lives, so don't you think, the efficacy of these methods has stood the test of centuries and millennia?*

A : Yes indeed. So far as *yoga and meditation and a disciplined way of life* are concerned, they are extremely salutary for the spiritual way of life. And they are very natural for very *sattvic* people and they have done wonders to probably millions of people over the history of humanity, in moving them away from a grossly materialistic life to a more sublime, *sattvic spiritual life.* They have stood the test of time and nobody can deny that. Except that, for the *rajasic and the tamasic* people, such *meditation* and *yoga* might be too difficult in the beginning, but progressively as they apply themselves more and more and as they grow older even, these time-tested traditional methods may also start working for them.

Q : *What is the difference between self-denial and ignoring the self?*

A : Now in *self*-denial, you are aware that the *self* is pouncing upon you (who are the awareness, the *Atma*) like a beast going after its prey. It is upon you and it come up with some incessant craving and it is insistent and persistent in that craving and wants the satisfaction of the desire and you have set yourself up as a kind of policeman and you are dialoguing with yourself and you say, 'No, I'm not going to give you this food and I will put you on a diet of fasting' and then you seek an escape from that craving by indulging in some other activity, by telephoning a friend , by taking up a book and trying to read, by going to a movie theatre and trying to watch a film or immediately engrossing yourselves in your office work or something like that, so that you succeed in an attempted denial of the life of the gross *self.* This is *self*-denial.

And what could be ignoring the *self?* Now ignoring the *self* is a kind of a more passive approach while *self* denial is a more active kind of a thing. In ignoring the *self* you could be aware of what the *self* is doing, it is riding on a curve of craving, but then *you pretend that the craving does not exist.* You do not set yourselves as a policeman in order to *self* chastise and in order to punish the *self* and you don't consciously flee from that, but you ignore and you leave it aside.

Now this will work if the craving is moderately strong and of low proportion. If the craving is very intense, then the method of ignoring the self is not going to work. Because the craving will become stronger of the two forces and the craving *self* will kind of impose itself on 'you' who are in truth the awareness and then you have to take a call on whether you yield to it, yield to *Sakti* or resort to the previous path of *self*-denial. So *these are slightly different methods, self-denial being very aggressive and active, whereas ignoring the self is being more passive and because it is a passive/ weaker method, it will work only if the craving is also weaker.*

----

20. Right Watching of *what is* (Sakti)

1. No effort,

2. No judgment,

3. Total detachment,

4. No criticism,

5. No *self* - improvement,

6. Compassionately watching the *self* in order to understand It.

Q : *You are defining right watching of what is by the absence of any effort. Is it that effort will try to correct and improve what is, especially when that what is.is displeasing to us? And may be also, because effort will try to superimpose a 'what should be' situation, which is socially more acceptable? Or, even the effort can take the form of denial of what is?*

A : To understand how an effort to observe *what is*, will cause a modification of *what is*, let us consider a simple illustrative example. If a certain seeker is a very jealous individual, and becomes jealous, every time he hears of success coming to one of his friends, that seeker needs to deeply observe and understand *the arising of jealousy, and the source of this almost automated, mechanical repetitive reaction of jealousy,* every time he hears of someone succeeding. To get to this deep understanding, he needs to first of all accept this jealousy within himself, and *must somehow see the vital importance of observing this jealousy and learning all about this jealousy,* instead of trying to change this *what is.*

Now if he has an ideal that *he should not be jealous*, or that 'he is never jealous' (path of denial), then what will happen to him is that, it will become impossible for him to observe this jealousy, impossible to learn anything about this jealousy- why it arises so repetitively, what its consequences are and in this way, no *self*-knowing will ever happen to him. He will be all the poorer for it, simply because without *self*-knowing, there can be no true spiritual or religious life.

Effort in the observation of *what is,* always arises from a motive, open or hidden, and such motives, will at best prevent us from facing *what is*, which, in this particular case is jealousy. A desire to change *what is*, because of fear of *what is*, or a desire to modify *what is* (because *what is* may be socially shameful), will never help us to observe and study jealousy. The detached observation of jealousy and the study of jealousy will reveal a lot of secrets about jealousy, secrets which will heal jealousy and which will end jealousy.

If the observation is motiveless, then, *what is*, will reveal itself, through insights, and this will put us in a state of peace, a state in which we come to know clearly who we are, in terms of the happenings in consciousness. Proceeding in this way, we may come to *die to jealousy*, in the sense that, jealousy never again happens to us.

In all this, we need to be tremendously honest with ourselves, need to be interested in learning about ourselves, for then alone, this may be the path of spiritual flowering or spiritual awakening.

So, desire, will power, effort, *self*-control and ideals are not the way, instead, honesty, sincerity and a willingness to observe dispassionately - these things will save us.

Q : *One can also ask a more fundamental question, as to why we make an effort at all?*

A : Going to the root of the matter, it seems to me that the very intention to make an effort may be only to improve *what is,* or to deny *what is* at one level. But fundamentally, why are we doing this? Why are we trying to deny *what is?* Or, why are we trying to improve *what is?* Because, it seems to me that we are constantly striving to make ourselves more secure. Socially more secure, psychologically more secure, more secure in the family, etc. So the search for security and the craving for security, seems to be the ultimate ground from which all effort to modify *what is,* takes birth.

Q : *Coming to the second ingredient of right watching, namely, no judgment; we already have social approvals or disapprovals for various actions, some actions are considered good, some, bad, etc. So, the reason why we judge may only be to know where we stand, according to society's yardsticks, and the root of all judgment may be sourced in our craving for recognition, security and social approval.*

For example, a doctor may feel very good, if he, or she has saved a life, and this good feeling may evolve slowly into pride, or an exaggerated sense of greatness, which may be undesirable. On the other hand, if we have committed a sinful or selfish act, then the judgement may give rise to guilt and an inability to forgive oneself. So, one may become self-deprecating, or may acquire low self-worth.

How then do we free ourselves from the two kinds of consequences of judgment?

A : When we are looking at the act of a judgment of *what is* and then the two broad consequences of judgment of that *what is,* we see that one consequence is very euphoric, is very pleasurable, very *self*-gratifying and *self*- satisfying. While another branch of the judgment may give us, may put us into depression, may make us very *self*-deprecating and may make us very ashamed of ourselves. Being ashamed of our thoughts, actions, and our behavior, we should look into the question of how we can become free of both pleasurable as well as the painful consequences of judgment, how we can get out of this vicious cycle of pleasure and pain.

The whole of humanity seems to be orbiting in the cycles of pleasure and pain. We will discover by careful contemplation that we cannot have judgment still in existence and then freedom from the consequences of judgment. If we are to secure freedom from the consequence of judgment that will be possible only if judgment itself vanishes from our life. And judgment can vanish and will vanish only if we become somehow infinitely secure. So the question in a spiritual life is, can one become infinitely secure. And the contention here in the Tat Tvam Asi meditations, is that by anchoring to the Divine in the unmanifest aspect, will pave the way for our becoming infinitely secure. And it is then that we become free of every effort. Become free of every judgment and so on. Alternatively, by being the *Atma* and by abiding in it, we can also become infinitely secure. Then too, judgement ceases.

Q : *So, here again, we can raise the question of why we judge?*

A : We make an effort to get away from a painful *what is*. But ultimately we make the effort in order to become more secure. So similarly we are also judging ourselves because we wish to become socially secure. We wish to become psychologically secure, we wish to become very secure in the family, in all relationships. So it is the search for security that is the ground from which all judgments spring.

Q : *The 3rd and 4th ingredients of right watching have been identified as total detachment and no criticism. By this do you mean that we should not be attached, to what is, that we are looking at? In other words, we should not like it so much, nor should we hate it and sit in judgement over it?*

A : If we are attached, this means that we are either attracted by the *what is* as that '*what is*' may be giving us a lot of pleasure; or we may be repelled by that *what is*, because that particular *what is,* may be the ground for grief, regret and feeling ashamed and so on. Then both these are attachments. *Either being attached positively or being attached negatively.* If we are attached positively, then probably it is ground for pleasure or if we are attached negatively, then that is the ground for pain. Now either way, when there is pleasure, or when there is pain, nobody has told us in our tradition and in our religions that we have to learn from this cycle of pleasure and pain and that if it is possible we should bring this cycle of pleasure and pain to an end. Only because, the cycles of pleasure and pain, constitute the lower part of the human nature.

A time always comes in life when we have got to put them aside and ask the pertinent question whether there is a human drama, a human life which is beyond pleasure and pain? So, in order to go beyond pleasure and pain we have got to be detached from *what is*. We have got to develop an objectivity like how a scientist functions. Scientists, when they observe under the microscope or when they observe through the telescope, they are objective, and they put pleasure and pain aside and they see what actually is going on in that *what is*. So we have got to look in a similar way. We have got to see very dispassionately and very objectively. And then there is also criticism. Now we criticize something when it gives us pain. And every moment of this *self* is, an attempt to make itself more secure. So if we come with criticism, then we are not going to understand *what is*. So here the goal is to understand *what is* by looking at it and therefore criticism cannot be an approach either, just as attachment cannot be an approach. So both have to be put away.

Q : *The 5th ingredient of right watching is 'no attempt at self-improvement'. All our lives, from childhood, we have been told, not to be angry, not to be jealous, not to steal, not to tell lies, etc. All this implies self-improvement, and a way by which we could fall in line with society's norms and expectations, fall in line with the religious teachings. Now you are giving a contrary teaching, saying that, we should not try to improve ourselves. What then are we supposed to do, if we are not to improve ourselves?*

A : The important point for us to note is that in the traditional approach, we face a certain *what is* and that *what is,* is invariably ugly and difficult to contend with. It is either a heap of anger or a heap of jealousy or a heap of lust or hatred and so on. And since we never know what we should be doing with these negative energies, negative manifestations in our consciousness, we invariably try to cover them up. Put them under the table or look away from them in the hope that we will be rid of them, somehow. Now this could be an instinctive reaction, but this cannot be a mature approach at all. If we pause to think about these things deeply, it can be the first reaction, a childish reaction, but this cannot be a mature approach. So what we are trying to do here is, we are trying to face up to that *what is* and see that *what is* and

219

understand that *what is,* in just the same way as how a scientist will observe a bacterium under a microscope. You have to see it, *as it is.* Similarly observe the jealousy, observe the anger, *as it is.* Now when we do this, we actually observe it, *as it is.* Then a new opportunity opens up for us which could never ever have opened up in the traditional approach, where we try to fight with ourselves. Where we come on a path of *self*-control, *self*-chastisement, and *self*-flagellation, like there are a certain class of mystics in the Middle Ages whom we come across. Here it is not a question of penalizing ourselves and feeling guilty. Rather, it is a question of understanding the nature of these negative energies.

Nobody has ever told us in the traditional approach what will happen if we understood these negative energies deeply in a compassionate way. That is something which we have to discover in this retreat. We have got to look at these negative energies of greed, hatred, confusion, so deeply that these things will probably completely vanish from our consciousness leaving us in a beautiful state of peace. So here is another possibility which is completely unforeseen in the traditional religious approach. In the traditional religious approach, there is a lot of *self*-control, fighting with yourself and this leads to a lot of conflict. Ours by contrast, is the path of *self* - Knowing. This is an entirely new path, which has been opened up only since the last 80 years or so. It could be called, *amanaska yoga,* for want of a finer-grained equivalent. And in the last 60 - 70 years the master J. Krishnamurti's teaching has been consistently in this direction. And that is the central essence of *self* – Knowing, in these Tat Tvam Asi retreats.

Q : *6ᵗʰ Ingredient of right watching, compassionately watching what is, with a view to understand it. Do, you mean then that we must observe this what is, very objectively, like we are watching a movie? A movie in which we are also the characters?*

A : Yes. First of all there has to be a conviction that we have never done this watching before. Nobody told us the significance of this watching. Our parents did not tell us. Our elders did not tell us, our holy books did not tell us, our religious prophets and *gurus* did not tell us. So, we are attempting something which is new. And we have to have an *intellectual conviction* that this is a new ground that we are going to cover, the examination and the patient consideration of *what is.* Now, the kind of attitude and the mentality that is called for in the meditative observation of *what is* is very much like that of an intelligent mother who will actually be looking at her infant son or daughter and because she is all love, the mother will never criticize or condemn the infant and try to correct the infant as the infant probably makes a few mistakes in a an attempt to cross one of the milestones like walking or standing or so on. The mother is full of compassion, mother is full of empathy. Because the mother wants to understand the child. Just as the mother wants to grant the child the freedom in the same way we have to pay attention to this *what is.* That *what is,* however ugly it may be, could not have come into existence without a mandate of the Divine, even if it is lust, even if it is crime, even if it is the most obnoxious human qualities. So, we have to understand, go deeply into them and study them and then perhaps because of the empathetic observation and empathetic understanding, *something may happen to that what is.* That *what is* will probably undergo an unexpected metamorphosis, the satanic energy may well undergo a transformation to a Divine energy. That could very well be our deliverance. This whole metamorphosis of *what is,* cannot happen if there is no compassion, if there is no dedication, if there is no *shraddha* and devotion to the meditation, of observation of *what is.* One has to come to it like a loving mother comes to her infant, full of care, full of concern that the infant should flower in life. With the same attitude we should watch this *what is.* And then perhaps we will have our deliverance, the gate will open.

----

21. 'This Meditation cannot be Learnt from Another..'

"This meditation cannot be learnt from another. You must begin without knowing anything about it, and move from innocence to innocence."

- J. Krishnamurti in 'Meditations'[19]

Q : *Krishnamurti says, "This meditation cannot be learnt from another…", since we are all new to this kind of a meditation, will you be teaching us this skill in meditation?*

A : Yes, this is a *yogic* skill, just like swimming, cycling, driving a car and flying are skills. It is a meditative skill in consciousness, but the skill is not so important, as the learning about the *self,* which eventually leads to the calming and silencing of the *self.* We have already seen that the *self* is unique, the destiny is unique, and from this we inferred that our individual path is consequently also unique. Further, because of this uniqueness, we cannot learn from another, because another individual does not know us and our problems, only we ourselves can know ourselves and our peculiar problems.

If you depend upon me, or try to imitate or follow, no learning will take place. However as you attempt to meditate, you will fall down a few times, fail in the endeavor, then will come the skill, and the learning about the ways of the *self.*

----

22. First and Second Seeing

1. Practice **first seeing**, but without effort, and dispassionately *(choiceless awareness)*.

2. Practice **second seeing**, but without effort, and dispassionately *(choiceless awareness)*.

3. ***What is*** - is the fruit of *karma*, mandated by the Divine, ***what should be*** *is the projection of the self, because it does not know how to deal with this problematic,* ***what is***.

Q : *Concerning, first seeing, what do you mean by, first seeing, because you seem to be emphasizing the adverb first. Say also something about seeing, which you are incidentally using for the first time.*

A : We have already dealt with seeing *per se*, seeing is observing in meditation, by being the *Atma. Seeing means observing and understanding a thing as it is. Not as we would like it to be. That is seeing.* And first seeing is when *what is,* is happening in a flecting way, suddenly there could be a flash of anger or there could be surge of bad temper or a surge of jealousy and the question is, can we observe it as it is taking place? Not later. As it is taking birth. And the whole thing will be over in a fraction of a second. So the question is, are we capable of this first seeing? For this first seeing, we should be very well rooted in the present (be the *Atma*). As the surge of the jealousy or the surge of comparison with somebody else, the whole thing is gone in a fraction of a second. Can you observe this process? How it takes place and how it moves on? That is direct seeing, when that *what is,* is a momentary fleeting affair. Not a long drawn out thing, but it is a sudden fleeting thing. You are going for a walk, you suddenly see a shaft of jealousy darting forward in the mind. *You see it dispassionately, without wanting to correct it, then you understand jealousy and you know where it is coming from. That is first seeing.*

Q : *Concerning, second seeing, what do you mean by this second seeing?*

A : The second seeing is when there is a certain pattern in your life. There could be a pattern of fear, or it could be a pattern of not being able to express yourself even though there are desires in your heart. Not having enough self confidence to articulate one's desire. Or, there could be a pattern of hatred, pattern of enemity, of intolerance or impatience, whatever it is. And you know vaguely and you know partially that this pattern has been repeating and so every time when it repeats there is pain, but you did not care to attend to it. So now you have an opportunity to put the whole thing on a table and look at the whole range pattern as it kept recurring in your life over 20, 30, 40 years. You see a whole pattern, what havoc it has been playing in your life. How relationships have been broken and how you have become so miserable. Seeing the whole thing, the long range pattern in time. The repetitive pattern over decades. That we may call the second seeing, which is in contrast to the seeing of a momentary happening, momentary, *what is.*

Q : *You are saying that what is, is always a karmic manifestation, mandated by the Divine. What is your basis for saying this?*

A : The basis is really found in the Hindu scriptures that anything which comes into existence has to be mandated by the *Divine*, otherwise it just cannot come into manifestation. And so if there is a problematic or a happy *what is,* which has come to stay, let us say it is going to stay for a few weeks or a few months or a year, then that *what is,* is certainly the fruit of our *karma,* or rather, the collective *karma* of the whole of humanity.

And because the Divine itself carries a special name, in the scriptures, in the *Upanishads,* as *Karma dyakshaha,* i.e., as the dispenser, distributor, of *karma,* different *karmas* manifest at different times in the lives of different individuals. This requires an extraordinary computational machinery and the Divine seems to have the wherewithall, to organize and distribute the good and bad *karma.* So that *what is,* is certainly a manifestation of this *karma* and it will give us happiness if it is the fruit of good *karma* and it will give us pain, conflict, loss and unhappiness, if it is a result of negative *karma.*

So as a result of the first seeing and the second seeing we will probably become very comfortable with *what is* and hopefully, we may have also learnt the difficult lesson of not avoiding or ignoring the *what is.*That *what is,* may be destined to stay for some months or even some years. Because we have befriended that *what is,* and have become comfortable with that *what is*, because we lost fear of that *what is*, living with that *what is,* will no more be like living with a beast. On the contrary, it may be a bearable experience on the whole, fruitful, in so far as learning is concerned. You may just accept it as a part of the Divine dispensation. All of this will be the fruit of first seeing and second seeing. So we have to take this *what is,* as the *prasada* of the Divine as actually a blessing of the Divine and as a fruit of our *karmic* manifestation. Then probably we will have greater clarity in not wanting to avoid it or ignore it.

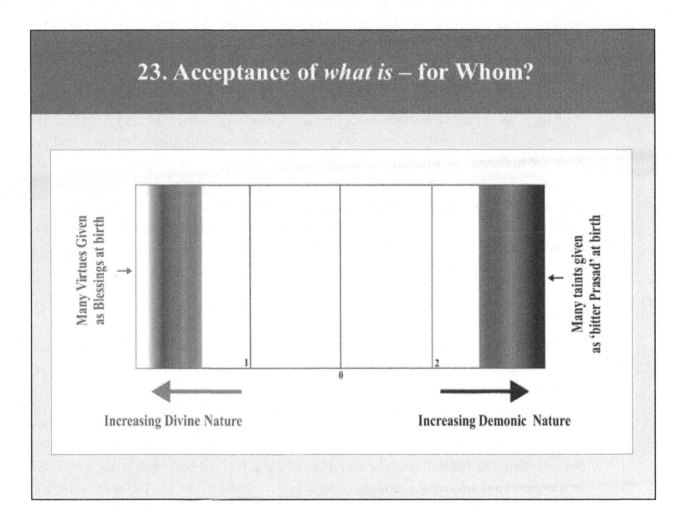

Q : *We were talking about seeing in the previous topic, so in this topic, are we concentrating on what we are seeing in our human nature, like, extremes of human nature, and even extreme Divine nature, as is found in saints and very spiritual people and extreme demonic nature, as is found in the notorious criminals, perverts and tyrants of history?*

A : This happens to be a very important theme in our spiritual life. Yes, to answer the question, we are seeing our human nature and we should remind ourselves at this point that we are in the third day and are moving through the process of *self* -Knowing and taming of the *self*. Till now s*elf* - Knowing has been concerned primarily with knowing the activities of the *self*. Now the activities of the *self* is just one thing, because, they are actually driven by the Divine energies in us and the demonic energies within us, as both are always present.

And there is an important part of *self* - Knowing, which will lead us to fathoming of our *swabhava* or our innate nature, how we are architectured by the Divine. Has the Divine architectured us as *devas* (angels) or has the Divine architectured us as *asuras* (*demonic* entities)? So we have got to know that. And to know that, is actually a second huge step in *self* - Knowing. So in *self* - Knowing, one part is knowing the activities of the *self,* the becoming, the endless *self* seeking and then the everlasting search for security and pleasure and so on.

And then we come to another aspect of *self* - Knowing which is understanding the Divine architecture and understanding our *swabhava* or our innate nature. And we have got to figure out whether we are dominantly Divine in our temperament or we are dominantly demonic. Of course we can also be 50% Divine and 50% demonic that is also a possibility. But the other extreme possibilities of extreme Divine nature and extreme demonic nature are more interesting to study, especially the extreme demonic nature. Because that is more hard to understand and more hard to tame and to cope with. So we are going to go into that more deeply.

Q : *You seem to have broadly classified humanity into two categories. One category, seems to pertain to human beings, who are fundamentally so Divine, that the path of idealism is easy for them and works for them. And another category of human beings, in whom the demonic energies are so strong that idealism can never work for them. Am I right?*

A : Yes. So we have to understand our innate nature, the innate nature of the *self,* as I said in the answer to the previous question, by going beyond *self* – Knowing, by going beyond the mere fathomingof the activities of the *self*. We have got to go from there to another kind of *self* - Knowing which is deciphering the Divine architecture in ourselves and our temperament, whether we are more demonic or we are more Divine.

We have got to know this. Because, if we do not introspect and look at ourselves, probably we will never know this. Because we could actually be demonic but all the time we are trying to cover up the demonic nature with idealism and saying 'no, no', I'm reforming myself, I'm trying to become a better human being every day and if that never happens, then we have got to take a more ruthless perspective on that and then probably come to recognize that the demonic nature is very strong, in which case, a different kind of healing medicine will have to be administered to us, so that the demonic nature is tamed.

The next goal in the third day after *self* - Knowing is taming of the *self*. So how are we going to do this? But even before we move to that taming of the *self*, we have got to know our temperamental constitution. So that is what we are trying to do here, to drive home to ourselves very very honestly whether the Divine nature is dominant in us, or the demonic nature is dominant.

If the Divine nature is abundant, then idealism will work for us. Like for example, let's say the Divine nature has blessed us with a lot of good qualities but has also given us a strong will power. Through *self* - Knowing, we observe that some demonic energies give us a tendency to lie or a tendency to run after pleasure in eating and pleasure in sex or give us a tendency towards seeking worldly power and so on.

As the religious and spiritual life tells us that these are not conducive to the real happiness within us, we have the option of using our *will power* to correct the demonic energies. So, we may do this by *sublimation*, that is by purifying, by refining, by dedicating these dark energies to something more nobler and sublime or we may do this by *suppressing* the dark energies or by controlling the dark energies using our *will power*. We are able to do this, only because, we also happen to have the necessary *will power*. So we use *yoga*, we use meditation, we use prayer, and we may dedicate ourselves to some spiritual movement and or start doing a lot of *Karma yoga*. In this way, we may eventually be able to bring our demonic energies under control and if that happens, then we should know that idealism has worked for us and that we are dominantly Divine beings.

However, if the demonic nature is very strong, then even our will power, and our *self* - control, our suppression, our sublimation, will not work. Then, we have to wake up and admit to ourselves, if not to others that the demonic nature in us is very strong and the Divine nature has no hold over the demonic nature. So this discovery of our *swabhava* or our innate nature is part of s*elf* - Knowing. And without this we will not be able to move further in this retreat, so each of us has to be honest and each of us will have to find out where we stand in the spectrum, either on the extreme right side or towards the left of the spectrum.

Q   :   *So, what is your commentary and suggestion for the idealistic kind of people and for the other kind of people for whom ideals never work?*

A   :   As I said, if we have got a dominant Divine nature, then idealism is going to work for us and how will we know this? Only by trial and error, only by experimenting with ourselves. Thus, we should try idealism, for example, let us say an idealistic person, a person who has got a lot of blessing, finds himself being very jealous and because he has the knowingness in him, he is a little ashamed that he is so jealous, but, he tells himself that he should not be jealous and he goes into *yoga* and he makes a confession of it to his *guru* and the *guru* prescribes a meditation perhaps and he starts meditating and he starts controlling the jealous energies, starts suppressing jealous energies and in one way or the other he may be able to drive the dark jealous energies under the carpet. So these are idealistic kind of people.

You ask yourself, Am I in that box of the idealistic people? Do I belong to that category of people, the idealists? Do I have noble ideals in my life?

Now if idealism never works for you and you are not ashamed to admit this and you are honest enough to tell yourself, yes it's never worked for me and I'm fighting with myself, I'm in tremendous conflict and I'm never able to eradicate my dark energies; then we have to look for another method of meditation in order to do something with the dark energies, with the demonic energies so that they do not become tormentors in our life.

So what is the new meditational method, which will save us? This new method has to obviously be very different from that for the idealists and it should be far more effective for us, than the old labor-intensive and struggle-intensive traditional methods of purifying, of refining, of controlling, of suppressing, of sublimating. And that new method which will be more pertinent to people with heaps of demonic energy, will have to first of all work in an entirely different way, instead of putting those dark energies of a wild *self* under the carpet.

They have to face up to the difficult and dark *self* and we must say to ourselves, with a lucid conscience and with deep feeling, 'yes, I am a slave of this mental pattern. I am a slave, I don't know what to do with myself'. In this fashion, we have got to face up to our dark energies and we have got to make a frank admission that 'I am also all these dark energies' and then will begin the next step of studying the dark energies.

So, studying it deeply with compassion, because that is part of *self* – Knowing, and when there is complete acceptance, then you will find that the dark energies function not in such an untamed and tumultuous way, because we have now become friendly towards them. They do not prove to be so troublesome, they begin to flow on a more even keel and this is where we ought to get. And all this is taming of the *self.*

----

24. Two Kinds of Seeing *what is.*
First Kind: 'Just at that very moment'

To see, to watch, to observe **what is**, *just at that very moment*, when pleasure-seeking, greed, is happening. From such seeing arises:

(i) Insights into the nature of pleasure seeking, or greed, or self-centeredness, etc.

(ii) *Sakti* calms down temporarily.

(iii) Every time a successful seeing has happened, you come to abide in *Sivatva* - because *Siva* alone can see.

Sankara: It is probably a very serious mistake to have listed the above three benefits which will accrue to the one, who is able to see in this way. 'Mistake', because, the *self* then latches on to these benefits and it's prime concern becomes one of acquisition of these benefits.So long as the *self* is going to make it's success, it's prime concern, seeing cannot happen at all, so any mention of what may happen as a result of seeing, carries the risk of proving to be counter productive. To see, as the *Atma*, or the awareness, in this vein, implies, a complete absence of all desire to achieve something, through such seeing. *Someone one has to be free of the ghost of this desire, greed, craving, in the beginning itself, rather than at the end of it.*

In the Hindu tradition, this absence of; desire, greed, craving is what you may call renunciation, or detachment. Detachment from what? From the desire to succeed in this meditation. There has to be an interest, which is not *self*-centered, yet at the same time, one must also have this detachment, right at the beginning itself - then seeing happens and one starts learning about the *self*.

----

25. Second Kind of Seeing *what is*

Second Seeing : Observe dispassionately all that *Sakti* has been doing.

This is also watching of **what is**, except that, this **what is** as a pattern has been happening over a longer period of time, rather than being confined to a 'given moment'.

Dispassionate observation, just as you watch a TV programme.

Sankara: As a species, we seem to live a superficial life, that is, we live on the surface only, without being able to penetrate into the depths of our feelings and stirrings. If we probably paid enough attention and are able to become intimate with those bothersome feelings and stirrings, the chances are that life may indeed take an unexpected liberating turn…*Consider this real life example, where the second seeing is extremely pertinent.* He was 40, from a northern city, sensitive and intelligent, married with two children, a boy and a girl. At work, he was treated shabbily, without any regard to his feelings - his ambitious boss had no time to waste on his feelings. Though he was an asset at work, this was never recognized. He had made an initial attempt to quit, but this was unsuccessful, so now, he was even more trapped. To build a new life would mean nothing short of jumping out of a moving train, with the attendant risk that the transition may land him in the dump. There was also the trap of social respectability which came from financial security in the present job. As against these outer glories and temptations, there was the inner confusion, fear, and the quandary of wanting to get out, to be free, yet not having the courage to take that much needed step into the unknown. He was drifting, without taking any decision, twelve precious years had already passed in this way. This quandary of not knowing, how to jump out, how to take a leap into the unknown, for setting himself free, the attendant fear of what the future might bring, in the event of his jumping out - this dilemma was his *what is*.

---

26. Krishnamurti's Choiceless Awareness of *what is*

When there is:

(i)   No effort in observation,

(ii) No desire or intention to change or get rid of what you are observing,

(iii) No judgment,

(iv) No condemnation,

(v)   No criticism, *no desire to improve **what is**,*

(vi) No motive, hidden or open;
      *then the awareness of **what is**, is choiceless.*

The master Sri J. Krishnamurti's life time work.

Sankara: *Choiceless awareness of what is,* is J.Krishnamurti's special vocabulary. A more comprehensive term, may be given for bridging the existing gulf between Krishnamurti's *self* - Knowing and traditional Self - Realization (which we will go into on the fifth to the seventh days). This is *amanaska yoga.*So-called, because, through this *yoga*, or meditational skill, the *manas*, or consciousness, is calmed, silenced, so it becomes void. This is also the calming and silencing of the *self*. When we come to this *choiceless awareness of what is*, we are bound to fail in the initial attempts, as invariably, we are very prone to making effort, in one form or the other all the time. In *choiceless awareness of what is*, effort has no place, as such effort, if present, will divert, deflect, and modify that *what is*, into *something other than what is.*We had called such a thing, *what should be*, which is an ideal, something projected by the *self*, for it's own security. After failing a few times in this *sadhana* (meditational practice), we will eventually, learn to watch *what is*, without the interference of effort. To call this a meditational skill is also 'risky', because then, this *amanaska yoga, this choiceless awareness of what is,* will also appear to the calculating and greedy *self,* as another opportunity for 'spiritually growing'. Thus, rather than *choiceless awareness of what is (amanaska yoga)*, leading us to freedom from the nuisance of the *self,* it may be the *self,* whch, eulogizing the glory of *choiceless awareness of what is*, very subtly, starts clinging to it, rather than, suffering dissolution.Thus, one has to be extremely aware of one's line of approach, lest one suffer *self*-deception, in the name of *self* - Knowing.

27. Wrong and Right Watching in *self*-Knowing?

1. As you start watching, 'wrong watching' comes to pass first! One part of *Sakti*, the controller, the *self,* tries to control and watch the ugly part of *Sakti*. In this no learning, only conflict.

2. Right watching, a *new pole* in consciousness is created, this is *being*. Now this *being* was buried till now in the coils and heap of *Sakti*.

Q : *You are talking of wrong watching vis-à-vis right watching. If I am permitted to go back to the devas-asuras model, am I right in thinking that wrong watching would happen when a devic energy is watching, an asuric energy, and trying to suppress or get rid of it?*

A : You are correct, this is exactly what wrong watching would be- a *devic* energy, trying to control or suppress, or eradicate an *asuric* energy that is socially disapproved. We have already dealt with many examples like jealousy, lust, hatred, lying.

Q : *Right watching by contrast - would it mean that we watch everything, in a dispassionate and objective way with no intention to correct or modify what is? Would this then mean that we are watching things as pure awareness, represented by the Divine at the top of the Atmic pillar-in the devas-asuras model?*

A : Yes, such right watching is characterized by absence of effort and will be possible only for pure awareness that is, for the *Atma*, represented by the Divine at the top of the central pillar. Now you may wonder, how you could get there. Your question is absurd, because you have always been at the top, but have never used this subtle faculty.

----

28. Where was 'Being' Till Now?

2a. Right watching, a *new pole* in consciousness is created, this is *being*. This is timeless. Now this *being* was buried till now in the coils and heap of *Sakti*.

2b. Svetasvatara Up.[22] says:

"Sukshmadi sukshmam kalilasya madhye"

"Subtler than the subtlest, in the midst of confusion."

Sankara: In the early years of the spiritual life *(dharma and moksha)*, we may not have any significant awareness about our *being* nature, for much of the life in the consciousness country is centered only on *becoming*, which is a movement of *Sakti*. Not that *Siva* or *being* is far far away, impossible to reach. In fact, often in life, we are in *being*, in *Sivatva*, peaceful, serene and unresponsive to the mad goings on in life. So it should be noted that we are certainly not strangers to our *being* nature, although we do not seem to recognize this aspect of ourselves. The *Svetasvatara Upanishad* has been invoked, to point to this very subtle *being* nature. The *Upanishad* says, this *being* or, it's root, our *Atmic* nature is subtler than the subtlest, somehow buried in the coils of confusion (of *Sakti*). So, right in the consciousness country, as we settle down within ourselves, we are free of the coils of confusion of *Sakti*, and that *being* nature is the *Atmic* country, hereitself.

----

29. Blessings from *self* - Knowing

From such *seeing* arises these Blessings:

1. Insights into the nature of pleasure seeking, greed, anger, jealousy, self-centeredness, etc.

2. *Sakti* calms down temporarily.

3. Every time a successful *seeing* has happened, you come to abide in *Sivatva* - because *Siva* alone can see.

Sankara: As I may have mentioned elsewhere during this retreat, the very mentioning of these blessings, may come in the way of *self* - Knowing not resulting in these fruits. I should have probably added another conditional clause. Namely, that, these blessings will accrue, provided there is continued *innocence*. The danger in making these blessings known beforehand is that the *self*, may well become greedy for the blessings and may start pursuing them, in which case, naturally the blessings will not fructify at all. Why is this so? Because the activity of the *self*, whether it is gross or subtle, will close the door on these blessings. In other words, *detachment* from desires and the fruits of our actions is very essential in *self* - Knowing. This is an additional ingredient which is not already present in *self* - Knowing, which is the reason, detachment is being specifically mentioned here and its importance highlighted.

----

30. More Blessings from *self* - Knowing
- Through Choiceless Awareness of *what is*

4. You begin to understand *for the first time in your life,* the *self,* its motives, its pursuits, its manipulations, its agendas, its games, etc.

5. You become compassionate to the *self,* though it has been like a beast. Conflict ended, integrity established.

Sankara: Prior to *choiceless awareness of what is,* fructifying, there was one kind of life, even in *dharma and moksha,* one in which, there was total ignorance about the *self*-centered manner in whch the *self* was functioning. Whereas, after *choiceless awareness of what is (amanaska yoga),* turned out to be fruitful, one is somehow, vastly different. Because, one has seen the activities of the *self,* in a very impartial way, almost asthough, one has no relationship with that *self.* After having secured that marvelous opportunity of seeing the *self* at work, in all relationships and in the market place of life; one is almost dumbfounded, as to how, in all the ten thousand years of the Hindu tradition, we had completely missed out on this precious jewel of *amanaska yoga.* One's feeling and compassion for man, almost goes into a conflagration, only in the wake of having seen fully the activities of the *self.* It must be understood that unless, one (the *self*) actually suffers and learns to die, compassion for oneself and for all, may not arise at all. All of what we are talking here can become very real, only when a seething misfortune in one's inner life has taken hold of us. Without the blessing (in disguise) of such a misfortune in our inner life, it is very doubtful, if we will ever come this far in *dharma and moksha.*

31. Blessings from Taming the *Jiva*

6. With the taming of *Sakti, Jiva* also becomes more peaceful, *Siva & Sakti* are harmonized.

7. You get rooted in *Siva*, and enjoy your *beingness*. From now on, you become self-composed and a stranger to boredom.

8. You will be able to meet life, from your *beingness*, always feel good within.

Sankara: In topics 29, 30 and 31, we are seeing life, through the eyes and consciousness of the *sthitha prajnya;* one in whom, not only, *self* - Knowing has actually happened, but also, the farther milestone of the calming and taming of the *self* has been crossed. Such a *sthitha prajnya*, naturally becomes an outsider to this world, even though, within this world, he functions in the most responsible way, as though, all that happens to others, also happens to himself. Life, which was formerly, anything but delicious, undergoes a radical shift. After *amanaska yoga* fructified, a new mysterious life seems to start. He now acts only spontaneously, never with ulterior motives. He lives his life, entirely without conflict and a sense of divisiveness, he is not the old pleasure seeking creature. This sense of divisiveness and conflict was the hall mark of his former life. One feels that the milestone of the *sthitha prajnya* can be crossed, more easily, when a great misfortune lands in one's life and then one is also fortunate to secure the guidance of an *Advaitic* master or at least the writings of an *Advaitic* master. All seekers may not be fated to develop and blossom into *sthitha prajnyas*. So, those, for whom this is hard, they may have to find instead, more fulfillment in *artha and kama*.

32. Untamed *Sakti* is 'Fast', *Siva* is Timeless

One part of you has always been *Siva*, You have always been 'outside' time. But you did not care to know this. **'Time', happens to you like cool or hot air blowing on your face.**

Now, start watching *what is* (*Sakti* in movement). In this kind of *self* - Knowing meditation, initially, you will find it hard to watch *(to see)*, while something is happening in *Sakti*. **After *Sakti* has 'done' something only, you become aware.**

Q : *Talking of a tamed Sakti and an untamed Sakti, I get the impression that Sakti will be untamed, only so long as She is the dominant form of energy. The moment the Presence of Siva, so to speak, rises on the horizon, Sakti automatically gets reigned in and becomes tamed - is this what is happening?*

A : Yes, consciousness has got two independent kinds of modes. One is being and that is, what we have identified as *Siva or* awareness which is essentially timeless and which is *Atma*. And the other is kind of reflection of the timeless *Atma* and the timeless *Siva* in the field of consciousness, that is *Sakti*, which is one aspect of the reflection in the mirror of body-mind. So it's more like *Siva* is the potential energy and *Sakti* is the kinetic energy. It so happens that in our material life in which we are largely unaware of who we are, we are more in the becoming mode and very little in the being mode, and in that state *Siva* is kind of eclipsed by *Sakti and She* is more dominant and there is no awareness of what is going on because we are ourselves moving in the train, so to speak, rather than standing on the platform and watching the train arriving and departing. The train is a thought, a feeling which is breezing into consciousness, which is kind of radiating out of the *Atma.*

So the question which you have asked, the moment the presence of *Siva* becomes strong, then automatically the *Sakti* is tamed? Yes, *Sakti* is slowed down for sure which is the taming and the presence of *Siva* kind of clips her wings and makes her slow down and then alone even observation becomes possible.

Q : *I'll quote from the present topic, in order to bring my Q into proper perspective: "In this self-Knowing meditation, initially, you will find it hard to watch (to see), while something is happening in Sakti. After Sakti has 'done' something only, you become aware."*

Why is it difficult for Siva, to observe this fast Sakti - did He go missing? What happened to Him? Because His very nature is only witnessing awareness, how did He miss this witnessing - when Sakti is fast?

A : We have to firstly remember and firmly grasp the three *gunas* or the three modes in which the living energy of consciousness can exist. The *gunas* are the three fundamental modes of all living and non-living forms, whether in *yoga,* or *ayurveda* or in Hindu psychology, or even in atomic and elementary particle physics. We have already met with them towards the end of the first day.

When *Sakti* is so wild, so dynamic and so diffuse, then the living energy of consciousness is more in the *rajas* mode, or in the *restless* and overactive mode. This is not the only mode for the living energy of consciousness to be in. For example, it can also be in the dense, lethargic, inattentive and a kind of slumbering mode, a mode in which learning is impossible. And this is called the *tamas* mode. Apart from these two modes, the living energy of consciousness can also be in the well poised, spiritual, happy and intelligent mode, called *sattva.* Thus, like all other things in nature, the living energy of consciousness, can be in three states or three modes, and these are called *gunas,* or 'natures' or modes.

At any given time, the living energy of consciousness will strongly be in one mode (the dominant mode), and weakly in the other two modes. Importantly, all three modes will co-exist, with one mode dominant, and the other two modes weaker. *Sattva* alone is spiritual and intelligent, while *tamas* and *rajas* modes are not.

However excess of *rajo guna or* excess of the *tamo guna* will eclipse the intelligence and joy, inherent in the *sattva guna.* And the combination of *rajo guna* and *tamo guna* is also undesirable and results in aggression and darkness. It is more of *tamo guna* especially, that creates darkness, thereby eclipsing *Siva,* who is beyond the three *gunas.* So *Siva* is not present at all, because the whole thing is only becoming and

239

there is hardly any being. *Sattva* is closest to *Siva*, and when *sattva* is very weak, *Siva* cannot make His presence felt.

Now the Hindu scriptures have a beautiful way of describing where *Siva* is actually placed. He seems to be missing and so they say that the *Atma (Siva)* is '*sukshmadi sukshmam, kalilasya madhye'*. i.e., *Siva* or the *Atma* is subtler than the subtlest and in the midst of chaos, in the midst of confusion, buried in the coils of chaos and becoming, buried in the coils of *Sakti.*

So unless the coils of becoming are kind of ripped apart and they are pushed aside, the underlying luminous awareness will not come into relief. So, the moment we remember that we have another dimension to our consciousness, namely, the *dimension of being* and *the dimension of awareness* and we initially make an effort to recollect ourselves and to observe the moment in consciousness; there occurs a polar shift in consciousness and though initially the effort is detrimental to actual observation, yet, by and by, by trial and error we will soon find that we do manage to be *choicelessly aware* of what is going on, namely, *what is.*

So we turn inward and we observe what is going on. So we settle in the *Siva* nature, we discover the nature of *awareness* and the nature of *being* which is normally missing. The dimension of our life, which is the *spiritual*, which is normally unrecognized and normally, undiscovered and missing, suddenly it becomes our real nature. So this happens by *amanaska yoga sadhana*, by the *choiceless awareness* of *what is,* we come to uncover the hidden *awareness* and the *hidden state of being* and then immediately *Sakti* which was fast and untamed till then, starts undergoes taming.

----

33. Obstacles Hindering
Choiceless Awareness of what is

1. You may not have courage to face *what is*.

2. Unable to face *what is*, you will try and superimpose a *what should be* on the ugly *what is,* **which you have been avoiding**.

3. If you are very 'dense' (too much *tamas*), you will try and avoid facing *what is*.

Q : *Let us take the most common problem in our lives. This is admittedly in relationship, where we get hurt and we hurt the other with whom we are related. Then we play games of dishonesty, we pretend, we tell lies, never disclosing to the other, how we actually feel in any given situation. Because we may be thinking that this is a common human condition and human nature - this hypocrisy, this double talk, this lack of integrity - we may not be paying enough attention to all this. In other words, is it really a lack of courage to face an ugly what is? Or, rather, the human family as a whole, being largely unconscious of its fallen condition, refrains from taking any pains whatsoever, to improve this rotten condition?*

A : There are actually two things involved here. When one has got a glimpse of *what is*, and then finds that, this *what is*, is very scary, nightmarish, because it is socially very rare and may be socially disapproved and so on; you may be ashamed of yourself in being in that *what is*. So the instinctive reaction will be to avoid facing that *what is* and not have the courage to stand up to that *what is*. So this is one possibility.

And quite distinct from this possibility, is another kind of a phenomenon which happens in relationship with *what is* and that is a phenomenon which is driven by our

241

apathy and by our indifference to *what is.* Because we don't find anything wrong and objectionable to that *what is,* because, in the first place, nobody told us to even look carefully at that *what is.* And because it is not kind of brought into relief in our society and the awareness and healing of the wounds in our consciousness are not given sufficient importance, we just slur over it, we just throw a blanket over it and pretend, or at any rate, go about as though, this shocking *what is,* does not exist at all.

Now, if you are confronted by a teacher or by a psychologist and you yield gracefully and become vulnerable to that confrontation, then upon impartial examination you will find that the ultimate source of this apathy and reluctance to face up to this *what is,* is the taking for granted that this is part of the human drama and that gives us a justification and a mandate that we need not bother, need not do anything about it. Please observe that this is an entirely different kind of response to a challenging *what is,* and it is not the condition in which we lack the courage to face the *what is.* This is a completely different kind of equation between us and the *what is,* so we need to differentiate between the two scenarios.

Q : *Is 'what should be', always the opposite of what is and always something which is socially respectable and therefore having greater, survival value? If this is so, are we not always functioning under social pressure, rather than in an authentic and original way?*

A : Yes, survival is probably the most important thing in so far as the *self* is concerned. And the whole of society and the whole of civilization have been patterned in such a way that the *security* for the *self* and the survival and preservation of the *self* are accorded the highest importance. None but the philosophers and very unusual spiritual teachers or psychologists who do research, may even dare to call this to question - whether the *self* should actually renounce this *self* defensive mechanism in its pursuit of survival and security, for its own greater wellness? Yes, because an ugly *what is,* is socially not respectable, we do not want to look at that *what is,* and everybody has thrown a blanket on that *what is* and even we are doing it unconsciously because it is a thing not examined, a thing which we are not aware of.

We actually lead a somewhat unconscious life, without adequate awareness about our inner life and always running on the track of survival. Yes, and that is why the projection of *what should be,* over *what is,* is such an automatic process, which is no more under the vigilant eye of our awareness. Unless and until somebody gives us a teaching and we open up to it and we are wakeful enough to open up to it, we may never make a discovery for ourselves that this *what should be,* is often diametrically opposite to *what is.* That *what should be,* has come into place only because it gives us greater security and a greater protection for the *self.* With what should be, superimposed on the disgraceful *what is*, the *self*, becomes free of the necessity for *self*-examination, which in any case seems to be a difficult thing for the *self*, it is far easier for the *self*, just to go on the well laid out track of hypocrisy and *self*-denial.

Q : *You have described the third obstacle to the choiceless awareness of what is, as 'being dense' and you have also added, 'too much tamas' in brackets. Are you saying that being dense, makes one too lazy, insensitive and not having the energy to exert oneself, and to perceive? So, is all this also tamasic nature?*

A : Yes, *tamo guna* in consciousness is also one of the obstacles. *Tamas* is a mode of living consciousness and we have to identify that *tamas* as mental lethargy, inaction and indifference. However, we have to be aware, that apart from *tamas*, there is another mode called, *rajas*, which is excessive activity, excessive aggression or restlessness and willfulness, as an attitude in life. If *rajas* is present and we perceive *what is*, then we may want to replace the ugly *what is*, with which we are uncomfortable, so we project a *what should be* and that is one mechanism whereby the *what is*, is not perceived and some substitute for it is sought.

The *tamas* mode of consciousness, when it is present, creates another alternative to avoid *what is*. So, what exactly is this alternative? We do this by just turning a blind eye, by pretending that, that *what is*, does not exist or by refusing to look at it. And that refusal to look at it, the utter insensitivity to one's own inner condition, that is what we may call, 'being dense'. This would mean lacking the sensitivity and lacking the swiftness of consciousness, the swiftness of the body to do something about it. So when we are *tamasic*, we postpone and we are not quick to act and not alert enough to do, what we have to to day, but, we will say we will do that tomorrow and finally we will never do it. So *tamas* is another mode in the human consciousness, which will be an obstacle in the *choiceless awareness of what is*. Just as *rajas*, when it is in consciousness will also be an obstacle, because, it will surely hinder our *choiceless awareness of what is*.

243

34. Untamed *Sakti* 'Dominating' *Siva*

Kali dancing on Siva *(Modern Period)*

Acknowledgement: 'Myths and Symbols in Indian Art and Civilization', Plate 69, Heinrich Zimmer, Bollingen Series / Princeton, 1972.

Sutra on the Spiritual Fall

Yatato hy api Kaunteya puruṣasya vipaścitaḥ |
Indriyāṇi pramāthīni haranti prasabhaṁ manaḥ ||

||Bhagavad Gita II.60||[7]

The turbulent senses do violently enslave the true Self, even of a clear-sighted discerning *mumukshu*.

Q : *In this very perplexing picture, are we seeing a powerful rajasic Sakti, dominating Siva, the awareness? What would be the consequence of this?*

A : The picture itself actually conveys to us what the consequence will be and you can see that *Sakti* is like a virago, quite wild and unrelenting. She has completely subdued and eclipsed *Siva* who stands for awareness, and the timeless aspect of consciousness, namely the *Atma*. Now when this kind of a situation arises in consciousness whereby *Siva* or the *Atma* is eclipsed, then the individual in question will also have no awareness either. Instead, the individual will exist only in the becoming mode, that is, as an entity in *Sakti* only, which will be either excessively *rajasic* or excessively *tamasic*. If it is excessively *rajasic*, then the person will be over active, over aggressive and too much in a *becoming* mode and if it is excessively *tamasic*, then the person will be extremely physically and mentally indolent, lethargic, insensitive and prone to inaction and postponing things. In other words, the person will not have enough energy to act. He will be more deadened and unresponsive like a stone, so in

244

that condition too, awareness is eclipsed. So these are the consequences when *Sakti* is wild and *Sakti* is untamed.

Q   : *When this kind of situation happens in consciousness, that rajas or tamas are too strong, then one has no awareness to observe what is, isn't it? And then, is the Bhagavad Gita sutra telling us, that under these conditions, even wise beings will be carried away and enslaved by sensory impressions?*

A   : True, when *Sakti* is so wild and stronger than *Siva,* then *Siva* inevitably gets eclipsed. Then the *rajas* or *tamas* will be so strong that *Siva* who is even beyond *sattva,* as the *Trigunatitha (i.e.,* beyond the three *gunas),* becomes inaccessible. Then *Siva* has no chance to kind of come into relief. Under such circumstances, *Sakti* who is working through the senses and working through thoughts and feelings at a frenetic pace will do what She likes and that could be pursuit of pleasure or some other aggressive kind of thing or some other very malefic kind of thing like some criminal activity and so on. In that case the individual, whose essential nature is the *Atma,* will have no discriminatory power, will have no awareness and will just become a victim of the *rajasic or tamasic Sakti.*

The *Bhagavad Gita sutra* actually says that when this *Sakti* is so strong, then automatically the senses also will be so strong and then the senses will actually enslave the awareness. Will hijack the awareness and the person will have a spiritual fall. The *sutra* says that this kind of a spiritual fall can happen even to people who are very ardent in the spiritual path, and who are persevering steadily on the spiritual path, those who are very disciplined - even they can be occasionally be hijacked by these turbulent senses and the underlying *Sakti.*

Now we must not be so surprised by this phenomenon. We just need to look at the eclipses which the luminaries face in each passing year of time when the sun undergoes a solar eclipse and the moon undergoes the lunar eclipse and this is in the nature of things itself. But given a little bit of time, the eclipsed and darkened luminaries, the sun and the moon, do recover from the eclipses and they do regain their old brightness, old glory and their capacity to guide humanity is fully regained. Just as the eclipses happen, similarly even sages and wise people may momentarily slip and fall by the temptations that the senses offer to them. But then if they have indeed stabilized in wisdom, they will quickly get up from the fall and they will go about their old serious approach in pursuit of the Divine and the truth.

Q   : *You are speaking of turbulent senses. Do you mean to say, the senses will be wild and turbulent, only when Sakti is turbulent?*

A   : We have got to understand the consequences of *Sakti* being turbulent. When *Sakti* is turbulent then consciousness is naturally in a flurry, it is frenetic, it is wild and there is no pause between thought and thought. Because this consciousness drives the senses, we will be too hasty to act, we may be too hasty to speak and this is usually called rash actions or this will sometimes be called indolence or apathy or inaction too. Inaction is sourced in the *tamas* mode and excessive action is sourced in the *rajas* mode.

Now let us go back momentarily to the metaphor of the Bhagavad Gita in which Krishna who stands for the *Paramatma* is seen to be the chariot driver and Arjuna who is also in the chariot is the little *self* and then the chariot itself is the body and the five horses stand for the five senses. Now under normal circumstances if Krishna is well in tune, because he is the awareness, he is the *Paramatma*, then the chariot is under his control. So the body and senses become completely obedient to the master who is the charioteer, the *Atma*, who is also *Siva*. Now, consider the case where the master by a twist of fate becomes momentarily a weakling, a powerless weakling, and then the horses which are the senses take the law into their own hands and they begin to gallop in a mad fashion.

So that is exactly what will happen to us if *rajas* and *tamas* become dominant in consciousness. The chariot which is our body, mind and our senses goes amok like a wild elephant going amok and then awareness is eclipsed and therefore becomes non-functional, powerless and the *self* which is also in the chariot will be equally confused and will not be in an equipoised state. So when *Sakti* is turbulent naturally it is going to manifest as turbulent, uncontrollable senses. Then sorrow begins in life.

----

35. 'Tamed' *Sakti – Sthitha Prajnya's* Consciousness

The *Jiva* should elevate itself by the *Atma* alone. Let not the *Jiva* lower itself; for the *Atma* alone is the friend of the *Jiva,* whereas the *Jiva,* alone can be it's own enemy and the enemy of the *Atma.*

- Bhagavad Gita:VI.5[23]

Siva – Sakti (Bengal), X century A.D.

Acknowledgement: 'Myths and Symbols in Indian Art and Civilization', Plate 69, Heinrich Zimmer, Bollingen Series / Princeton, 1972.

Q : *This topic shows that, you are referring to the Bhagavad Gita, VI Chapter, 5th sloka. What is the content of this sloka?*

A : Actually in other retreats I had given this *sloka* because I consider this to be extremely important, because, a lot of people think that Krishna is the *Avatar* and they have to take refuge in him, in his personality. So the Krishna cult has developed in India. But Krishna's whole teaching is entirely different. He never asked us to take refuge in his human personality and in his human form, instead he gives us a recipe for getting a union with the *Paramatma.* And that is the *sloka* in chapter 6 (*sloka* no: 5) [23]:

उद्धरेदात्मनात्मानं नात्मानमवसादयेत् ।

आत्मैव ह्यात्मनो बन्धुरात्मैव रिपुरात्मनः ॥   ॥६ ॥५ ॥

Uddhared ātmanātmānam nātmānam avasādayet |
ātmaiva hy ātmano bandhur ātmaiva ripurātmanaḥ || ||6.5||

Meaning of the *sloka* is that we should be self-reliant on the path of *Jnana yoga* or the path of understanding as a means to achieving the Divine within ourselves. One is enjoined to be one's own teacher. So to put it simply: "The *Jiva* should elevate itself by the *Atma* alone. Let not the *Jiva* lower itself, for the *Atma* alone is the friend of the *Jiva*, whereas the *Jiva* alone can be its own enemy and the enemy of the *Atma*". [23]

Now the *sloka* speaks about two selves, like the Tat Tvam Asi birds, like *Siva & Sakti*. So obviously, *Siva* is the higher Self and *Sakti* is the lower *self*. Paradoxically, we are both. But we live our life in complete unawareness of the fact that we are also *Siva* and for the most part, we live only the life of *Sakti* and we don't seem to adequately live the life of *Siva*. And in a retreat like this the whole *sadhana* has to be in the direction of bringing *Siva* into relief. That *Siva*, who is behind the scenes, to bring that *Siva*, which is the essential and core part of ourselves, into full relief, that is the content of the *sloka*.

Q : *So, can I infer that this tamed Sakti is not fighting with herself, or in other words, She is her own best friend, and that She has come home to Siva?*

A : You are right, this *Sakti* is not fighting with herself. *Sakti* will fight with herself only if She is fragmented into two or three or four different things and they are all in opposition with each other, then She will fight. Then the force of *duality* and *maya* will be strong. But where *Sakti* is completely well integrated and has become *whole* because *Siva* has come into the picture, She will naturally be docile and tamed and will not be fighting with herself. So She will be her own best friend and absolutely a good friend, because She has come home to *Siva*, who is her Lord and master. This is also the state in which, *Siva* comes into relief and *Siva's* presence which is intelligence *(prajnya)* begins to manifest.

The topic also represents the *sthitha prajnya's* state of consciousness, which is an extremely important teaching from the *Bhagavad Gita*. *Sthitha* means stable and *prajnya* is intelligence sourced in the *Divine*. So the *sthitha prajnya* is one whose consciousness has fallen silent and because the consciousness has fallen silent, that consciousness is automatically yoked to the *Divine*, the *Atma* or *Siva*. So this mythic picture, the religious sculpture also signifies the *shtitha prajnya's* state of consciousness. We should at least get this far in our meditative journey where *Sakti* becomes silent and gets yoked to *Siva*.

Q : *If we observe closely the expression on Siva's face, it is so beatific and also compassionate. Don't you think the sculptor has done good justice to Siva being an embodiment of ananda and isn't He also seen to be full of compassion, karuna?*

A : You are right, the face of *Siva* - if you come close to the picture and observe carefully - you will find to be extremely beatific and the emotion called *ananda rasa* is seen on His face. He is in ecstasy. And this is His natural state, because He is *sat, chit and ananda*. He is existence and beatitude and He is awareness (*chit* is awareness). And the sculptor has done full justice in bringing out the *ananda* aspect of *Siva* and the *karunamaya* aspect of *Siva,* that is, His nature is full of *karuna* or in other words, compassion.

Here I like to add, that in the ancient Hindu civilization, there were 64 art forms and every art form was a means to find the Divine and yoke into the *Divine*. And *sthapatya Veda* or *sthapatya shastra* or *shilpa shastra* was a system of knowledge and understanding of how one is to give beauty and correct proportion to art forms. And if one dedicates oneself completely to the art form and then one becomes engrossed and immersed in the sculpture, then that also becomes a route or passage to *moksha*. So if you find the Hindu sculptures doing tremendous justice, then we have to understand that this is so, only because the artisans, the sculptors and the artists who worked with these forms, for them it was a religion, not just a profession or a vocation. It was not just a means of livelihood, nor was it just a skill, it was a traditionally well-established means to realize the Divine. It was a means to realize God. And that is why it has the obvious stamp of excellence and perfection.

Q : *Some of these temple sculptures, are often misinterpreted as being erotic, that is having sexual overtones. Now that we have come to this topic, where a god and a goddess are seen to be in an intimate embrace, should we not understand at this stage as to why there is the presence of erotic sculpture in Hindu religious art and Hindu temple architecture? We see even to this day erotic sculpture in the temples of Halebid and Belur (Karnataka) and also in the temple in Konarak (Orissa)?*

A : This is an extremely significant question that may spring up in the minds of all people who are fascinated by India's obsession with the Divine and the spiritual life. You may also not find any satisfactory answers in the religious literature. I have pondered this question intermittently for many long years.

When I was probably 16 or 17 years of age, my father had taken us on a tour to temple sites in the state of Karnataka in South India and at that time we visited the temples in Belur and Halebid. This place is about 450 Km from Chennai and we had gone by car. During our tour we observed these sculptures and at that time, I was a teenager and an older cousin of mine was with me; so, I asked him and my father this same question which you are now asking me. And they could not give me the answer to that question, they were themselves puzzled.

So I pondered over this question myself. I did not read any books on this subject. So, what I am going to tell you now is not from any books that I have read or any seminars that I attended. I got this particular answer as an insight. Now, any religious culture whether it is Buddhist or Jaina or Hindu or Christian gives a very important place for celibacy and chastity. And the saints of the religions whether they were Jains or Hindus or Buddhists or Christians, or belonging to any other faith, must have attempted to live a life of celibacy and chastity. Surely, there must have been saints who tried to eschew all desires and all sensory indulgences by fighting with their lower sensate nature, all in the hope of finding the Divine and in the hope of finding everlasting bliss.

And surely, there should have also been a few exemplary cases of saints and sages, to whom celibacy, came as a blessing at birth itself, *and those exceptional cases would have never struggled to be celibate and chaste.* So, we have to understand that the saints and sages fall into two neat categories. Firstly, the natural saints and sages, for whom celibacy is absolutely natural, these must have been in the minority. Then secondly, the majority of the saints and sages, struggling with their lower nature and trying to be celibate and chaste. The latter category will probably succeed only with age and never when they are still young and their bodies are still in good vigor.

Now, in any religion when they go for the quest of achieving the Divine, they go too far to achieve it and they have to pay a price for that. And you already see that the two religions from India, the Buddhist and the Jaina religions, which are actually the religions of renunciation, imply that you have to completely eschew and renounce worldly life and obviously sex, which is part of sensual pleasure.

Then your material life and the life of the body takes a beating and if that takes a hard beating, then it will show a dwindling in the numbers in the population. And if the kings in the kingdom who are ruling the civilization are alerted to such a happening, then it is for the kings to again probably use religion as a mandate to give a religious sanction once more for the sexes to co-habit together, so that the progeny may come forth and the race be furthered.

Now, that India has been long obsessed with celibacy and chastity is known to Indologists and philosophers, who have studied India deeply. And it is also seen in the horoscope of India as an exalted *Ketu* on the most effective point of the seventh house of sexual relationships. Now astrologers know this very well that whenever you have *Ketu* or *Saturn* on the cusp of the seventh house, that is an indication and signification of celibacy or complete abstinence from sex.

So India did have this tendency, which is seen in her birth chart, so a time must have come when the pendulum must have swung to one extreme position, threatening the continuity of the race itself. Therefore the wise kings of that period must have been suitably advised by philosophers of that time. I'm sure the kings at that time would have wanted to get a religious sanction or a religious mandate for saying that it is quite alright, and that even sex is after all, part of the human drama and human life. And therefore their new message to the people should have been in this vein: 'Don't take all this so very seriously anymore, now we are in peril, as our population is dwindling'. So they put the erotic sculpture in temple architecture.

Because in India when anything gets a religious mandate, then the people follow it. For Indians religion is the highest thing, the voice of God and the voice of truth. So for even any simple material thing, unless there is a sanction and a mandate coming from the religion, people will not take recourse to that.

So the instance of erotic sculpture being in Belur and Halebid and in Konarak in Orissa are probably instances of time periods in Indian history, when the kings of that age had to take recourse to religion in order to certify that sex was not forbidden by the Divine. Because at one point, too much of abstinence from sex would have led to dwindling of the human population. It was at that point in time, this erotic sculpture must have been brought in as an urgent remedial measure, by the ruling kings to resolve this problem in a decisive way.

Q : *Does this topic represent a meditative state of consciousness, one in which consciousness is almost still, or at any rate, very sattvik, and with a minimum of the grosser gunas, rajas and tamas?*

A : Yes. As the posture of *Sakti* represents, *Sakti* has no restlessness at all. Nor is She indolent. She is tuned into the Divine, tuned into the ground from which she has emanated as an independent energy. This mythic representation of *Siva & Sakti* in religious sculpture actually points to the *sthitha prajnya's* state of consciousness.

Prajnya means intelligence that is sourced in awareness and *sthitha* is that intelligence which has become stabilized. So this *sthitha prajnya* state is one in which the awakened intelligence is not flickering, but has become very stable and very steady. And that happens only when *Sakti* has come home to roost. With Her coming home, all Her madness and all Her activity is at an end and that is when *Siva* the primal intelligence has an opportunity to come into relief and make His presence felt. So the sculpture actually represents the meditative state in which consciousness has become very silent, has become very unruffled, when the *gunas, rajas* and *tamas* are at an all time minimum.

36. 'Move from Innocence to Innocence'

"This meditation cannot be learnt from another. You must begin without knowing anything about it, and move from innocence to innocence."

- J. Krishnamurti in 'Meditations'[13]

"Innocence is incapability of getting hurt."

- J. Krishnamurti

Q : *Is Krishnamurti referring to choiceless awareness of what is?*

A : Yes, this is what he is referring to.

Q : *Then why does he maintain that it cannot be learnt from another?*

A : He is saying that - that it cannot be learnt from another - only to emphasize that this is far more intricate, subtler and deeper than taking a *mantra* given by a *guru* and meditating on that *mantra* till one has *samadhi*. In *choiceless awareness of what is*, one enters into this meditation and it goes on and on and is very creative and non mechanical, watching every reaction of the *self*, without ever criiticising, ever judging, but assimilating every auspicious thing therein and every inauspicious thing also, as part of *what is*. In this there is no room for becoming, no spiritual enrichment... No one can hold your hand and walk you through this meditation, you will have to walk on a solitary path, all alone-because, you alone know your consciousness and your peculiar, problematic *what is*.

We may also question Sri J. Krishnamurti, in so far as the validity of his statement is concerned. I have found that, it is possible to help others when they are receptive and capable of great learning. This is what I am trying to do in this retreat.

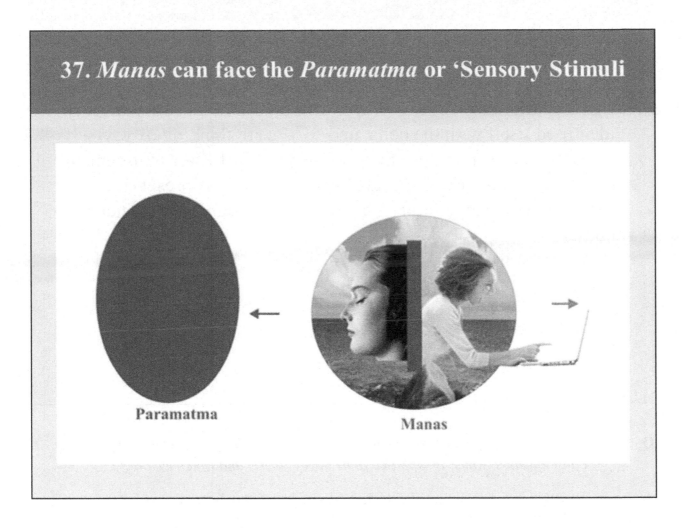

37. *Manas* can face the *Paramatma* or 'Sensory Stimuli

Paramatma

Manas

Q : *As manas is the feeling nature, why have you brought in the manas, in so far as facing the Paramatma is concerned?*

A : *Chitta*, is the general flow, causing time, it is a display of *Adi Parasakti*, in this individual body. *Ahankara* and *buddhi* are not good receptacles to face the *Paramatma*, so we are left only with the tender *manas*, which is our Mo, our feelings.

Q : *In the part of this picture, corresponding to introversion with closed eyes, what is one to do, when no words, no pictures, no thoughts arise, it is just an empty screen and a void?*

A : When no words, no pictures, no thoughts appear to you, who are the witness, then indeed, there is only silence and emptiness. Then, feel the conscious presence, the 'I' that you are, and abide in it, with a sense of mystery and wonder.

38. Disconnect 'I am' from your body-mind

"The knowingness that you are ('I am'), has mistakenly identified itself with the body, and so you are thinking of yourself as this body. But you are that 'knowingness of I am'. Strengthen the conviction that you are that 'conscious presence', the knowingness that you are ('I am'), the beingness, and not the body."

- Sri Nisargadatta Maharaj[27]

Q : *So, this presupposes that each of us, must have a pretty clear idea of the 'I' consciousness, which is supposed to be always there, and which we are?*

A : Yes, this may be the first and the last step in the journey inwards.

As this 'I' consciousness, which Maharaj calls, 'I am ness' does not abide in itself, as being, but instead, is outgoing as becoming, the activity of thought must subside to a certain extent, for each of us to succeed in getting hold of ourselves, as the 'I' consciousness. Once you have discovered the essence of your being as this, 'I' consciousness, many things will fall into place. This, 'I' is the core of inner goings on.

----

39. The Witness Consciousness ('I am ness') is Inherently Unstable in the face of Sensory Calls

Sankara : "The *advaitic* texts, as well as your own experience, if you are a true *mumukshu*, will be seen to confirm the fact that the witness consciousness, 'I am ness' is inherently unstable, especially when *pratyahara* (withdrawal of the senses from the sense objects) is not part of the *sadhana* of the *mumukshu.*"

Q : *The witness state is that of Siva, or of the Atma, or of awareness; whichever way you want to put it. As in our inner life, we seem to have no option, but to be 'amphibians'. Sometimes living in 'water' (abiding in the witness, or in awareness) and sometimes 'transferred' and pulled away on to the 'land' (getting into the activity of Sakti or consciousness). So, is the mentioned inherrent instability, sourced in this dual nature of Siva & Sakti, of awareness and consciousness?*

A : You have put it correctly, it is because of the 'contamination' of *Siva* by *Sakti*, that we are inherently unstable in the witness state. We have to understand that *Sakti*, who is paradoxically, an aspect of *Siva*, creates the illusion of time and 'rocks' the witness state. At the same time, life will be very dull and uninteresting, without this play of *Sakti*, which produces infinite variety, from the one source of *Siva*.

Q : *You seem to also suggest in this topic that there is some kind of an antidote, for the poison of this inherent instability. That withdrawal of the senses from the sense objects, which is called pratyahara and daily meditations (to be described hereafter), will certainly make the abidance in the witness state, more stable?*

A   :   Yes, there is a kind of *sadhana* that has to be done, in order to calm and tame *Sakti (self)*, yet even after this calming and taming, you will be astonished to find that, the *self*, has not entirely given up its defence mechanism. In fact, the moment a *sadhana* is commenced, the *self* will start feeling more secure, and will try to get some gain out of this *sadhana* - that is, 'becoming' commences again. For this reason of the interference of the *self*, the *sadhana* has to be done in a rather oblique way and is necessary for the final fulfillment of human life.

40. Equilibrium of the *Jiva and Atma*

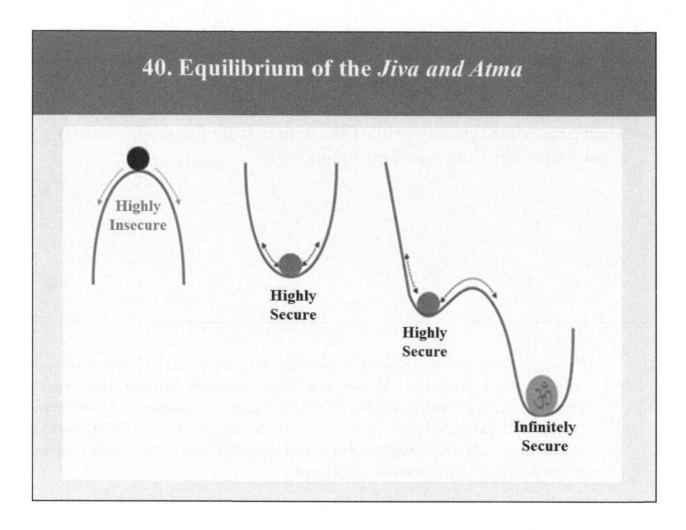

Q   :   *You are speaking here of some equilibrium of the Jiva and Atma. Can you clarify, what this so-called equilibrium is?*

A   :   Our true identity always rests with the *Atma*, the birthless and deathless awareness. However, because this awareness has somehow got associated with this extraordinarily sophisticated body and also as a result, got associated with consciousness, which is the result of the nervous system and the body, the awareness, gets covered by *maya* and so forgetting our true identity, we consider ourselves, to be a man or a woman, an engineer or a doctor, a father or the mother, a husband or a wife, and so on. All of these earthly identities are *anatmas*, false selves, or our life as a *Jiva* whereas the underlying imperceptible *Atma* alone is our true nature, our true identity.

Q : *Will you please explain the three different equilibrium diagrams?*

A : The bowl in the middle shows stable equilibrium of the 'I', you see a 'dark grey ball' (shown green in the original picture, and referred to as the green ball in the audio commentary too) in that bowl, it is that conscious presence or the 'I' in the pure form. As sensory calls impinge on this 'dark grey ball', it will at best make a few oscillations, be disturbed temporarily, yet also reasonably quickly return, very naturally to its equilibrium position. The 'dark grey ball' in this bowl therefore represents, a *sthitha prajnya* or a mature spiritual individual, who has stabilized wonderfully in the witness consciousness or in the *Atma* or in the awareness. In this state, the 'impurities', which are nothing but the false associations and attachments of the 'I' are at a minimum.

The left figure emphasizes the absence of any stability, but a perpetual fickleness and unsettled and insecure nature - this is the state of someone, who knows only consciousness, which is subject to time, and who does not ever come into the 'awareness country'. It is what physicists would call, unstable equilibrium. The individual's sense of *self*, is shown as the 'black ball', which is not the 'I', in its pure form, but only an *anatma* or *Jiva* arising out of the association of the 'I' with something or the other. The important thing for us to understand is that, stability corresponds to inwardly feeling secure, whereas, instability corresponds to the feeling of inner insecurity. So, the left diagram, stresses the fact that as long as we remain in the 'consciousness country' alone, there is no peace for us, no security what ever, instead only a perpetual insecurity. All of this is shown by the 'black ball' (shown red in the PPT slide (topic), and referred to as the red ball, in the audio commentary).

On the right you see a deeper 'esoteric' aspect of the stability of the *sthitha prajnya*.

It has happened to Nisargadatta Maharaj and Ramana Maharshi that sometimes, even the *sthitha prajnya's* 'I', develops an instability, in that, consciousness is sucked back to *Parabrahma* and also emptied in the process. This is classic inward death. This is a massive purgation of consciousness, which would tantamount to 'death' of consciousness. There after, there will be a rebirth and renewal. This is shown on the extreme right, with the symbol *Aum*.

----

41. *Ganesha* as the *Paramatma* in Creation

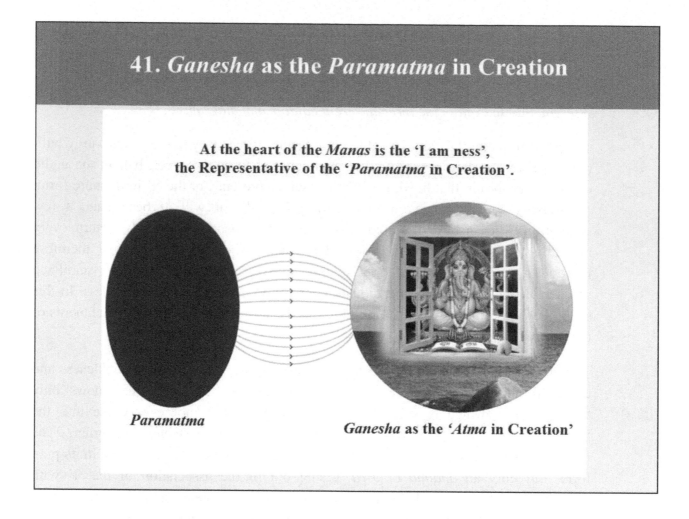

**At the heart of the *Manas* is the 'I am ness',
the Representative of the '*Paramatma* in Creation'.**

Paramatma

Ganesha as the '*Atma* in Creation'

Q : *What Maharaj calls, conscious presence and what Ramana Maharshi calls, 'I', is this what you are describing as the 'I am ness'?*

A : Yes.

Q : *Are you saying that in the Hindu spiritual literature and in the Hindu religion, Ganesha stands for the pure 'I'?*

A : Yes, this is precisely my point, so we have to get hold of this, pure 'I', bereft of all attachments and associations. *Ganesha* is this *Atma*, which is really who we are, when we are stripped of all the hundred false coverings.

Q : *Is the Atma knowable?*

A : No, being imperceptible, on account of being the subject, you can never know it, like you know apples and mountains and all other sense objects.

Q : *Is the Paramatma or the Parabrahma, namely, 'That', knowable?*

A : Not at all, but, we may infer the existence of the Divine, by It's acts of Mercy and Kindness, more over, as *Atma* and awareness, we are 'That', post Realization.

Q : *What are the golden field lines connecting the Atma or Ganesha to Parabrahma?*

A : These are always invisible, but any happening in the *Atma* is immediately conveyed to the Source and the Source then responds compassionately. Sometimes, instead of us appealing to the Source, the Source for unfathomable reasons, stretches out a helping hand and comes to our rescue, even when unasked. This was the classic and stunning case of Sri Ramana Maharshi, *moksha* without any seeking, so it is a two way invisible connection. We will go more into this on the seventh day.

42. Stable Abidance in 'I am ness' is Liberation

"Once it is understood, that 'I am ness' is purely 'I am ness', formless, and not that shackled body form - then no liberation is called for. To be stabilized in that *beingness*, which has no name and form, that is itself, liberation."

- Sri Nisargadatta Maharaj[28]

Q : *So the middle diagram in the centre showing the dark grey ball (shown green in the original PPT slide), this is the sthitha prajnya's consciousness, his 'I'?*

A : Yes, so from the point of view of Maharaj, that is *moksha*, liberation, no more sorrow.

Q : *So, the main problem seems to be, disassociation of the pure 'I' from all things, including the identification with the body?*

A : Yes, this is what it amounts to. You have to be interested in this quest, first of all, you have to be a seeker and then will come that moment, when it dawns on you that, you have always been in the final state, the pure 'I'.

43. The World exists in 'You', in the 'I am'

" 'I am' is itself the world. It contains the entire world, that should be your conviction. **Just as in a dream, when you feel that you are 'awake', but actually you are not, and your world at that time is the dream world.**

"Similarly, this knowingness (in the waking state) contains this so-called real world; this conviction must come. **The truth is that there is no diff between dream consciousness and waking consciousness, as all consciousness is one.**"

- Sri Nisargadatta Maharaj[29]

Q : *How does Maharaj say that 'I am' is itself the whole cosmos?*

A : It is so, because, the world happens in the consciousness of a human observer and without a human observer there are no galaxies and no universe. If you start thinking about this, you will understand how, this is the truth. Perhaps we can discuss this later.

Q : *Maharaj seems to be making an analogy between the dream world and this world, which science claims to be objective and also real. Just as the dreamer wakes up to find his dream world utterly imaginative and unreal and is often thankful for the same; in the same way, upon waking up from this dream of the waking consciousness, does the Jiva, lose only his imagined world of relationships, which is based entirely on the assumption that one is the body, or does the Jiva lose the physical world as well?*

A : When we move from awareness, as the witness, after we have stabilized there, to the root of awareness, which is *Pure Awareness* or *Parabrahma*, we certainly will find that the world of relationships, which was based on dreaming, as well as the physical world, supported by the witnessing awareness, both are lost.

---

44. Maharaj: 'I am' *(Atma)* is the Greatest Miracle

"Your consciousness, 'I am' *(Atma)* itself gives rise to this world., which is a unified field. **But it may be objected to, as there is such an infinite variety of shapes and colors in that world. How can reality then be said to be not two, *Advaita*?**

"It is because all these differences exist only in your consciousness, 'I am' *(Atma)* as appearances. The source is the same consciousness, 'I am' *(Atma)*, but the manifestation exhibits so much variety!"

- Sri Nisargadatta Maharaj[34]

Q : *Is Maharaj saying that 'I am', the Atma is the greatest miracle, only because, though it is One Atma, One Essence, yet, It has given birth to this infinite diversity with infinite number of living and non-living forms?*

A : Yes, the wonderful thing is this deeply hidden, seemingly insignificant and infinitesimal, essence, the *Atma*, it has begotten this splendorous cosmos, the macrocosm. For this reason, it is a great wonder.

---

45. Self-Realization is vulnerable to *Maya*

"The Truth that 'I am Brahman' is realized from the scriptures or by the Grace of the Master, **but it cannot be firm in the face of obstructions.**

"Ignorance, uncertainty and wrong knowledge are obstacles resulting from long standing habits in the innumerable incarnations of the past which cause trouble, and then the fruits of realization slip away. Therefore root them, out by: (1) hearing the Truth, (2) reasoning and (3) meditation (abidance in the *Atma*)."

- *'Kaivalya Navaneetham'* [24]

Q : *We have all been under the impression that Enlightenment, like that of the legendary Buddha, once gained, will stand us in good stead, for the rest of our life. Now I see that, this has been another 'maya', in populist perception.*

A : The layman, may have any preconceived opinion about Self - Realization or Enlightenment, but this will always be different from the truth about Self - Realization, with which we are all becoming familiar.

Q : *Thus, in the light of these mandates from Kaivalya Navaneetham, are we to suppose that Self - Realized beings are also expected to do their share of house-keepiing, or putting their house in order, almost on a daily basis?*

A : Yes, the truly great Self - Realized people are always humble, they will easily spot their pit falls and either by choiceless awareness, or by *sravana, manana* and *nidhidhyasana* and they will be purifying themselves as often as is needed.

Third Day (Chapter - III), 2nd 'Tat Tvam Asi' Meditation

Observing and accepting the *Jiva.*

Learing to be compassionate to the *Jiva.*
Seaparating the what should be from the *what is*.
Driking the pain in relationship.
Suffering the pain and forgiving.

Chapter IV

By being the *Atma,*
Calming and Silencing of the *Jiva (self), happens*

Let us Recapitulate the Important Ground Covered in the Last Three Chapters

Topics 1 to 7

Q : *This is the fourth day and we have the meditational challenge of calming and silencing the Jiva (self). Usually, teachers talk of the self or of the Jiva. Here you have emphasized that the self belongs to the Jiva. So, we need some clarification about the way in which you are using the two words, self and Jiva.*

A : In *Advaita* literature, the *Jiva* is used to describe the man encased by the *maya* of algae (go to the algae man metaphor, Ch. I, topic 18). J. Krishnamurti uses *self* to signify the *self* of the *Jiva,* though in his vocabulary, *Jiva* is absent. Sri Nisargadatta Maharaj understands how the term *Jiva* is used in the traditional literature of India. Sri Ramana Maharshi, being extremely familiar with the spiritual vocabulary of the *Advaita* tradition and the ancient Saivite tradition of Self - Realization (texts in Tamil and Sanskrit), uses the term *Jiva*, as it is used in these traditions. However, he uses, Self, a modern term, instead of the traditional, less understood *Atma*.

Although we are talking of the *self* of the *Jiva,* we might also use the term *Jiva* and the *self,* synonymously, as equivalent things, since the essence of the *Jiva* is indeed the *self* only.

In this context, an extremely pertinent *sutra*, from Maharshi Patanjali, one of the founding fathers of the Sanskrit language, along with Panini, comes to mind. It is about the importance of our sensitivity to words and how we use them in our work: "Every word, when perfectly grasped, and when skillfully applied, leads to the fulfillment of our aspiration, be it in heaven or on earth."

---

1. Fulfillment in *Artha and Kama*, must precede entry into *Dharma and Moksha*

1. Generally, *artha and kama* Journey (of the *Jiva*) is completed by 60 or 65 years. Then, *Jiva* seeks *dharma and moksha,* just as the same *Jiva* was seeking *artha and kama* till 60 or 65 years.

2. Sometimes *dharma and moksha* journey may commence when young, or *artha and kama* journey may commence after 60 or 65!

3. Astrologers know when, what journey begins and ends.

Q : *Recapitulating an earlier topic on the goals of life, isn't it but natural that the Jiva has to be fulfilled in the artha and kama journey, from the 20th year to the 60th year roughly?*

A : Correct. This is the normal pattern, so that the hungry senses have been satisfied and even satiated as the body grows old. However, we may also remember that if the *Jiva* is not reigned in, sometimes it's appetites in *artha and kama* may also become insatiable. It must somehow dawn on the *Jiva*, that there should be an ending of the *artha and kama* journey, one way or the other.

Q : *You seem to draw attention to the possibility of the dharma and moksha journey, preceeding the artha and kama journey. Is this from an observation of life? What is the basis of your data?*

A : The Indian sage, Veerabrahmam from Andhra Pradesh (19th Century), got married and had four children, after the full maturity of his Self - Realization. In the case of the American mystic, Bernadette Roberts now still living, it was after completion of many contemplative years at seminaries, that she decided to marry and raise a family. Also from my astrological practice, I have many examples of people, whose Rahu dasa (materialistic season of life) commences after 60. So, there are substantial grounds for the 'topsy turvy' order of the goals of life. For Ramana Maharshi, there was in fact, no *artha and kama* journey at all, since he secured *moksha* at 16 years of age.

2. The 'Creeper' *(Jiva)* and the Supporting 'Tree Trunk' *(Atma)*

Q : *I see that, you are ever on the look out for new metaphors to drive home the same eternal truth of the Jiva and the Atma, what is common ground between them and what is different. You started with the ocean and the wave, then the two birds of the*

Mundaka Up, then the man enmeshed in algae, and now, you have come up with this. So, many examples, only to create conviction in us?

A   :   It has been brought home to us by Adi Sankaracharya that it is human nature to undertake a *sadhana* or a practice and carry it through to its logical conclusion, only when we have an irrevocable *intellectual conviction* that what we are doing is necessary and is going to be absolutely fruitful and that it is something of measureless salutary value [4]. So, we have to approach the same truth of the *Jiva* and the *Atma* from so many angles so that all doubts are disspelled and one is ever ready to embark on this practice without the slightest hesitation. This is really the idea.

Q   :   *One understands by now that the Atma, represented by the tree trunk here is the very ground of the inner life of human beings. But what exactly are the creepers?*

A   :   The creepers stand for the numerous false notions we have about ourselves. These are well accepted notions though they are completely erroneous from the spiritual point of view. In contrast to the *Atma* which is our true Self, these give us *anatmas*, that is, false selves. We will see more of this in the next topic. A typical creeper would be what one thinks, as to what one is. For example one may think of oneself as a man or a woman. This is utterly absurd from the spiritual point of view because one is the *Atma* and one is neither of these. One might get angry because one considers oneself to be the father or the mother or husband or the wife, etc. However, one is none of these. One is the *Atma*. Thus there are several false impressions we have of ourselves, all these are *anatmas*, here represented by creepers.

----

3. The Two Birds-Revisited: Awareness vis-à-vis Consciousness

"Awareness is primordial, it is the original state, beginningless, endless, uncaused, unsupported, without parts, without change. Consciousness is on contact, a reflection against a surface, a state of duality. There can be no consciousness without awareness, but there can be awareness without consciousness, as in deep sleep. Awareness is Absolute, consciousness is relative to its content. Consciousness is always of something. Consciousness is partial and changeful. Awareness is total, changeless, calm and silent. And it is the common matrix of every experience."

- Sri Nisargadatta Maharaj[16]

Q : *As the title itself suggests, Maharaj's statement seems to be, exactly the mythic picture of the 'two Tat Tvam Asi birds', cast in the form of words. Where, awareness would refer to the witnessing bird or the Atma, and consciousness would refer to the eating bird, the Jiva (self)?*

A : Exactly. I would like to make one additional point. All these *sutras,* whether they are from Sri Ramana Maharshi, Sri Nisargadatta Maharaj, Sri J. Krishnamurti, Bhagavad Gita, Ashtavakra Gita, Kaivalya Navaneetham, would touch sincere seekers, so they will do well to commit these *sutras* to memory and then internalize them in their hearts. For example, Maharaj's *sutra* on awareness and consciousness, may be mapped on to the two Tat Tvam Asi birds, in order to enliven that metaphor even more. Put simply, consciousness is a drama or film that awareness can see.

Q : *If I understand correctly, may we think along the following lines in order to better understand the sharp contrast between consciousness on the one hand and awareness on the other? Let us think of two levels of a house, the ground floor and the first floor. The ground floor provides the support structure for the first floor. The first floor can be imagined to be the level of consciousness, where there is always a duality between*

270

oneself and another, as a thought by its very nature is dualistic. Awareness is not dualistic, so if one moves from the first floor to the ground floor, it would amount to moving from consciousness which is dualistic, to awareness which is completely outside consciousness, being a mere witness of every happening in consciousness. One can choose to live in the first floor, namely live in the plane of thought, which is divisive and dualistic and hence the breeding ground for enormous pleasure and enormous pain as well. On the other hand if one moved to the ground floor, one is already in a completely different field, one is an outsider to the happenings in consciousness, one is the observing intelligence, so one can neither be the self, nor can one be the 'other'?

A : You are absolutely right, this is yet another powerful metaphor. The more clearly we understand these metaphors, the more easily we will be able to migrate or jump from the field of consciousness to the field of awareness. This is such an important distinction, though subtle, that if we do not grasp this difference and if we do not practice being conscious inhabitants in the consciousness country and then, in the awareness country, we will not make progress in this retreat.

----

4. What are the Creepers on the Tree?

- They are your *'self'*-creating' thoughts:

- 'I like my mother', 'I like movies'

- They are the many strands of the *Jiva* as various attachments, likes and dislikes.

- *Creepers* are formed in childhood, from the Tree or I *(Atma)*. Then the I *(Atma)* is forgotten, we live as *creepers,* as the *Jiva.*

Q : *Looking at these metaphors in the topic, are we supposed to infer that in the case of great saints and sages, who have had a very strong spiritual inclination from a very tender age, that, somehow, for them, either the creepers fall away, or they do not form, or that the Atma is so brilliantly lustrous, that it just burns up the creepers, so that the Jiva is transformed into the Atma, by the very destiny of these special people?*

A : In the case of Sri Ramana Maharshi, the *Atma*, 'burst forth', ripping away whatever creepers were present, when Ramana was just 16. Another example is Tirugnana Sambandar, who had the first mystic experience of drinking milk from the Divine Mother at age three, and who attained *moksha*, soon after marriage at age sixteen. In the Christian world too, child mystics do exist, in fact they should exist in all nations and in all religions. These people may be considered to be exceptionally blessed at birth itself, so that the question of *sadhana*, does not arise at all.

Q : *Is every creeper, only an association of the 'I' with a certain experience, namely a memory?*

A : Yes, this is so, that is why it is so important to renounce the idea that you are the body, because it is the basis for a million other false perceptions. Apart from this root illusion, we also have other false associations.

---

5. The Human Birth: From I *(Atma)* to *Jiva*

- Self-Realization is 'remembering' who we were when we were born as a human.

- Self-Realization is 'reversing', the transformation, the I went through, when it lost knowledge of its true nature and mistook its transformed version *(Jiva)* to be its true nature, 'I'.

- *For 'remembering' and 'reversing', the Jiva (self) must fall silent.*

Q : *When the baby is born, the baby is given an identity, which is body-centered, with a name and form, with emphasis on other bodies, father and mother, grandparents, etc. So, this is like, eclipsing the inborn Atmic identity, so that the Jiva 'takes birth'. Isn't this very unfortunate for all of us?*

A : Indeed, this forgetfulness is called in the scriptures as *mula-avidya* (root ignorance) and in Christianity it is called original sin. *Mula-avidya* or original sin implies loss of innocence and innocence can only come from the *Atmic* identity. Having lost the *Atmic* identity we have entered into the world of duality, ignorance and conflict. By migrating back to the *Atmic* country, this mistake of *mula-avidya* or original sin can be nullified.

Q : *All of us as Jivas, should be interested in this quest isn't it? So, this retreat gives us the opportunity to reverse the identity, from the Jiva to the Atma?*

A : Indeed, that is why we are stressing that people who have crossed the milestone of their 60th or 65th birthday are better candidates for undertaking this inward journey from the *Jiva* to the *Atma*. Sometimes, even for people in the younger age bracket, because of misfortunes, the inner journey may suddenly commence. It may also suddenly bear fruit as in the case of Sri Ramana Maharishi or having suddenly begun it may go on and on in a slow or in a medium pace untill one lands in the *Atmic* country.

6. Disconnecting the 'I am' from your body-mind 'Key' to Calming and Silencing of the *Jiva*

"The knowingness that 'you are' ('I am' *(Atma)*), has mistakenly identified itself with the body, and so you are thinking of yourself as this body.

"But you are that knowingness of 'I am'. Strengthen the conviction that you are that 'conscious presence', the knowingness that you are ('I am' *(Atma)*), the beingness, *and not the body.*"

- Sri Nisargadatta Maharaj[27]

Q : *The title is confusing, when you say, disconnect 'I am' from the body-mind. Could you explain how this is to be done?*

A : At birth we were only the *Atma,* did not even know who we were, this is the state of innocence in which all babies are. In this state there is no division between *self* and another. As the body lives in the world, it succumbs to *maya* and the illusory *self* is formed, the *Jiva*. Thereafter the *Atmic identity* is completely forgotten and is overwritten. Now, how to go back home? One has to correctly identify who one is, after negating every false identity of oneself. One is not the body, one is not a man or a woman, one is not a husband or a wife, or a father or a mother, one is not a professional, or a doctor or an engineer. One is none of these, but one is '*something*' in consciousness, a thing which seems to be alive, something which enjoys and suffers, one has to start here and trace out what is the core of this inner thing, the 'I am'. Then you will come to an irreducible core which is absolutely outside time and this is of the nature of awareness and witness and peaceful existence, provided you are able to come this far, retreating into yourself. By abiding here, every day for half an hour, you will more and more get the conviction you are this mysterious existence and the awareness, which has nothing whatever to do with the body. This is how you may disconnect from the body.

Q : *Sri Nisargadatta Maharaj, we hear is one of the greatest Self-Realized masters India has produced, so he cannot certainly be wrong. Nevertheless, when he says, that conscious presence, 'I am' has mistakenly identified itself with the body, the question arises, by what force, did the 'I am' make this mistake? Was it a Divine mistake? Then, if the Divine made the mistake, was it an intentional mistake? And all Jivas seem to suffer and enjoy, because of this Divine mistake?*

A : The *Atma* or the Divine made the mistake, as man perceives and understands this. The force by which this mistake happens, arises from the Divine itself, so in one sense the Divine is itself the 'mischief maker'-from our human point of view. Thus in *Advaita* one often makes the paradoxical statement that *Brahman* and *maya* are the two sides of the same coin and they are paradoxically inseparable. The only consolation for us in this paradox is that, when we migrate to the *Atmic* country, we have more or less permanently escaped from the mesmerizing force of *maya*. But even here in the *Atmic* country, one may not be forever peaceful and forever keep *maya* at bay! Like the luminaries (i.e., the sun and the moon), which succumb to eclipses but are otherwise always luminaries; the inhabitants of the *Atmic* country too, namely the *sthitha prajnyas,* though they may have secured the freedom from *maya,* they too may also suddenly succumb to *maya* during a momentary fall. But like the luminaries, they will recover from such a fall in no time. It seems to be an intentional mistake on the part of the Divine, in so far as man is able to understand this phenomenon. The Divine seems to be in an extremely 'playful' mood and the whole of creation seems to be a fruit of this play. The play has a name in the Hindu scriptures, it is called *leela,* which means the Divine play.

----

7. *Jiva's* Ignorance, Sustains Chattering, Craving and Confusion

- *Jiva*: *self*, experiences duality, is in time
- Self: 'I', sees no duality, is outside time
- *Jiva* is an unfaithful and distorted reflection of the Self, is a false Self *(anatma)*, when not purified. When purified It is *Atma=Brahman*.

'Naked' or Pure 'I'(Self), clothes itself through associations and attachments and becomes the *Jiva (self)*. Hence the Self must 'dissociate'.

Q : *So, are you saying that as the Jiva learns, as it gets more self - Knowing, it acquires a stronger sense of Self; as peace, calmness, intelligence, certainty, imperturbability, assurance. And once it gets this, then all the old mischief is at an end?*

A : Prior to *self* - Knowing, *Jiva* is just a lot of 'noise', pleasure seeking every moment, or seeking for security, but this whole search is absurd, because the *Jiva* itself is illusory, as the *Jiva* imagines itself to be the body, which is absurd and paradoxcically the unmasked *Jiva* is infinitely secure. So the activity of the *Jiva* is senseless and based on ignorance as to who the *Jiva* is.

The *Jiva* has come into existence through the natural process of having a body and associating with it, and thus undergoing a transformation from *Atma* to *Jiva*, and this happens to all. This of course is due to *maya*. The reverse process, of the *Jiva* getting metamorphosed into the *Atma*, through purification, is unfortunately not an automatically happening process. However, rude shocks in life, facilitate this reverse transformation, as they will create an introversion of the *Jiva (self)*.

Q : *As self - Knowing dawns, does the ignorance get corrected and the mad activity of chattering, craving and confusion - does it all stop?*

A : Naturally, for these can exist only along with ignorance. When the *Jiva* undergoes a metamorphosis to the *Atma,* none of this can exist. However, unless, one pays deep attention and has dedication, the metamorphosis may not happen.

Q : *Does the Jiva, which seems to be an 'individualized' version of the Atma, some kind of a defective 'toy model' of the Atma; always have a sense of division and separation with all perceived objects, even one's own body?*

A : Yes, the characteristic of the *Jiva (self)*, is precisely this divisiveness, this separation and a *self* enclosing tendency. The *Jiva* cannot but always perceive the world as itself *(self)* arrayed against the 'other'. Because of this, the master J. Krishnamuti calls this *self,* 'evil' and has beautifully explained why he calls it this way.[32] Hence it is important to realize that the *Jiva* or the *self* cannot be 'reformed', retaining all of its mad activities. Reformation of the *Jiva* or the *self* is like trying to change a cunning fox into a wise elephant. Reformation will happen, only when the *Jiva* is calmed and silenced, that is, when all its activities have come to an end.

Q : *I would like you to clarify for all of us, why, you keep saying all the time, the Jiva and its self?*

A : I use the two terms, *Jiva* and the *self,* interchangeably. The former term is from the Hindu tradition, the latter from J. Krishnamurti's usage. There are two huge examinations to be passed in the spiritual life. One is to gather knowledge of how the *Jiva (self)* comes into existence, maintains itself and how it is at war with the whole world. The second examination is, notwithstanding the demon of the *self,* being ourselves, if we dig deeper into this *self,* we find lurking thereunder, the immortal *Atma,* so the second challenge for us will be to realize how we are indeed that *Atma* only, whereas the *self* has arisen as a cover or a mask over the *Atma,* because of our bodily existence. This is called, Self - Realization. The first challenge is referred to as *self* - Knowing. The essence of *Jiva,* which is the limited human consciousness, is indeed the self defensive mechanism of the *self.* So, because the *self* is the very essence of the *Jiva,* we can use these two terms interchangeably.

In the Self - Realization literature of the *Advaita* masters like Sri Ramana Maharishi and Sri Nisargadatta Maharaj, *self* does not have any significant place, because it is understood that when we go to a master who teaches Self - Realization, we are so mature that this little *self* has already calmed and silenced itself. So it is not a problem to be addressed in the Self - Realization chapter of the spiritual life. Often this assumption is completely wrong, which is the reason, Self - Realization does not happen, because the calming and silencing of the *self,* has not happened.

However, since the spiritual life often begins when the *self,* is still confused and agitated, it is appropriate that we must begin with Krishnamurti, rather than with Ramana Maharishi or Nisargadatta Maharaj. Krishnamurti throws the greatest light on the *self* and shows a way to calm and silence it. Krishnamurti does not use the expression *Jiva*; Ramana Maharishi and the *Advaita* tradition uses *Jiva* to denote the essence of the seeker, the 'I' in the human condition.

Any teaching in the spiritual life must be respectful of the conventions already familiar in the spiritual life, in so far as naming of various things is concerned. For example if everybody has agreed to call a horse a 'horse', we cannot bring in a new teaching wherein horses are referred to as 'donkeys'.

Q : *Going back to an earlier topic, in which Sri Nisargadatta Maharaj was speaking and saying that this conscious presence, 'I am' made a mistake, in identifying with the body. Is this Divine mistake, all these associations and attachments of the 'I' with other things, so that, the 'I' is deluded into thinking, that it is not the 'I', but rather the Jiva only?*

A : Yes, indeed as man sees it, this is a mistake committed by the Divine. What for has the Divine done this? Without this mistake life with its immense pleasures and immense pains will not exist. The problem with us is, we want to get drunk on the pleasure, but want none of the pain. Unfortunately this is not possible since pain and pleasure are two sides of the same coin. Once we have fallen in love with the Divine in its unmanifest aspect, then we will keep a safe distance from both pleasure and pain, so that the peace in the heart, in the *Atmic* country is not ruffled.

Q : *So, the famous enquiry of Sri Ramana Maharshi, 'Who am I?', is that the train we all have to board, to go from the identity as the Jiva to our true identity as the Atma?*

A : For *mumukshus*, certainly, yes. As mentioned already, spiritual life has two parts or two chapters. Both are important. The first part is *self* - Knowing. The second part is Self - Realization. Ramana Maharshi's teaching pertains to the second chapter, whereas Krishnamurti's teaching on *self* - Knowing pertains to the first chapter. In the second chapter Ramana Maharshi's teaching has the potency to deliver us.

----

8. What 'Practice' Will Calm and Silence the *Jiva*?

- Calming and silencing of the *Jiva* will happen by *choiceless awareness*, enquiry and understanding.

- 'Practice' will not calm and silence the *Jiva,* on the other hand, practice may offer 'security' to the *Jiva,* pamper it, nourish it, in *dharma and moksha.*

- *So, the purpose of sadhana (practice) must only be to enquire into the Jiva and Self and cultivate detachment.* The purpose is not to reveal the Self, which you have always been.

Q : *Why do you say, practice or sadhana will not calm and silence the Jiva?*

A : The *Jiva* is a dream, though nobody, but people like Nisargadatta Maharaj and Ramana Maharishi may have pronounced this shocking verdict. The *Jiva* imagines to be something and is in pursuit of a goal which it has imagined and thinks that just as you can board a bus and travel to another city, by doing a series of actions, you may be able to arrive at the so called 'wonderful destination'. This is the misleading imagination of the *Jiva.* Following up on this imagination, the *Jiva* cither does *sadhana* or wishes to do *sadhana.* Real *sadhana* will be the ending of the *Jivahood, which happens by the choiceless awareness of the activities of the Jiva.* And when the *Jivahood* is renounced and we move to the *Atmic country* then it will become clear by repeated observation that much of the activity of the *Jiva* is based on concepts and reactions which are false and uncalled for. In the *Atmic* country such concepts and reactions do not exist. Only in the field of consciousness, where the *Jiva* is, all the things are prone to problems.

Q : *On the other hand, you say, that practice will offer security to the Jiva, can you explain, the connection between practice and security?*

A : As mentioned already, the *Jiva* is in a dream, imagining itself to be in a path and having to do something in order to move forward on that path. All this is the imagining of the *Jiva*. This will not help because even after hundred years of this *sadhana*, the *Jiva* will be an inhabitant in the consciousness country only. Unless the *Atmic* dimension comes into existence, we will not even be able to understand what right *sadhana* is. The security comes from the *Jiva's* dream and belief that it has done *sadhana* for one hour everyday, 'so now I'm better off, I'm a more advanced disciple'. All this is a dream in the consciousness country, where the *Jiva* lives. Here all that the *Jiva* can do is to seek security in the kind of activities mentioned. This process in time is called 'becoming'…..

Q : *You are implying that, while the conventional practices may not at all help in calming and silencing the Jiva, another kind of subtle practice, seems to be recommended and implied. What is this subtle practice?*

A : This subtle practice is vacating the consciousness country and moving to the *Atmic* country. And being a witness to all happenings in the consciousness country. This is the beginning and the end of the spiritual life. This is Krishnamurti's *freedom first and last through choiceless awareness.*

----

9. You are the *Paramatma* Bird

So you must 'negate' the eating bird *(Jiva)* as your identity.

Q : *By the statement, 'we must negate the eating bird (Jiva)'s identity', are you suggesting that, we should try getting rid of the limiting idea that 'we are the body'?*

A : The *Jiva* has so many refuges, shelters or hiding places, it wears so many masks and to begin the new life the *Jiva* must be liquidated from every one of these refuges, hiding places or shelters. The idea that it is the body is an important shelter, an important hiding place, an important illusion, so this must be dispelled by enquiry and very close observation. Then the *Jiva* has so many other false impressions about itself, as to who it is. These are called *anatmas* or false selves. The notion that one is a father, a husband, a mother, a daughter, an engineer a doctor, a good or a bad man, etc., all are illusions or false selves; which are like cloaks on the *Atma*. As we peel them off the *Atma* will come into relief and we will know our true identity, as awareness, as being, as the witness.

Q : *Then if we are not the body, who are we?*

A : One should not give an answer to such a question for the simple reason that the *Jiva* will cling on to this answer, make it a belief or faith, become contented and then make no further original discovery of its own. So one has to find out who one is. This is the enquiry in 'the second chapter' of the spiritual life.

Q : *We were seeing till now two birds, now suddenly you are showing only one bird and instead of the other bird, you are showing light. What are you trying to express?*

A : A metaphor is a metaphor only. It tries to convey the abstract truth in a simple way using images, because we will think that there are actually two birds, we introduce the adjective 'Tat Tvam Asi' for the two birds just to drive home the point that these are not two independent birds, but one and the same bird, which can exists in two countries, the consciousness country and the awareness country. Because awareness is awareness, not any physical or material thing, but the light which sees, without a seer, to convey this truth that brilliant flash has here replaced the witness bird.

10. 'Pond Water Contaminated by Algae': Metaphor

Clear water = *Atma* = 'I', Algae *(Jiva's maya)* = Feelings of duality, *maya*, ambitions, pleasure and pain, hurts, etc.

Q : *We have seen this topic before. Looking at it afresh, do you think, the extent of this contamination will be different in different people?*

A : Of course! The more ignorant one is, more the contamination and the more lucid you are, less the contamination.

Q : *More the contamination, more the pain in life?*

A : More pleasure to begin with. And this more and more pleasure will invariably end in a tragedy, which is the impossibility of continuing that pleasure, which is pain. So more the contamination, more the pleasure and more the pain.

Q : *After the cleaning of consciousness, through choiceless awareness, and learning about the Jiva (self), do you think, Jiva becomes calmer and more silent?*

A : Think of the man with the algae enmeshing him (Ch. I, topic 18). We had said that his body represents the *Atma* and the enveloping algae was the *maya* and the ignorance. So now the *Jiva* is the man with all the algae. The *Jiva* attempts to observe itself. This is possible because the *Atma* is at the heart of the *Jiva*. As the *Jiva* observes itself, awareness comes into play and learning happens and if one has the desire (*Jiva, has the desire*) to achieve some end through this choiceless observation, then the learning will be unfruitful. But if there is intense interest and no accompanying surging desire, then the *Jiva* will be calmed and silenced.

Q : *How does the Jiva get into maya?*

A : This is a Divine doing and the tragicomedy is that, as the *Atma* is the Divine itself in creation, it is the Divine which has got entangled, but of course as a human being. The moment the Divine creates the world, this *maya* and entanglement come along. It is very sweet and delicious, but soon turns bitter - this is the Divine conspiracy, so that you have to spit it out, in the end.

Q : *One understands that hurts and pain are contrary to Atma's blissful nature, so these are contaminations all right. But how are aspirations and ambitions also contaminations?*

A : Many people are not going to like this answer, because every aspiration and ambition is fundamentally *self*-centered. So it implies a blindness as to who we are and this ambition invariably will lead to stepping on other people's toes and causing them great pain and importantly being so obsessed and preoccupied with the ambitions and aspirations that one necessarily has to lose all peace and all intelligence. This lesson is learnt invariably, only after a fall, never while the game is still going on.

----

11. A Model of the *Jiva* in *Maya:* Metaphor

Man's body = *Atma,* sticking algae = *maya* (illusions), *self,* mass of human memories, hurts, experiences, attachments.

Q : *Is this just a reiteration of the previous topic (pond water contaminated by algae)?*

A : We have to go slowly here, for this metaphor has two different meanings. The body represents the *Atma,* the true Self, which is 'hidden' and the algae represents the multiple false selves (i.e., the *anatmas*), shrouding the *Atma.* This is one interpretation so that we may all get the intellectual conviction of the importance of purification.

The same metaphor can also mean the following. The body represents the erroneous thinking of the *Jiva* that it is the body. And the algae represent all the mischief and illusions and other false selves of the *Jiva.* In the usage of this metaphor in this second way, there is no room for the *Atma,* but the metaphor brings into life the root illusion which is the *Jiva's* wrong thinking that it is the body.

Q : *You have again brought in the word self and referred to it as the sticking algae. Will you explain how this self is different from the so-called Jiva, if it is different at all?*

A : *Jiva* is a term found in the *Advaitic* literature of India. For example Adi Sankara has said *Jivo Brahmaiva naa paraha,* this means that the *Jiva* only is *Brahman* or the

Divine, not anything other than this. When is this true? Only when the *Jiva* is purified, for then all the algae is stripped clean and the *Atma* shines. In the writings of Krishnamurti, the term *Jiva* is not used, but *self* is used. In truth *Jiva* is the *self* or if you want to be more meticulous, you can call the *self* the very essence of the *Jiva*. So it is the *Jiva's self.*

Q : *Honestly speaking, this seems a most wonderful metaphor, coming to think of it. However, you have referred to the body of this man as the Atma, whereas, everywhere else, you are saying, that the very identity of the Jiva that it is the body is the curse on mankind. Are these usages not contradictory?*

A : These usages are not contradictory because they are mentioned in different contexts. We always have to look at the context and inner meaning of the metaphor. Please remember the context and inner meaning of all these metaphors, once you remember the context, you can never be confused or misled.

12. Water Without Contamination by Algae

Q : *Looking at this absolutely clear pond, can such an ideal state be reached?*

A : When there is integrity for the *Jiva*, and the *Jiva* has no private and secret agenda of its own and has *nirguna bhakti* (the seventh or highest *bhakti*) to *Parabrahma*; the pond will be without any blemish, as in this picture. This state of purity arises, when the *Jiva* has no more refuges and shelters, which protect the life of its illusory existence. Then the clear pond, would stand for aloneness, which Krishnamurti has explained clearly: "Uninfluenced, innocent, free, and whole, not broken up. When you are alone, you may live in this world, but you will always be an outsider."

I feel that as long as the *Jiva* has too many fanciful desires, ambitions, aspirrations, goals, what is more likely to happen to the *Jiva*, is only further entanglement in duality and *maya*. In this case, the clear pond will never become a reality. If, on the otgher hand, the *Jiva* has suffered a great misfortune, which has served to open the eyes of the *Jiva*, then renunciation and a turning away from the world can happen more easily. Also when a *mumukshu* or seeker has an exemplary master, who has inspired the *mumukshu*, the necessary renunciation can also come without too much difficulty.

With renunciation, perfect inner integrity and freedom from *maya* is possible. Under such conditions, the 'clear pond' becomes a reality.

---

13. We Have Begun from the 'the Other Shore'- Revisited

"In all this movement you must somehow begin from the other end, from the other shore, and not always be concerned with this shore or how to cross the river.

"You must take a plunge into the water, not knowing how to swim. And the beauty of meditation is that you never know where you are, where you are going, what the end is."

- J. Krishnamurti in 'Meditations'[13]

Q : *In this beautiful meditation from Sri J. Krishnamurti, we must realize that most of us suffer from the fear of the unknown, so how would you expect us to take the plunge, as it were and reach out to the other shore?*

A : We have two dimensions, a human dimension, to which all your logic applies, the fear, etc., and fortunately, we are also a timeless being, a witness, with infinite Divine possibilities. Because, we are always with a swarm of thoughts and feelings, we are never able to know ourselves, as we are, without these thoughts and feelings. This witness is our deeper nature, and this whole retreat is devoted to the discovery of this essential nature, awareness. This is also who we are. If the *Jiva* hears these words, 'infinite possibilities', the *Jiva* is tempted, it wants to have this powerful thing and this kind of an aspiration is actually an obstacle, which will come in the way of our abiding

287

as the awareness for this awareness is automatically reached when the *Jiva* become void, not when it is pampered and fattened with many aspirations.

Q : *So, is it like pressing the 'emergency button', which may be always there, but which we are unaware of?*

A : Yes, we are unconscious of the mechanism of how some of our difficult problems get resolved. We call that grace, result of prayer, blessing, etc., and in attributing this to grace, what we have done is to externalize a power which is inherent in us all. This Divine source is our very Self, the *Atma*. We do not know this, we cannot be aware of it as we can be aware of the sun and the moon and the trees, for the latter are sensory objects. This retreat is intended to help us to get at this treasure, which we are already. It is not a new treasure or a new blessing which will come to you from the outside world, from another external source.

Q : *Why does the master J. Krishnamurti say the, "the beauty of meditation is that, you never know where you are, where you are going, what the end is?*

A : Our limited human nature makes us everlastingly seek security, we need to be constantly assured that we will find some great treasure, if not now, at least in the future, etc. However, when our Divine nature comes into play, as it surely does in these meditations, then we are naturally going to be fearless, rather than afraid. In fact all creative minds have this enormous courage and spirit of adventure-without this, they would never have discovered, all the wonderful things they discovered. Theirs was a journey into the unknown. So, master J. Krishnamurti says, this is the nature of these meditative journeys, they are mysterious journeys into the bosom of truth, into the unknown.

----

14. Ignorant People, negate the *Atma* and accept only the Eating Bird *(Jiva)*

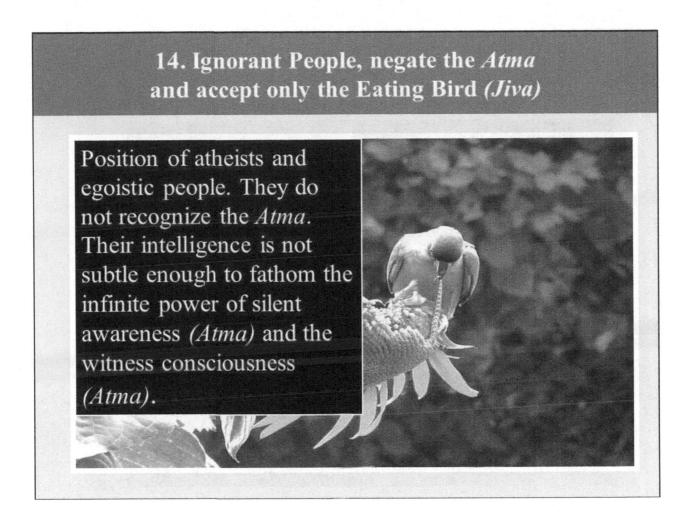

Position of atheists and egoistic people. They do not recognize the *Atma*. Their intelligence is not subtle enough to fathom the infinite power of silent awareness *(Atma)* and the witness consciousness *(Atma)*.

Sankara: If the *Jiva* is badly entangled in the body-mind (as exemplified in the algae-man metaphor, Ch. I, topic 18) and has become restless, with hardly any proper sense of self; then it is very hard for such a worrying, brooding and excessively cerebrating *Jiva*, to be calm, and discover another distinct dimension of itself, namely, the 'I am', the 'conscious presence'. In this circumstance, it will be most natural for the *Jiva* to declare that, 'it des not perceive any other higher agency, other than itself, in its own kingdom, or in some neighboring territory'. This declaration and finding of the *Jiva*, cannot be disputed!

However, the *Jiva* is ignorant of the potentiality of another way of life, which is available to it, and which it will easily slip into, if it will only undergo, taming, calming and silencing. Then, the *Jiva's* activities subside, and it will then feel, peace and love, as its own state of 'I am', or conscious presence. It is this, which is called the *Atma*. When the *Atma* is undiscovered, it is natural for the *Jiva* to deny its existence. In fact all atheists and materialistic people, deny the existence of the mysterious and seemingly 'non-existent' *Atma*. The above topic exemplifies this ignorant disposition of the brooding *Jiva*.

289

15. The Living Silence was misinterpreted by the Buddha

This 'living silence' was misinterpreted by the Buddha as 'sunyata' (void). *So there is no 'Divine' in Buddhism. Buddhism is not a theistic religion.* Hinduism is obsessed with the Divine.
So, Adi Sankaracharya 'drove out' Buddhism from India. Hinduism represents this by the *Siva Linga*, Islam by the Kaaba Stone (Allah). Christianity by the Father in Heaven.

Q : *What is the white star on the Jiva?*

A : The white star represents the purified, calmed, silenced *Jiva*.

Q : *What is the difference between the stand of Advaita Vedanta: where Parabrahma is the Absolute and sunyata of Buddhism?*

A : The Buddha was an original thinker who was daring enough to negate the authority of the *Vedas*. This was the reason Buddhist thought was exorcised from India during the life time of Adi Sankaracharya. A long line of seers, had verified in the *Vedic* tradition that the *silence* of the great void was the abode of Supreme Intelligence and Supreme Compassion. Because it is unmanifest, both the Buddha and Buddhist tradition failed to take note that the source of life is a great void. In the Hindu tradition which is obsessed with the Divine, in both the manifest and the unmanifest aspects, the greatest emphasis is placed on the compassionate nature of the great void. Recognizing the great void to be the Father and Mother of all sentient beings, He is addressed as He, a merciful Godhead, *Karunakara*, *Apadhbandava*, *Bakthavatsala* etc. The Buddhist tradition is poorer because of the poorer conception of the unmanifest Divine.

16. Under what Conditions will the *Jiva* be Calm and Silent ?

1. When the power to *the fan* is switched off! Can energy supply *(Prana)* to the *Jiva* be switched off ?

2. By the 'identity' shifting from *(Jiva)* to the true Self ?

3. Deep faith, humility, cultivation of virtue, study of scriptures, detachment, *self*-Knowing, calms and silences the *Jiva* ?

4. *However, Jiva should work to save the life of the body, when a tiger comes to kill us, for example.*

Q : *You have drawn an analogy between the power supply to a fan and the pranic energy to the Jiva. Implied in this, is the fact that unless, there are sensory inputs (movies, conversations, food, work, play), the Jiva cannot be sustained. Where does pranic energy come from?*

A : This comes from *Sakti* or the Divine, which orchestrates the body and the Universe.

Q : *Thus, as in pratyahara, when the senses are de-plugged from their sense objects, does the Jiva have a greater chance of falling silent and being calm?*

A : *Pratyahara* is not enough for de-plugging, because the *Jiva* will wallow in the memory lane, in loneliness and this is enough to sustain the *Jiva*.

Q : *You say, that when the identity shifts from the Jiva to the Atma, then Jiva falls silent, this does not seem to be a proper answer. So, how is the identity to actually shift?*

A : The *Atma* for all practical purposes, because it is buried under a heap of *anatmas, avidya and maya*, is an 'atrophied organ', in a manner of speaking. Just as we would bring an atrophied organ back to life, by beginning to exercise it, in the same way the atrophied *Atma* can be exercised, the moment the *Jiva* endeavors to observe itself. As it endeavors repeatedly, the atrophied *Atma* comes into full relief as the observing awareness. Ultimately, the *Jiva* is transformed into a *sthitha prajnya* just as a big fat caterpillar is transformed into the butterfly.

Q : *Is knowing the Jiva (self) more important than the calming and silencing of the Jiva?*

A : Knowing the *Jiva* and detachment are both of the greatest importance in both *self* - Knowing as well as Self - Realization.

Q : *In the last fourth point, are you trying to suggest that even this Jiva, whose frenetic activity is an obstacle to moksha, has its appropriate role in life?*

A : Of course, the *Jiva* is nothing but the caricature of the *Atma* within the highly limited framework of the body and consciousness. Or, you can also call it the reflection of the *Atma*, in the mirror of the body and consciousness, without which we cannot function as human beings. To be human in the mundane sense is to be the *Jiva*. But to be human in a noble and Divine sense is to be the *Atma*, we are actually both, with one or the other more dominant.

----

17. *Jiva* 'falling' Calm and Silent is Hindered by:

1. Fear, jealousy, body-centered desires, survival, powerful *vasanas, samskaras.*

2. Attachment to body, wealth, family, social and professional prestige, prevents this.

3. No awakening to sorrow within oneself.

4. Do not pay enough attention to *inner life.*

5. *When Atma's calmness, intelligence (Atma sakti) is used for pursuing success of Jiva.('calm worldly people')*

Q : *All of these five factors, which seem to come in the way of the Jiva's calmness and silence, are they part of the journey in 'artha and kama'? In this sense, is it not natural that these above five factors do have a place in life?*

A : Yes, in *artha and kama,* all of these factors will surely, time and again spring into action, especially so, when the *Jiva* is deeply engrossed in the *artha and kama* journey. As we are in the context of *dharma and moksha* (the farther reaches of the spiritual life), these five factors, ought not to operate. If by chance, they do come into play, it only shows that one is not sufficiently dedicated and devoted to the spiritual quest, or that one is not mature enough.

Q : *Let us say, these five factors are still operational; then do you mean to say that the seeker will not be able to reach the goal of moksha?*

A : Where *moksha* is concerned, *moksha* is not Kashi or Rameswaram to which we can make a pilgrimage so as to 'attain it'. You are already in the final state which is the *Atma.* Because of *maya,* this knowingness is prevented, that is all. So long as these factors are operational, how can there be yearning for *moksha*, which is a very important qualification for coming upon *moksha*.

Q : *We do not really question ourselves, as to who we are, or even become aware that we are having a lot of sorrow in our lives. Is it that, we are frightened to do so?*

A : Many factors are at work in our lives. Spiritual life (which is actually our inner life), is in truth, something almost last on our list. Society also does not encourage us to tread this path of inner awakening. Thus, if at all, we make a beginning, we must be very courageous souls, for whom the truth and the calling will supersede social compulsions. Thus, with many odds, going against our favor, we are apt to be indifferent and give the spiritual life, much less importance than it rightly deserves.

Q : *So, looking at all these factors, there is a lot of home work that is called for, before we can make any progress in the spiritual life (inner life). This clearing of the home work will open the doorways to harmonious relationships in every walk of life and very significantly will bestow upon us a robust sense of self-worth and self-confidence, thereby enriching even our material life. Correct?*

A : Yes, the *sthitha pragnya's* state is the answer to hundred human problems, without getting here every solution will be fragmentary and will not last.

----

18. 'Scorched Seeds, Do Not Sprout'

"As *seeds of latent impressions scorched by fire* do not sprout any more, so with *taints scorched by the fire of understanding* - the Self meets them no more."

- Mahabharata, XII.204.16a

Q : *This theme would be a natural sequel to the theme of 'home work', we were just talking about. Whether in our material life or in the inner life, we are often plagued by certain nagging thoughts. These often drain away our energy, because we just do not know how to deal with them, and the home work that we were talking about, seems to entail paying very close attention to these patterns of enmity, hatred, lust, fear, guilt, regret, possibly carried over from childhood or even previous lives. Are these not the very things of which we were supposed to be choicelessly aware?*

A : Yes, one has to observe all these happenings in consciousness, with interest, very keenly so that we realize what the limitations of *Jivahood* are. Unless this *Jivahood* is let go in its entirety there will be no radical transformation.

Q : *What exactly are the 'seeds', you are alluding to?*

A : These seeds are our traumas, *vasanas*, old attractions and attachments to sense objects, seeds which come to us again and again and come upon us, initially giving huge pleasure, but the pleasure turning into pain, in its wake. It can be anger, greed,

295

jealousy, lust, comparison with others, cheating, telling lies, playing the game of one-upmanship, etc.

Q : *If we are consciously and choicelessly aware of either the origin of the nagging thoughts, or the mere thoughts themselves, then, would that meditation, be sufficiently powerful to scorch those seeds?*

A : One may have to be with the seeds, nurturing them, giving them space to express themselves, studying them very keenly without any sense of judgement or condemnation or guilt and in this way as the light of awareness falls on the seeds, again and again, the seeds will give up their stories and they will get scorched in that fire of understanding.

Q : *If this meditation of choiceless awareness has been brought to a finale, may be even many a time, or, even, say, during the ensuing several months; would not the individual concerned, be invigorated and begin to live in the present, rather than be haunted by such nagging thoughts?*

A : More importantly, and I do not think I have emphasized this point sufficiently yet, *choiceless awareness of what is* is not certainly some 'dependable system' that can be practiced for half an hour everyday, so that the *Jiva* will feel good and secure and so that in the thinking of the *Jiva* this is a way for getting *moksha*. On the contrary, when the *Jiva* through its greed and attachment to success, tries to convert this *choiceless awareness of what is*, into a system that will pave the way, for it, to deliver success; it is then that *choiceless awareness of what is* will no more be fruitful. As you walk through life you do not know when a shaft of jealousy will dart forward in your consciousness and how long it will torment you. But when this happens, you have to be vigilant, take interest and watch. When such a watching will be called for the next time, no one can tell. So *choiceless awareness of what is*, will happen as and when challenges confront you in your day to day life. To answer your question, as the *Jiva* learns through the light of awareness, the old life, bereft of vitality will fall away and the trees and animals will all come alive and they will endear themselves to us.

Q : *This sutra seems to have great importance in psychopathology, where the psychologist or the psychotherapist has to deal with people who have such haunting persistent thoughts, as those people may be traumatized. Would you say that, such people, can be helped by making them face their personal reality, through choiceless awareness, so that the seeds of negative traumas in their consciousness are scorched by the fire of understanding, feeling, repenting, etc.?*

A : This seems to be a question of importance. Where an individual does have such seeds of negativity, those seeds may be weak or they could be strong. Weaker seeds are easier to handle than stronger seeds.

The latter must be handled much more sensitively and the counsellor and friend, may be required to spend a lot of time, and this kind of a therapy, may not be successfully conducted, if commercial gains alone is the basis of clinical practice. Where dedication and devotion and service are paramount, these cases can be taken up, without haste dictating terms.

Also some cases may be so hard that, even talking together will be of little help. In that case, psychiatric treatment with medication may be called for and a more personal therapy can come in only at a later stage, when the individual feels much better.

19. What Life Situations foster *Jiva* becoming Calm and Silent?

1. 'Death-like' physical/psychological crisis/suffering.

2. Surrender: (i) to life; (ii) to *what is;* (iii) to the Divine.

3. A spiritual, 'astrological cycle' commencing.

4. When one crosses 60 or 65 years and when the life cycle is completed and fulfilled.

5. Unless *Jiva,* 'shuts shop', Self, as silence, intelligence, enormous courage, will not manifest.

6. *Jiva* becomes 'exhausted' by too much effort and conflict.

Q : *How would you qualify, 'death-like' suffering?*

A : Death-like suffering will happen when what the *Jiva* held close to its bosom, as its beloved, as its cherished trophy, when this is taken away from the *Jiva* through the twists and turns of fate, then death-like suffering befalls us. It is death-like, because the old life has to die to give way to the new. Examples are death of a family member, diseases like cancer or aids, the birth of a mentally retarded child, losing a child in an accident, an accident in which one gets paralyzed for life, a divorce, a colossal business suffering, a family breaking up, dishonor and disgrace in public life; every one of them is an example of death-like suffering.

Q : *What is the difference between surrender to what is and surrender to life? Don't they mean the same?*

A : There are many kinds of surrender, they depend on the maturity of the *Jiva*. A person who is in the path of *self* - Knowing may be fortunate if he secures a surrender to a boiling *what is*. A person who has been beaten very hard in life, time and again and who has not been exposed to religion or a spiritual life, in utter helplessness and desperation may resign himself or herself to all that which is going to happen in the future also and such people may be considered to be the ones who have surrendered to life. What about people who surrender to God? Because this is what we hear most of the time. Not that the people know what God is, but religion presents the face of God as a point of anchorage and refuge for the *Jiva* and if the *Jiva* has the blessing of faith, then the *Jiva* will have no difficulty in anchoring to this God or deity. In this case we say the individual has surrendered to God.

Q : *Can you give us an example of a spiritual astrological cycle?*

A : If Jupiter is a benefic planet in an astrological chart and the position of Jupiter in both the Rasi chart and the Navamsha chart is in spiritual houses, such as the 4th, 5th or the 9th; then when the *dasha* (season) of Jupiter commences and has a run for 16 years, these would be spiritual years. Likewise, when the *dasha* of the lord of the 9th house is in session it can run for a few years, depending on what the planet is, then too a spiritual season of life can begin and this will turn out to be a blessing.

Q : *What is the basis for the supposition that life can be fulfilled at the age of 60 or 65?*

A : Astrologically the important slow moving planets of Jupiter and Saturn return to their natal positions after 60 years. So this is a completion of a big cycle. One retires at this age more or less. One's children are grown up and are no more dependent on the individual and the children learn to stand on their own feet. The life of pleasure and marriage which ran on for nearly 40 years will also come to fulfillment and will be satiated. Thus from many points of view 60 - 65 is a turning point. If we are wise and intelligent, we will start renouncing and will start becoming detached as we are closer to death at 60 than we were at 30 or 40. So this is a season for looking inward and pursuing the answers to the difficult spiritual questions of life. The risk is that one may succumb to faith which is not the answer to the great questions of life. The real answer is enquiry on our own part.

Q : *Do you think Jiva 'shutting shop', is just putting an end to its mad activities of decades, or because, Jiva has become weary and reached 'old age'?*

A : The *Jiva* can become nauseated with its own meaningless life or may be beaten so hard that it is obliged to retreat into the spiritual life. Or great renunciation might dawn as a blessing and a new spiritual season may begin in life. The word, 'spiritual' is very ugly, I do not like to use it at all, nevertheless use it, for lack of an alternative. This inner life is so sacred and so mysterious that all words, fail to capture the fragrance of that sacredness. Anything can happen, depending on the changing moods of the Divine, with the change of the *dashas*, the astrological seasons.

20. The Witness Consciousness ('I am' *(Atma)*) is Inherently Unstable in the face of 'Sensory Calls'

The scriptures, as well as your own experience, will be seen to confirm the fact that the witness consciousness *is inherently unstable, in the face of sensory calls,* especially when *pratyahara* (withdrawal of the senses from the sense objects) and detachment are not part of your spiritual practice.

So we have to place greater emphasis on purifying the Jiva in many ways.

Q : *Can we say that this inherent instability is much like a small boy, unable to balance on his bicycle, in the early stages, but with continued practice, he can ride his bicycle, paying attention to the happenings in the road (witnessing), without falling off?*

A : Yes, you got it, this is what is meant by *inherently unstable.*
Practicing to witness will be like attaching training wheels to the boy's bicycle.

21. *Atma* Must 'Withdraw Its Investment'

1. *Atma's* real nature is *ananda* (causeless joy), *chit* (awareness), *sat* (truth-existence).

2. 'Finding the body to be a source of *pleasure* (which seems-like joy)', the *Atma* has come to 'make an investment' *in this 'fund' or bank (of the body)'*.

3. Because of too much pain and loss in this 'investment', *Atma must now 'pull back' the 'investment'*.

4. Learning and detachment will enable this 'withdrawal of the investment'. Result: intelligence, joy, end of suffering.

Q : *Let us first understand, the nature of the Atma, which seems to be outside time and space. We can accept that this is joy or ananda, also accept that awareness and prajnya as chit, but what exactly is 'sat'? Is 'sat' a short form for satya?*

A : *Sat* is truth and existence (being), referring to the *Atma*. It cannot be understood unless one 'settles in the *Atma*'. It is incorruptible and imperishable, we have dealt with these strange implications of the *Atma* in this retreat. *Sat* stands for all of these.

Q : *Considering the fact it was the Atma only which consented to incarnate as the Jiva with a body, etc, how do you now say that the Atma must 'withdraw its investment'?*

A : In this partnership between the *Atma* and *Sakti*, *Sakti* took the form of the body, along with the consciousness, subject to duality, namely *maya*. In this partnership when the *Atma* incarnated, *Sakti* had the lead role, she was dominant, while *Atma (Siva)* was the 'sleeping partner'. Scriptures use the very apt terminology, power *(Sakti)* and power-wielder *(Siva, Atma)*. As the *Atma,* though behind the scenes, It is the power wielder, and can get disgusted, because the pain, coming along with the body and earthly life, surpasses the pleasure eventually, so the *Atma* certainly wants to withdraw the intimate association with *Sakti*. Dissolving the partnership with *Sakti*, which would mean death, would of course be an extreme step. If dissolution is ruled out, the next best choice for the *Atma* would be to recover its own lost ground. The *sthitha prajnya* is one in whom the *Atmic* ground is recovered, as far as is possible, without dissolving the partnership.

Q : *You are saying that, the more clearly one understands this whole process, the more whole heartedly, one can plunge into the sadhana, is this it?*

A : Of course we have been harping on that a hundred times that understanding holds the key and it is not as mysterious as it has unfortunately come to be perceived – because you are already the owner of the wealth and in fact you are that very wealth itself. So conviction is of paramount importance, nothing beyond conviction, because you are already 'That'. The moment you are prepared to swear that you are 'That', no body needs to recognize you and you need no recognition. Recognition is only necessary for the *Jiva* and not for the *sthitha prajnya*.

Q : *So fruits of the withdrawal are ananda, intelligence, end to suffering?*

A : Yes, these are the bounties of a good victory. More cannot be asked for at this stage, as the partnership is still continuing.

----

22. *Jnana*, without Detachment

"As gold unrefined does not shine, so the understanding of an immature man attached to the world does not shine forth."

- Vishnu Sahasranama

Q : *Why is attachment so notorious an obstacle, coming in the way of liberation of the Jivatma?*

A : It is attachment to body, people, food, status, wealth, name and fame and all the pleasures of life, which has basically landed the *Jiva* into this terrible mess of sorrow. So, if we are to reverse this malady, must we not withdraw the causes, which produced the malady in the first instance? The cause is attraction and attachment to all these things, so we have to negate these supports. But as these were intensely enjoyed by the *Jiva*, in *artha and kama* spheres, we must give some time, say up to 60 or 65 years, then as the body wears out, attachment will also turn into its very opposite, namely detachment, because, those whom *Jiva* loved, they will be the cause of pain.

As some detachment is also good in the younger years, we may enjoin some spiritual detachment, keeping the individual's spiritual well-being in later years in full-view.

302

Fourth Day (Chapter -IV), 1st 'Tat Tvam Asi' Meditation:

Calming and Silencing of the *Jiva*

In this meditation, we have to again, identify the 'burning' *what is*, then commence 'first seeing' and then 'second seeing'. The witness watches (sees) the *Jiva* at work. In this way, we come to understand the *Jiva*, its miseries and its hopes. Under the watchful eye of the witnessing awareness, the calming and silencing of the *Jiva happens*, when the *Jiva* understands that struggling, competing, is futile. When the *Jiva* learns to keep silent, then the calming and silencing has *happened*. Wisdom on the *Jiva's* part would be to stop struggling in life, to jump out of the rat race.

If there is faith in a master, and strong affection for him, and an appreciation of the value of the teaching, or faith in the Divine and an adoration of the Divine, then progress on the path will be fast. There has to be a combination of enquiry, devotion and seeking. *Passivity and blind dependence on the master or God is worthless, except as a useful beginning at the kindergarten level.*

----

23. Self-Realization is vulnerable to *Maya* - *Kaivalya Navaneetham*

"The truth that 'I am Brahman'(Tat Tvam Asi) is realized from the scriptures or by the grace of the master, *but it cannot be firm in the face of obstructions.*

"Ignorance, uncertainty and wrong knowledge are obstacles resulting from long standing habits in the innumerable incarnations of the past which cause trouble, and then the fruits of realization slip away. Therefore root them, out by: (1) hearing the truth, (2) reasoning and (3) meditation (abidance in the *Atma*)."

- Kaivalya Navaneetham[24]

Q : *In one of the previous topics we met with the rather rare insight that the abidance in awareness or as the pure 'I' (witness consciousness) is inherently unstable in the face of sensory calls. Here in the text 'Kaivalya Navaneetham', are we then having a confirmation of our thesis?*

A : Yes! A very authoritative confirmation.

Q : *This important warning from 'Kaivalya Navaneetham', is it meant for those who have passed the examination of moksha and have been 'certified' as, 'jivanmuktas', that even they cannot take their blessing for granted, and that, if a sufficiently strong sensory call or sensory distraction were to come upon them, they may well topple and come tumbling down?*

A : Yes! This warning is also for *jivamuktas*, who have come to abide in the witness consciousness and who have become detached from the world and who are on the path of austerity, negation of the sensory life; even they can topple and fall. Therefore one has to be eternally vigilant.

Q : *Hence, this sadhana of sravana, manana, and nidhidhyasana, seems to be recommended for all true seekers, even after jivanmukti? Also, if some jivanmuktas are of the impression that 'I have crossed over to the other shore', that this will be a testimony for maya already having begun to gobble them up?*

A : Yes, the very thought, 'I have crossed over to the other shore' cannot be sourced in anybody but in the *Jiva*. A *sthitha prajnya* who is poised in awareness will never get this thought; unless he has fallen. The moment somebody opens his mouth and says, 'I have got it', he has perhaps fallen from the precipice by 10,000 feet.

----

24. A Model of the *Jiva* in *Maya*

Man's body = *Atma,* sticking algae = *maya* (illusions), *self,* mass of human memories of experiences, hurts, ambitions, attachments.

Q : *The veiling effect of maya is seen in this excellent metaphor. In the light of the warning given by Kaivalya Navaneetham, are we to infer that the accumulation of 'new maya' is always an easy possibility, for an individual, who does not practice pratyahara, after jivanmukti, but rushes into the world of sensory calls and sensory distractions?*

A : Yes, new *maya* will always be a danger even for *jivanmuktas.* So one has to be ever humble, ever keeping the sensory distractions at bay, even when one is not tempted by any of them for it is in the very nature of *maya* to make a visitation on all and sundry, especially, on whoever is functioning in the thick of the world.

Q : *In a country like India, since thousands of years, there have always been ashrams of sages and saints, dedicated to the spiritual goals of life and these ashrams were always far away from cities. Looking at this metaphor and the warning from 'Kaivalya Navaneetham', we are able to appreciate the setting of all ashrams in seclusion and solitude, away from the madness of city life. What is your view on this?*

A : It makes profound sense that the sages and saints of India lived in seclusion, practicing *pratyahara* and keeping at bay all distractions of a city life. Without this context, their

306

spiritual life could not possibly be nurtured or even preserved. At the same time to live in such extreme seclusion, where one is relatively untroubled by all the temptations of life, may not always be the best of solutions. There are sages like Sri J. Krishnamurti and Sri Nisargadatta Maharaj who come into the thick of the world and the madness of the world, to teach. And there are sages like Sri Ramana Maharishi, Sri Nithyananda Maharaj, and Swami Samarth, who eschewed the world and peacefully lived in their own *ashrams*. There is no uniform blue print which all sages and saints can follow. How can that be, that would be absurd. Each sage and each saint lives according to his calling and the inner prompting from the Divine.

Q : *The question also arises, as we gaze at this wonderfully apt metaphor, whether, not accumulating the dross of maya, in the process of day to day living is inherently an impossibility, so then, what option do we have, for periodically parting company with the newly accumulated dross of maya?*

A : Serious spiritual seekers and sages are known to live in the mountains, in the Himalayan ranges, far away from the cities - where sensory stimulation is inevitable. It is very sensible to meditate on a daily basis, meditate, not in a habitual manner, but with great depth and beauty, as recommended by Sri J. Krishnamurti or by Sri Ramana Maharshi. Such daily discipline and practice, will certainly act as a deterrent for the pollution of the *Atma*, by *maya*, and by the *self*, by the human drama, generally speaking. Just as we will clean our house on a daily basis, we will also have to clean our consciousness and wipe the dust off the mirror of the *Atma*. In fact in Patanjali's *ashtanga yoga*, *saucha*, in the sense of '*bahyabantara suchitvam* (inner and outer cleanliness) is an integral part of the *yogic* way of life.

----

25. Antidote for *Maya*
- *Kaivalya Navaneetham*

"Checked by incantations *(sthambhana)*, fire will not scorch. Likewise, defective realization will not put an end to bondage. Therefore devote yourself to hearing the truth *(sravana)*, clear contemplation *(manana)* and abidance in the *Atma (nidhidhyasana)* and root out ignorance, uncertainty and wrong knowledge."

- Kaivalya Navaneetham[24]

Q : *As I had asked in the context of another such topic, pertaining to a sutra from 'Kaivalya Navaneetham', here again, we see enormous stress on the three-part sadhana of sravana, manana and nidhidhyasana. One understands sravana, which is listening to the teaching, manana is contemplation, thinking it out, understanding it. 'Nidhidhyasana' is vague, what is its real meaning?*

A : Here, I like to sound a note of caution; one should never be intimidated by the Sanskrit terminology. One should look at the context and see whether you agree with the given meaning of the Sanskrit term. Just to know Sanskrit is not enough, one should also know that particular discipline of knowledge in which that particular term is being used. Here the discipline is Self - Rrealization or *Atma vidya*. The usual meaning of the term '*nidhidhyasana*' is meditation, but this is as vague as it can possibly be. Sri Ramana Maharshi gives the exact meaning of '*nidhidhyasana*' as it is used in the discipline of Self - Realization. In this context it means to abide in the *Atma* as the *Atma* and to enquire, whence came this *Atma*? To wonder about the origin of this *Atma* and to again and again abide as *Atma* in the *Atma*. In traditional spiritual literature this '*nidhidhyasana*' is equated with *Atma anusandhana* – meaning enquiry into the *Atma* by abiding therein. Etymologically, *'nidhi'* means treasure, a place which is a reservoir or repository of valuable things. *Adhyasana* is the act of settling into the *nidhi*. The *nidhi* here is the *Atma*.

Q : *As we study the teachings and practice and move away from ignorance, uncertainty and wrong knowledge, will we be getting a rock like conviction and brilliant clarity, along with a tranquil and pure 'I'?*

A : Yes! Because the pure 'I' is the *'nidhi'*, the treasure house of all the treasures.

Q : *Where, a seeker, is not being personally tutored by a Self - Realized master and is not easily in touch with a Self - Realized master, the chances for ignorance, uncertainty and wrong knowledge are all the more isn't it? In modern times, where the pace of life has been accelerated, in spite of attending good retreats, where authentic teachings are heard (sravana), yet without repeated satsang with a Self - Realized master, one may not reach the goal of jivanmukti isn't it?*

A : Answer to the first question is - Yes. Answer to the second question is also - Yes.

The *sadhaka* or the disciple has always to make his own enquiry. Often it happens that he runs into by-lanes, which are not pertinent to the main line of enquiry. If he were to struggle by himself, without being overseen by a Self - Realized master, the chances are that the discovery of the mistakes might be very slow and the correction also slow. When an experienced eye is watching over the progress made by a *sadhaka*, the correction is immediate, so time is not lost and the process of learning becomes more efficient. The *sadhaka* should never believe blindly what the Self - Realized master tells him. He must always question intelligently, rather than arrogantly and with proper knowledge, arrive at his own inferences and this will be tested by the master too. The process goes on like this.

----

26. Again *Kaivalya Navaneetham* on *Maya*

"Ignorance veils the truth that the Self *(Atma)* is *Brahman* and shows forth multiplicity instead; uncertainty is the confusion resulting from the lack of firm faith in the words of the master; the illusion that the evanescent world is the reality and that the body is the Self is wrong knowledge. So say the sages."

The Bhagavad Gita also calls attention to *maya*.

Q : *So, in this topic we seem to get a clearer idea of what 'ignorance', 'uncertainty' and 'wrong knowledge', really are?*

Since all of us see and then believe multiplicity and diversity, instead of the unity of all life, so all have ignorance and wrong knowledge isn't it?

A : Yes, the whole of humanity, rich and poor, young and old, foolish and intelligent.

Q : *When we see two scriptures emphasize the same principles, then our conviction is strengthened isn't it?*

A : Yes, when you meet the same *sutra* in two different scriptures say in the Bhagavad Gita and in *Advaita bodha deepika* for example, we are apt to remember that the theme is recurring and so it will get committed to memory. A good disciple or *sadaka* will always take pains to memorize certain *sutras*. The idea of repeating these *sutras* mentally or silently within the mind, or in a murmuring fashion is to make it enter very deeply into *chitta* so that it may be realized there and it will uproot wrong knowledge and uncertainty.

Q : *The greatest obstacle (ignorance and wrong knowledge) seems to be the sensory delusion that we are the body? So, probably one has to make the maximal enquiry here?*

A : Mere enquiry is not enough. The enquiry must go deeper, one must see what the scriptures are saying and one must argue with oneself and with fellow seekers like how scientists do in all discussions, so that the truth becomes a matter of our own discovery and conviction, not a mere belief, nor a possibility, nor even a hypothesis, nor even a speculative thesis.

27. How to Perceive an Ending

"What is worn out, broken, loosened, powerless, disturbed, crushed, or destroyed, *consider that a new beginning.*"

Yoga Vasishtha [on misfortune]: [VI/1-16-33][25]

Sankara: Because *prajnya* is not awakened, you are unable to see beyond the ending, so you weep, when something comes to an end. When *prajnya* is awakened, you will know, this ending to be the seed for a new beginning, so there will be no disturbance in you at all. Generally, neither excitement nor despondency.

28. What should you do as *Jiva*?
Or, What should you do as the Witness?

1. Every human being, every created object is already connected to the source, *Parabrahma*. Like the seed within the mango.

2. Every *mumukshu* (seeker of *moksha*) must do his own exploration as the witness *(nidhidhyasana)* to discover.

3. Monumental mystical experiences will not repeat. Do not seek them even. They will even fade in your memory and consciousness. Faith is necessary but not sufficient. But insightful understanding and enquiry will blossom into conviction and abidance in the *Atma*.

Q   :   *It appears that the lesson that is repeatedly coming home to us, in almost every topic is the same, namely that the Divine, as our Atma is ever present at the core of our being. Am I right?*

A   :   You are on the dot, so do not run after any mirage of God, why should you, when Godhead *(Brahman, Parabrahma)* is present as the essence of your being?

Q   :   *Another lesson that is coming home to us, in a recurring fashion is this, that while the apples of grace may seem to fall into our lap, because of prayer, faith, worship, etc., abiding in the Atma, is the highest spiritual deed, that surpasses, prayer, faith, poojas, worship, reading of the scriptures. Would you go with me?*

A   :   Yes, this is the right *sadhana* in Self - Realization. Every other *sadhana* is besides the point, because it sustains ignorance and the life of the *Jiva* in the consciousness country. **"As a *Jiva*, you have no work in Self - Realization, but as a witness, you have all the work".** And this distinction is of paramount importance, as stressed by Sri Nisargadatta Maharaj.

Q : *That mystical experiences are also maya and will not take us home. Would you consider this view correct?*

A : Yes, all the *advaitic* masters like Sri J. Krishnamurti, Sri Nisargadatta Maharaj and Sri Ramana Maharshi negate experience as a way and as a path. The reason for this is only the *Jiva* can have experiences and since the *Jiva* has to be liquidated for the new life and the *Atma* to begin, what is the point in enriching the *Jiva* with experiences and making it more proud, conceited and boastful?

---

29. *Jiva's Dharma* : Humility, straight forwardness...

Amānitvam adambhitvam ahiṁsā kṣāntir ārjavam |
Ācāry'opāsanaṁ śaucaṁ sthairyam ātma-vinigrahaḥ ||

Bhagavad Gita XIII.7[26]

"Humility (freedom from self-importance), unpretentiousness, non-violence, patient forgiveness, straight-forwardness, service to the teacher, cleanliness, steadfastness, self-restraint." All of these are necessary qualifications for life in *dharma and moksha.* These virtues are difficult for the *Jiva,* but very natural for the *sthitha prajnya.*

Q : *May we say that, as the Atma is already pure, no further purification is called for. Yet, as the Jiva is horribly polluted, especially in the ways of thinking, and in consciousness and in the inner life, these noble qualities when practiced in our inner and outer life, will they kind of clean the dross of maya and ignorance (I am thinking of the algae in the pond)?*

A : Yes, absolutely, it is audacious to suppose that *sadhana* will purify the *Atma*. What it will do is to minimize the pollution to the *Jiva*, and even this may be insufficient as what is called for is a complete annihilation of the *Jiva* or at any rate atleast a silencing which will have some durability.

Q : *Will the sthitha prajnya, more or less, have all of these qualities, as natural traits, for which he need make no effort what so ever?*

A : Right, these are natural for the *sthitha prajnya*, in the beginning, when he is 'twice born', but *maya* can also accrue to him, as he walks the streets of mundane life and looks at the cinema posters and watches the television!

30. *Jiva's Dharma* : Sensitivity to death, old age,...

Indriy'ārthesu vairāgyam anahaṅkāra eva ca |
Janma-mṛtyu-jarā-vyādhi-duḥkha-doṣ'ānudarśanam ||

Bhagavad Gita XIII.8[26]

"Indifference to the objects of the senses and also absence of egoism; contemplating the reality of birth, death, old age, sickness and sorrow." All of these are necessary qualifications for life in *dharma and moksha*. These virtues are difficult for the *Jiva*, but very natural for the *sthitha prajnya*.

Q : *The detachment from sense objects of various kinds and selflessness in thought, word and deed are usually not even thought about. Thus a mumukshu, who practices this way of spiritual life, should be an extremely sensitive individual, attentive to all the minor sensory calls and unless, he is a sthitha prajnya, would this not be difficult?*

A : Assume he is starting on the spiritual path, for such a one, all these restraints may seem hard. But if someone has seen death of a dear one, seen much suffering within oneself or in the family, then it is easier to come upon these sensory restraints.

Q : *What will happen as we sincerely and deeply ponder over the fleeting nature of human life, how short and fragile it is, on the nature of old age and even death?*

A : Surely, then we will not be so attached to our 'success', we will not fight with others with a sense of divisiveness, we will become more humble, calm and perceptive, we may even turn inward, something that is of the very essence of the spiritual life.

31. *Jiva's Dharma* : Detachment, equanimity,...

Asaktir anabhiṣvaṅgaḥ putra-dāra-gṛhādiṣu |
Nityaṁ ca sama-cittatvam iṣṭ'āniṣṭ'opapattiṣu ||

Bhagavad Gita XIII.9[26]

"Detachment and non-identification with one's son, wife, property and the rest, and constant equanimity and 'distance' from both the pleasing and the displeasing things in life." All of these are necessary qualifications for life in *dharma and moksha*. These virtues are difficult for the *Jiva*, but very natural for the *sthitha prajnya*.

Q : *Here the prescription for dharma from the ancient scripture of the Bhagavad Gita is so rigorous and uncompromising. Modern gurus, do not seem to insist on such excellence in the cultivation of virtues, why is this?*

A : In the Hindu tradition, the *guru* is considered equal to God, as our highest well-wisher. He guided, starting from a tender age of seven, or so. The *guru* knew the family, all the difficulties of the personality, and was a personal life coach, like a beloved parent, and having the time to groom the disciple. In modern times, *gurus* are not so accessible, to spend so much time and to get close to a *guru*, is next to impossible, not to speak of receiving guidance, which is even more remote a possibility. Times have changed, and so standards may have declined. Nevertheless, in ashrams throughout India, where, seekers gather at the feet of the *guru*, greater attention on the seekers may be possible, but even here no one can tell, how much time the *guru* will have to spend overseeing the development of any disciple and what the *guru's* own views on personal guidance are.

Q : *The mumukshu is enjoined to be detached from the son, wife, home, property, by being equanamous in both pleasing and displeasing circumstances of life. This one sutra seems to be enough and calls for perpetual vigilance. Though this may fall on deaf ears, during the artha and kama spheres of life, for most of us; yet, there must be seekers, who come on such an austere path, even in their younger years isn't it?*

A : Real seekers are few. But in very difficult times, such as during diseases, wars, poverty, much spiritual growth can occur, as such misfortunes, will have the effect of routing the *Jiva* from the consciousness country.

----

32. Moving from Innocence to Innocence

"This meditation cannot be learnt from another. You must begin without knowing anything about it, and move from innocence to innocence."

- J. Krishnamurti in 'Meditations'[13]

Q : *Why does J. Krishnamurti, differing from an ancient Hindu tradition, make this scary statement that this meditation, cannot be learnt from another?*

A : We have to be vigilant about the use of spiritual terms, for they may mean many different things. As we said earlier, there are many kinds of meditations in the Hindu, Buddhist, Jaina and Christian religious traditions (I am not familiar at all with the Islamic traditions). Sri J. Krishnamurti is here talking about, 'choiceless awareness of *what is*', which is his special original contribution towards the ending of sorrow, towards the purification of the *Jiva*, so that the *Jiva* may realize the *Atmic* nature (in our terminology).

Only, you know your own consciousness, it is very very private, where the dark zones are, where you may never have been before and, another, even the *guru*, may not take the pains to hand hold you and lead you from darkness to light. Since, it is your own consciousness, you alone are competent to work in this field, observing everything and learning, and as this kind of 'Krishnamurti' learning is a lifelong affair, no one but yourself can do this.

Q : *Looking at the master J. Krishnamurti's words, this kind of a meditation seems to be a journey into the unknown, much like a researcher, enquiring endlessly and passionately, all in silence?*

Also, moving from innocence to innocence, seems definitely to imply, that as we go deeper into these meditations, we become incapable of judgment, a mean dirty tendency to which we humans are sadly prone, so we plunge this way into the unknown depths, quivering with devotion and deep feeling?

A : J. Krishnamurti's meditations are all done by the witness, not by the *Jiva*. Such choiceless awareness will lead to the calming and silencing of the Jiva, provided, there are the ingredients of seriousness, detachment and surrender to what is.

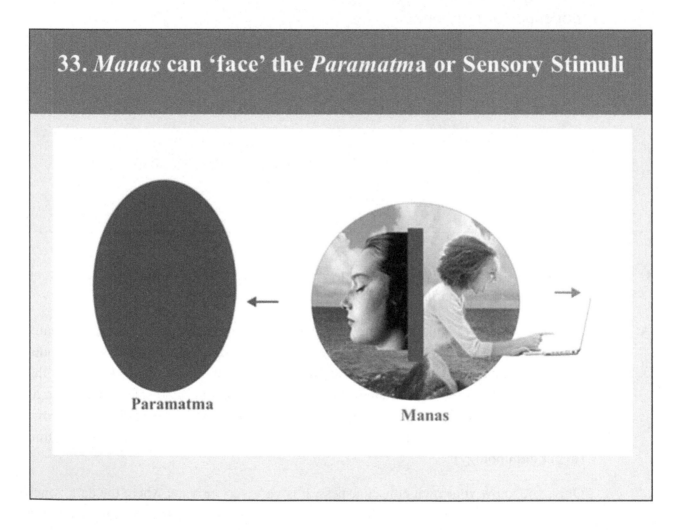

33. *Manas* can 'face' the *Paramatma* or Sensory Stimuli

Paramatma

Manas

Q : *When we shut our eyes, we will either see some pictures, popping up from our past memories or future imaginings, or we may start chattering, since we are the chattering Jiva! If no thoughts and feelings are seen to be coming, then there is only a blank* *screen, nothing to see really, but what is still here is only the 'conscious presence' of the 'I', of ourselves, so are we to sink into this 'conscious presence' or abide in it?*

A   :   When thoughts have subsided more or less we have a new opportunity and this opportunity becomes more spectacular, conducive to learning if we are not on the verge of dreaming. Some images may be flashing and the important point is the images are all illuminated. Where did this light come from to illuminate all these images? This is the eternal light by which we are able to see all thought and all feeling, it was never switched on and it can never get switched off. It is perpetually on. One has to wonder about this happening. When all thoughts have subsided, there may be absolutely nothing for us to see by way of a spectacle in our consciousness. At this stage no distractions are possible, so we can just abide in the conscious presence and it is likely to become deep, as nothing is coming to unsettle it. This is the kind of abiding in the *Atma* that we have to do. Doing is not enough, there must be learning. All this is *nidhidhyasana*, which is the perfection and final practice in traditional *advaitic* meditation.

Fourth Day (Chapter - IV), 2nd 'Tat Tvam Asi' Meditation

Jiva knows only duality, abiding in the *Atma*, you become an 'outsider' to consciousness. The master Krishnamurti once said, 'Live like a guest in a stranger's house'.

Abiding in the *Atma*, you become innocent, because, you have left behind duality.

Chapter V

By Being the Atma,
the Awakening of Intelligence *(Prajnya), happens*

1. Beginning from the other shore... Revisited

"In all this movement you must somehow begin from the other end, from the other shore, and not always be concerned with this shore or how to cross the river.

"You must take a plunge into the water, not knowing how to swim. And the beauty of meditation is that you never know where you are, where you are going, what the end is."

- J. Krishnamurti in 'Meditations'[13]

Q : *This is a beautiful meditation from J. Krishnamurti, nevertheless, we must realize that most of us suffer from the fear of the unknown. So, how would you expect us to take the plunge, as it were and reach out to the other shore?*

A : We have two dimensions, a human dimension, to which all your logic applies, the fear, etc. However, we are also a timeless being, a witness, awareness, with infinite Divine possibilities. Because, we are always with a swarm of thoughts and feelings, we are never able to know ourselves, as we are, without these thoughts and feelings. This witness is our deeper nature, and this whole retreat is devoted to the discovery of this hidden nature called the *Atma* or awareness. *Atma* is the realm of all possibilities.

Q : *So, is it like pressing the 'emergency button', which may be always there, but which we are unaware of?*

A : Yes, we are unconscious of the mechanism of how some of our difficult problems get resolved. We call that grace, result of prayer, blessing, etc. However, this Divine source is also our very Self. We do not know this, we cannot be aware of it as we can be aware of the sun, moon and the trees. This retreat is intended to help us to get at this

322

treasure, which we are already. It is not a new treasure or a new blessing which will come to you from the outside world, from another source.

Q : *Why does Krishnamurti say, "the beauty of meditation is that, you never know where you are, where you are going, what the end is?"*

A : Our limited human nature makes us everlastingly seek security, we need to be constantly assured that we will find some great treasure, if not now, at least in the future, etc. However, when our Divine nature comes into play, as it surely does in these meditations, then we are naturally going to be truly fearless, rather than afraid. *In fact all creative minds have this enormous courage and spirit of adventure, without this, they would never have discovered all the wonderful things they discovered. Theirs was a journey into the unknown.* So, the master Sri J. Krishnamurti says, this is the nature of these meditative journeys, they are mysterious journeys into the bosom of truth, into the unknown.

Q : *Why does Krishnamurti say, "Somehow in all this, you must begin from the other shore, from the other end, and not always be concerned about this shore or how to cross the river"? As we are standing on this shore, so how do we start from the other shore, this looks like an impossibility?*

A : You are on both shores, all at once and this might sound strange at first sight. As a *Jiva*, with its ridiculous ignorance and *maya*, it thinks it is on this shore. As an *Atma*, you have always been only on the yonder shore. Remember also what the master Sri Nisargadatta Maharaj has said: 'You are already in the final state.'

You are taking the metaphor of the two shores too literally and have forgotten the *Atmic* nature of the *Jiva*.

----

2. *Prajnya*, What is It?

1. You already have this wealth of *prajnya,* it is the essence of the 'witnessing bird' (the *Atma*), which is your true nature. To awaken this *prajnya,* the *Jiva (self),* must fall silent. Then, *prajnya* has a chance to manifest in the field of that silence.

   Etymology, intelligence which is awareness, 'intelligence of those established in the witness-consciousness *(Atma)*'.

2. ‖ *Prajnyanam Brahma* ‖   - Aitareya Up, Rg Veda

Q : *So, the prajnya which is Atmic intelligence, is always there, except that it has been beclouded by the frenetic chattering of the Jiva. This seems to imply that, only when the Jiva falls silent, do human beings actually become capable of listening, for the very first time in their life?*

A : Absolutely. Being unconscious we are perpetually in a frenzy of self-defense and self-aggrandizement and because intelligence is not awakened, it never even occurs to us that this way of living is so sterile and senseless. If people can just 'listen' this will be a great spiritual achievement indeed. But it becomes possible only when the noise of the *Jiva* has subsided.

Q : *The capacity to listen to so important, yet so rare in the world. In actual life, I find that most people do not listen, because they are in a web of daydreaming. Their minds are wandering all the time, they are so preoccupied with too many desires and too many distractions.*

Then, can we also say that life begins only when prajnya is awakened?

A   :   True. People are too much in *maya*, so the *Jivas* are noisy, thus obstructing the flowering of intelligence. J. Krishnamurti has said, 'life begins when thought ends'.

Q   :   *How would you assign the correct meaning for the Upanishadic sutra or mahavakhya: 'Prajnyanam Brahma'?*

A   :   As *prajnya* is the primordial intelligence belonging to the *Atma*, or to 'That' *(Brahman)*, *Prajnyanam Brahma* ought to mean, that; 'That', referred to here as *Brahman,* is in fact, this very auspicious intelligence *(prajnya)*, which is also the primordial awareness.

---

3. Who is a *Sthitha Prajnya?*

- In Chapter II of the Bhagavad Gita (BG), the *sthitha prajnya's* consciousness is described. *Prajnya* is *Atmic* intelligence, *sthitha* means stabilized, meaning, this *prajnya* is not 'flickering' any more but steady and stabilized in the *sthitha prajnya*.

- *self* - Knowing also leads to the awakening of intelligence.

- The Awakening of Intelligence by J. Krishnamurti,
London Victor Gollancz Ltd, 1973.[8]

Q   :   *Can you describe the sthitha prajnya again?*

A   :   The senses and consciousness are very awake in a *sthitha prajnya*, because *prajnya* or *Atmic* intelligence is awakened. The flashes of insights will also be more luminous and many more in number. The *sthitha prajnya* has settled in the *Atma*, bereft of conflict and there is constant inner wellness or joy.

4. *Prajnya* is '*Atmic* Intelligence'

"There is no *(Atmic)* intelligence in him, who is not yoked to the *Atma*, nor is there any feeling of devotion or contemplation. For one who is not devoted thus (or, for one who does not contemplate this), there can be no inner peace and how can there be inner joy and well-being, when there is no inner peace."

- **Bhagavad Gita II.66 [7]**

Q : *We see that whether it is joy (ananda) or intelligence, or peace, or anything else, it is only the Atma, which can truly be our refuge, could this be the reason, at least in this Advaitic teaching that we are all driven to the Atmic country?*

A : Yes. In agriculture one hears of dry land and wet land. Dry land is dry and arid, with no rivers and canals flowing there, so we cannot grow crops which need plenty of water. Wet lands are those which can have bountiful crops, because there is abundant water from a river or through rains, etc. The *Atmic* country is like fertile wet land and consciousness country is the dry land. The *Atmic* country is silent, deep and profound. The consciousness country is like the market place, full of noise and confusion.

----

5. The Two 'Tat Tvam Asi' Birds - Revisited

Atma (Self), witness, 'conscious presence', 'I am ness'

Atma, in disguise as the '*Jiva*'- limited and body-mind centered

Q : *Now this topic speaks of two Tat Tvam Asi birds of the Mundaka Upanishad. As a Hindu, I am somewhat aware that the Upanishads are part of the Vedas, the deepest scriptures of the Hindus. However when this retreat is offered to Western seekers, how would people understand these Sanskrit terms, and even the meaning of 'Upanishads' and 'Mundaka'. Should you not be giving us the meanings of these terms, so that even Hindus like us, may have an even clearer understanding?*

A : It will be good if seekers do understand the meanings, especially the etymological meaning of these Sanskrit terms, *Upanishads* and *Mundaka*. But this is actually not so necessary for our present purposes here, of *self* - Knowing and Self - Realization. Nevertheless, for the sake of completeness, let us go into this.

The term *Upanishad*:

Upa is composed of two parts which is U + Pa - meaning '*near the feet*'. And '*nishad*' means sitting beneath the feet-implied that these are the feet of the master.

It is suggestive of a disciple or a *mumukshu* sitting at the feet of a Self-Realized master, having humbled himself and having the very essential quality of humility. So sitting at the feet of a master is symbolic of the extremely humble posture, for without this humility no learning is possible. It is a teaching which is received and centered on the *Atma* and on *Brahman*. *Atman* is the deeper aspect of the I-consciousness and *Brahman* is the unmanifest Divine. So the *Upanishads* teach us about *Atman and Brahman*, i.e., *Atmavidya* (knowledge or learning about the *Atma*) and *Brahmavidya* (knowledge or learning about *Brahman* or the Divine).

In India, the *Vedas* are the ancient spiritual corpus of the Hindus. *Upanishads* are considered to be the *Veda siras* - the crown of the *Vedas* or *Vedanta* - the highest peak of the *Vedas*, which is naturally centered on Self - Realization.

Coming to the adjective *Mundaka:*

The word means 'shaven off'. Why is this adjective used here? It is probably used because to shave off the head, which is what the *sannyasis* do in India, is symbolic of renunciation of the ego, the *self*. Renunciation of the idea that one is the body, that one is the *self* and shaving off of the head or tonsure is a symbolic and ritualistic act, signifying, 'the casting away of the *self*', or individuality, or the notion that 'we are the physical body'.

So, *Mundaka Upanishad* will probably indicate an emphasis which is based on detachment from the body, detachment from the *self*, without which this teaching may not get internalized and come home to us. So detachment and renunciation of the idea that we are the body, that we are the *self*, are central to this *Upanishad*. And this is a teaching given by a particular sage, and every *Upanishad* is a teaching by a particular sage. The key thing here is that no two teachings actually are the same, because every sage speaks from his own realization. So that is the reason there are so many *Upanishads*. There are more than 100 or 200 *Upanishads* and each of them has equally legitimate insights, which that particular sage had in his life and which he is presenting to us in the form of teachings and these teachings will be helpful to us in our own pursuit and discovery of the truth of the *Atma* and *Parabrahma*.

Q   :   *Are the two Tat Tvam Asi birds seen in this picture, metaphors for some teaching in this Upanishad? If so, what exactly do they represent? Most importantly, why are you describing these birds as Tat Tvam Asi birds?*

A   :   At the outset, I wish to emphasize that every one of us will benefit by memorizing this mythic picture or this metaphoric representation of the truth, which is an analogical understanding of the truth. Yes, indeed it is a metaphor. You will see that one bird is very engrossed in the act of eating, which is symbolic of sensory-gratification and the pursuit of pleasure which is such an integral part of the human drama. While the other bird is not involved and not engrossed in the act of the pursuit of pleasure; instead it seems to be detached and only witnessing the whole act of the pursuit of pleasure, the search for sensory gratification, the search for survival, the search for emotional and economic security. This other bird is a complete outsider to this whole drama and is only a witness and probably has got the capacity to learn and the capacity to negate the life of the lower bird. If we like we may call the bird which is engrossed in the pleasure seeking and search for security as *Sakti* and the other wise bird which is just watching everything, as *Siva.* And I have given the particular name Tat Tvam Asi birds because in truth there are not two birds. There is just one bird, capable of being in both states, so we are both the birds.

This is one of the most important principles in this retreat - that we have a body and mind centered *self* (our human nature), and another Self, awareness, the *Atma,* that is imperishable, unborn, deathless, and timeless, pointing to our Divine nature. So we will have to commit this picture to memory, like we had recommended committing to memory, the previous ocean-wave metaphor. The ocean-wave metaphor is also a Tat Tvam Asi metaphor, likewise these two birds.

The eating bird represents the *Jiva (self)* which enjoys and suffers, the witnessing bird represents the timeless awareness *(Chit),* the *Atma,* a higher spiritual potential we all have, and which we use far too inadequately. So it is, if we may use these terms, a powerful faculty, which is unrecognized and used unconsciously and insufficiently. Every human being has two dimensions or two aspects, a very manifest human aspect, and a veiled Divine aspect. The witnessing bird represents the hidden Divine aspect of every human being, and the pleasure-seeking and eating bird represents the human nature of every human being. In Ch. I, topic 2, we have already dealt with the human nature vis-à-vis the Divine nature of every human being. 'Tat' refers to our *Atma,* which in fact is our Divine nature, 'Tvam' refers to the core of your so-called human nature, and 'Asi' means 'are', so 'Tat Tvam Asi', the *Upanishadic sutra* says, the very essence of each one of us is the Divine Itself. *The two birds are thus different aspects of ourselves, the eating bird, the mask, the self, and the witnessing bird, the somewhat veiled Divine nature, the Atma or the witness consciousness. Thus we are both the birds, simultaneously and obviously this is a paradox. Hence the present adjective Tat Tvam Asi is quite appropriate.*

Q   :   *So, this is yet another way of driving home the same point of Tat Tvam Asi, that we are the Divine - not as the body, but as the root of our consciousness?*

A   :   Yes, that is the hint that is being given by this particular metaphor - that we are both. We are the pleasure seeking entity, we are the entity seeking survival and security perpetually and feeling insecure in this whole endless process. That is the *Sakti* bird. But we also have to discover and realize that we are also the witnessing bird, we are intelligence which is now buried. So the teaching will help us to know that we are both the things. When we understand the teaching deeply, then the seeming contradiction between the *Sakti* bird and the *Siva* bird will completely disappear and we will know/ realize that there are no contradictions and that we are both aspects of consciousness, hence the truth of Tat Tvam Asi.

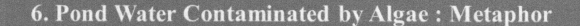

6. Pond Water Contaminated by Algae : Metaphor

Clear water = *Atma* = ' I ', algae (*maya*) = illusions of duality, attachments, hurts, memories, pleasure and pain

Q   :   *We have seen this picture before. Looking at it afresh, do you think, the extent of this contamination will be different in different people?*

A   :   Of course! The more ignorant one is more the contamination and the more lucid one is less the contamination.

Q   :   *More the contamination, more the pain in life?*

A   :   More pleasure to begin with. And this more and more pleasure will invariably end in a tragedy, which is the impossibility of continuing the pleasure, which is pain. So more the contamination, more the pleasure and more the pain.

Q : *After the cleaning of consciousness, through choiceless awareness and learning about the Jiva (self), do you think, Jiva becomes calmer and more silent?*

A : Think of the man with the algae enmeshing him (Ch. I, topic 18). We had said that his body represents the *Atma* and the enveloping algae was the *maya* and the ignorance. So now the *Jiva* is the man with all the algae. The *Jiva* attempts to observe itself. This is possible because the *Atma* is at the heart of the *Jiva*. As the *Jiva* observes itself, awareness comes into play and learning happens and if one has the desire (i.e., *Jiva* has the desire) to achieve some end through this choiceless observation, then the learning will be unfruitful. But if there is intense interest and no surging desire, then the *Jiva* will be calmed and silenced.

Q : *How does the Jiva get into maya?*

A : This is a Divine doing and the tragicomedy is that as the *Atma* is the Divine itself in creation, it is the Divine which has got entangled, but of course as a human being. The moment the Divine creates the world, this *maya* and entanglement comes along. It is very sweet and delicious to begin with, but soon turns bitter so that, you have to eventually spit it out.

Q : *One understands that hurts and pain are contrary to Atma's blissful nature, so these are contaminations all right. But how are all our aspirations and our ambitions also contaminations?*

A : Many people are not going to like this answer, because every aspiration and ambition is fundamentally self-centered. It implies a blindness as to who we are and such ambition invariably will lead to stepping on other people's toes and causing them great pain. Also importantly, being so obsessed and preoccupied with the ambition and aspirations, makes one necessarily lose all peace and all intelligence. This lesson is learnt only after a fall, never while the game is still going on.

----

7. Water Without Contamination by Algae - Revisited

Q : *Looking at this absolutely clear pond, can such an ideal state be reached?*

A : When there is integrity for the *Jiva*, when the *Jiva* has no private and secret agenda of its own and has *nirguna bhakti* (the seventh or highest *bhakti*) to *Parabrahma*, then the pond will be blemishless like in the picture. Where there is sincerity, devotion, faith and dedication, it is as impossible a thing, as you imagine it to be.

----

8. 'Tamed' *Sakti* : Mythic Metaphor

Siva – Sakti (Bengal), X century A.D.

Acknowledgement : 'Myths and Symbols in Indian Art and Civilization', Plate 34, Heinrich Zimmer, Bollingen Series / Princeton, 1972

One should raise one's lower *self (Jiva)* by one's higher Self *(Atma)* alone. Let not one lower oneself *(Jiva)*; for the higher Self *(Atma)* alone is the friend of lower *self*, and the lower *self* alone is the enemy of the higher Self *(Atma)*.

- Bhagavad Gita: VI. 5[23]

Q : *This picture shows that, you are referring to the Bhagavad Gita, Ch. VI, 5th sloka. What is the content of this sloka?*

A : Actually in other retreats I had given this *sloka* because I consider this to be extremely important - a lot of people think that Krishna is the *avatar* and they have to take refuge in him, i.e., in his human personality. So the Krishna cult has developed in India. But Krishna's whole teaching is entirely different. He never asked us to take refuge in his human personality and in his human form, instead he gives us a recipe for getting into a union with the *Paramatma*. And that is the 5th *sloka* in Ch. VI:

उद्धरेदात्मनात्मानं नात्मानमवसादयेत् ।

आत्मैव ह्यात्मनो बन्धुरात्मैव रिपुरात्मनः ॥   ॥६ ॥५ ॥

uddhared ātmanātmānaṁ nātmānamavasādayet |
ātmaiva hy ātmano bandhur ātmaiva ripurātmanaḥ || ||6.5||

Meaning of the *sloka* is, that we should be self-reliant on the path of *Jnana yoga* or the path of understanding, as a means to achieving the Divine, within ourselves, as the core of ourseloves. One is enjoined to one's own teacher. So to put it simply, 'the *Jiva* should elevate itself by the *Atma* alone. Let not the *Jiva* lower itself, for the *Atma* alone is the friend of the *Jiva*, whereas the *Jiva* alone can be its own enemy and the enemy of the *Atma*'.

Now the *sloka* speaks about two *selves*. Like the two 'Tat Tvam Asi' birds, like *Siva* and *Sakti*. So obviously, *Siva* is the higher *Self* and *Sakti* is the lower *self*. And we are both. But we live our life in complete unawareness of the fact that we are also *Siva*. We only only living the life of *Sakti* and we don't seem to adequately live the life of *Siva*. And in a retreat like this the whole *sadhana* has to be in the direction of bringing the *Siva* into relief. That *Siva* who is behind the scenes, to bring that *Siva* which is the essential and core part of ourselves into full relief so that *Sakti* also falls into place. That is the content of the *sloka*.

Q : *So, can I infer that this tamed Sakti is not fighting with herself, or in other words is her own best friend and that she has come home to Siva?*

A : You are right. This *Sakti* is no more fighting with herself. *Sakti* will indeed fight with herself only if she is fragmented into two or three or four different things and they all are in opposition with each other - then she will fight. Then the force of duality and *maya* will be strong. But where *Sakti* is completely well integrated and has become *whole* because *Siva* has come into the picture; that *Sakti* will naturally be docile and tamed and will not be fighting with herself. So, She will be her own best friend and absolutely a good friend. Also, because She has come home to *Siva* who is her lord and master. This is also the state in which, due to the silence of *Sakti*; *Siva* comes into relief and *Siva's* presence, which is intelligence *(prajnya)* begins to manifest.

The picture also represents the *sthitha prajnya's* state of consciousness, which is an extremely important teaching from the Bhagavad Gita in Ch. II. And *sthitha* means stable and *prajnya* is *Atmic* intelligence sourced in the Divine. So the *sthitha prajnya* is one whose consciousness has fallen silent and because the consciousness has fallen silent, that consciousness is automatically yoked on to the Divine who is the *Atma* or who is *Siva*. So this mythic picture, the religious sculpture also signifies the state of the *sthitha prajnya*. We should at least get this far in our meditative journey where *Sakti* becomes silent and gets yoked to *Siva*.

Q : *If we observe closely the expression on Siva's face is so beatific and also compassionate. Don't you think the sculptor has done good justice to Siva being, embodiment of ananda and He is seen to be karunamaya (full of karuna or compassion)?*

A   :   You are right, the face of *Siva* - if you come close to the picture and observe it carefully - you will find to be extremely beatific and the emotion called *ananda rasa* is seen on His face. That is, He is in *ecstasy.* And this is His natural state, because he is the *sat-chit-ananda.* He is existence, awareness and beatitude (*chit* is awareness), so that is the natural state of *Siva.* And the sculptor has done full justice in bringing out the *ananda* aspect of *Siva* and the *karunamaya* aspect of *Siva.* That is, His nature is full of *karuna,* in other words, compassion.

Here I would like to add, that in the ancient Hindu civilization, there were sixty four art forms and every art form was a means to find the Divine and yoke into the Divine. And *sthapatya Veda (sthapatya shastra), shilpa shastra* were systems of knowledge and understanding of how one is to give beauty and correct proportion to art forms, in architecture and sculpture respectively. And if one dedicates oneself completely to the art form and then one becomes engrossed and immersed in the sculpture, then that also becomes a route or passage to *moksha.* So if you find the Hindu sculptures doing tremendous justice, then we have to appreciate that this is so, only because the artisans, the sculptors and the artists who worked with these forms, for them, it was a religion, not just a profession or a vocation . It was not just a means of livelihood, nor was it a vocation, nor was it just a skill, it was a traditionally well-established means to realize the Divine. And this is the reason, why it has the obvious stamp of excellence.

Q   :   *Does this picture represent a meditative state of consciousness, one in which consciousness is almost still, or at any rate, very sattvik, and with a minimum of the grosser gunas, rajas and tamas?*

A   :   Yes. As the posture of *Sakti* represents, *Sakti* has no restlessness at all. Nor is She indolent. She is tuned into the Divine, tuned into the ground from which She has emanated as an independent energy. This mythic representation of *Siva* and *Sakti* in religious sculpture, actually points to the *sthitha prajnya's* state of consciousness.

Prajnya means intelligence that is sourced in *prajnya* or awareness and *sthitha* is that intelligence which has become *stabilized.* So this *sthitha prajnya* state is one in which the awakened intelligence is not flickering, but has become very stable and very steady. And that happens only when *Sakti* has come home to roost. And with her coming home to roost, all Her madness and all Her activity is at an end and that is when *Siva* the primal intelligence has an opportunity to come into relief and make His presence felt. So the sculpture actually represents the meditative state in which consciousness has become very silent, has become very unruffled and the *rajas* and *tamas* are at an all time minimum.

----

9. Intelligence (*Prajnya*) as Sensitivity

1. Sensitivity to yourself

2. Sensitivity to family members

3. Capacity to feel every situation

4. Sensitivity to your own sorrow

5. Sensitivity to sexual attraction

6. Sensitivity to the whole of nature

7. Sensitivity to the Divine

Q : *This topic presupposes that the person has to be silent within and therefore having space within himself, so as to be receptive to life, in all its movements, so that he is also in a position to empathize with whom he is face to face with. Is this not so?*

A : When one is the *Jiva*, there is obviously no space within, consciousness is over crowded and polluted. Over crowded with too many thoughts and polluted because of a sense of divisiveness of the *self*, anger and a sense of separation from the whole world. In *Atmic* country there is plenty of space because everything is silent, hence the *sthitha prajnya* who is poised in the *Atma*, is like the one who is hospitable, with the doors of his house open for all to come in and be honored. He has space, the *Jiva* has no space at all. This inner space is the key to the new life. From this inner space is the scope for sensitivity to oneself, to the family and to society, to nature and to the whole movement of life. It is limitless.

Q : *A sthitha prajnya will obviously have all of these sensitivities - just because he is Atmically rooted. Don't you think so?*

A : That is the secret. That is his power. From the ground of the silence arises that intelligence which is called *prajnya*.

Q : *In the recent enormous calamity in Chennai, due to excessive rains, we have seen many examples of people, who have rallied round, those in deep trouble and those who have selflessly thrown themselves into service, thus rescuing the drowning people. Will you consider these as examples of sensitive behavior? And if so, how come they had sensitivity, without their prajnya being awakened?*

A : There are many factors which may be working here. Firstly, in a crisis of this proportion, the defense mechanisms of the *Jiva* are eroded, and the *Jiva*, responds from the *Atma*, at least temporarily, because it has come almost face to face with death. Secondly, people do not have the same level of sensitivity or insensitivity, so there are always some sensitive people, and if they are touched, they will respond from the *Atma* - but this is a temporary goodness, which may not last. Thirdly, many people may be helping, because they do not feel good within themselves, and this is an opportunity for them to jump and do something, so that they have a nice feeling. People who are socially important and who are being watched by the media, are rarely spontaneous, and often do things, just to appear good in the public eye. Even those who acted from the *Atma*, they will go back to being the *Jiva*, so you see, the phenomenon is very complex, with many different kinds of forces motivating people.

The sensitivity of the *sthitha prajnya* is wholly different, sometimes, he may not act at all, and may not even intercede in a collective crisis, like what you cited.

Q : *What is sensitivity to yourself?*

A : The first sensitivity to oneself is to one's sorrow. One has to awaken to this first, without awakening to this sorrow, one cannot be sensitive at all. One has to awaken to this sorrow, accept it, bow down one's head to it, and drink the sorrow, so that nothing of it is left. Then one is ready to be open to the whole of life. If one is angry or jealous or comparing oneself with another or lusty - to perceive all of this in wonderment, *without having the desire to correct it, or feel guilty, or condemn it or chastise it; this is wisdom and choiceless awareness.* You do not know when sorrow will come, but when it does comes the *Jiva* will be devastated, all its desires will be dashed on the rocks, at such times the *Jiva* has no option but to die. This is what J. Krishnamurti calls *dying to an experience*. It is the greatest purification we can have in life, because in this dying there is a complete parting of company with the past and its burdens. From this arises greater sensitivity to oneself.

Q : *What may be sensitivity to the Divine?*

A : The Divine has to *be felt*. For you can never know the Divine. You can see the handy work of the Divine in the mountains and in the stars. By looking in silence, our heart will melt and tears of devotion will roll down from our eyes. This can happen when you just look at a tree or look at a small plant or flower. All of this sensitivity to the whole of nature (seen as the handy work of the Divine), is sensitivity to the Divine.

10. When can this Intelligence be Awakened?

When the 'chattering bird' *(Jiva)* is at its wit's end, when a 'death-like' crisis stares the 'chattering bird' *(Jiva)* in the face, then there is a possibility of the awakening of intelligence. Such a 'crisis' is only an outer necessary condition. It is not enough, there has to be a sufficient condition, over and above the necessary condition, for this awakening of intelligence to *happen*.

Q : *From what you are saying here, when there is a crisis for the Jiva, can the Jiva suddenly shift from maya to the Atma?*

A : What the *Jiva* invariably does is this. It survives by anchoring and taking security in various relationships, in ownership, in possession, in skills, in wealth and status. When one anchorage is uprooted by the vagaries of fate, if the *Jiva* has its eggs distributed in many baskets, it will cunningly develop affection for the basket which is not being disturbed and it will veer towards that basket. This shifting of security and anchorage can be seen in the whole of our human life. If the *Jiva* is so placed that all its eggs are in only in one basket and that basket too breaks; then the world comes crashing down on the *Jiva's* head. This is the crisis point, and depending on the solace offered by the

Jiva's faith or by family, the *Jiva* can be healed and anchored to a new life. If the *Jiva* is so fortunate that it has got spiritual tendencies, then in a crisis such as this, with good guidance, the *Jiva* can secure a foothold in the *Atmic* country, which will be the beginning of the new life. The *Jiva* has the determining power, the *Atma sakti*, even though it is an inhabitant in the consciousness country only. Which way the *Jiva* will use its *Atma sakti*, nobody can tell. *Jiva* has to decide for itself what it will do with this unsuspected power.

Q : *You are speaking of two conditions, one following the other, to be fulfilled, for the awakening of intelligence. The first condition, you have called the 'necessary' condition and the second the 'sufficient' condition. The outer 'necessary' condition, you have indicated, what about the 'sufficient' condition?*

A : We go into this 'sufficient' condition in the following topic.

11. When every 'Security', 'Refuge' for the *Jiva* fails, only then....

In such a crisis, the 'chattering bird'*(Jiva)* will go on struggling, go on trying, but all gates will be closed, no gate will open. Then a teaching or a *guru* will open the gate of *choiceless awareness of what is,* or by some other *yogic* means, then the old life falls away and a new life commences.

This is a journey into the unknown. In all this, you have to be your own teacher, as every refuge would have failed you and you would not be able to connect to spiritual masters, as your own discovery will be near at hand. (This is the sufficient condition.)

Sankara: We use the expression, *turning inwards*. This turning inwards is the first milestone that must be crossed, before the process of *self* - Knowing may commence. The *self* is often very stubborn like a bull, insisting on its own kind of solution, for its perceived problem. Because the *self* is opinionated and self-enclosed, it is hard for the *self* to open itself to what the wise people in the world have to say about its condition of misery. It is not enough to turn inwards, this has also to be sustained, namely, after having turned inwards, the *Jiva* has to continue to be inwardly turned. In this way, after the *Jiva* has made the intial turning inwards, if it can sustain the inward perception, then it will start learning about itself (sufficient condition). It is this which is really the beginning of *self* - Knowing. Unless every effort of the *Jiva*, to solve the problem, according to its peculiar understanding fails, the *Jiva* will not be able to turn inward. After *self* - Knowing starts fructifying, the *self* is likely to fall silent, and once this happens, the *Jiva* will find, new insights flowing in, a new intelligence will be in evidence, along with awakened senses. We have called this intelligence, *prajnya.*

12. The Seeds of Honesty and Humility are Important for 'Freedom' *(Moksha)*

The awakening of intelligence will happen when we realize, there is nothing fresh and original in us, when we are 'dead' within, when we honestly admit, we have discovered nothing for ourselves, that we have never enquired, that all is 'algae' only. Then from the seed of this honesty, this profound humility, this willingness to stand alone; begins the journey into the unknown, a journey in which the 'chattering bird' *(Jiva)*, has no role whatever. The *Jiva* can at best communicate this to the world, that's all. This intelligence is from *Parabrahma*, coming through the 'witness' *(Ganesha)*.

Sankara: In modern times for various reasons, survival pressures on every individual, exerted by society, have intensified. Generally, the individual is quite unconscious of these pressures and compulsions, until he comes to the point, where he meets with a significant failure in his life. From that point onwards, he will find many of the social courtesies, even within his own family withering away, he then has to contend with his crisis, himself. In Western society, which is more individualistic, people have to contend with their life crises, themselves. One has to suffer alone. But as we have not been taught the salutary value of suffering, we suffer unwillingly and incompletely, never developing in the process of this solitary suffering, any ennobling, learning experience. At the end of it all, it is much like a wasted precious opportunity. The words of the poet, T.S. Eliot, come to mind, "We had the experience, but missed the meaning." The importance of humility and absolute honesty are underestimated in the spiritual life. The truth is that, only those who are extremely honest with themselves and have become humble, only they may be able to make a pilgrimage to *moksha*, in the shrine of their hearts. The other people, smitten by frivolity, a lack of seriousness, who do not know themselves deeply and well enough, their pilgrimage may be aborted by this or that outer circumstance.

13. Voluntarily Negate All Support Systems, that Sustain and Nourish the *Jiva.*

"Let even *Hara (Siva), Hari (Vishnu)* and the Lotus born Brahma be your instructor, **but unless, you forget all**, you cannot be established in the Self."

- Ashtavakra Gita[37]

"Better than viewing Him as 'other', indeed, the noblest attitude of all, is to hold Him as the 'I' within, the very 'I'.

- Sri Ramana Maharshi's 'Upadesa Saram'[46]

All this means, you will have to stand alone, not bolstering your *self*, **by leaning on anything, so that you will abide in yourself (this standing alone is the grand negation of the** *self***).**

Q : *By 'support systems' are you referring to family, job, status, wealth? How are you supposed to negate these?*

A : Oh, what a wonderful question this is! In India there are widely different spiritual traditions, spiritual teachings and paths. This week-long course in *self* - Knowing and Self - Realization is meant for the courageous, who have set for themselves the highest standards in the spiritual life. It is meant also for those who are incapable of being blind followers because of their power of determination, intelligence and courage. Naturally, such people can cut their own paths and will be original. I have been emphasizing throughout that in traditional Hindu society the pursuit of *moksha* began after 60 or 65, when worldly responsibilities naturally came to an end, when the passions in the body greatly cooled down, when even *maya* became more relenting and was letting go. At that age, around 60 or 65, one should have no hesitation in practicing detachment from family and seeking the Divine since anyhow the reality of death will be becoming brighter and brighter with every passing year. Some spiritual people may become detached even when they are younger or may be spiritually so disciplined that they will be following certain ethical principles like *pratyahara*, a humanitarian approach to life, even when young. In the light of these observations, we will know by the time we are 60 that, family, wealth, job and status, are ephemeral our realities, which come and go, so we will not *cling to them* in desperation, to create for ourselves, a sense of *self*.

Q : *The negation of all gurus and masters, implicit in the sutra from the Ashtavakra Gita, what would it mean in practical terms?*

A : So long as one is following somebody, whether it is a *guru* or a mentor, without actually thinking and understanding what the *guru* is talking about and what his teaching is, one must be considered to be completely in the dark. If one has begun to think and enquire for himself, the *guru* or the master's teachings may be helpful to a lesser or a greater degree depending on the suitability of that teaching, for the temperament of the individual. In all this journey, since it is fundamentally a journey into the unknown, and nothing but integrity and honesty will work, sometimes one may have to change one kind of teaching because of its unsuitability and change to another spiritual tradition or to another spiritual master in order to continue with the journey more fruitfully and with integrity.

Q : *Is Ramana Maharshi, referring to Parabrahma, when he uses the term, 'other'?*

A : The essence of Ramana Maharishi's teaching is that the *Atma* (our feeling of 'I') is *Parameswara*, the Supreme Being. Usually, we have the implicit impression that the Divine, is not certainly us (as we understand ourselves), but is somehow, something 'other' than us, something mysterious and Infinite, while we consider ourselves finite, as we take ourselves to be the body, etc. Here, the Maharshi, is dispelling this notion which is widely held. He annihilates the distance between ourselves (now as the 'I') and the Divine, and is saying, that the Divine is this mysterious, 'I', only. He is leaving

342

us with this puzzle, which we will then have to take up and solve ourselves, as seekers or *mumukshus*.

He gives guidelines and an exacting teaching, which seekers and his disciples were following. Though a silent sage, by and large; yet, he was no passive *guru*, he was profoundly learned, profoundly humble and an example for the whole world of the highest possible spiritual life that a human being could possibly lead. Not only was the style of life the most austere, even the teaching was the most exalted. It was the same *advaitic* teaching which was given by Adi Sankaracharya, long long ago, but now coming in a new, original way.

14. When *Sakti* Dominates, *Siva* Cannot Shine as Intelligence

So, long as the *chattering bird (Jiva)* is very busy and never falls silent, it can only come up with silly survival solutions, arising from comparison with others, from fear or greed.

When this *chattering bird (Jiva)*, falls silent, *Siva* can shine as intelligence.

Therefore, for the awakening of intelligence, the mad activity of the *chattering bird* must subside.

Acknowledgement : Harish Johari's 'Chakras' and 'Tools for Tantra'. Inner Traditions, India.

Q : *Here Siva & Sakti are shown as two gods, but in human form. Now I would think that the eternal truth or the Divine source, is not a human form at all, so is this mythological representation only an artist's representation of a truth, which our minds may never be able to grasp?*

A   :   Yes, you are right. All Self - Realized teachers have emphasized that the eternal truth cannot be captured by the mind or through words, *'avang-manasa gochara'*, meaning 'not reached by words, by speech *(vak)* and by feelings *(manas)* even. The prefix, 'a' in Sanskrit, serves to negate words, speech and mind and feelings.

Human beings have an innate urge to communicate their discoveries, and this is usually done through speech or song, or writing or through the careful and skillful use of words. And sometimes, the eternal truth can also be communicated through dance form and through various art forms - as in these mythic pictures.

In India, art has always been a kind of handmaiden of religion, whose concern is always with the eternal truth. All the classical arts in India have been religious in spirit and in intention. And art can take a great variety of forms of expression: painting, singing, dancing, drama, and writing - all are forms of art only. Indian classical music and classical dance are religious in spirit. The *sapta swaras* (sa, ri, ga, ma, pa, da, ni) are bound up with the five mnifestations of *Siva*.

When a lot has been sung, spoken and written about the eternal truth, some illumined teachers have also chosen silence as a language, way of living itself, also as a language in which to communicate the eternal truth. *Dakshinamurti* is that manifestation of *Siva* as the silent teacher. Sri Ramana Maharshi also spoke very very little, generally.

Mythology (in the *puranas*) has actually been an independent vehicle for conveying the eternal truth. This anthropomorphic form of *Siva & Sakti* conveys something - not the literal masculine and feminine forms - something completely spiritual - so the mythic picture conveys a *sutra*, an eternal principle of how the timeless *(Siva)* is the 'Power Wielder', whereas the changeful, movement of energy in time and as time is the 'Power' which our senses see. *Sakti* is this Power. In fact, the *Sanskrit* word *Sakti* means energy or power. And *Siva* is the source, behind that Power, but He is unmanifest, invisible - so we can make the fatal mistake of supposing Him to be non-existent - because He is not a sense object, only *Sakti* is the sense object.

Q   :   *In this beautiful picture, we see Sakti in the foreground, looking bright and resplendent and dancing with abandon, ecstasy and freedom. However, in the background, we also see Siva, in a faintly ashen color, but involved with Her in some protective way, just as a mother would be very concerned about her infant. So does this mean that as the Power Wielder, He is Her benevolent master and because of His benevolence, He has granted freedom to Her to do what She likes, and goes with Her wherever She wants to go? Is this understanding right?*

A   :   In fact, *Sakti* is called *Swatantriya Sakti*, meaning independent Power or independent energy and She can keep this independence as long as She wishes, till She has the realization that She is after all, 'only shining in borrowed feathers' and so decides to return Home to *Siva*, Her, beloved master. So there is an extroverted movement for *Sakti* and then following this, there is also an introverted movement of *Sakti* - Her homecoming. We may also think of *Siva* as the Sun and *Sakti* as sunlight.

All our desires, aspirations, cravings, feelings, thinking is the dance of *Sakti*, and in all this, *Siva* is behind the scenes, He is non-interfering and watching as a witness. *So, the dance of Sakti & Siva is happening in our consciousness, within us. It is not a physical romantic or sensual dance.* If *Sakti* is life, *Siva* is 'life of that life'. *Sakti* is becoming, *Siva* is being. *Sakti* is time, *Siva* is timelessness, eternity, death, silence, the beginning and ending of life.

Q : *If this dance of Siva & Sakti is happening in our consciousness, then why is this dance being depicted on a Himalayan terrain?*

A : The floor on which the dance is happening is the Himalayan terrain - this just shows that the dance has transcendental and cosmological origin, mysterious and beyond human comprehension, even though it may be transpiring in the micro-cosmic realm of our limited human consciousness. This dance of *Siva & Sakti* must also be applicable to the cosmos, but in this retreat, we focus on the dance within the human consciousness.

Q : *So, could I conclude that this dance of Siva & Sakti is a metaphor, quite similar to the two birds of the Mundaka Upanishad? Then obviously the watching bird is Siva and the eating bird is Sakti-right?*

A : You have asked two very interesting Qs. Yes, indeed, the dance of *Siva & Sakti* is a metaphor, much like the two 'Tat Tvam Asi' birds. And yes, indeed, it is the witnessing bird that is *Siva*, and the engrossed eating bird is *Sakti*.

Q : *Another intriguing question also comes up. Why do we see so many snakes on Siva's body?*

A : This is a very good question which deserves clarification. The snakes are also metaphors, but not just metaphors too, they represent the mysterious and secret *kundalini* energy in the *chakras* and *nadis*, a power which is awakened only as one approaches and comes closer to *Siva*. You will remember that at the Amrit Desai Yoga Institute at Salt Springs, Florida, we had the opportunity to listen to a seeker, who had all these experiences, exactly as seen in this mythic picture of *Siva & Sakti*. In fact, it is such *kundalini* experiences, which are behind these mystic art forms of *Siva & Sakti*. Such experiences do befall serious seekers, especially when they are doing sustained *sadhana* in an *ashram*.

However, the emphasis in this retreat is not on *kundalini* experiences, because in *Jnana yoga*, the path of understanding, there is no place for *kundalini* experiences, though they may befall some seekers.

15. When *Siva* become dominant....

This is the *Atma* (Pure 'I'). That is, *Siva* has come into dominance ('conscious presence' has become strong). *Prajnya* or intelligence has been awakened. Then, just watching of all inner and outer happenings takes place — but without a 'centre', without a watcher.

Acknowledgement : Harish Johari's 'Chakras' and 'Tools for Tantra'. Inner Traditions, India.

Q : *Sakti in this picture seems to correspond to the Jiva bird, while Siva, naturally to the Atma bird or, the Paramatma bird. The Jiva bird, seems to have voluntarily yielded, to the presence of Siva, and the tejas or glow is the 'conscious presence' of our Atma. Having said all this, will this mythic picture, correspond to the sthitha prajnya, and to one who has settled down as the Atma, rather than as the Jiva?*

A : Yes, this is a portraiture of the *sthitha prajnya's* state where the *Sivatva*, the quality of being *Siva* and the *prajnya are awakened.*

Q : *As this mythic picture stands for the sthitha prajnya, it seems to imply that Sakti or the activity of thought and feeling is greatly diminished in the sthitha prajnya? Or, has it actually come under the control of Siva (Atma)?*

A : *Sakti* becomes obedient and a servant of *Siva*. Previously, She was a virago, disobedient and an authority unto herself and unrecognizing of *Siva*, so long as the *Jiva* was in the consciousness country. In the *sthitha prajnya* state, *Sakti* works receiving mandates from *Siva*. *Siva* gives the inspiration and the goal and *Sakti* executes the same. So there is great harmony between silence and action.

Fifth Day (Chapter - V), 1ˢᵗ 'Tat Tvam Asi' Meditation

Keep on watching *Sakti*, without trying to control Her. Those whose *Sakti* is not troublesome anymore, may close their eyes, and feel who they are, not by thinking, nor by feeling, but by being. If you truly abide in being, this will give a strange feeling, because this is new to you and unfamiliar. You have to digest the fact that, this being is who you actually are. This means giving up the idea that you are the body and so many other concomitant things. Every meditation has a soft and soothing musical background.

----

16. The Caterpillar *(Jiva)* will 'Metamorphose' into the Butterfly *(Atma)*

Acknowledgement :
http://amazingdata.com/the-metamorphosis-of-butterflies/

Sankara: Topic speaks for itself. This is yet another metaphor. The released butterfly is the *Atma*. The gluttony of the caterpillar corresponds to excessive feeding on sensory pleasures in the terrain of *artha and kama*. There is obviously a world of difference between the caterpillar and the butterfly. It is only the butterfly which has freedom, not the caterpillar. Just as the caterpillar *(Jiva)*, has to be 'sacrificed', before the metamprphosis to a butterfly can happen; so too, the *Jiva*, has to learn to die to all its experiences, and must be calmed and silenced, before it can pave the way for the realization, that it is in fact, the *Atma*. Every metaphor, opens a door, gives an insight, and will help us to solve the puzzle of our being the *Atma*.

----

17. Intelligence *(Prajnya)* sourced in *Parabrahma*

1. In people with more *sattva guna* (good, calm and peaceful people), good thinkers, creative people-this intelligence can be seen to be at work, you can verify this. *However it is outward turned, so cannot discover the Divine.*

2. *Prajnya* is that same intelligence, same awareness, but has *turned inwards* and become fascinated with the source of intelligence, *Parabrahma*.

Q : *You have said, some people, the creative ones or the gifted ones, are more intelligent by birth, than the rest of humanity. What is the reason for this inequitable distribution of intelligence?*

A : All human qualities are seen to be inequitably distributed, not just intelligence. Astrologers have a very clear way of ascertaining the intelligence of any individual. The strength of the Su, Ju and VH lord determine intelligence, also two divisional charts, called the *Panchamsha* and the *Vimshamsha*. These determining variables, will be different in different human beings, so intelligence is inequitably distributed.

Q : *When you say, the intelligence of creative people is outward turned, are you meaning that these gifted people are only looking and studying nature, the arts and sciences in one form or other and that they will not have the inclination to turn inwards and gain self-knowledge?*

A : Yes, this is what I mean, when I say that their intelligence is outward turned and engrossed in either in sense objects, or in concepts and formulae, which are pleasing to the intellect *(buddhi)*; or in artistic and musical forms, which is pleasing to our ears and our feeling nature *(manas)*.

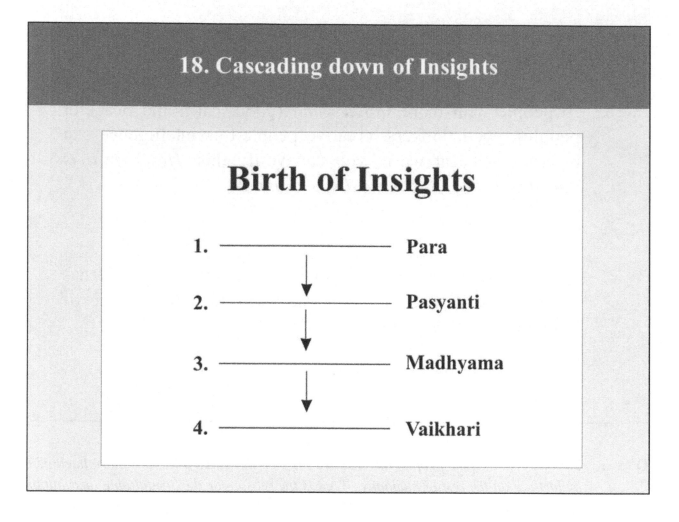

Q : *Are these four stages, the flowing down of insights, from the highest level to the lower level?*

A : Yes, from the *Paramatma* and from, beyond 'I am', down to the spoken word.

Q : *Then, does 'Para' correspond to the Atma?*

A : Here, I must clarify something very important. *Para* is beyond the 'I am ness', because the light by which we see anything in consciousness comes from beyond the 'I am ness'. The light comes through 'I am ness', so *Para* correspond to the *Atma*, which are at the inner most level, and that *Atma* itself is *Parabrahma (Para)*.

Q : *Have you brought in these four stages, just to drive home the point that, Atma, the starting point, is like the 'crown of Siva', from which Ganga water begins its downward journey?*

A : Something like that. If consciousness is kept lucid and clean and relatively bereft of the pollution of *maya*, by abidance in 'I am ness', then when the connection to the *Atma* has happened by abidance therein, this facilitates the flow of intelligence from *Para* (the *Atma*), right down to the spoken word. We think it comes from the mind which is of course utterly wrong, mind being consciousness.

19. *Sthitha Prajnya*, the Awakened One

1. In the Bhagavad Gita, this awakening of intelligence is called *Buddhi yoga*. *Buddhi* here means intelligence, awareness.

2. "One anchored to this intelligence, abandons the effects of both 'good' and 'bad' actions, even in this very life. Therefore persevere for this anchorage to intelligence. *Yoga* is really skill in action (in the day to day life), while anchored to this intelligence, awareness."

Bhagavad Gita: II.50, Buddhi Yukto Jaahatiha....[7]

Q : *Is buddhi the intellect or the intelligence? I am asking this question, because, we learnt on the second day that consciousness, which is the field of the Jiva's inner life, and a field of duality at that, has four essential 'organs', 'ingredients' or 'faculties'. (1) manas, the faculty of feeling, (2) buddhi, the faculty of the intellect, with thinking and analysis as its functions, (3) ahankara, the faculty of egoism or 'self' and finally (4) chitta, the whole 'motion picture'-like flowing movement of consciousness, which creates the illusion of time and memory.*

A : I am glad, you have raised this question and sought this clarification. Yes, in that topic we are using that word as the intellect only. However the same word is also used to point to intelligence in the Sanskrit language, and even in Tamil and Telugu, the languages I speak and know. In Bhagavad Gita, Ch. II, *sloka* 50, *buddhi* means definitely only the *Atmic* intelligence.

Q : *Here too, the stress by Bhagavan Krishna seems to be only on abidance in and as the Atma only, since it is this Atma, which is also the seat of intelligence (prajnya) as well as awareness?*

A : Correct, this is right.

Q : *So, then, being poised in this Atma, as the Atma, in this BG sloka II.50, we are being asked to act, intelligently, is this then the the definition of 'skillful action'?*

A : Yes, skillful action is a consequence of abidance in the *Atma*, which is awareness, as such abidance makes us pay attention to all things.

Q : *This sutra II.50, from the Bhagavad Gita, implies that, while being poised in the Atma, as the Atma, it is also possible to engage in action in the world, for example speak or drive, or answer e-mails, or write. Surely this is very different from being poised in the Atma as the Atma, in a silent meditative state with the eyes closed?*

A : Yes, I am glad, you have raised this very pertinent question, because, engaging in all the day to day activities that you mentioned, calls for greater skill and stability in the abidance in the *Atma*, as the *Atma;* than when you so abide in the *Atma*, with eyes closed. This skill comes with practice, and as thoughts subside and distractions with them; skillful action, while poised in the *Atma* as the *Atma*, will also become a spontaneous and natural thing.

----

20. Being Aware, Paying Attention

1. Have you settled in the 'witness consciousness' (Pure 'I')? Are you discontent to be the ugly *chattering bird (Jiva)* ?

2. This awakening of intelligence, *implies the ending of self-centered activity of the chattering bird (Jiva). Then senses will be awakened! Have you noticed how the senses function now?*

3. Are you sensitive to nature, to trees, to people?

Q : *You speak of the power of discontent, as an important motivating factor, for shifting from the Jiva to the Atma. This discontent can arise, only with acute awareness of the mischief and sorrow of the Jiva, happens, isn't it?*

A : Some topics ago, we were talking of the necessary and sufficient condition, for the 'transformation' from *Jiva* to *Atma*. We had identified a boiling crisis in our outer life as a necessary condition. Now we see that these agonies of discontent, also have the power to act as a sufficient condition for the 'transformation' to the *Atma*.

Q : *The endless involvement in self-centered activities, in one form or other, seems to be going on in the life of the Jiva. This is probably, an inevitable part of our human nature. Don't you think, awareness alone of this condition, can create a discontent and nausea, which may then act as a trigger or a sufficient condition for the transformation to the Atma? And that, when there is a lack of any awareness of the self-centered nature of the Jiva's activities, we will never reach the triggering point of discontent and nausea?*

A : Right, so the beginning of the journey back home is always through an awareness of the limitations and follies of the *Jiva*. One must be fortunate to receive such a direct teaching as to retreat back to the *Atma*. I say this because often various other teachings are prescribed which continue the troubled life of the *Jiva* in the consciousness country, by offering supports in consciousness country itself. So long as one lives in the consciousness country one is prone to duality and conflict. It is natural for the *Jiva* which has suffered so long, to seek asylum in a land where the afflictions coming from duality will not be there.

Q : *You are speaking of something new, the awakening of the senses, you have not spoken about this before. Is this all part of being a sthitha prajnya?*

A : Right, the *sthitha prajnya's* consciousness is calm and silent, he is wide awake. Any input into the senses reaches him and he is amazed by the whole of nature and responds readily to any challenge in life. Smells, sights and sounds, all become very keen and the *sthitha prajnya* delights in these. In this too, there is the mystery of the Divine. As a *Jiva* the senses are all clogged because of too much of cerebral activity and too much of thinking. Not about lofty things, but about all trifles and silly survival concerns.

Q : *And without the awakening of the senses, will there be no sensitivity to nature?*

A : Definitely not. Thus the *Jiva* by definition cannot be sensitive to nature. Then you may ask what about all the nature lovers, who want to take care of the forests and the animal kingdom. They respond in that sensitive fashion because even the *Jiva* has the *Atma* at the very center, but they might not have migrated to the *Atmic* country. People with a strong Sagittarius Asdt and a strong Ju, are known to be lovers of wild life, trees and the whole of nature, but this love of nature and this sensitivity, is sourced in the structure of their destiny, not in having crossed over to the *Atmic* country.

----

21. Tests for the *Sthitha Prajnya*

1. What is the nature of your surrender? Either you can surrender to the Divine, or to *what is*.

2. Without surrender to *what is* (or the Divine), and without realizing the utter futility of the works of the seeking bird *(Jiva)*, you will not come to abide in the *Atma* (conscious presence, pure 'I'), as the *Atma*. Have you come this far?

3. You will be unruffled totally, you will be reborn, *dwija*, 'the twice born'.

Sankara: Seekers and *mumukshus* may be somewhat puzzled by the term surrender - here in a course, which is ostensibly centered, not on *Bhakti yoga*, but rather only on *Jnana yoga*. In traditional *Bhakti yoga*, it is recommended to the *Jiva*, that it must surrender, to the Divine, for securing peace. Though, conceptually, the *Jivas* accept the existence of the Divine, as they have never contemplated on the nature of the Divine, the question, may not even occur to them, as to how, one may surrender, without having a clear idea of the Divine, either conceptually, philosophically or through an experience. Nevertheless, under stress of an obsession or driving desire, *Jivas*, investing their belief and faith in the Divine, whom they have never known, may still surrender to their Divine.

If, one has taken the teachings of the master Sri J. Krishnamurti, and one has not had any exposure to any religion, then a *sthitha prajnya* in the making, may be extremely fortunate to surrender to *what is*, rather than surrender to the Divine. The *Jivas*, are invariably under the delusion that by going on thinking, and 'problem solving', they will succeed in solving their particular problem. As there are a class of problems, which cannot be solved by endless thinking, but rather, only by, the cessation of thinking itself; when a weary *Jiva*, exhausted by too much thinking, consciously gives up its mad thinking activity, then there is peace. This alone is surrender, and the *sthitha prajnya* is thus born. From this point onwards, awareness and *prajnya* start shining, and the life of the *Jiva* comes to an end. Thereafter awareness and *prajnya* direct the life of that *sthitha prajnya*.

22. 'Renunciation' happens for a *Sthitha Prajnya*

1. Renunciation of 'sense of agency'.
   'I have done this', 'I have done that', etc.

2. Renunciation of the 'fruits of all action', performed by the body, by the *Jiva,* etc.

3. Conversely, by renouncing the 'sense of agency' and the 'fruits of action', performed by the body and *Jiva,* you have a good chance of 'rolling back' as the *Atma* (pure 'I'), and it is then that the *sthitha prajnya* is born.

Q : *Even abandoning our sense of agency, such as 'I only did this', 'I only did that', etc., may not be so hard. What seems to be even harder is turning away in our consciousness, from any thinking about the fruits of our actions - whether after we have acted, will we succeed or not, etc. This turning away, implies, that we no longer consider, those things, as defining the 'self', the 'mine' isn't it?*

A : Right, the *sthitha prajnya* has turned away from the fruits of all action, they do not interest him any more. And any questions about the fruits of his actions will seem absurd to him. Because his *self* is not in his actions. It is in his being, as the *Atma.*

Q : *Should not one practice these things in the beginning and gradually we will get success in that practice?*

A : Indeed, this would be part of the right *sadhana*. Unfortunately too much of *sadhana* is on the material plane, in terms of social work, doing good to society, but with consciousness completely polluted and with no peace there. This is no good, when one is oneself in such pain and confusion, to go out and do good to the world, does not seem very sensible. Most often, because we have no proper identity for the *self* and we feel guilty about our wealth and acquisitions, to purge this guilt and to create a better feeling within ourselves, we indulge in all these socially commendable activities.

23. Withdrawal of the Senses

Yoga, meditation, contemplation, observation of *mouna*, fasting, solitude, spiritual retreats – all of these facilitate withdrawal of the senses *(pratyahara)* from their sense objects.
                                                        - Bhagavad Gita II. 58[7]

Q : *This is a very interesting metaphor, in that, one picture depicts, extroversion and the other introversion. By, extroversion, I mean thoughts and feelings are going out as cravings, and by introversion what I mean is that all thought and feeling, which was an outgoing craving before, now subsides and awareness, freed from thought, 'rolls back' to its natural home. In this analogy, should we consider the shell as the*

Atma, and the four limbs as the four organs of consciousness, namely manas, buddhi, ahankara, chitta?

A : You have put it quite correctly, yes this will be one interpretation for this tortoise metaphor. Yes, indeed, the hard shell, may be imagined to be the *Siva Linga*, the *Atma*, and the out going limbs of the tortoise, may be likened to the 'consciousness', which spreads, like a vapor in expansion and diffusion, through thinking and feeling, which calls for an activation of all the four faculties of consciousness. The moment you start thinking and memories rush in, the expansion and diffusion of consciousness starts. This idea of 'consciousness' diffusing and going out of the *Atma* and manifesting as the universe, as a projection is not my idea, it is also used by Sri Ramana Maharshi, and by all *Advaitins*.

Q : *However, the title of this topic, 'withdrawal of the senses', is really calling our attention, not so much to the idea of the shell of the tortoise as the Atma, and the limbs of the tortoise as 'consciousness'; but rather to the limbs of the tortoise being likened to the senses, which go out to the sense objects, or which can be pulled back from the sense objects, back to their natural calmness. Can you go through with this interpretation further, for all to see?*

A : Okay, it is natural for the senses to dart like arrows towards the target, which has to be a sense object. For example, for the sense organs of the eyes, a beautiful face may be a sense object, or for the sense organ of taste (tongue) and the sense organ of sight (yes), the sense object, may be a delicious sweet of which you are always very fond of. The moment the eyes see the sweet, the mouth waters and the hands go forward to take hold of the sweet! This is an example of the limbs of the tortoise going out. For a *sthitha prajnya*, *pratyahara* will happen like this: he will see, being poised in the *Atma*, the sweet, and the first thought, the first surge of wanting to take it, because he sees, the outgoing energy is withdrawn, pulled back, so the hand may not go forward to take the sweet. This will correspond to the limbs of the tortoise, being pulled back from the sense object. In this way, the senses will get trained to retreat from the sense objects, back to the *Atma*. Often, when the *sthitha prajnya* sees the sweet, he may be actually looking at the sweet, and no desire to eat the sweet may arise.

----

24. *Pratyahara* and the *Sthitha Prajnya*

Yadā saṁharate cāyaṁ kūrmo'ṅgānī'va sarvaśaḥ |
Indriyāṇī'ndriy'ārthebhyas tasya prajñā pratiṣṭhitā ||

Bhagavad Gita II.58[7]

Sankara: In the above tortoise metaphor, we learn from the Bhagavad Gita, how we are to understand the *sthitha prajnya*. The *sloka* says, just as the tortoise contracts it's limbs into the shell, in like fashion; if, an individual withdraws his senses from the sense objects; then, in such an individual, the *Atmic* intelligence is well established (i.e., such a one is the *sthitha prajnya*). The classical Hindu texts, like the Bhagavad Gita, or the Upanishads, are the time-tested wisdom of the sages since thousands of years. It therefore becomes mandatory to check our own modern understanding and realization, against the *sutras* from these ancient texts, as these provide the reliable yardsticks, which will sober and humble us.

----

25. 'Consciousness is the Prison, Something External'

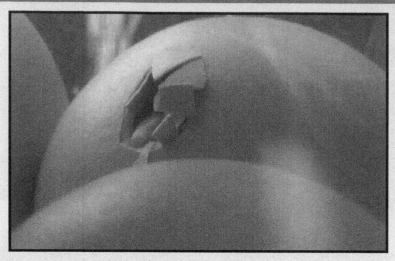

"The egg-shell is 'consciousness', the 'prison' within which all the futile activities of the *Jiva* go on. 'Consciousness' is something which happens to you, something external, alien, superimposed"

- Sri Nisargadatta Maharaj[35]

Q : *Is not the birth of the sthitha prajnya, which is indicated here the same as the Jivahood, getting metamorphosed into Atmahood? So then, the chick, within the prison of the shell is the Jiva? And the chick which has come out is the Atma?*

A : Yes, that is right. All these are just some aids from Maharaj, for you to start thinking for yourself. The *sutra* of Maharaj will startle you, for you have been under the impression that, all that happens in consciousness, happens verily to you, for this is where our prime identity is, as a *Jiva*. However, when, you have 'walked out' of Jivahood, be refusing to struggle, refusing to be rowing the boat of 'becoming', then you come to rest in awareness, as awareness. Then your position is very well 'protected', for then thoughts happening in consciousness country are like rain showers falling on an umbrella, you hear the pitter patter, nothing more, nothing is happening to you!

----

26. "You Cannot Step Out of Consciousness"

- Sri Nisargadatta Maharaj

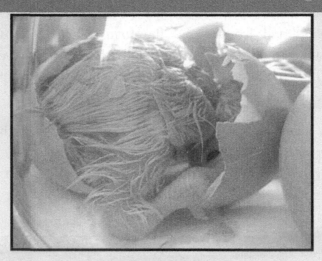

"Then, suddenly, you are free of consciousness, really alone, with nothing to intrude. And that is your true state. Consciousness is an itching rash, that makes you scratch. Of course, you cannot step out of consciousness, for the very idea of stepping out is in consciousness".[35]

Q : *My question is, does this freedom mean, the process of duality which is all pervasive in relationship, 'the, you and the me', has stopped?*

A : After freedom, lies, self-defensive postures, games, conflict, hypocrisies, all of this falls away, only truth, love and intelligence remains, this sweetness comes into relationship too.

Q : *In the previous picture, a crack in the egg shell was seen to begin with, what does this correspond to, in so far as the life of the Jiva is concerned?*

A : It represents a crisis. It starts with the imaginary world of the *Jiva* falling apart.

Q : *When does the egg shell fully and irreversibly crack?*

A : *Jiva*, after endless struggling, realizing the futility of its efforts, says, 'Now, I'll not struggle any more, let anything happen, even I can die, I am not bothered.' Then the activity of the *Jiva* ceases. Which was the agency, which pressed the button of transformation? - It was the *Atma*, the *Atma* superceded the *Jiva* and closed the case. Till this point was reached, the *Atma* as *Siva* had no chance, *maya* or *Sakti* was in control, and She is an independent Power. This marks the chick coming out, the *sthitha prajnya* being born. In Christianity, we have the born again Christians, who, I guess, may have all gone through a similar process.

Please note that the chick which has gained freedom, is not the *Atma, per se* which is anyhow birthless, and deathless, but the *Atma* which was drowned and submerged in the consciousness country - this is freed and the *sthitha prajnya* is this freed awareness or *Atma*. The imprisoned *Jiva,* which has now metamorphosed into the *sthitha prajnya,* is the liberated chick.

The *Jiva* has many identities, all are false selves only, so they are called *anatmas*. The *sthitha prajnya* has the *Atma* as his true Self (witness, awareness), though for functional purposes, the *self* or *Jiva* may appear to be there for eating, communicating, driving, for transacting the day to day affairs.

27. "Consciousness is a Kind of Fever"

"But if you learn to look at your consciousness as a kind of fever, personal and private in which you are enclosed like a chick in a shell, out of this very attitude will come the crisis which will break the shell."
                                            - Sri Nisargadatta Maharaj[35]

Sankara: This is just another metaphor, illustrating a transformation from imprisonment in consciousness to freedom (awareness). Maharaj has put it in an easy and original way. For most people, for the whole of humanity in fact, this fever lasts an entire life time and yet, no one actually seems to realize that it is a fever and the maximum effort may be only to reduce the fever a little bit, by taking some suitable medicines! None seem to aspire to eradicate the fever, once and for all. J. Krishnamurti, probably wondering at this human condition, is known from very reliable private sources, to have said in intimate conversations: "What a strange world, what a strange world".

28. 'The Act of Negation' of the *Sthitha Prajnya*

Prajahāti yadā kāmān sarvān Pārtha mano-gatān |
ātmany evātmanā tuṣṭaḥ sthita-prajñas tado' cyate||

Bhagavad Gita II.55[7]

"When a man completely negates, O Partha, all the desires in his consciousness and is contented by his Self, abiding in itself, then in such a one it is said that the '*Atmic* intelligence' has been awakened."

Q : *We can negate something perceived in consciousness, only when you have 'died' to a certain old nagging experience or old craving or addiction. Then, when that thought, repeatedly comes again, it may be easy to negate it. But what will happen, if an old addiction or tendency in thought, comes upon us in consciousness and it is strong?*

A : Then we may have to yield to it if it is too strong or, if you are poised in the *Atma* we may be completely unperturbed and we will not even respond to this sensory call.

Q : *Then, can we say that, nothing in the field of consciousness, which is the field of duality, has any more attraction for us. Is then, the negation of new sensory calls also possible?*

A : It depends on the individual - but we should not forget the warning given by *Navaneetha Kaivalyam* that even *Jivanmuktas* may be caught unaware by *maya* and may trip and fall.

Q : *Does the state of the sthitha prajnya imply that he is at peace, when in solitude, rather than being bored?*

A : Oh my God! Boredom does not exist in the dictionary of *sthitha prajnya* and he does not know what this boredom is at all.

Q : *This sutra also throws up a very important question and I am asking it, as you have emphasized, negation here. Krishna Paramatma is saying, 'when a man completely negates, all the desires in consciousness... does this not throw up the following situation?*

Either we may have undertaken a responsibility, a professional or educational responsibility, or a family or even a social responsibility; or we may have been willy nilly pushed into such a painful responsibility, by social and traditional pressures and then plunging into it in the beginning and enjoying it, we soon come to realize how it has killed off our soul, so we are exhausted, then the negation would also mean throwing away such a self-imposed or society-imposed burden on ourselves, which means we negate it and end that chapter of our life?

A : Something, you have voluntarily undertaken or something society has dumped on you, becomes a huge burden, then what happens generally is that you delay throwing off the burden, because of fear, absence of a right teaching in your life, because of mental laziness, because in your foolishness, you are looking for certainty of the future, which never exists. Then, if the right teaching is there to guide you, you will have to negate such a life and such a burden, not for pleasing others, but for bringing peace to the *Jiva*, which longs for this peace. *All this is, not only negation, but awakening of the Jiva to its sorrow.*

----

29. The *Vasanas* of the *Sthitha Prajnya*

Viṣayā vinivartante nirāhārasya dehinaḥ |
rasa-varjaṁ raso' py asya paraṁ dṛṣṭvā nivartate ||

Bhagavad Gita II.59[7]

"The sense-objects 'drop off' from the embodied soul, who has come on the path of austerity, where the sense objects are concerned, leaving only the 'taste' for them still lingering; but even this lingering taste also wanes away, after the embodied soul, having actually 'seen' the Divine."

Q : *What are Vasanas?*

A : *Vasana* means fragrance. Say fragrance of a flower, or of a perfume or of some nice food which is being freshly cooked. Think of you getting the fragrance of lilies or jasmine or of roses, but you never see any of these flowers anywhere around you, this would be an example of a *vasana*. Sometimes people have various desires, various attractions to various kinds of activities or studies and no one knows why these attractions exist. Sometimes it may be an aversion and not always an attraction. When such attractions and aversions exist with unidentifiable causes, these are *vasanas* from past life or from early childhood.

Q : *If a residue, or vasana is left lingering, without being completely scorched, then is there certainly the possibility of that temptation coming again?*

A : Yes, ofcourse.

Q : *How does the sthitha prajnya deal with these vasanas?*

A   :   He will deal with these *vasanas* in an unperturbed way, he will not be disturbed. Sometimes he may even gracefully yield to those *vasanas*, if they exert too powerful a pull on him.

30. *Sthitha Prajnya's* Integrity

The *sthitha prajnya*, has heightened sensitivity, full of deep feeling for nature. He has no conflict, no suffering in any relationship. He will be learning all the time.

The *sthitha prajnya* is obviously one who has awakened senses (because the *Jiva* has fallen silent). He is highly sensitive, as his *Atmic* intelligence, deals with all problems in relationship, and not through the 'bag of tricks, lies and manipulations', with which, the *Jiva*, was attempting to resolve all human problems, previously. The *Jiva* was only surviving, after having compromised integrity. *The sthitha prajnya's power is not only his prajnya, but also his integrity: alignment of thought, word and deed.*

Q   :   *Does it mean that, for the sthitha prajna, all problems in relationship are resolved, once and for all?*

A   :   Absolutely! This does not mean that he may not quarrel or he may not shout at anybody. The *Jiva's* will be displeased with my answer, because in their thinking the *sthitha prajnya* has to be perfect and immaculate!

Q   :   *All the old bag of tricks, lies, manipulations, and ulterior motives are gone for ever?*

A   :   Lies, tricks, ulterior motives and manipulations are unknown to this *sthitha prajnya*. This is not his country, he is utterly innocent, and awakened.

Q   :   *The sthitha prajnya is never a survivor? Even though the Jiva could have lived a life of survival?*

A : The *sthitha prajnya* never survives. He has no need for it, because the thought of the future will never come to him. Past and future are burnt and buried, hence he is joyous *(ananda)*. Even if there is pressing economic crisis, he will face up to it courageously, will eat less, if that is necessary.

Q : *You are placing great importance on the integrity of the sthitha prajnya, and seem to recognize this as a very potent power - this integrity?*

A : We are unaware of the power of integrity. There are certainly people in the world, even *Jivas* who have integrity and because they have integrity, they are connected to the Divine, much more than the others. But they know it not. They have a ridiculous idea of the Divine, that it is Mount Kailash and as big as the galaxies. They do not know that it is as small and as anonymous as their awareness, their *Atma*. Those who have integrity, even as the *Jiva,* their lives will be special. Because the power of the Divine will come through in their lives. They will walk with theirs heads held high and they know no fear.

Q : *Coming back to the calmness, silence and intelligence of the sthitha prajnya, are we to suppose then, that being a sthitha prajnya, is indeed the only durable solution, for all the miseries in life?*

A : Of course! All other solutions are silly or short lived. You correct a problem and you think you have solved it, no sooner another problem will start and there is no end to these piece meal solutions.

----

31. How a *Sthitha Prajnya* Responds to Desires

Āpūryamāṇam acala-pratiṣṭhaṁ
    samudram āpaḥ praviśanti yadvat |
Tadvat kāmā yaṁ praviśanti sarve
    sa śāntim āpnoti na kāma-kāmī ||

Bhagavad Gita II.70[7]

"He into whom, all desires enter, even like the ocean, that is ever being filled by the rivers, but still remains steady and unperturbed within its bounds; such a person attains peace, not he who runs madly after his desires."

Q : *So, while the sthitha prajnya is generally unperturbed, is it possible that he may also respond to desires, accepting them, like Jivas?*

A : Yes. He may yield to a desire if it is strong enough, but he will not fight with it. He will not practice virtue, never. He is nevertheless virtuous!

How a *Sthitha Prajnya* Responds to Desires - Illustration

Sankara: One thing is for sure, the current of desire will come slowly into the vast ocean of the *Atma*, in the case of the *sthitha prajnya*. He will not be excited or depressed, like breeze coming in through one window and going out through the other, these desires may breeze in and may also bereeze out-he has nothing to do with them and normally will not at all interfere with their flow. In this way, his peace and *prajnya* will remain completely unruffled, much like the ocean not being ruffled, as rivers flow into it. This is the meaning of the Bhagavad Gita *sutra* in topic 31, above.

----

32. *Sthitha Prajnya's Vasanas*

"*Vasanas* which do not obstruct Self-Realization remain after Self-Realization. In *Yoga Vasishtha*, two classes of *vasanas* are distinguished; those of enjoyment and those of bondage. The former remain even after *mukti* is attained, but the latter are destroyed by it. Attachment is the cause of binding *vasanas*, but enjoyment without attachment does not bind and continues even after *sahaja (mukti)*."

- Sri Ramana Maharshi [36]

Q : *Vasanas of enjoyment, I do understand, like the enjoyment in eating, drinking, playing sports, sexual enjoyment, playing cards, swimming, reading, cycling. What are vasanas of bondage?*

A : Attachment in relationship to wife, son, daughter, parents. Attachment to name and fame, wealth, status, to property, these are *vasanas* of bondage. These *vasanas* formerly had given to the *Jiva*, a sense of *self*, which of course was false. In the *sthitha prajnya*, these *vasanas* get burnt, or rather have no 'resting place', since he has 'vacated' 'the whole field of consciousness', and lives in awareness or the *Atmic* country.

Q : *Can you give an example of a master, who was Self - Realized, and yet had a kind of habit, which continued even after Self - Realization.*

A : Many examples are available to illustrate this principle given by Bhagavan Sri Ramana Maharshi. Sri Nisargadatta Maharaj, used to smoke and that habit continued, even after Self - Realization. Likewise his *guru* was also Self - Realized,

Sri Siddha Rameshwar Maharaj also used to smoke, after Self - Realization. Sri Shirdi Baba, also used to smoke the hookah, after his early Realization.

Fifth Day (Chapter -V), 2ⁿᵈ 'Tat Tvam Asi' Meditation

By Being the Atma,
The Awakening of Intelligence *(Prajnya), happens*

Chapter VI

By Being the Atma,
You discover *Parabrahma* (the unmanifest Divine)
and His 'All Merciful' nature (He is *Karunakara*)

Note : Some topics in this Chapter are also there in the Chapters III and IV

Topic 3   = Topic 21, Ch. IV;
Topic 8   = Topic 34, Ch. III;
Topic I 4 = Topic 22, Ch. IV;
Topic I 7 = Topic 25, Ch. IV.

1. Journey beyond Belief and Faith

1. Belief and faith in the Divine are two ways of relating to the Divine, in our state of individuality, ignorance, as the chattering bird, i.e., as the *Jiva*. This may be alright for a 'beginning', but this lacks depth, clarity, commitment and seeking of the complete truth of the Divine.

2. Even people of faith do not know: Who is the Divine, what is the Divine, where is the Divine?

3. We can answer the second point only when we become a *sthitha prajnya*, i.e., when intelligence *(prajnya)* is awakened.

Q : *The first point is very interesting. Does it show us that there is a religion and a God for the Jiva state of humanity and another religion and God for the sthitha prajnya or the Atma state of humanity?*

A : Yes, of course, though you will not find it as clearly stated as here. The *Jivas* are afflicted by fears and desires and they need a sheet anchor to give them security which the *Jivas* think, is necessary. The *sthitha prajnya* has no such fears and insecurities, even if desires come, he does not feel an ownership over them. So whether they are fulfilled or not, he really cares not. So, these *sthitha prajnyas* certainly, for this very reason, do not have a desperate dependence on the *guru* and the personal God, which are the customary refuges of the *Jivas*.

Q : *And from the point of view of the sthitha prajnya, the religion and God of the Jiva - are they insufficient, for him? Is it implied that he needs a more robust, more profound religion and God, which he can cherish and reconcile with his Atmic state?*

A : Yes. This is why the teachings of masters like Ramana Maharshi, J.Krishnamurti and Nisaragadatta Maharaj are entirely different from the teachings of other masters who

374

offer nothing more than a comforting solace in the field of duality, the field in which the *Jivas* live and function.

Q : *Then are you implying that the teachings in this retreat, belong to the sthitha prajnya category?*

A : I'll never assert anything, make no claim, for such a stand will be so immature. It is for you to enquire and find out. If I give you an answer, all of you, if you repose your faith in me and are following all that I am saying closely, you will probably start clinging to that answer, because, you may consider that to be the truth. My intention is to provoke and disturb you, because I see that, you have got stuck at the milestone of faith and there you have gone to sleep. Why did this stupor overcome you? Only because probably, you are not a true seeker-you were merely searching for security, which most masters are providing for their followers. My purpose is to make you think and make you discover, so that eventually, you will be your own teacher-constantly learning from all your failings and the failings of the people whom you are observing.

Q : *And because prajnya is not awakened in the Jivas, there cannot be the question of discovery of the Divine? It has only to be a matter of belief or faith?*

A : Belief and faith are enough for the *Jivas* because they will not ask questions. All their questions pertain to their fears and desires. They will never ask fundamental questions about the Divine. Because they are not infact seekers of the Divine, they have turned to the Divine because of their helplessness and only because they have the impression that when the refuge is sought in the Divine, the Divine will protect. By contrast the *sthitha prajnya* will give his life for the truth and for the union with the Divine.

Q : *Would you go with me when I say, that Hindu Advaita and Buddhism, are religions, which require prajnya, for the understanding of what they offer by way of religion?*

A : Certainly, this is the truth. Once Ramana Maharshi was asked, 'For whom is his path of *Atmic* enquiry intended?' He replied saying, 'It was for noble and mature souls'.

----

2. The *Sthitha Prajnya* is also Vulnerable to *Maya*

The *sthitha prajnya* is poised in the 'witness consciousness', the 'I am ness', the *Atma* as awareness, but because of sensory distractions *(maya)*, that are always there for an embodied *Atma*, the *sthitha prajnya* has to do some additional *sadhana* to 'shut down' the *Jiva's (self's)* activities. Once this is done, the *sthitha prajnya* is well-established in the witness consciousness. However, without *pratyahara*, detachment, and dedication to the goal, the *sthitha prajnya* will not become well-established.

Q : *The Jiva was always in the field of consciousness, which is the field of 'you and me', i.e., the field of duality. In such a field, the Jiva has the possibility of becoming a prey to maya, more easily. What about the sthitha prajnya, whom, we thought, had basically 'crossed over' to the blessed Atmic country - is he too prone again to this madness of maya?*

A : As the *sthitha prajnya* has 'crossed over' from the consciousness country to the awareness country; i.e., from the field of duality (consciousness) to the other field of non-duality (awareness), he cannot be as badly influenced by *maya*, as when he was still only a *Jiva*. Nevertheless, since he is not a pure timeless *Atma*, but an *Atma*, with a bodily association ('dehin', or embodied soul), he has to, so to speak, also 'pay a price' for having a body as a 'vehicle'. So when some old *vasana* of the *sthitha prajnya* come back, they may cast a spell on him, though not as badly as they did, in his former existence as a *Jiva*.

With more *sadhana* however, the *sthitha prajnya*, will be able to beautifully stabilize in the *Atma*, as the *Atma*, without succumbing too much to sensory calls from the consciousness country, which is, in a manner of speaking, a neighbouring country.

Q : *Then, after crossing over from consciousness to awareness, do you mean to say, there is more dedication to the spiritual life that is called for, something even, which the sthitha prajnya has to do, as a way of life?*

A : Wonderfully pertinent question. The *sthitha prajnya*, will be what J. Krishnamurti had once described, as 'a guest living in a stranger's house' - that is how, he is likely to conduct himself, as he walks and talks in his earthly life, loving, but never, never expecting anything in return. There will be a new way of life for the *sthitha prajnya*, something that will go on, throughout his life. And there may also be other times, when the *sthitha prajnya* must retreat from worldly life (in which the senses will always trouble us), and go into meditation for a week, fortnight or a month at a stretch. So, the life of the *sthitha prajnya*, is, in one sense profound, endless and mysterious.

3. *Atma* must 'Withdraw It's Investment'

1. *Atma's* nature is *ananda* (causeless joy), *chit* (witnessing awareness, *prajnya*) and *sat* (truth - awareness - joy in being).

2. 'Finding the body to be a source of pleasure (which 'seems somewhat akin to *ananda*)', the *Atma* has come to 'make an investment in this bank (of the body)'.

3. Because, eventually, there is too much pain and loss in this 'investment', *Atma* must now 'pull back the investment'.

4. Learning and detachment will enable this 'withdrawal of the investment'. Result will be intelligence, joy, permanent end of suffering.

Q : *Let us first understand, the nature of the Atma, which seems to be outside time and space. We can accept that this is joy or ananda, also accept that awareness and prajnya as chit, but what exactly is sat? Is 'sat' a short form for satya?*

A : *'Sat'* is truth and existence, which refers to the *Atma*, which is one with *Brahman*. It cannot be understood unless one has fully taken his being as the *Atma*. It is incorruptible and beyond time, we have dealt with these strange qualities of the *Atma* in this retreat before. *'Sat'* stands for all of these mysterious excellences.

Q : *Considering the fact it was the Atma only which consented to incarnate as the Jiva with a body, etc., how do you now say that the Atma must 'withdraw its investment'?*

A : In this partnership between the *Atma* and *Sakti*, *Sakti* took the form of the body, along with the consciousness, subject to duality, namely *maya*. In this partnership when the *Atma* incarnated, *Sakti* had the lead role, she was dominant, while *Atma (Siva)* was the 'sleeping partner'. Scriptures use the very apt terminology, Power *(Sakti)* and Power-Wielder *(Siva, Atma)*. As the *Atma*, though behind the scenes, is the Power Wielder, It can get disgusted, because the pain, coming along with the body and earthly life, surpasses the pleasure eventually, so the *Atma* certainly wants to withdraw the intimate association with *Sakti*. Dissolving the partnership with *Sakti*, which would mean death, would of course be an extreme step. If dissolution is ruled out, the next best choice for the *Atma* would be to recover its own lost ground. The *sthitha prajnya* is one in whom the *Atmic* ground is recovered, as far as is possible, without dissolving the partnership.

Q : *You are saying that the more clearly one understands this whole process, the more whole heartedly, one can plunge into the sadhana, is this it?*

A : Of course we have been harping on that a hundred times that understanding holds the key and it is not as mysterious as it has unfortunately come to be perceived - because you are already the owner of the wealth and infact you are that wealth itself. So conviction is of paramount importance, nothing beyond conviction, because you are already 'That'. The moment you are prepared to swear that you are 'That', no body needs to recognize you and you need no recognition. Recognition is only necessary for the *Jiva* and not for the *sthitha prajnya*.

Q : *So fruits of the withdrawal are ananda, intelligence, end to suffering?*

A : Yes, this is a signal victory, this settling in awareness and being detached, more cannot be asked for, as the partnership is still in place.

----

4. Understanding without Detachment is Worthless

"As gold unrefined does not shine, so the understanding of an immature man attached to the world does not shine forth."

-**Vishnu Sahasranama**

So, the *sthitha prajnya*, must cultivate detachment. For some this is a blessing at birth itself, for others, it must be sought after, cultivated. The petty *Jiva (self)*, may be scared by the word, detachment!

Q : *Why is attachment so notorious an obstacle, coming in the way of liberation of the Jivatma?*

A : It is attachment to body, people, food, status, wealth, name and fame and all the pleasures of life, which has basically landed the *Jiva* in this terrible mess of sorrow. So, if we are to reverse this malady, we must, must we not, withdraw the causes, which produced the malady in the first instance? The cause is attraction and attachment to all these things, so we have to negate these supports. But as these were intensely enjoyed by the *Jiva,* in the *artha and kama* spheres, we must give some time, say up to 60 or 65 years, then as the body wears out, attachment will also turn into its very opposite, namely detachment - because, all those things which *Jiva* loved, those very things will turn out to be the cause of pain.

Because, some detachment is also good in the younger years, we may enjoin some spiritual detachment, keeping the individual's spiritual welfare in later years in mind. What is detachment in all this? Attachment is preoccupation in thought and feeling with those sense objects, to which you may be attached. For example if a mother is attached to her daughter, or a father to his son, then, the mother or father will all the time be thinking about the child, because they consider that child as part of the *self*.

When, you disconnect with the son or daughter, through wisdom, then the useless thinking and feeling will stop and you will have peace - this is detachment.

5. Incomprehensible Ways of the *Parabrahma*

1. In the case of Ramana Maharshi, he was not even a seeker, yet the *Parabrahma* stripped off *maya* from the *Jiva* in a single Divine 'swoop', and he suddenly realized he is the Self *(Atma)*. The old identity of the *self* as the body *(Jiva)* disappeared. This miraculous happening in the Sri Ramana Maharshi's own words is reproduced in the commentary.

2. We are not so fortunate, so have to systematically 'seek and find'. Million paths for million seekers. Never compare with other seekers, as you are unique.

The *moksha* of Sri Ramana Maharshi is described in his own words:

"It was in 1896, about 6 weeks before I left Madurai for good (to go to Tiruvannamalai - *Arunachala*) that this great change in my life took place. I was sitting alone in a room on the first floor of my uncle's house. I seldom had any sickness and on that day there was nothing wrong with my health, *but a sudden violent fear of death overtook me*. There was nothing in my state of health to account for it nor was there any urge in me to find out whether there was any reason for the fear. *I just felt I was going to die* and began thinking what to do about it. It did not occur to me to consult a doctor or any elders or friends. I felt I had to solve the problem myself then and there.

"The shock of the fear of death drove my mind inwards and I said to myself mentally, without actually framing the words: 'Now death has come; what does it mean? What is it that is dying? This body dies.' And at once I dramatized the occurrence of death. I lay with my limbs stretched out still as though *rigor mortis* has set in, and imitated a corpse so as to give greater reality to the enquiry. I held my breath and kept my lips tightly closed so that no sound could escape, and that neither the word 'I' nor any word could be uttered. 'Well then', I said to myself, 'this body is dead. It will be carried stiff to the burning ground and there burnt and reduced to ashes. But with the death of the body, am I dead? Is the body I? It is silent and inert, but I feel the full force of my personality and even the voice of I within me, apart from it. So I am the Spirit transcending the body. The body dies but the Spirit transcending it cannot be touched by death. *That means I am the deathless Spirit.*

"All this was not dull thought; it flashed through me vividly as living truth which I perceived directly almost without thought process. 'I' was something real, the only real thing about my present state, and all the conscious activity connected with the body was centered on that 'I'. *From that moment onwards, the 'I' or Self, focused attention on itself by a powerful fascination.* Fear of death vanished once and for all. The ego was lost in the flood of Self-awareness. Absorption in the Self continued unbroken from that time. Other thoughts might come and go like the various notes of music, but the 'I' continued like the fundamental *sruti* note ['that which is heard' i.e., the Vedas and Upanishads] a note which underlies and blends with all other notes.

"In the vision of death, though all the senses were benumbed, the *Aham sphurana* (Self-awareness) was clearly evident, and so I realized that it was that awareness that we call 'I', and not the body. This Self-awareness never decays. It is unrelated to anything. It is Self-luminous. Even if this body is burnt, it will not be affected. Hence, I realized on that very day so clearly that, that was 'I'." [12]

Q : *From the case of Ramana Maharshi, it is obvious, that moksha came unexpectedly and suddenly, uninvited. You have explained on the very first day, that the time for moksha is only after 60 or 65, when the body is weakened and when maya is also weakened. So, your main point seems to be that it can happen in a million different ways, and at different time frames and that we should never compare ourselves with others, since each of us is unique?*

A : Yes, this realization of our uniqueness is of paramount importance. Usually, by comparing ourselves with others, we become jealous, miserable creatures. For example, consider what Krishnamurti is saying: 'Thought in its attempts to be honest, is comparative and therefore dishonest.' By comparing ourselves with others, we also fail to look at ourselves. In other words, this comparison, blocks *self* - Knowing and as *self* - Knowing is the door through which we may enter the awareness country, all such comparison will ensure that we remain only mediocres, in the consciousness country.

Q : *You have brought in this realization of the Maharshi, which is clearly an understanding, rather than an experience and secondly, you may have introduced this in this retreat, as we have a pilgrimage to Tiruvannamalai, the Maharshi's ashram. Is there more to it?*

A : Yes. It is my perception that after Adi Sankaracharya, the next great teacher of the same *Advaitic* truth is Sri Ramana Maharishi. In many of the Upanishads it is said that without austerity and the pursuit of truth, you cannot get this. The Maharishi is a brilliant shining example of this Upanishadic verdict. It is recommended to all seekers that every day they should read atleast one or two pages of what the Maharshi has written or what Maharshi has translated from the ancient Hindu scriptures, if they have indeed matured as *mumukshus.*

6. Who, Where, What is the Divine?

1. Distinguish between the idols of gods in the temples, human beings, saints, the gurus, various sacred objects, like pictures *(sri murtis)* of the Divine; and the unknowable Divine. You have taken the former to be the Divine, that has been your faith. At best these are pointers only.

2. Man has made 'toy models' of the Divine. The Divine is always in the realm of the unmanifest, unknowable, beyond the senses and your consciousness. *But, you as the Self (Atma), can travel beyond faith, and actually discover the unmanifest Divine (Parabrahma).*

3. Who, where and what is this Divine? Find out.

Q : *Am I right in inferring that your drawing our attention to the sharp distinction between, so many 'forms of God' (Like vigrahas in temples, forms of masters, saints, sages, sacred objects, like Kailash, sacred symbols, etc.) and the unmanifest absolute aspect of the Divine, is only to drive home the important point that the former forms* *are all 'sensory objects' only, whereas the unmanifest Divine alone is the true aspect of the unknowable Divine, with which we are one - though we may not know this, because of maya?*

A : As we have said elsewhere, the Hindu religion, or for that matter any other religion must always be in two tiers. The lower tier caters to the needs and appetites of the *Jivas*. Whereas the upper tier caters to the further journey of the *sthitha prajnyas*. Adi Sankaracharya first cast Hinduism in this two tier format. In other religions also, there is an esoteric aspect of that religion, meant for very evolved and noble souls and that upper tier is this esoteric aspect of that religion. Every religion must have such a two fold teaching.

Q : *You have emphasized that man as sthitha prajnya, can indeed come upon the Divine as the unmanifest Parabrahma and are you implying that this discovery is impossible for the Jiva, even when he is an apostle of faith?*

A : Impossible, yes, because faith will not get you here. Faith may be innate, Divine-given, as seen in the Horoscope, or faith may be materialistic, based on desires and fears of the *Jiva*. We must also examine to see if it is the *Jiva*, which has faith, or if it is the *sthitha prajnya*, who has faith. We have to suspect the *Jiva's* faith, because the *Jiva* is after all only an inhabitant in the consciousness country.

Q : *So, how do we start on this treasure hunt? First of all, must we not have an intense yearning for this, even before we start?*

A : Intense yearning is very important. Without it how will you get going? Initially the seeking will be outward turned and then will come a critical point in the journey when it will dramatically turn inward. Without the journey turning inwards, there is no hope of discovery of the *Atma* and 'That'.

---

7. Antidote for *Maya*

"Checked by incantations *(sthambhana)*, fire will not scorch. Likewise, defective realization will not put an end to bondage. Therefore devote yourself to hearing the truth *(sravana)*, clear contemplation *(manana)* and meditation *(nidhidhyasana* – abidance in the *Atma)* and root out ignorance, uncertainty and wrong knowledge."

- *'Kaivalya Navaneetham'* [24]

Q : *Why are you flashing this topic, out of context, when we should be hearing more about the discovery of the Divine?*

A : All is not perfect in our life, sometimes even the teacher will be capricious, so this topic has come here. It warns us about the pitfalls entailed in the discovery of the Divine. It tells us that we must be diligent in the study of the scriptures, which for Hindus, are the Bhagavad Gita, Upanishads and *Brahma Sutras*, or we must study closely the Self - Realized masters, for without such study, we have no right foundation for the discovery of the Divine.

Q : *Discovery of the Divine, what are the traditional qualifications for going on this journey of discovery?*

A : The tradition gives so many pre-requisites and I refrained from giving the full list only because I did not want to sound discouraging. Among the qualifications, the capacity to suffer the suffering that the destiny has given us, the capacity to trust the teacher, to have faith in him, the willingness and the yearning to control the senses and to turn inward, the importance of respecting every form of life and being careful in thought, word and deed, not give too much importance to success and be drunk on that, not to be gullible but to enquire - all of these are pre-requsites. You need not be discouraged that you may not have some of them. *One has to be patient and the greatest consolation for you is that already you are in the final destination (Atma), though you may not know this truth.*

8. *Sakti 'Dominating' Siva*

Kali dancing on Siva *(Modern Period)*

Sutra on the spiritual fall

Yatato hy api Kaunteya
puruṣasya vipaścitaḥ |
Indriyāṇi pramāthīni haranti
prasabhaṁ manaḥ ||

- Bhagavad Gita II.60[7]

The turbulent senses, will even violently hijack and eclipse the true Self -even in the case of a *mumukshu* who is very perceptive and persistent.

Acknowledgement: 'Myths and Symbols in Indian Art and Civilization', Plate 69, Heinrich Zimmer, Bollingen Series / Princeton, 1972

Q : *We are supposed to be on the path of discovery of the Divine, in its unmanifest aspect. You called this Parabrahma. You only clarified that this would be possible only for the sthitha prajnya, and not for the Jivas. How does the sthitha prajnya come upon the Divine-should you not be telling us about this, rather than digressing in matters of how people have spiritual falls? May be after clarifying my point, we can take up this present topic?*

A : The *sthitha prajnya* is a very keen observer of his life both inner and outer, like a good experimental scientist. His laboratory is his inner and outer life. If he had the distractions of thought and the pulls of the senses, he would never have had this attentive nature which is so characteristic of him. Miraculous happenings will come to pass in his life and they will be correlated with his aspirations. While millions of human beings miss the correlation and the connection between the happening in their life and their own aspirations; the *sthitha prajnya* because of his unwavering awareness, picks up this correlation exactly like a scientist who makes a discovery in his laboratory. To come upon this Truth, one must be very silent inwardly and the *sthitha prajnya* is such an inwardly silent human being. So he is qualified to make this discovery. The *Jiva* on the other hand is inattentive and first of all he has no quest of the Divine, so he is not even in the 'race', so to speak.

Q : *In this very perplexing picture, are we seeing a powerful rajasic Sakti, dominating Siva, the awareness? What would be the consequence of this?*

A : The picture itself actually conveys to us what the consequence will be and you can see that *Sakti* is like a virago, quite wild and unrelenting and has completely subdued and eclipsed *Siva* who stands for awareness, and the timeless aspect of consciousness, namely the *Atma*. Now when this kind of a situation arises in consciousness whereby *Siva* or the *Atma* is eclipsed, then the *Jiva* in question will also have no awareness either and instead, the *Jiva* will exist only in the becoming mode, that is, as an entity in *Sakti* only, which will be either excessively *rajasic* or excessively *tamasic*.

If it is excessively *rajasic*, then the *Jiva* will be over active, over aggressive and too much in a *becoming mode* and if it is excessively *tamasic*, then the *Jiva* will be extremely physically and mentally indolent, lethargic, insensitive and prone to inaction and postponing things. In other words, the *Jiva* will not have enough energy to act. So he will be more deadened and unresponsive like a stone, so in that condition too, awareness is eclipsed. So these are the consequences when *Sakti* is wild and untamed.

Q : *When this kind of a situation happens in consciousness, that rajas or tamas is too strong, we have seen in the previous topic, obstacles hindering the choiceless awareness of what is, that one has no awareness to observe what is, isn't it? And then, is the Bhagavad Gita sutra telling us, that under these conditions, even wise beings will be carried away and enslaved by sensory impressions?*

A : Yes. When *Sakti* is so wild and stronger than *Siva*, then *Siva* inevitably gets eclipsed. Then the *rajas* or *tamas* will be so strong that *Siva* who is even beyond *sattva* and *trigunatitha* (i.e., beyond the three gunas), becomes inaccessible. Then *Siva* has no chance to kind of come into relief. *Under such circumstances, Sakti who is working through the senses and working through thoughts and feelings at a frenetic pace will do what she likes and that could be pursuit of pleasure or some other aggressive kind of thing or some other very malefic kind of things like some criminal activity and so on.* In that case the individual, whose essential nature is the *Atma* will have no discriminatory power, will have no awareness and will just become a victim of the *rajasic or tamasic Sakti*.

The Bhagavad Gita *sutra* actually says that when this *Sakti* is so strong, then automatically the senses also will be so strong and then the senses will actually enslave the awareness and will hijack the awareness and the *Jiva* will have a spiritual fall. The *sutra* says that this kind of a spiritual fall can happen even to evolved souls, who are *sthitha prajnyas*, who are very ardent in the spiritual path, and who are persevering steadily on the path, those who are much disciplined - even they can be occasionally hijacked by these turbulent senses.

Now we must not be so surprised by this phenomenon. We just need to look at the eclipses which the luminaries face in each passing year of time when the Sun undergoes a solar eclipse and the Moon undergoes the lunar eclipse and this is in the nature of things itself. But given a little bit of time, the eclipsed and darkened luminaries, the Sun and the Moon, do recover from the eclipses and they do regain their old brightness and old glory and their capacity to guide humanity is fully regained. *Just as the eclipses happen, similarly even sages and sthitha prajnyas may momentarily slip and fall by the temptations that the senses offer to them. But then if they have indeed stabilized in wisdom, they will quickly get up from the fall and they will go about their old serious approach in pursuit of the Divine and the truth.*

Q : *You are speaking of turbulent senses. Do you mean to say, the senses will be wild and turbulent, only when Sakti is turbulent?*

A : We have got to understand the consequences of *Sakti* being turbulent. When *Sakti* is turbulent then consciousness is naturally in a flurry, it is frenetic, it is wild and there is no pause between thought and thought. Because this consciousness drives the senses, we will be too hasty to act, we may be too hasty to speak and this is usually called as rash actions or this will sometimes be called indolence or apathy or inaction too. Inaction is sourced in the *tamas* mode and excessive action is sourced in *rajas*.

Now let us go back momentarily to the metaphor of the Bhagavad Gita in which Krishna who stands for the *Paramatma* is seen to be the chariot driver and Arjuna who is also in the chariot is the *Jiva* and then the chariot itself is the body and the five horses stand for the five senses. Now under normal circumstances if Krishna is well in tune, because he is the awareness, he is the *Paramatma*, then the chariot is under his control. So the body and senses become completely obedient to the master who is the charioteer, who is the master, the *Atma* and who is *Siva*. Now, consider the case where the master by a twist of fate becomes momentarily a weakling, a powerless weakling, and then the horses which are the senses take the law into their own hands and they begin to gallop in a mad fashion.

So that is exactly what will happen if *rajas* and *tamas* become dominant in consciousness. The chariot which is our body, mind and our senses goes amok like a wild elephant going amok and then awareness is eclipsed and therefore becomes non-functional, powerless and the *Jiva* which is also in the chariot will be equally confused and will not be in an equipoised state. So when *Sakti* is turbulent naturally it is going to manifest as turbulent, uncontrollable senses. And then sorrow begins in life.

9. *Sthitha Prajnya's* Discovery of *Parabrahma*

A *sthitha prajnya* will find amazing happenings in his life, they are 'miracles', but he will never realize that they are miracles, and may never even search for an explanation, as to how these wonderful things happened to him. Many years later, when he studies the scriptures, he will come to understand effortlessly, that he, as the *Atma* has been yoked to the Divine, since many years!

Now for the benefit of *sthitha prajnyas* and *Jivas*, I am saying something about *maya* - for preparing you for the deeper spiritual life.

Sankara: Watching the flowing in of aspirations and the consequent, fulfillment of the same aspirations, through an unexpected and 'miraculous' Divine doing, the *sthitha prajna*, will start wondering if even the desires, which humans consider to be their's, may not be their's after all. He will wonder in this particular vein, because, he himself, never strove to bring in those desires, nor was there any seeking to fulfill them. Nevertheless, the fulfillment happened, all by itself, and the 'perfect' way in which the fulfillment happens, will be seen by the *sthitha prajna*, as a clinching testimony to Divine intervention. He will be stunned at the perception that now arises in him that he is himself the sanctioning authority *(Anumanta)* [25], in this way he arrives at the astounding truth of 'Tat Tvam Asi', namely, 'That Thou Art'. He then knows, through a direct experience that, 'That', the unmanifest Divine, can never ever be known. In Ch. II, topics 29, 30, we had dealt with the *Anumanta* aspect of the Divine.

10. What is *Maya*?

Icchā-dveṣa-samutthena dvandva- mohena Bhārata |

Sarva-bhūtāni sammohaṁ sarge yānti Parantapa ||

- Bhagavad Gita VII.27[40]

"O scion of Bharata's lineage! From their very birth, all beings are *deluded by 'duality'*, springing from the instinctive feelings of attraction & aversion for the pairs of opposites."

Q : *When a baby is born, the Atma is unpolluted by maya, but as the baby grows up, very soon the baby is given an identity of a name, names of parents, names of grand parents, and as the child grows, sense of duality arises, because, already the child thinks it is the body. So long as the Jiva lives in this field of consciousness, which by definition, is afflicted by duality, that is, through a sense of separation between self and another; there will be maya isn't it?*

A : Right. *Maya* is inevitable and is a source of immense pleasure, so it is very sweet for the *Jiva*, except in the unfortunate circumstance when the pleasure giving *maya* turns into unbearable pain. Hence, we have to enjoy this *maya*, at the same time keep a certain distance from it so that we do not suffer when it is time for pleasure to turn into pain. Sometimes, pain is also inevitable and at such times, we will do well to drink the cup of suffering. Drinking this cup of suffering is a great art in life, for in the wake of it we become more mature.

11. Bhakti* Minimizes the Negative Impact of *Maya*

Daivī hy eṣā guṇamayī mama māyā duratyayā |
Mām eva ye prapadyante māyām etāṁ taranti te ||

- Bhagavad Gita VII.14[40]

"Verily this Divine illusion of mine, made up of the three *gunas* is difficult to cross over; those who take refuge in 'me' alone, cross over this illusion." *'Me' refers to the Atma* (Self), *the swarupa, of 'Krishna', as well as 'ourselves'.*

*Nirguna Bhakti

Sankara: Many so called spiritual people, think Krishna is a human being, with that particular dark complexioned body. Here, he is telling us, that those who take refuge in 'him' alone, will be able to cross over the illusion of *maya*. He is not speaking here as a human. 'By himself', he means the *Atma*, the *Paramatma*, so one has to understand the inner meaning of the Bhagavad Gita. There is no necessity to surrender to the human called Krishna. What is necessary and very important is the anchorage to the unmanifest Divine, which Krishna represents.

The *gunas* produce 'variety' and 'multiplicity on the background of the one screen of the *Atma*. The *Atma* alone is unchanging, everything else that is formed on it goes on changing. Because of the incessant change, the *Jiva* gets fooled.

12. Spiritual Falls - 'Get Up and Start Walking Again'

Indriyāṇāṁ hi caratāṁ yan mano' nuvidhīyate |
Tad asya harati prajñāṁ vāyur nāvam ivāmbhasi ||

- Bhagavad Gita II.67[7]

Whichever of the senses is pursuing their sense object, if the consciousness ('*manas*', or *Jiva)* gets engrossed in that sense-faculty, then, that sense faculty carries away his '*Atmic* intelligence', in just the same way, in which a gale would carry away a boat, (moving) on the waters. *(prajnyaparada)*

Q : *Is this topic referring to the repercussions of excessive pleasure seeking of the Jiva? What would happen to such a Jiva, who gets into the reckless pursuit of pleasure, in an addictive fashion?*

A : Yes, this *sutra*, pertains to just such situations, where the *Jiva* gets addicted to a certain pleasure and insists on repeating that pleasure, till there is the calamitous descent of pain, as a consequence of all this.

Q : *Why, a calamitous descent of pain?*

A : Calamitous, because the *Jiva* was completely covered by *maya,* and had no idea of the consequences of such pursuit of pleasure. The nature of pleasure seeking is such that, when we go to the end of that pursuit, then there will be the very opposite of what we have sought. This arises from the fact that pain is the shadow of pleasure and one can never have pleasure, without a concomitant pain. The *Jiva* in its *maya* and blindness, exceeds all limits, and this excess precipitates the very opposite. You can see this phenomenon of descending calamities, whenever, any thing is carried too far, be it in the life of an individual, or even in the life of a nation.

Q   :   *How does such excessive indulgence in anything, imply an eclipsing of the Atmic intelligence (prajnya)?*

A   :   The *Jiva*, lives in the consciousness country only. Though the *Atma* is at the core of the *Jiva*, yet it is also covered over by *maya*, so already there is a veil on *Atmic* intelligence in the consciousness country. When the *Jiva* plunges headlong into pleasure, this creates an even thicker covering of *maya* on the *Atma*, resulting in an eclipsing of the *Atma* and with it also an eclipsing of that *Atmic* intelligence. This is the mechanism.

13. 'Ship-wreck Sutra' : Illustration
Bhagavad Gita II.67[7]

This seems to be the essence of the previous *sloka* from the Gita, describing spiritual falls. The message seems to be that we should digest spiritual falls, face them and not be disheartened.

Q   :   *This must be part of the life of the Jiva, in the terrain of consciousness, which is fraught with duality. If there is this powerful sensory impact, then one does lose one's*

Atmic intelligence. Could this be the reason then, why the Jiva, is incapable of making an original discovery of the Divine in its unmanifest aspect-because of the failure of Atmic Intelligence?

A : That is correct. The *Jiva* is a pleasure seeker and without the diet of success and sensory stimulation, the *Jiva* will fall down dead. In so many ways *Jiva* is fortunate in so far as materialistic enjoyment is concerned. It is however bereft of love and intelligence. What it calls love, is at best possession, infatuation or sensory attraction. To know love it has to migrate into the *Atmic* country, which it has not done.

Because of the veiling of the *Atmic* intelligence by *maya*, I say emphatically that it is impossible for the *Jiva* to come upon the Divine, in its present deluded state in consciousness.

Q : *Once again the Bhagavad Gita is also seen to use a very telling metaphor of the shipwreck, so beautifully portrayed in the above picture, to convey how one becomes a mudha, or a fool, who has lost the Atmic intelligence. Are these some of the sutras, you have been wanting the Indian mumukshus (seekers) to memorize?*

Secondly, are you suggesting that this kind of a loss of Atmic intelligence can also happen to the sthitha prajnya?

A : Yes, I had recommended that some of the Bhagavad Gita *sutras* be committed to memory, so that it may be easy to remember them again and again and then also apply them to our life situations.

To answer your second question, yes, even a *sthitha prajnya*, may lose the *Atmic* intelligence, when a powerful sensory call comes upon him in an area, where he is very vulnerable, because he has some *vasanas* which may still be coming upon him. However, unlike the *Jiva*, who may be under the spell of that sensory call for days on end, the *sthitha prajnya* will quickly get up from his 'spiritual fall', and without any regret, or guilt, go about his life as the old *sthitha prajnya*. In other words, *he will die to the experience*, to use the vocabulary of the master Sri J. Krishnamurti.

If the *sthitha prajnya* came to his *Atmic* state, through choiceless awareness of *what is*, he may have the rare gift of *dying to an experience*, so that no residue is left in his consciousness, and he may then get on with his life, without any guilt, regret or remorse. As I have explained in this retreat elsewhere, these once in a way falls are rather akin to the eclipses of the luminaries, the Sun and the Moon, which happen periodically. Just because the eclipses happened, though they held the luminaries, temporarily captive, they did not succeed in creating the taints on the luminaries. In like manner, these falls which may come upon a *sthitha prajnya*, or even a

Jivanmukta, do not necessarily show any imperfection in the state of the *sthitha prajnya*, or the state of the *Jivanmukta*. These falls, should be viewed more compassionately and with a deep understanding of the power of *maya*, which is but an inseparable aspect of *Parabrahma Himself.*

---

14. 'Emptying' the Content of Consciousness Necessary for Discovery of *Parabrahma*

Baggage of the *Jiva*

1. Opinions and perceptions, beliefs and views, attachments, '*anatmas*' (caste, community, nationality, color, race, language).

2. Knowledge, information, news papers, cell phones.

3. Constant 'survival mode'- earning money, future, security.

4. Craving for pleasure, sensory gratification.

5. Anger, jealousy, hurts, resentment.

Q : *In all these dispositions and movements in consciousness, you seem to suggest that the Jiva is hiding, 'surviving' and so what are we to do, if we are mumukshus, to wind up all of these activities, so that we can live in peace and in freedom, as the Atma?*

A : First step is watching the activities in consciousness, studying the *self,* which is secretive, which is survival oriented, which is planning. There must be *self* - Knowing in J. Krishnamurti's sense. Once this happens you will get all further guidance from within. Secondly, to keep *maya* at bay, a disciplined way of life is called for. Austerity is important. *Sravana, manana and nidhidhyasana* is very important. This is the kind of *sadhana* a *mumukshu* will have to do.

Q : *So the baggage of the Jiva will have to be thrown away, either deliberately, because the Jiva has realized the burdensome nature of such baggage, or the Jiva is forced to abandon its baggage, by a violent shock-either way, you seem to be saying that unless this baggage is discarded, there is no hope of the discovery of the Divine?*

A : So long as there is a baggage to which the *Jiva* is attached, it will never get an inclination to enquire into the Divine, for the simple reason that, such a baggage will preclude the awakening of *Atmic* intelligence or *prajnya*. This *prajnya* awakens, only when the *Jiva* has become empty and not pursuing any goal, overtly or covertly. Thus, emptying the content of consciousness, which is the same thing as throwing away the baggage, is what opens the door to the Divine. However, take note, this may sound somewhat scary to the *Jivas*.

---

15. 'Support Systems' for the Jiva are Impermanent

"Look upon friends, lands, wealth, houses, wife, gifts and such other good fortunes, as a dream or a juggler's show, lasting for no more than three or four days."

-Ashtavakra Gita[37]

"Detachment and non-identification with son, wife, property and the rest, and constant equanimity towards both the pleasing and the displeasing things in life".

- Bhagavad Gita XIII.9[26]

Q : *What has been your idea in showing such demanding sutras to people who may still be young?*

A : We are brought up on illusions, which are sanctified by society. But honestly, for our own happiness and welfare it will be very good, if we learn the great lessons of life, when we are still young, rather than being unable to digest them when we are much older. Can't you conceive of young people, who are wiser than the older people-who are supposed to be wise. Much sorrow in life can be avoided, by teaching the younger generation the basic nature of life that it is impermanent, that it is a passing show. After all the whole of the Buddhist world stands on the solid perception that life is impermanent, since death, loss, disease, all are causes for change and upheavals.

Such detachment is anyhow necessary and has to come to us, by the time we are 60 or older. By then we would have seen many family members dying, but often, we may not have learnt the important lessons, the experiences may not have translated themselves into wisdom, through detachment.

16. From *Jiva* to *Atma*

1. The purified and silenced *Jiva* will yield to its root, which is *Atma*, which is intimately connected to *Parabrahma*. But, you will not know this, because *Atma* is not a knowable sensory object, but only peace, as conscious presence - this is awareness or *Atma*.

2. This is the *sthitha prajnya's* state in the Bhagavad Gita.

Sankara: Among *mumukshus*, there are those, who have a natural profound detachment, they will discover, 'who they are'-as *moksha* or Self - Realization is really about discovering who we are. I feel that without detachment and consequent turning away from the world and all its temptations, this discovery will be impossible. Either one must be fortunate enough to have great sufferings, great misfortunaes, so that one has good grounds for turning away from the world. Or, the Divine Itself must come after us and embrace us, as happened in the case of Sri Ramana Maharshi. When one turns away from the world, one becomes innocent and in many instances, also unknowing. This, innocence of the *sthitha prajnya*, is not an incapacity or weakness, rather, it is the greatest strength, a human can have in life. Then as the master J. Krishnamurti, would say, 'Then, you need not take care of life, life will take care of you.'

17. The *Jiva* can commence a new 'becoming' in *Dharma and Moksha*

1. The *Jiva* can search for some wealth, like *moksha* in the spiritual life. Because *prajnya* is not awakened, it does not know, it already has this wealth. *So, it can again get into that 'becoming' which will build that old individuality, old maya in an even more respectable form, but which will breed disappointments, sorrow, hurts, etc.*

2. To prevent this, the scriptures warn about the *Jiva* using *sadhana* for strengthening itself.

Q : *Here in this topic, we seem to examine the position of the impure and ignorant Jiva, attempting to take up a spiritual life. Is this the lesson for us: That, as all that the Jiva knows is only struggling as the individual, which has identified itself with the body, and thus getting caught in the process of 'becoming' which is the process in time?*

A : The *Jiva's* spiritual life is based on duality and is not wrong. It is a prelude and a slow preparation for the nobler and more exalted spiritual life as a *sthitha prajnya,* in the morrow. It is part of the whole process of unfoldment in a human being's life. Though the *Jiva* is in the field of duality, because consciousness is subject to duality, there are a number of opportunities for the *Jiva* to purify itself, by coming onto one or another spiritual path. Humility, self-abnegation, faith in the teacher, love and obedience to parents, these are wonderful preparations for the more advanced spiritual life. So, the spiritual life of the *Jiva* need not be in vain. It is the foundation for something nobler and greater which is bound to come with the passing decades of life.

Q : *And is it to correct the assumptions of the Jiva, and prevent it from beginning yet another journey in 'becoming' that, the Jiva is asked to study the scriptures, so that the Jiva will not mistake this 'becoming', for being on a path of Self - Realization?*

A : The warnings given by *Ashtavakra Gita* are really meant for *mumukshus,* they are not meant for *Jivas* who have still a long way to go in the country of consciousness. The *Jiva* living in consciousness has no option but to get into 'becoming'.

Spiritual 'becoming' in this sense must not be condemned. Instead, we have to understand that because the *Jiva* is in the caterpillar stage, which is a stage of gluttony, the *Jiva* will be entertaining hosts of desires and will be ever seeking their fulfillment. A time will however come sooner or later when the gluttony stops and the caterpillar is metamorphosed into the butterfly. Then, the butterfly will simply fly away in freedom. So, the *Jiva* can be permitted to trudge along in this path of spiritual 'becoming' and we need not impose on the *Jiva* the high standards of total detachment, which are meant for the *mumukshus.* Because this is a retreat in Self - Realization I will be doing you all a gross disservice, if I treated you entirely only as *Jivas* and never deemed you to be *mumukshus.* As *mumukshus,* high standards await you, I did not want to hide this fact from you, hence these *sutras* from the *Ashtavakra Gita.*

----

18. The Way to Discover *Parabrahma*

The *sthitha prajnya* to proceed with his natural 'discovery' of the unmanifest Divine, he must be free of all conflict, and must accept every corner of his life peacefully. He must be choicelessly aware of *what is*. If some sensory infatuation or addiction, from his former life as a *Jiva*, pursues him, he will have the wisdom, never to fight with this, but accept even this as His Will, and yield to this gracefully. The *sthitha prajnya* will ever remember who he is, namely the *Atma*, and will abide in that, he will avoid sensory extroversion, he will spend time with himself, he will devote time for *sravana, manana and nidhidhyasana*.

Q : *What is said here in this topic about the life of the sthitha prajnya is very beautiful indeed. One gets the impression that he lives in the world, yet seems to be an outsider, 'as a guest in a stranger's house', to use, J. Krishnamurti's words. Isn't this a radical shift, from the way people live, by socializing too much, by thinking too much, by indulging too much?*

A : The *Jiva* has two options, either he can wallow in worldly life, caught up in the dualistic field of consciousness, enjoying much pleasure and inevitably reeling under the pain which always follows pleasure, like a shadow. Or, getting away from this life of individuality, with its pleasures and pains, he must retreat into his true nature, the *Atma,* the conscious presence, after he has 'put his house in order', as a *Jiva.* By this process, he would graduate to be a *sthitha prajnya,* which means, he has turned away from *maya* and the life of duality. In the latter life, there is no agony and pain of any kind, only peace, understanding and the courage to stand alone and go your way. As he lives like this, certain miraculous happenings happen to him, due to his intimate connection with the unmanifest Divine, but even he may not know of the connection, because he is living his life of innocence, and may not have read the scriptures. Adi Sankaracharya had maintained that unless a seeker comes on the path of *Jnana*, of *sravana, manana and nidhidhyasana, Jivanmukti* will not be attained. The *Jivanmukta* knows that the *Atma,* is the same as Absolute Reality, which is called *Brahman.*

Q : *Regarding the remnants of some addictions and sensory indulgences, that may come upon him, periodically, even as a sthitha prajnya, what would be 'right' action for him, under these conflicting conditions.*

A : A *sthitha prajnya* does not have conflict, in his former life as a *Jiva,* he might have fought with himself, struggled to improve himself, but he never fights with himself, after coming home to the *Atma.* Even if some *vasana* from the older life were to come upon him, like the pull of eating, or smoking or drinking or sexual gratification, he will watch everything, as though he was not involved. He lives in this way, in complete wholeness, with total integrity, which is his virtue, of which he will not even be aware. He will yield gracefully to the sensory pulls, but will not feel guilty or ashamed. He will understand everything, all at once.

Q : *If he were to have a spiritual fall, how will he perceive this and how are we to grasp this contradiction?*

A : We have just examined this possibility and have 'digested this contradiction', turning to the Bhagavad Gita, which has throw much light on this contradiction.

----

19. The *Jiva*, can get attached to *Sadhan*a

"The ignorant *(Jiva)* constantly take to the practice of concentration and control of the mind. The wise abiding in their real Self, like persons in sleep (so deeply peaceful), do not find anything else to be done."

- Ashtavakra Gita[37]

Q : *What is 'taking security'?*

A : The *Jiva* has already identified itself with the body, this mistake has to be corrected, as this is a consequence of *'mula avidya'* or root ignorance (or 'original sin' in Christianity), which is an integral part of Divine creation. We have already studied the two *sutras* from the Bhagavad Gita on *maya,* inherent in consciousness, in the form of duality of 'the me and the you', with attendant likes and dislikes. Because, the *Jiva* functions in this field of duality, something appeals to the deluded *Jiva,* so it starts thinking, 'Oh how wonderful, I have found the truth, now I am going to follow this, and practice every day, so that I become strong'. All this is the way of the *Jiva,* it is 'becoming' and the *Jiva* has taken security in a certain path, which appeals to it, all this may be at best a prelude to the transition to the *Atma,* but this will not lead to Self - Realization, because the *Jiva* has the wrong foundation, that, it is the body.

Q : *So, then, is this the reason, this becoming is discouraged and negated and instead, the only sadhana prescribed by Ramana Maharshi is sravana, manana, nidhidhyasana?*

401

A : Right. The kind of examples of *sadhana* we have considered, involve activity or various spiritual practices which are physical or devotional activities but enquiry and understanding did not have any role in all of these activities. At the end of these activities the *Jiva* feels that it has become richer in spiritual merits etc., and in this way this self-satisfaction of the *Jiva* only gets fortified and built up. Such fortification and strengthening of the *Jiva* is not the goal in *moksha*, instead the goal is to liquidate the *Jiva* so that the *Jiva* will have nothing of which it can feel proud and self-satisfied. With *sravana, manana and nidhidhyasana*, the liquidation of the *Jiva* has commenced, in all earnestness.

---

20. The Negation of *Sadhana* - because this *Sadhana* strengthens the *Jiva*

"An ignorant person *(Jiva)* does not attain liberation by repeated practice, which is an 'activity'. The blessed one, devoid of all activities, stands free, through mere understanding."

- Ashtavakra Gita[37]

Q : *What comes through clearly in this sutra from the Ashtavakra Gita is that the Jiva may have the temptation to plunge into one spiritual activity or the other, for this is all that the Jiva knows-namely 'becoming'- 'I want to become Self - Realized, I want to get moksha'. So is this the warning for seekers that such practice and such activity is not going to give Self - Realization?*

A : This is actually a good question because usually *Jivas* do not seek Self - Realization and if they have come so far that the goal of Self - Realization has become real, and the calling for the same has become strong, then the *Jiva* would have to come on the path of *sravana, manana, nidhidhyasana.*

However, it does happen that even though the *Jiva* might not be properly speaking a *mumukshu,* yet because of *maya* and compulsion from the spiritual organization with which he is affiliated, he may venture into some *sadhana* which is in the nature of some 'becoming'. At this point two possibilities arise. Some one may point out to him that this 'becoming' kind of a *sadhana,* which he has taken for the enrichment of his individuality, is in truth no *sadhana* at all. But only a process of 'becoming' which will give some self-satisfaction. Or, he may continue in the 'becoming' *sadhana* for very many years. It seems to me that those for whom the vitality giving cosmic life energies are very strong in their horoscope, this kind of an activity is a very natural thing. So, the temperament befits this kind of a 'becoming' *sadhana.* So, the 'becoming' continues till a turning point is reached, whereupon the *Jiva* turns inward and may be fortunate to graduate as a *sthitha prajnya.* Once a *sthitha prajnya,* all 'becoming' is ofcourse out of his life.

The *sutra* from the *Ashtavakra Gita* will make profound sense for *mumukshus* who are quick to realize that they too are in the trap of 'becoming' and the *sutra* may knock them out of this slumber. For other *Jivas* who are not *mumukshus,* but engrossed basically in *artha and kama,* some kind of a spiritual 'becoming' is not certainly bad and may even be part of the human drama of having to walk on the ground of *maya* for many years.

Q : *Also, the emphasis in the Ashtavakra Gita sutra, is on understanding, which is also the 'thing' emphasized by Ramana Maharshi, Nisargadatta Maharaj and Krishnamurti?*

A : One has to be told again and again that understanding is really the key thing. It is the source of all creative work in the sciences as well as in the arts and humanities and we do not see how it cannot be central even in the spiritual life. So the *Ashtavakra Gita* emphasizing understanding should atleast be a further impetus for us to take the path of understanding more seriously than we have taken till now. I'm sure if some one had come up to you and convinced you of the importance of understanding, then you too would have given up your negligence and come right onto this path of understanding.

----

21. Right *Sadhana?*

"If your watchfulness is deep and steady, ever turned to the source *(Parabrahma)*, it will gradually move upstream, till suddenly it becomes the source. Put your awareness to work, not your mind (consciousness). The mind (consciousness) is not the right instrument for this task. The timeless can be reached only by the timeless. Your body and your mind (consciousness) are both subject to time. Only awareness is timeless, even in the now. In awareness, you are facing facts, and reality is fond of facts."

- Nisargadatta Maharaj[38]

Q : *Is it because, we are the Atma, already, that emphasis is placed repeatedly in all the scriptures on the discovery of this Atmic essence, and the understanding of it, rather than on any practice and sadhana?*

A : Exactly, this is the reason. I want to remind you at this stage that in the view of Sri Ramana Maharshi, even a *mumukshu* after abiding in the *Atma* should not rest contented, but turning to *sravana, manana and nidhidhyasana*, he should draw inspiration from the scriptures and do his *sadhana* as a '*nishkama karma*' and not for getting some fruit, which any how he already has. The emphasis by Ramana Maharshi is on *nidhidhyasana*, namely having reached the railway station of the *Atma*, to discover that it is our home and to settle down there and enquire how this sanctuary of the *Atma* came into existence at all. And to meditate on this mystery. In this step the Maharshi has gone beyond Sri Nisargadatta Maharaj, who also enjoins that we abide in the *Atma*, since we are the *Atma*, and this is indeed *nidhidhyasana*, but, Maharaj, does not stress on the preceding steps of *sravana and manana*, as emphatically and as repeatedly as Ramana Maharshi does. In my view, a good *mumukshu* should never be like a frog in a well, content with drinking the water of that one well alone, he should enquire about other waters and other wells and other rivers and taste them too if an opportunity comes in his way. In this way, the *mumukshu* will have a much broader canvas and will be fortunate to receive the guidance from many exalted masters.

Q : *Maharaj is also stressing that we should work, as the witness, and not as the Jiva. This seems to be extremely significant, as much of the spiritual sadhana going on in Ashrams and spiritual missions, seems to be assignments given to the Jiva and not to the witness, and the Jiva is only too glad, because it sees all of this sadhana, as a means to make itself 'spiritually' more glorious- so a sanctified becoming?*

A : Yes, Maharaj's words are very significant, we must all see the danger of accepting assignments given to the *Jiva* in us, and be wary of such assignments, because such assignments will enrich the *Jiva,* whereas, the *Jiva* has to be liquidated, rather than enriched and made more secure.

I have always maintained that the works of Sri Nisargadatta Maharaj are equal to a thousand Upanishads. For example, see here, how he stresses on the witnessing awareness, and the unimagined potentiality it holds, a potentiality, which we would never have guessed or suspected:

"Look at your self steadily, it is enough. The door that locks you in is also the door that lets you out. The 'I Am' is the door. Stay at it until it opens. As a matter of fact, it is open, only you are not at it. You are waiting at the non-existent painted doors, which will never open."

Q : *Is awareness timeless?*

A : You have to discover that it is so, not believe it. As you keep watching, you will arrive at the truth of it, yourself.

Sixth Day (Chapter - VI), 1st 'Tat Tvam Asi' Meditation

Discovery of *Parabrahma*, by identifying His 'All Merciful' Nature

----

22. Turn your back: '*Neti Neti*'

"Let even *Hari*, *Hara* or the lotus born *Brahma* be your instructor, but unless, you forget all, you cannot be established in the Self."

- Ashtavakra Gita, Pg 156 [37]

You should have started listening to yourself. From this arises learning, from this learning, *Jiva* ends its foolish activities ('dying'). In the new life: water, trees, space, everything, become mysterious and things, you have not got used to.......

Q : *We had seen that the Jiva 'takes security' by depending upon external things and seeking the Divine' as though the Divine is different from it and is present only externally, in temples and in the form of the masters and gurus. Is all this being negated here by this sutra of the Ashtavakra Gita?*

A : Of course! Emphatically.

Q : *And what is the real significance and meaning of 'neti neti'?*

A : '*Neti, Neti*' is an Upanishadic phrase, indicating, 'not this, not this'. It is a statement of negation. When someone suggests erroneously, that 'this is the *Atma*', then you negate this by saying, '*neti, neti*'.

Q : *There is a sharp distinction made between 'religion followed and practiced' as against 'religion, internalized and realized'. All the negations we have seen, are for the 'blind following of religion' isn't it?*

A : What is the use of following a religion, when your heart is dry and you have discovered nothing for yourself? Unless all the *anatmas*, i.e., false selves are negated, how can we come upon the subtle *Atma*, which is our bedrock identity?

23. The *Paramatma*, Completely Reached

Jit'ātmanaḥ praśāntasya Param'ātmā samāhitaḥ |
śīt'oṣṇa-sukha-duḥkheṣu tathā mān'āpa mānayoḥ ||

- Bhagavad Gita VI. 7[23]

When the *Jiva* has reached tranquillity, in all the pleasures and pains of life, and likewise in all circumstances of honour and dishonour; then already the *Paramatma* has been completely reached.

Q : *Going back to the metaphor of the 'man enmeshed in algae (maya)', would the calming and silencing of the Jiva and its self in the contexts of pleasure and pain as well as, honor and dishonor, amount to the enmeshing algae (maya) dropping off?*

A : Yes, indeed, in terms of the metaphor of the 'man enmeshed in algae *(maya)*' this calmed and silenced *Jiva*, would correspond to the algae dropping off, almost completely.

Q : *Does this then mean that, the sthitha prajnya, who has become calm and unruffled in honor and dishonor, who has settled in the Atma as the Atma, has unknowingly run into the territory of the Divine, Parabrahma?*

A   :   Quite right. This is the most mysterious truth and there will be miraculous events which happen in your life, to offer testimony for the *Atma* being one with *Parabrahma*. This *sutra,* helped me clinch my own discovery of the *Atma* being that *Brahman,* 'That', *Parabrahma*.

---

24. 'Have I a Tongue or Not?'

"One may think of the Self without space, but not space without the Self. One may deny anything, but not the Self.

"**To doubt the existence of the Self is as ridiculous as the doubt expressed by a man: 'Have I a tongue or not?'**"

- Vedanta Panchadasi, Ch. III.20[39]

Q   :   *People who are too extroverted, may find it hard to locate and identify the Self (Atma), and could this sutra be intended for such people?*

A   :   It is intended for all, because *maya* is universal, as Krishna says in the Bhagavad Gita.

Q   :   *Does this also mean that even space, which is such a subtle thing, exists only on the bedrock of the Atma? And could space itself, be the full externalized form of the Atma, just like a peacock, can open and spread out its beautiful multi colored plumage, in the same way, the Atma, through the projector of the body, gives us its full cosmic display of its majesty and grandeur?*

A   :   What a great poet you are! And yes, this is the truth that the *Atma* is the bedrock of the entire cosmos with its impenetrable mystery and majesty.

408

25. *Atma's sakti* is in Thinking. One must think Auspiciously for the Good of All.

"One who considers oneself free, is free indeed. And one who considers oneself bound, remains bound. As one thinks, so one becomes, is a popular saying in this world, which is true"
(Yad bhavam, tad bhavati)

- Ashtavakra Gita[37]

Q : *When the Atma, like a tortoise curling its limbs within its shell, abides within itself, we seem to have awareness (and prajnya), truth-existence and inner wellness (bliss). But, when the Atma opens out, like an umbrella, we have consciousness and sakti, which is movement and thinking, which is inherently dualistic. Is the Ashtavakra Gita saying that, with this Atma sakti, one has the option of building a heaven or building a hell, depending on how this Atma sakti functions in the field of consciousness?*

A : Yes, examples are not wanting to illustrate this *sutra* that a heaven or a hell can be built, so powerful is man. If we are wise, we will build a heaven. If we are driven by dark energies which is not an impossibility, we may very well build only a hell. And sometimes the strange thing is that in the name of building a heaven, we may build a veritable hell.

Q : *Is Atma sakti, what the Christian religion calls, free will?*

A : Exactly, you got it.

----

26. *Jivatma* before God Realization

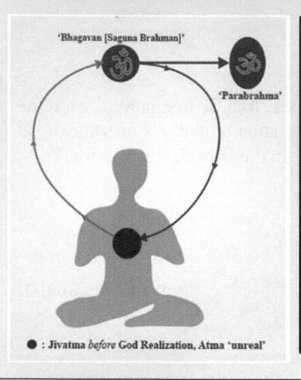

'Bhagavan [Saguna Brahman]'

'Parabrahma'

● : Jivatma *before* God Realization, Atma 'unreal'

The devotee to begin with is only the miserable *Jiva*. In this ignorance, the *Jiva*, seeks some strength, some grace, to make himself happy and fulfilled. In actuality, he has no proper sense of Self, which is why he suffers. He accepts and believes that the chosen formful aspect of the Divine is the true Divine. The real unmanifest Divine is not even in his dictionary.

Q : *Does the Jiva in the initial stages of the spiritual life, have no deep sense of Self?*

A : If the *Jiva* is *sattvic* and the Sun and the 4th house Lord have some strength then such *Jivas* will have a sense of the *Atma* or sense of the Self. If on the other hand if the *Jiva* is too *rajasic* and the Sun and the 4th house Lord are weak, then the *Jiva* is unlikely to have a good sense of Self.

Q : *Will such a Jiva, who is a novitiate in the spiritual life, even grasp what the unmanifest Divine will be?*

A : In due course yes, may not be immediately as this may be hard.

Q : *So, having blindly accepted some picture of God, he just talks to that picture, that idol in the temple, just as you and I talk?*

A : Exactly, with some possible fear, with definitely some devotion and definitely with some amount of faith and/or conviction - even in his state of *maya*.

Q : *From the point of view of Self - Realization and these advaitic masters, this seems to be too childish an approach.*

A : We should not make such judgements, it is a process of growth. In the beginning stage, we were all babies at a certain time and our mothers were feeding us and were washing our bottoms. Many years later only we attained what might be called some kind of maturity.

Q : *Does the pink patch (shown black here) represent the Jiva's poor sense of self?*

A : That is right, it shows the poor sense of self.

Q : *As there are no connecting lines between the Jiva's heart and Parabrahma, does this mean that 'Parabrahma' is not real for him?*

A : Yes, It is outside his world view, unreal for him.

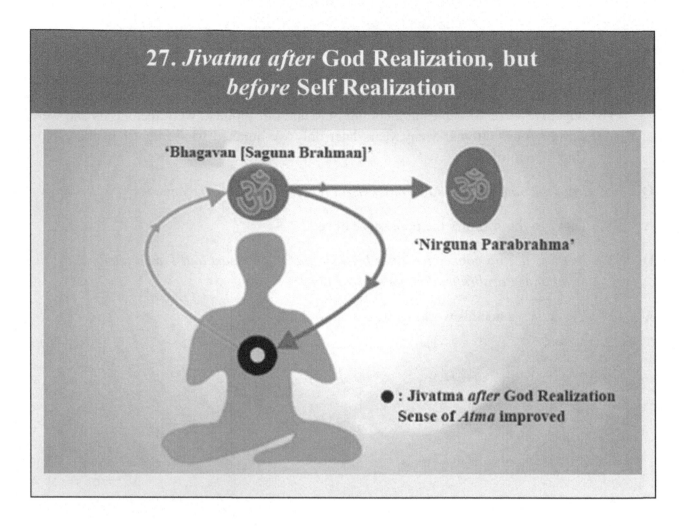

27. *Jivatma after* **God Realization, but** *before* **Self Realization**

'Bhagavan [Saguna Brahman]'

'Nirguna Parabrahma'

● : Jivatma *after* God Realization
Sense of *Atma* improved

Q : *What do you mean by God - Realization?*

A : The *Jiva* under the pressure of fear, unfulfilled desires and the urgency to achieve accepts and becomes comfortable with the belief that there is an external power which can solve all his problems. It is of course so distraught at this stage that he can never conduct an enquiry into the Truth or the Divine. This belief matures into faith and the *Jiva* will then get attached to his master, or to his God and to his religion. If he has one or two powerful experiences or dreams in which his God or master comes to him, that is enough for him to give his heart to his God or master. In his state of ignorance in the consciousness country, if you ask me, I will say this is a good enough step in progress. Inspite of this progress and *bhakti*, he will still not know, who God is, what God is and where God is.

Q : *You say, the sense of Atma, after God - Realization has improved. Is it because, this blessing from the master or the Divine experience, was successful in separating the Atma of the Jiva from the maya, which was covering the Atma?*

A : Yes, he would have also become more introverted because of the many blows in life, so a sense of Self develops, but it is still too weak.

Q : *Another question arises: after this so-called God - Realization, can this Jiva, conceive of the Divine as the unmanifest?*

A : Why are you obsessed with the Divine as the un-manifest. Don't you know that this is the last and the greatest stage? A lot of ground has to be covered in duality and you have to graduate as a *sthitha prajnya*, before one can sensibly talk about the unmanifest aspect of the Divine.

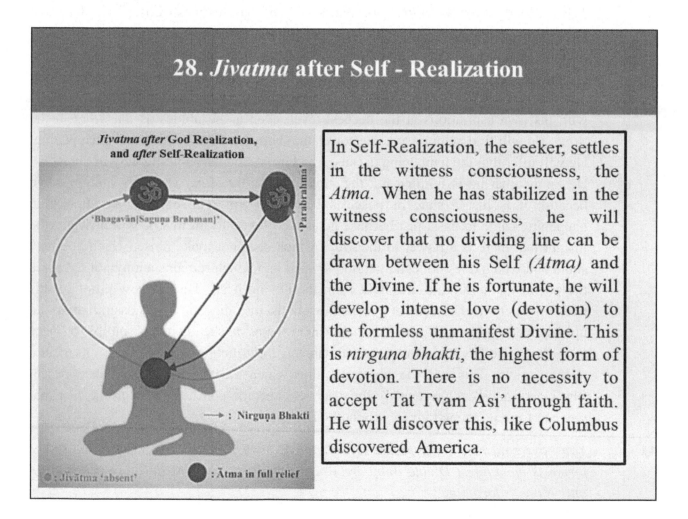

28. *Jivatma* after Self - Realization

Jivatma after God Realization, and *after* Self-Realization

'Bhagavān[Saguṇa Brahman]'

'Parabrahma'

⟶ : Nirguṇa Bhakti

◉ : Jivātma 'absent'   ● : Ātma in full relief

In Self-Realization, the seeker, settles in the witness consciousness, the *Atma*. When he has stabilized in the witness consciousness, he will discover that no dividing line can be drawn between his Self *(Atma)* and the Divine. If he is fortunate, he will develop intense love (devotion) to the formless unmanifest Divine. This is *nirguna bhakti*, the highest form of devotion. There is no necessity to accept 'Tat Tvam Asi' through faith. He will discover this, like Columbus discovered America.

Q : *You say that one has to settle in the witness consciousness or Atma and stabilize in that state, for only then can a seeker discover that there is no dividing line between his/ her consciousness and the unmanifest Divine. So does this mean that we can never form any conception of the Divine, because in its true form it is unmanifest?*

A   :   Yes. In truth, the Divine does not lend itself to conceptualization and imagery. If at all the Divine does manifest to you in a specific form like that of the *murti* of your *guru* or in the form of one of the dieties of your religion, like *Vishnu or Siva or Ganapathy or Jesus Christ*, or in the form of one of the saints; you are likely to make the mistake of taking the Divine only to be that one particular 'form'. This will be limiting the Divine, when it is infinite in its possibilities of manifestation. On the path of *Jnana* or understanding, one is extremely comfortable with the Divine in this unmanifest, incomprehensible aspect and all seekers of *moksha* must become comfortable with this. In Buddhism, the unmanifest aspect is described as *sunyata* (void).

The difficulty for the *sthitha prajnya* is this; he has to be so observant of all the happenings in his inner and outer life; inner life in the form of thoughts, reactions and aspirations and outer life in the form of happenings and events which are amazing. He has to look for happenings, without actually looking for them with the desire, especially when they land into his life uninvited. He must correlate such happenings with his own aspirations at the deepest level, even as he abides as the *Atma* in the *Atma*. He will find an unmistakable correlation between an aspiration and a happening. He will infer that the happening is caused by him. As he was abiding only in the *Atma.* He knows that he is nothing but the *Atma*, and as the *Atma* is totally unimpressive because it is just a state of peaceful being, he will wonder how an impossible happening came to pass, just because he aspired for it. From this he will arrive at the insight that there is a power in the *Atma*, which does not make noise, which does not shout and which does not call attention to itself and which remains anonymous. This is the power of the Divine, different from the Divine itself. He has now proof of this power in action. The rest of his homework is just digesting and assimilating the unimaginable power of the Divine, which seems to be switched on by a mere aspiration. The Divine is formless and nameless, but the power can express itself in a million ways. This will be his conclusion which will give him immense peace. The Upanishads declare exactly this truth. So become comfortable with the fact that you can form no mental images about the Divine.

Q   :   *You have said that if the seeker is fortunate he will develop intense devotion to the formless unmanifest Divine. Why are you emphasizing that this devotion will happen only if one is fortunate?*

A   :   One knows this truth which can be sometimes painful, that this intense devotion to the Divine in the unmanifest aspect, is not given to all. Either it is given at birth itself, and will blossom at a certain stage in life, or it may not be given at birth itself. If this is given as a blessing at birth itself, and astrologers know this so well, then an additional dimension in the relationship between the seeker and the Divine will flower which is the dimension of devotional adoration. The *Nayanmars* are wounderful examples of this devotion. Without this dimension one will still make the discovery that the *Atma* itself is the unmanifest Divine. 'Tat Tvam Asi' and *Aham Brahmasmi* represent this truth. But, the emotional effervescence which adds intensity to this discovery may not be present or may be only weakly present. In any case the discovery stands by itself, it does not need the additional aura of the devotional adoration to mandate the discovery.

Q : *You say that there is no necessity to believe and to have faith in Tat Tvam Asi and accept it as a great truth given by the Upanishads. Then do you mean to say that the seeker actually comes upon this monumental discovery originally?*

A : Not all seekers, but only the *sthitha prajnyas* who are peacefully resting in the hammock of the *Atma* will be able to discover the truth of 'Tat Tvam Asi'. They of course need not believe in it or have faith in it, like the Upanishadic seers, they too have become the 'seers'.

---

29. Your Own Answers to Three Questions

1. Who is the Divine?

2. What is the Divine?

3. Where is the Divine?

Prajnya (awakened intelligence) will do the 'tracking' and the discovery of the Divine.

Q : *Your point is that even apostles of faith, whom we may meet in our day today life, will not know the answers to these three root questions. These people of faith may be found among our circle of friends and family. They are usually anchored to the one fixed* *form of the Divine, namely to Jesus Christ or to Rama or Krishna. But, Jesus Christ, Rama or Krishna, are like 'sense objects', supported by the respective histories, scriptures etc. Thus you saying that the journey made by these apostles of faith till this point of anchorage to these avatars or deities is incomplete and needs to go further?*

A : Exactly! My point is that if you have faith you are lucky and fortunate, there can be no doubt about this. But you will still be only a second hand person, as this faith is not even an advanced milestone in the spiritual journey. It is a necessary milestone, but comes quite early in the spiritual journey. The real spiritual journey starts from the milestone of faith, but does not end with that milestone. The Divine is still a mystery at this milestone and the apostles cannot answer any of these questions. If they say that the Divine is Christ or Krishna, then their understanding is extremely limited and people on the path of *Jnana* and understanding will laugh at their achievement. They need to travel further, by putting these questions to themselves, whereupon they will find that they know not the answers. The journey begins from this point onwards. Impatience, desire for spiritual achievement, ambition in the spiritual life will be sure enemies on this path. Patience, freedom from the desire to achieve, abidance in the *Atma*, and surrender to the Divine even in the limited form, will turn out to be monumental blessings.

----

30. Neither 'Existent' nor 'Non-Existent'

Jñeyaṁ yat tat pravakṣyāmi yat jñātvā'mṛtam aśnute |
Anādimat paraṁ brahma na sat tan n'āsad ucyate ||

- Bhagavad Gita XIII.12[26]

Bhagavan Krishna : "I shall enunciate 'That' which has to be known, knowing which, one attains immortality. It is the beginningless **Supreme Brahman** - which is spoken of as neither existent nor non-existent."

Q : *Throughout this retreat you have emphasized that it is important to turn ones back on all worldly considerations, for one honestly to step on to the path of the seeker. Why do you bring in this insistence?*

A : We know that the *Jiva* is body-centered, greatly concerned about survival, name and fame, financial security etc. Usually the activities of the *Jiva* continue throughout life even after 60 or 65, which implies that the true spiritual life never really begins. At least after 60 or 65, handing over responsibilities to our children, we have to truly turn away from all our material quests mentioned above and turn inwards so that the life of the *Jiva* may truly come to an end. Without the life of the *Jiva* coming to an end and you abiding in the *Atma* as the *Atma* and without your having the necessary detachment, how can you ever make any original discovery which will be truly yours and which will open the new life? So, it is very important to turn away from obsession with the world in one form or another, so that abidance in the *Atma* becomes a reality. With this abidance the spiritual life begins and importantly, learning commences.

Q : *How can you discover your immortal nature, that is your birth less and deathless nature by knowing 'That'?*

A : Even before we know 'That', we have to learn to live as the *Atma*, for only then we can know that the *Atma* is birth-less and death-less and the *Atma* was never born and shall never die. To convince yourself of this, having tasted the *Atma* by being the *Atma*, you have to apply every one of the *sutras* from the Bhagavad Gita to verify if these are truly also your *sutras*. For example, the *Atma* cannot be burnt by fire, cannot be wetted by water, cannot be dried by wind, will you actually give an attestation to the *sutra* elements? Are they also your truths? You have proceeded in this vein to gain a conviction of the immortal nature of the *Atma*. This will give you immense peace, because you have known who you are. So, even though the *sutra* says that by knowing 'That' you discover your immortality, you need not even go that far. It is enough to know the *Atma* as your true nature, that itself will drive home to you that you are unborn and undying. It was only the body that was born and the body will surely die. We have to disassociate ourselves from our body-this is the really important thing.

Q : *'That' the unmanifest Divine is portrayed in this sutra in ambiguous terms, namely that one cannot say whether 'it' exists and one cannot assert that 'it' does not exist. What is the basis for this ambiguity?*

A : To prove that something exists, we have to take the person who is asking the question to that object and show him the object. The object in this case is not the sensory object, such as we are used to. Instead it is the unmanifest Divine, which only each one of us has to discover for himself or herself. Therefore, we cannot say that the unmanifest Divine exists, like we can say that the Sun and the Moon exist. Now those who observe their life very closely like the *sthitha pragnyas,* they will know for sure that there is an aspect of the Divine which is absolutely unknowable, belonging to the realm of the unmanifest and that this aspect of the Divine, though itself is inaccessible to our senses, creates events which are undeniable and which imply its existence. For this reason we cannot even deny the existence of 'That'. Because of these facts, 'That' cannot be denied, yet it cannot also be proved. This mysterious, unmanifest and unknowable Divine is our Father and Mother.

----

31. *Siva (Arunachaleswara)* and *Sakti ('Maya' or 'Avidya Rupini')*

Sri Apeethakuchambal Sametha Sri Arunachaleswara Swamy

Q : *This is a very beautiful form of the Divine Father and Divine Mother, both unmanifest, yet why has man given a form to the unmanifest Divine? And who are these deities? Where are they in India?*

A : The unmanifest Divine is obviously abstract and there are mathematicians, physicists and good thinkers who may be extremely comfortable with the unmanifest nature of the Divine. They do not ask for a form full aspect of the Divine at all. But they are in the meagre minority. The vast majority of humanity are not abstract and subtle thinkers, for their benefit, we need to convey the unmanifest Divine in a much more tangible and pictorial form so that consciousness, which is dualistic and the field in which they actually live, can grasp this intangible truth. This is *Siva* as '*Arunachala*' and the *Adi Sakti* of *Siva* as '*Apeethakuchambal*' portrayed here in the form in which the unmanifest Divine had chosen to take in the life of 'saiva saints'. They are deities in Tiruvannamalai, a center of *Siva* worship. This is the unmanifest aspect of the Divine who actually bestowed *moksha* on Sri Ramana Maharshi when he was only 16 years old, thereby completely negating *artha and kama* for the young lad.

419

Q : *Why is the Adi Sakti of Siva called Maya or Avidya rupini?*

A : This we shall see in the subsequent topic which takes up this question.

32. Atma and Atma Sakti (Siva & Sakti)

"In one's own Self *(Atma)*, which is no other than Brahman (another name for the unmanifest Divine, called *Parabrahma*), there is *a mysterious power (Sakti)* known as '*Avidya*' (ignorance), which is beginningless and not separate from the Self *(Atma)*. Its characteristics are veiling and presentation of diversity."

– Adi Sankara's Viveka Chudamani[41]

Note: This mysterious power is also called '*maya*' or '*Avidya rupini*'.

Q : *This is absolutely astounding and compels us to be silent when we contemplate this mind boggling and impossible to understand truth that, within the belly of this unmanifest Divine is lying dormant, this infinite serpent of power, which has created the world of diversity and confusion, why has the Divine power created this madness?*

A : You have to find out the answer to this question yourself. It is the question which can engage your attention as long as you live, you can give a thousand answers and yet you will not be exhausting the mystery behind the infinite power of *Adi Sakti*. She performs all the miracles and through her the aspirations of the devotees are appeased and fulfilled and through her dance this world of duality is sustained. If one comes to abide in the *Atma*, rather than still wallowing in pain and ignorance in the field of consciousness, one will know that *Adi Sakti* does this for her own sport/*leela*. You will understand *leela* (Divine play), once your life in the *Atma* commences.

"In one's own Self, which is no other than *Brahman*, there is a mysterious power, known as *Avidya* (ignorance), which is beginning less and not separate from the Self. Its characteristics are veiling and presentation of diversity..."

- Adi Sankaracharya's Viveka Chudamani,
translated by Bhagavan Ramana.

Q : *You say that the Sakti of the Atma has two functions, one is veiling and another is presentation of diversity, where formally there was only unity? Will the sthitha prajnya discover all of these truths about the functioning of the Adi Sakti, just by abiding in the Atma and doing nothing, like a lazy person?*

A : Yes, *sthitha prajnya* by abiding in the *Atma* and doing nothing, but very attentive because he is now devoid of the duality of the consciousness will be able to fathom the *Adi Sakti*. So Adi Sankaracharya expressed this truth by the following words:

'That the *Adi Sakti* can be grasped by the eye of stainless intelligence *(prajnya)*, just by abiding in the *Atma* as the *Atma*'.

We have to note that the *sthitha prajnya* by no means is a lazy person. Laziness is sourced in *tamas*, whereas the *sthitha prajnya* is soaked in *sattva*, the *guna* favorable for the *prajnya* or intelligence to function.

Sixth Day (Chapter - VI), 2nd 'Tat Tvam Asi' Meditation

Subtler Discovery of *Parabrahma* and His 'All Merciful' Nature

----

Chapter VII

By Being the Atma,

you discover a two-way intimate bond with *Parabrahma*,

like that between you and your beloved Father/Mother,

through this devotional bond,

you will discover the truth of 'Tat Tvam Asi'

1. The Discovery of *Parabrahma*, and the Union of the *Atma* with 'That'

1. Even for devotees of some *guru* or God, learning about the Divine and the Self *(Atma)*, rarely happens, if at all.

2. If you have 'taken security' and 'dropped anchor' at the port of your *guru* or God, and are contented, then, you may never in your life make a discovery of *Parabrahma*.

3. To discover *Parabrahma*, you will have to be a skillful observer, like good scientists, and also walk in aloneness, without dependence on religious or spiritual authorities as the 'other'.

4. The discovery will be facilitated by reading the scriptures and contemplating on them.

Q : *Is it true that for devotees of various masters, gurus, learning about the unmanifest Divine and the Self (Atma) rarely happens, if at all?*

A : I raised this question just to provoke you people. There are a few masters who ask you to enquire and put you on the path like Sri J. Krishnamurti, Sri Nisargadatta Maharaj and Sri Ramana Maharshi and Adi Sankaracharya. There are also masters who do not encourage questions and if the devotees are only walking on the mundane terrain of *artha and kama*, and *moksha* is never a goal even in their thoughts, how can we expect them to come on a path of learning about the unmanifest Divine and about the Self?

Q : *For steadfast devotees who are anchored firmly to their gurus or their sampradayas or their deities, is it difficult for them to come on the path of learning, leading to the discovery of the Parabrahma?*

A : Most devotees come to a *guru* or God in times of distress, if the *guru* or God is inspiring and is able to create trust and faith, then the mind of the devotees is convinced and they drop anchor at the port of such a *guru* or God and may not unsettle themselves ever again in a lifetime. This is quite a common phenomenon in India, where the devotee never thinks for himself, because he is actually not a true seeker, but will be content only to be attached to the *guru* or to the deity. If this is the case, then they will not set out on the original path of discovery because their journey has been arrested at the milestone of finding solace in religion rather than finding the greater blessing of salvation in religion.

Q : *You emphasize skillful observation such as what scientists are supposed to do. This we can understand very well and without this, discovery and anchorage to the Parabrahma may be impossible. The phrase 'walk in aloneness without dependence on the other', obviously portrays a very solitary journey. Is this the journey that the sthitha prajnya undertakes, without any company, in isolation and solitude and in unrelenting seriousness?*

A : Yes, it has to be a solitary journey if it has to be true journey at all. Why is this so? This is an inward journey where you cannot have a companion, a fellow traveler and your life is not the same as the life of anybody else. So it is not a journey like a collective pilgrimage to Kashi or to Jerusalem, full of entertainment and a feast for the senses. The solitary journey of the *sthitha prajnya* is the only true journey. It calls for maturity, courage and grace from the Divine. This is the last journey of mankind, the noblest and the greatest. At the end of it we reach home.

----

2. Deepest Mystery about *Parabrahma (Parameswara)*

1. Though *Parabrahma* is *acala*, unmoving and in eternity, an auspicious *Sakti* also arises from *Parabrahma (Parameswara)* - called *Adi Parasakti* or *Parameswari*, the Divine Mother.

2. 'In one's own Self, which is no other than *Brahman*, there is a mysterious power known as *Avidya* (ignorance), which is beginningless and not separate from the Self. Its characteristics are 'veiling' and 'presentation of diversity'.

- Ramana Maharshi's translation of 'Drik Drisya Viveka' [14] (Adi Sankaracharya's).

Q : *When you say Parabrahma is acala - unmoving and beyond time and yet is associated with an auspicious Sakti, which creates space and time, isn't even the unmanifest Divine, simultaneously two things rather than one?*

A : Yes! *Siva & Sakti* are two independent aspects of the Divine. The peculiar thing is that in every created object there is a presence of *Siva & Sakti*. This *Sakti* has come out of *Siva*. And *Siva* is again present at the heart of *Sakti*. And this flowing into each other converts the apparent duality into a mysterious unity. It is a mystery which we can contemplate endlessly throughout our lives and yet we would not have solved it, because thought cannot grasp it.

Q : *The name given to Adi Sakti as 'Avidya rupini' which means form of ignorance or maya is very interesting. Because we know that in the field of consciousness maya is fully at work and this is what life is all about, full of pleasure and full of pain. So the 'Avidya' aspect of Adi Sakti seems necessary. How do you account for the fact that Adi Sakti also manifests as Saraswati who is not 'Avidya rupini', but on the contrary is 'Vidya rupini', that is, Adi Sakti also takes the form of learning?*

426

A   :   This seeming contradiction between the two aspects is resolved when we remember that *Adi Sakti* is *'Trigunathmika'*, She is the essence of the three *gunas* and their workings and as She is even beyond, she is described as *'Trigunatmika para'* when the *Jiva* has closed down his shop. And the new life in the abode of *Atma* begins, then the *Atma sakti* now in the form of *Saraswati* becomes available. It was not available so as the *Jiva* was wallowing in the dualistic field of consciousness.

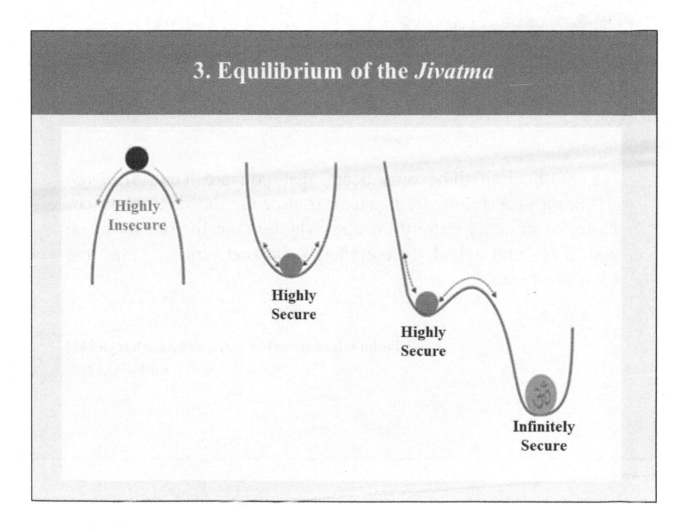

3. Equilibrium of the *Jivatma*

Highly Insecure

Highly Secure

Highly Secure

Infinitely Secure

Q   :   *Are these diagrams, illustrating how stable the Jivatma, and the Atma are?*

A   :   Yes, they show that the *Jivatma* is highly insecure, as insecurity is shown by 'instability'. The *Atma* by contrast is in stable equilibrium, that is, it is entirely secure, and nothing can rock and shake it.

Q   :   *In the last diagram, you have portrayed, a deeper equilibrium, beyond that of the Atma, what is this?*

A   :   I have been poised in the witness consciousness, since 1973 or 1974, this is the state of innocence, that of the *sthitha prajnya*. I do not know the extraordinary state which is indicated by the expression, 'infinitely secure', I know from the several writings of Sri Nisargadatta Maharaj and Sri Ramana Maharshi, that they have gone to the farthest limit, which is called, *nirvikalpa samadhi*. Hence the extraordinary clarity and austerity; originality and brilliance in their two teachings, respectively.

4. 'You are That *Brahman*', Feel this in thine own Heart-1

"Feel in thine own heart, that you are That *Brahman* (*'Brahma Tat Tvam Asi'*), which transcends the distinctions of caste, community, family lineage; which is not limited by name and form and which is completely beyond, space, time and sensory objects."

- Viveka Chudamani of Adi Sankaracharya,[41]
Sloka No:255.

Q : *Now, you have brought in the new term 'Brahman', formerly, you have used 'Parabrahma, to point to the primal umanifest Divine, beyond space and time. Why this change in the name of the Divine?*

A : *Parabrahma* is the primal source, which is unmanifest, and unknowable and the Godhead. In traditional *Advaita* literature, '*Brahman*' is also used to signify the 'absolute source' enveloping both the manifest world, as well as the unmanifest *Parabrahma*.

Q : *There is an emphasis on 'feeling' for the first time. The theme which showed, receiving with both hands, also invokes feeling. Why the reference to distinctions of caste, community, family lineage, name and form?*

A : We usually think of ourselves as the body, or as a person who was born to so and so, or as a person belonging to a certain country or to a certain community. Here it is pointed out, that these are all silly and superficial identities for the Self that we are, and that the true identity is only the Self, which is the *Atma*, which is also Godhead, *Parabrahma*. In *Advaita* literature, It is also referred to as *Brahman*.

Parabrahma or *Atma* is the abode of pure feeling, without any earthly associations. This manifests actually as an outpouring of love and is usually intense. Some people have this as a blessing, while others may not have this faculty so strongly activated. However *manas* and *Atma* also have feeling. This faculty of feeling is important for 'feeling' the truth of anything, be it in the arts, sciences, or in religious life.

Q : *What happens to a human being, Jiva, when he realizes this?*

A : The *Jiva* cannot have this realization, so long as he is enveloped in *maya*. Only the *Atma* can have this realization, then the organ of the tongue of a human body, will speak this truth, but you will think, that a human being spoke this truth. Rather, this is the truth of the *Atma*, 'spoken' by the *Atma*.

----

5. 'You are That *Brahman*', Feel this in thine own Heart-2

"That Supreme *Brahman*, which is absolutely beyond verbal comprehension; but which is within the reach of the eye of the intelligence of the enlightened *(prajnya)*; which is blemishless, indivisible compacted *awareness (chit)*; which is beginningless; That Thou Art. Feel and meditate on this truth in your heart."

- Adi Sankara's 'Viveka Chudamani', [41]
Sloka No: 256.

Q : *Adi Sankaracharya is saying that the stainless eye of prajnya (intelligence of the sthitha prajnya) can grasp 'That' - which otherwise cannot be understood. Is it through the stainless eye of prajnya that we can 'see' 'That' and by no other means?*

A : I have been able to 'see' 'That' only through the stainless eye of *prajnya*. I do not know of any other way of intuiting, 'That'.

Q : *How can the sthitha prajnya come to know that, that 'That' is blemishless, beginningless, and indivisible compacted awareness (chit)?*

A : As the *sthitha prajnya*, abides in the *Atma*, as the *Atma*, he will get the knowledge of 'That' and 'That' will also become his most beloved.

----

6. 'Hole in the Paper' *(Atma)*

"That which cannot be given name and form, for It is without quality and beyond consciousness - you may say, it is a point in consciousness which is beyond consciousness. Like a hole in the paper is both in the paper and yet not of the paper, so is the supreme state, in the very centre of consciousness and yet beyond consciousness. It is as if an opening in the mind through which the mind is flooded with light. The opening is not even the light, it is just an opening."

- Nisargadatta Maharaj[42]

Q : *Is this hole in the paper, the Atma, and is the paper, the space of consciousness?*

A : Yes, the hole in the paper, is what we have called, 'I am' or 'conscious presence'.

Q : *"The hole in the paper is both in the paper and yet, not belonging to the paper". Does this mean that awareness is also present in the field of consciousness, implicitly?*

A : Right, indeed, it is very much there, like ghee in butter. Think of the metaphor of the man enwrapped by algae. Therein we had said, the man's body was the *Atma*, the awareness. And the man with the algae wrapped around him was called the *Jiva*, which is the *self* in the field of consciousness.

Q : *If the paper is the field of consciousness, then isn't the hole, what we call awareness?*

A : Correct, that hole, is what we have been calling awareness, witness consciousness, 'conscious presence', 'I am'.

Q : *Where does the light come from?*

A : That comes from *Parabrahma*, which is beyond the *Atma*, comes from 'That', which we have called *Parabrahma*. This is again a *sutra* which should be memorized.

---

7. *Atma* (Self) and the Universe

"As waves, foam, bubbles, are not different from water, even so, the universe emanating from the *Atma* is not different from it."

-The Ashtavakra Gita[37]

Q : *Please convince us that the universe exists in the Self, the Atma, which we are.*

A : Is the universe in existence, without your being there to see it? Even if you are not there, another has to be there to attest to its existence, thus what is common to the two of you is the Self, so the universe has come upon the Self, as a dream comes upon you, in the dreaming state.

Would like you all to do a very small, but extremely significant meditation, just before you go off to sleep and as soon as waking consciousness has come upon you, in the morning. When you wake up in the morning, you will find that the world rises along with 'you'. So your *Atma* and the world are two sides of the same coin.

----

8. *Aham* sustains the World

"The word '*aham*' is itself very suggestive, the two letters of the word, 'a' and 'ha' are the first and last letters of the Sanskrit alphabet. The suggestion intended to be conveyed by the word is that 'It comprises all'. How? Because, *aham* signifies existence itself'."

- Ramana Maharshi[14]

Q : *Is this the point that went before in the previous topic?*

A : Yes, we have to note the etymology of '*Aham*' (1st person pronoun), that without the Self, there is no world.

----

9. The Self is the Canvas on which the World appears

"Just as the canvas is that whereupon the various printed figures appear, both of inanimate things like mountains and animate beings like men and animals; so also on the consciousness, which is the immutable Self (*Atma* or witness), the variegated world appears. Consciousness cannot be negated, even as the basic canvas, cannot be dispensed with."

- **Vedanta Panchadasi, Preface, xi [39]**

Q : *If this is the inference, that the Self (or, our human awareness) is the canvas, on which the 'the whole experience of the world' happens; do even the waking state experiences and the sleeping state as well as the dreaming state experiences impress themselves on the screen of this Self?*

A : Yes, everything, waking experiences, dreaming experiences, sleeping experiences, all are on the same screen of the Self, is it not?

If you are having difficulty in accepting this, it can only be due to the fallacy, which has probably become second nature to us, that rather than experiencing ourselves as the Self, we are experiencing ourselves as the body.

You can study your dreams more carefully, then you will find that, 'a dream world' comes upon the dreamer, who will be a character in the dream. Eventually when the dream is dissolved by a loud noise say, at that time, you will be in a position to appreciate that the dream world did happen to you and suddenly the dream world did also collapse. Once it has collapsed, the unreality of the dream and the dream world

434

will be evident. It is the same with the waking state. With abidance in the *Atma*, the shift in perception will happen.

---

10. After Settling in the *Atma*, or the Witness Consciousness...

1. Vexing duality will vanish. It will show its ugly face only when the calmed and silenced *Jiva* is again rudely stimulated by 'sensory calls'.

2. Then the witness consciousness will be destabilized. After this temporary 'fall', you have to do *nidhidhyasana* and *Atma anusandhana* (abiding in the *Atma*).

3. Slowly you will settle down in the witness consciousness. The new life begins.

Q : *So, even after abiding in the Atma or witness consciousness, one can again succumb to duality and become a Jiva?*

A : The possibility exists, depending on the *vasanas* and what kind of a life style and the sensory stimuli in the environment, prevails, etc.

Q : *To recover from the fall, will this be easy for a sthitha prajnya?*

A : Yes, not too difficult, as he will never wallow in the past nor get into day dreaming into the future. The fact that, he has come on the ground of the *Atma* is his great strength.

Q : *The new life that you are talking about is life lived as a sthitha prajnya, with pratyahara, or withdrawal of the senses from the sense organs, turning away from sensory stimuli, turning away from company of people caught in maya?*

A   :   Yes, for such a *sthitha prajnya*, the new life begins, but there is no gurantee, he must maintain vigilance at all times, he is peaceful fundamentally, intense and rooted in the present, so because of this groundedness, he is much more secure than the *Jiva*.

---

11. New Life: Unprecedented Clarity, Courage, Calmness

When you have settled in the
witness consciousness:
You effortlessly understand religion and scriptures. You attain
innocence.
"Innocence is incapability of getting hurt".
"Life begins when thought ends".
You have the new option of meeting life,
not from *self*, but from *Atma*.

Q   :   *What is characteristic of the Jiva is his 'survival tendencies'. Does the sthitha prajnya not make any attempts to survive?*

A   :   No, he accepts what life gives him, does his best, because he has no distractions and, every act gives joy, even drinking a glass of water, his is a life of contentment and inward integrity. A hall mark of the *sthitha prajnya*, is his 'unknowingness', because his peace, somehow co-exists with this unknowingness, his innocence. He does not become insecure, because of his inability to know.

Q   :   *The Jiva lives in fear, what about the sthitha prajnya?*

A   :   The *sthitha prajnya*, is a perfect stranger to fear.

Q   :   *The sthitha prajnya, does he judge?*

A : If he starts judging, he is slowly slipping into the muddy ground of consciousness. That is a sign for him to pull back to the witnessing awareness.

Q : *The Jiva is full of ulterior motives, dishonesty, comparison and secret planning. Does not the sthitha prajnya have these mean traits at all?*

A : What are you asking, after hearing so much, the *sthitha prajnya* is unselfish, honest, never compares, because he is infinitely secure, and no secretive nature.

Q : *Then this is extremely noble, the sthitha prajnya's life.*

A : Yes, indeed it is, it is the most important milestone to cross in the spiritual life. It is what Maharaj declares to be *Jivanmukti* or liberation itself.

12. Seeing the *Atma* in All

The Panchakośas & Ātma Tattva

Instead of a vexing duality, you will see the same *Atma*, and relationship will be child's play. When the *self*, gets hurt, then you will have to watch the *self* and learn. By *choiceless awareness*, *self* will once more become calm and silent.

Q : *Are you saying that, once one has settled in the witness consciousness (Atma), all relationships become so easy that you never have to lie, never play games, is this what this picture shows?*

A : Right, because you will see the same *Atma*, that you are, everywhere, so how can you treat yourself and another in different ways? Because, you have the constant blessings of inner peace and contentment, even if someone insults you, you will never react because the 'reaction' is the *self* in action.

Q : *The Aum symbol, is this the symbol of the Atma? And are the concentric circles, the five sheaths around the Atma, what we have already gone into?*

A : Yes, *Aum* is the symbol for the *Atma*, and the concentric circles in each case are the *pancha kosas*, the five sheaths.

Q : *Then will we treat all humans alike, whether they are high or low in our society, whether they are good or bad people?*

A : Yes indeed, and what is more, you will enjoy people, because each is the Divine, each is the *Atma*, deluded by *maya*, but a unique manifestation that is a name and a form, nevertheless.

13. Appears to be very very far, when It is actually very very near

'Bahir Anthas Cha Bhutanam...' [BG(XIII.15)]

Q : *Does this picture show the sthitha prajnya (a woman in this case) going about her work, peacefully, but because, she is innocent, she is incapable of judging, so when she goes to the market, and in that din, she meets a housemaid, she talks to her from her peace, because she may feel no separation from her, she sees the same Self, the Atma everywhere?*

A : Right, you have put it quite aptly, this is what it amounts to.

I have show two 'I's, they signify the *Atma*, and the *sthitha prajnya* is poised therein, and sees only that *Atma*, which incidentally is, 'That' everywhere.

Q : *What is the sloka in the Bhagavad Gita Sloka, that we are mentioning here as pertinent?*

A : When one comes on the path of *self* - Knowing and then moves to Self - Realization, one should study certain important works, just to get the bearings right. This has been emphasized by Sri Ramana Maharshi and Adi Sankaracharya and it is necessary, because the path is constituted by the three step process: *sravana, manana and nidhidhyasana. Sravana* is listening to the truth. In ancient days of the oral traditions, listening superseded reading, but in today's world, I would say, reading displaces, *sravana*, because reading also enables recapitulation, reading a second time, a third time and so on.

Coming to the *sloka* from the Bhagavad Gita : XIII.15, it says, " 'That' or the *Atma*, is *present within and without all beings*, both animate beings, like humans, animals, reptiles, insects, and also inanimate beings, like stones, water, air, fire, earth, space, stars, planets, etc. As It is very subtle to perceive, It appears to be very very far, when in truth, It is, in fact, very very near."

Q : *So, regarding the sthitha prajnya, has he vomited out the deadly poison of duality, which he was comfortable with, when he was a Jiva?*

A : Absolutely, upon settling in the *Atma*, as the *Atma*, the elimination of duality has happened, because in the *Atma*, as the *Atma*, he is not an individual, 'somebody', in opposition to a hundred 'others'.

----

14. Radha-Krishna

The *Atma* is in unison with *Parabrahma*, the unmanifest Divine, also called *Parameswara*. Unfortunately, *Parabrahma* is not a sense object to which the senses can cling. Yet the bliss of union, shown in mythic form here is so irresistible for the *Atma*, that Bhagavan Ramana Wrote:

"I came to feed on Thee, but Thou hast fed on me; now there is Peace, Oh Arunachala!

"Let me, Thy prey, surrender unto Thee and be consumed and so have Peace, Oh Arunachala!"

Q : *Usually, when we see a picture or the Sri Murti of Radha-Krishna, because human beings are in maya, they think this portrays love between the woman Radha and the God Krishna, who was a man. If they are spiritually more mature they will say, Radha represents the human soul or the Atma, and Krishna represents, the historical Divine incarnation. What is your own interpretation, which you are presenting to all of us?*

A : Clearly, both Radha and Krishna were historical human beings. If you study the life of Krishna, you would know that, Radha was attracted to Krishna, *not as a romantic beloved, but as a devotee will be attracted to God. This is impossible for other people to understand, unless they are also devotees of God, like Radha was.* Leaving aside, the historical aspect of this truth, I feel, we should concentrate on this *Sri Murti* of Radha-Krishna, because the artist has tried to illustrate the subtle principle of Self - Realization, implicit in the Upanishadic *sutra*, 'Tat Tvam Asi' (That Thou Art). In India, art was always a handmaiden of religion or *dharma*, and it was customary for religious truths to be portrayed in artistic works. This picture is one such example.

We see a physical embrace here, but have to understand that, *this is a rapturous embrace in consciousness, in the inner world, between the Atma (Radha) and the*

440

unmanifest Divine (Krishna). The embrace is so rapturous and 'tight', that no border can be drawn, between the *Atma* and the *Parabrahma* ('That'). You can see that one leg of Krishna has become one leg of Radha's, implying this is a borderless union between the *Atma* and 'That'.

Q : *Ramana Maharshi's words of 'rapturous union' with Arunachala, who is, 'That' seems to be an example of the purest love, in which nothing is held back.*

A : Yes, the strange thing is that Sri Ramana Maharshi, in spite of being a sage, a Maharshi, was also a devotee of the highest kind-here we are seeing the outpouring of *nirguna bhakti.* 'Arunachala' could not have meant the physical hill for him alone, it must have meant, the ineffable unmanifest Divine, 'That'. For his devotees, it could have been only the physical hill.

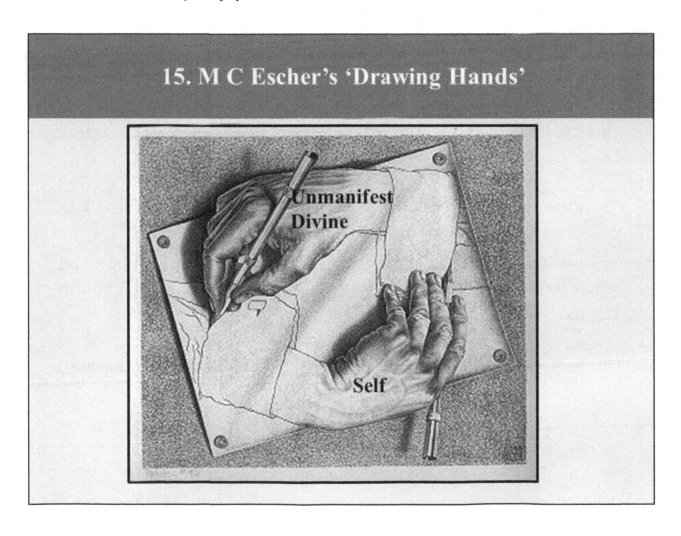

15. M C Escher's 'Drawing Hands'

Q : *What are you trying to teach through this enigmatic picture, which is one of the paintings of M. C. Escher?*

A   :   This too, like, 'Radha Krishna' portrays the truth of 'Tat Tvam Asi'. It is a metaphor for Tat Tvam Asi. The painting may be said to challenge the 'block thinking' in which the cause, has to have an independent existence, apart from the effect. Here, the effect (one hand) is also seen to be the cause (one hand). Both the *Atma* (Self) and the Divine ('That') in the unmanifest aspect, are on par, both are seen to be two aspects of a larger 'twin reality'.

Q   :   *Are all these metaphors and pictures, paintings, intended to inspire us to undertake this meditative journey to the Divine, by just abiding in the Atma?*

A   :   Your rational limited mind will naturally rebel against the supposition that the *Atma* is the same as *Brahman (Parabrahma)* - even without ever caring to know and abide in the *Atma*. So, to destroy that limited rational mind, I am attempting to create the opposite conviction that this indeed is the truth.

16. "One always is the Self"

"One ever is the Self. To ask oneself, 'Who and whereabouts am I?', is like the drunken man's enquiry, "Who am I?" and "Where am I?"

-Ramana Maharshi[14]

(In 'Ekatma Panchakam')

Q   :   *The suggestion has never been made to us, so emphatically before, except by the great sages, like Adi Sankaracharya and now Sri Ramana Maharshi that we cannot be anything but the Self. But honestly, we may be still in the delusion that we are the body, so the whole idea that one is the Self, is not really 'common sense for us' yet. For Ramana Maharshi it is 'common sense' and obvious. So, is this retreat, the 'first threat', or the first serious challenge to our delusion?*

A : You could take it that way, but merely taking it that way is of no use. As we discussed elsewhere, a lot of *sadhana* has to be done, not by the *Jiva*, who is trapped in illusion, but by the witness, the, I am ness, or the pure 'I'. By doing the *sadhana*, enjoined by the *advaitic* tradition, Sri Ramana Maharshi and Sri J. Krishnamurti and Sri Maharaj, we will become free of this delusion.

Q : *By comparing the man who does not know that he is the Self, to a drunken man, Ramana Maharshi seems to tell us that, maya has been so strong, that we are all practically inebriated (drunken with delusion)?*

A : Yes, we are like that, because *maya* is so delirious. Maharshi's metaphor is humorous.

----

17. The *Atma's* 'Reflection' is the *Jiva (self)*

"I am that conscious Self *(Atma)*, of whom the *self (Jiva)* is not independent, as the image in a mirror is not independent of the object reflected."

"Just as the reflection of the Sun on agitated waters *seems to break up,* but remains perfect on a calm surface, so also am I the conscious Self *(Atma), unrecognizable in agitated intellects* though I clearly shine in those which are calm."

- Hastamalaka (Adi Sankaracharya's disciple)[14]

Q : *This is one of the teachings which we have already seen before, and is so beautiful, because no one has correlated the Jiva with the Atma in such a simple fashion. That means, that so long as we have the body and the senses, the formation of this very troublesome thing called Jiva is inevitable-that there can no earthly human life without the Jiva ever?*

A : That is absolutely correct, this is a golden *sutra* in Self - Realization.

Q : *Hastamalaka's metaphor is thought provoking. It answers the question, why so few of us are able to identify ourselves with the Atma, while the vast majority of humanity, cannot make sense out of the statement that we are the Atma. Must we then infer that those who cannot identify with the Atma, have their intellects deluded by false perceptions?*

A : Yes, those who are unable to make sense of the statement that we are the *Atma*, are either too identified with the body, or too much in thought, so unable to be in the spiritual *sattva guna*, which alone is conducive to this kind of realization.

Q : *Was Hastamalaka Self - Realized, like Adi Sankaracharya, his Master?*

A : Yes, he was Self - Realized, that is another unbelievable amazing story, which Sri Ramana Maharshi told his disciples, when he translated a very important work of Sri Adi Sankaracharya, called *Viveka Chudamani*. The title means 'Crest Jewel of Discrimination'.

Here is that story, as Sri Ramana Maharshi told his disciples who were listening to him. "Adi Sankara, during his travels, was in the village Srivali, there a brahmin, by name Prabhakara came to him with his 13-year old son, who was dumb from childhood, with no likes and dislikes, no sense of honor and dishonor. And the boy was also completely inactive."[14] So, seeing this, Adi Sankara asked the boy a number of questions about his identity, and immediately the boy broke out, most eloquently, speaking the highest Truth of Self - Realization. Adi Sankara's disciples watching this, asked their master, 'how does it happen that without reading the scriptures and going through, *sravana, manana and nidhidhyasana*, this 13 year old boy became Self - Realized?'

Adi Sankaracharya, explained the paradox thus. "His mother left her two year old child in the care of a great and highly accomplished *yogi*, who was practicing austerities on the bank of the Yamuna river, while she went to bathe in the river with some women. The child walked towards the water and got drowned. Out of his compassion for his disconsolate mother, the sadhu abandoned his body and entered that of the child. That is why this boy has attained this high state."[14]

----

18. The *Atma (Siva)* and *Jiva (Sakti)*

Acknowledgement : Harish Johari's 'Chakras' and 'Tools for Tantra'. Inner Traditions, India.

Q : *Here Siva & Sakti are shown as two gods, but in human form, now I would think that the eternal truth or the Divine source, is not a human form at all, so is this mythological representation only an artist's representation of a truth, which our minds may never be able to grasp?*

A : Yes, you are right. All Self - Realized teachers have emphasized that the eternal truth cannot be captured by the mind and by words. *'a-vang-manasa gochara'*, meaning 'not reached by words, by speech *(vak)* and by feelings *(manas)* even. The prefix, 'a' serves to negate words, speech, mind and feelings.

Human beings have an innate urge to communicate their discoveries, and this is usually done through speech or song, or writing - through the careful and skillful use of words and sometimes, the eternal truth can also be communicated through dance form and through various art forms - like these mythic pictures.

In India, art has always been a kind of 'handmaiden' of religion, whose concern is always with the eternal truth. All the classical art in India has been 'religious' in spirit and in intention. And art can take a great variety of forms of expression - painting, singing, dancing, drama and writing. Indian classical music and classical dance are religious in spirit. The *sapta swaras* (sa, ri, ga, ma, pa, da, ni) are bound up with the five manifestations of *Siva*.

When a lot has been sung, spoken, and written about the eternal truth, some illumined teachers have also chosen 'silence' as a language, 'way of living itself' also as a language in which to communicate the eternal truth. 'Dakshinamurti' is that manifestation of *Siva* as the silent teacher. Sri Ramana Maharshi also spoke very very little, generally.

Mythology (in the *Puranas*) actually has been an independent vehicle for conveying the eternal truth. This anthropomorphic form of *Siva & Sakti* conveys something - not the literal masculine and feminine forms - completely spiritual-so the mythic picture conveys a *sutra*, an eternal principle-of how the timeless (this, is *Siva*) is the 'Power Wielder', whereas the changeful, the movement of energy in time and as time is the 'Power' which our senses see. *Sakti* is this Power. In fact, the Sanskrit word *Sakti* means energy or 'Power'. And *Siva* is the source, behind the Power, but He is unmanifest, invisible-*so we can make the fatal mistake of supposing Him to be non-existent-because He is not a sense object, only Sakti is the sense object.*

Q : *In this beautiful picture, we see Sakti in the foreground, looking bright and resplendent and dancing with abandon and in ecstasy, in freedom. However, in the background, we also see Siva, in a faintly ashen color, but involved with Her, in some protective way, just as a mother would be very concerned about her infant. So does this mean that as the 'Power Wielder', He is Her benevolent master, and because of His benevolence, He has granted freedom to her to do what She likes, and goes with Her wherever She wants to go? Is this understanding right?*

A : In fact, *Sakti* is called 'Svatantriya Sakti', meaning 'independent Power' or 'independent energy', and She can keep this 'independence' as long as She wishes, till She has the realization that She after all 'is shining only in borrowed feathers', and so decides to return home to *Siva*, Her beloved master. So there is an extroverted movement for *Sakti* and then following this there is also an introverted movement of *Sakti* - Her homecoming. We may also think of *Siva* as the Sun, and *Sakti* as sunlight.

All our desires, aspirations, cravings, feelings, thinking is the dance of *Sakti*, and in all this, *Siva* is 'behind the scenes', He is non-interfering and watching as a witness. *So, the dance of Sakti & Siva is happening in our consciousness, within us. It is not a physical romantic or sensual dance. If Sakti is life, Siva is 'life of that life'. Sakti is becoming, Siva is being. Sakti is time, Siva is timelessness, eternity, death, silence, the beginning and ending of life.*

Q : *If this dance of Siva & Sakti is happening in our consciousness, then why is this dance being depicted on a Himalayan terrain?*

A : The floor on which the dance is happening is the Himalayan terrain-this just shows that the dance has transcendental and cosmological origin, mysterious and beyond human comprehension - even though it may be transpiring in the microcosmic realm of our limited human consciousness. This dance of *Siva & Sakti* must also be applicable to the cosmos, *but in this retreat, we focus on the dance within the human consciousness.*

Q : *So, could I conclude that this dance of Siva & Sakti is a metaphor, quite similar to the two birds of the Mundaka Upanishad? Then obviously the watching bird is Siva and the eating bird is Sakti-right?*

A : You have asked two very interesting questions. Yes, indeed, the dance of *Siva & Sakti* is a metaphor, much like the two 'Tat Tvam Asi' birds. And yes, indeed, it is the witnessing bird that is *Siva*, and the engrossed eating bird is *Sakti*.

Q : *Another intriguing question comes up. Why do we see so many snakes on Siva's body?*

A : This is a very good question which deserves clarification. The snakes are also metaphors, but not just metaphors too-they represent the mysterious and secret *kundalini* energy in the *chakras* and *nadis,* a power which is awakened only as one approaches and comes closer to *Siva.* You will remember that at the Amrit Desai Yoga Institute at Salt Springs, Florida, we had the opportunity to listen to a seeker, who had all these experiences, exactly as seen in this mythic picture of *Siva & Sakti.* In fact, it is such *kundalini* experiences, which are behind these mystic art forms of *Siva & Sakti.* Such experiences do befall, serious seekers, especially when they are doing sustained *sadhana* in the secure environment of an *ashram.*

However, the emphasis in this retreat is not on *kundalini* experiences, because in *Jnana yoga,* the path of understanding, there is no place for *kundalini* experiences, though they may befall some seekers.

----

19. *Siva* becomes more dominant

In the *sthitha prajnya's* consciousness, *Siva* is more dominant, so *Sakti* is tamed and silenced.

Acknowledgement : Harish Johari's 'Chakras' and 'Tools for Tantra'. Inner Traditions, India.

Q : *Sakti in this picture seems to correspond to the 'Jiva' bird, while Siva, naturally to the Atma bird. The Jiva bird, seems to have voluntarily yielded to the presence of Siva, and the tejas or glow is the 'conscious presence' of the Atma, of ourself. Having said all this, will this mythic picture, correspond to the sthitha prajnya, and to one who has settled down in the Atma?*

A : Yes, this is a portraiture of the *sthitha prajnya's* state where the *Sivatva*, the quality of being *Siva* and the *prajnya* are awakened.

Q : *As this mythic picture stands for the sthitha prajnya, it seems to imply that Sakti or the activity of thought and feeling is greatly diminished in the sthitha prajnya? Or has it actually come under the control of Siva (Atma)?*

A : *Sakti* becomes obedient and a *dasi* of *Siva*. Previously she was a virago, disobedient and an authourity unto herself and unrecognizing of *Siva*, so long as the *Jiva* was in the consciousness country. In the *sthitha prajnya* state, *Sakti* works receiving mandates from *Siva*. It is *Siva* who gives the inspiration and the goal and *Sakti* executes the same. So there is great harmony between silence and action.

20. From Personal God *(Ishtha Devata)* to the Unmanifest Divine *(Parabrahma)*

1. When the *Jiva* is full of desires and fears, the personal God will act like a mirror which will 'reflect' and 'grant' these desires and 'offer protection' against these fears - which 'threaten' the *Jiva*.

2. When the *Jiva* is purified, calmed, and made innocent and whole (with integrity), then it is ready to know God, *not for fulfilling desires, and seeking protection from fears*. Then its God is 'That', viz., *Parabrahma, Parameswara, Atma*.

Q : *When the Jiva is in the consciousness country, the whole spiritual phenomenon of the personal God, 'granting' desires of the Jiva and 'offering protection' to the Jiva - through some external 'grace', which seems to come from the 'external' God, or guru or deity of the Jiva - isn't all of this, 'externalization of the grace', the Jiva's own making?*

I ask this question, because, the Jiva does have that very potent Atma sakti, but as the Jiva has still not found the ground of the Atma, it naturally has a very poor opinion about itself, so unable to accept its marvelous and powerful Atmahood and its exalted Divinity (which is the truth); the Jiva in ignorance, thinks in it's heart, 'I do not have this power', 'so let me go to that master, or that God, that God certainly has great power, that master certainly has great power, so he can certainly save me from this great difficulty, so let me go to them'. Isn't such thinking by the Jiva, if it is a conviction, itself sufficient, for the grace, to come from outside, rather than from within, from the Atma?

A : Yes, you have seen through the illusion in the belief and the thinking that the grace is from outside, when in truth, it can very well come from the *Atma*. We have to note at

450

this stage that the *Jiva* is deeply emnmeshed in *maya*, and this being the *Jiva's* condition, the deluded *Jiva* is in no state of spiritual maturity or spiritual intelligence, to realize that it is itself the source of power. So, rather than attempt to convert the *Jiva* into a *sthitha prajnya*, for whom all that you say will be self-evident, we must be wise, and allow the *Jiva*, to evolve and grow, at his snail's pace and in this deluded condition, he cannot but conceive of the grace as coming from 'outside', from his deity, his master or his God. As the vast majority of people are only *Jivas*, in ignorance and *maya*, we have to be compassionate enough, to allow the *Jivas* (who are not *sthitha prajnyas*), to unknowingly, project out their *Atma sakti* on to a deity or master, whereupon, the deity or master, will simply reflect this *Atma sakti*, which will now come as the grace from the deity, instead of from the well-spring of the *Atma*.

Q : *Thus, as Adi Sankaracharya had said, already thousands of years ago, religion can be in two tiers, a lower one, in which duality and division between the devotee and his God is inbuilt and held there by maya and a higher tier, in which the Self or the Atma is itself the unmanifest Divine.*

A : Yes, the lower tier religion is for the *Jivas*, and the higher tier religion is naturally for the *sthitha prajnyas*.

----

21. *Meenakshi - Sundaresvarar Kalyanam*

Sakti, giving up her restlessness and taking refuge in *Siva*, is reflected in *sanatana dharma* in many ways: in the legend of *Ardhanarisvara* and in the mythic image of *Meenakshi Sundaresvarar* 'Kalyanam' in Madurai.

Q : *I can see that the golden colored God is Siva, who is the blue colored body, to the right of Goddess Meenakshi?*

A : That is the God *Vishnu*, who is the *immanent aspect* of the *transcendent Siva*. To give clarity, different 'bodies' and different 'forms' are shown, in truth there is but one essence, in the unmanifest realm, called *Parabrahma*, or sometimes called *Brahman*. Goddess *Meenakshi* is in the centre.

Q : *So this wedlock is a symbolic thing, showing returning home of Sakti, after her independent 'roaming' in the world of maya, which She has only created?*

A : Correct, it is the celebration of the homecoming of *Sakti*, after she has renounced, her mad independence, which is also, comically part of the overall Divine plan.

Q : *Is sanatana dharma, another name for the Hindu religion?*

A : As you have sensed, yes, it is another name.

Q : *You also speak of Ardhanareeswara and His legend?*

A : *Ardhanareeswara* is another portraiture of *Siva & Sakti*, implying a strict and permanent inseparability of *Sakti* from *Siva* and vice versa. 'Ardha' means half, and

'*Naree*' means woman, so this mythic manifestation of *Siva & Sakti*, accommodates both *Siva & Sakti* in the same icon.

Q : *What is the significance of the antelope in the left hand of Siva?*

A : The antelope is known for its darting nature and swiftness, so it is *Sakti*, as She operates in consciousness-showing that this too is onl;y as aspect of the silence and peace of *Siva*, his handy work, despite having no inherent tranquility in its swift and capricious movements based on fear.

---

22. *Svetashvatara Up.* on the *Atma*

"As oil in sesame seeds, as butter in milk, as water in *srota**, as fire in fuel-sticks; he finds in his own being that One *(Atman)* - he, who sees Him (the *Atman*) through *satva* (truthfulness) and *tapas* (austerity). [I.15]

"He sees the all pervading *Atman*, as butter lying dormant in milk; when he is rooted in *self* - knowledge and *self* - discipline – which is the final goal of the *Upanishad*, the final goal of the *Upanishad*." [I.16]

- Svetashvatara Up.[22]

*Srota means dry river bed.

Q : *What a profound declaration on the Atma is this! It seems to be implied in this that the Atma, which unifies the whole of creation, is deeply buried, under the incessant activity of Sakti in consciousness?*

A : Yes, we have been discovering this and becoming comfortable with this very subtle truth of the *Atma*. It is subtle and It is hidden, but not difficult to realize, It is really who we are.

Q : *A question comes to mind: Does Krishnamurti ever talk of the Atma, I ask this question because he emphasizes awareness?*

A : No, as he was not a traditionalist, who had been brought up in the *Vedic* tradition; but on the other hand, much exposed to the West, he was not learned in the *Vedic* literature, nor was it necessary for him, because he was a *Jivanmukta*. He only stressed on awareness, never on the *Atma*. His teaching, must be considered to be a *species* which belongs to the genus of the Buddhist teachings.

Q : *What is very noteworthy in this Svetashvatara Upanishad is the plain emphasis on truthfulness and austerity. Can you say, why this is important, especially in the modern world?*

A : Whether you belong to the modern world or the spiritually refined ancient world or even a tribal primitive world, truth is truth, it will not bend to suit people of various *yugas* amd various civilizations. Austerity is important, because it implies, rearranging our life style, so as to have more time to be by oneself, rather than devoting more time to various kinds of sensory indulgences. It implies, simplicity and dedication to truth. I think, these are extremely important, if one is to discover the *Atma*, not as a distant brilliant star to be perceived and worshipped, but as the essence of oneself On the contrary, as we are the *Atma*, we can know who we are only by turning inwards.

Q : *The emphasis on self - knowledge and self-discipline is so strong, without that, we will not have Self - Realization, is it?*

A : I would say, these are important and are in fact qualifications, for that peace to have a lasting quality and certainty. In my case, I went through all this, it was part of my spiritual life. Austerity and truthfulness are of paramount importance, I reiterate this. I learn this from the master, Sri J. Krishnamurti.

----

23. The Upanishads on the Unmanifest Divine

"The One Unifier of the universe, by knowing Him as 'kind, benign' *(Śivam)*, one attains peace forever.

- *Svetashvatara Up.* IV.14[22]

"(Yes!), by knowing Him as 'kind, benign' *(Śivam)*, who is hidden in all things- like subtle ghee inside fine butter."

- *Svetashvatara Up.* IV.16[22]

Q : *Everywhere, we see only metaphors- like 'ghee hidden in butter', like 'butter hidden in milk', etc.*

A : This is the only way you can communicate, so subtle a truth.

Q : *Does Sivam means kind and benign?*

A : *Siva* means peace, auspiciousness, compassion. Hence also kind, benign.

Q : *What is the meaning of Svetashvatara?*

A : *Ashva* means horse, *sveta* means white, so the word means white horse, or pure horse, or *sattvic* horse.

----

24. *Svetasvatara Up.* on the Hidden Divine

एको देवः सर्वभूतेषु गूढः
सर्वव्यापी सर्वभूतान्तरात्मा ।
कर्माध्यक्षः सर्वभूताधिवासः
साक्षी चेता केवलो निर्गुणश्च ॥

Eko devaḥ Sarvabhūteṣu gūḍhaḥ
Sarvavyāpī Sarvabhūtāntarātmā I
Karmādhyakṣaḥ Sarvabhūtādhivāsaḥ
Sākṣī Cetā Kevalo Nirguṇaśca II   (Ch.VI,#11)

- Svetashvatara Up. VI.11[22]

Meaning of this *Sloka*

There is one Divine being, who is deeply hidden in every form; who is present every where; who is the inner Self of all beings; who is dispenser of the fruits of *karma*; who abides in all beings, as the witness, awareness, without attributes and qualities and who is all alone.

Seventh Day (Chapter -VII), 1ˢᵗ 'Tat Tvam Asi' Meditation

Discovery of Union of the *Atma* with *Parabrahma*

----

25. *Sthitha Prajnya* in Action

Karmaṇy ev' ādhikāras te mā phaleṣu kadācana |
mā karma-phala-hetur bhūr mā te saṅgo' stv akarmaṇi ||

- Bhagavad Gita II.47[7]

Your (dharmic) mandate is for work only; but never for its results. let not the results of your actions be your motive and concern, nor let your attachment be to inaction.

Q : *To give a sutra to be followed is one thing, and whether a sadhaka can and will follow the same is quite another matter. This is a well-known sutra in India, which is often quoted ('nishkaama karma' sutra, meaning, 'action devoid of self-centered motivation').*

The Jiva usually, dwells and dreams of the fruits, and in expectation of the fruits only, it acts. In this approach of the Jiva, there is great pleasure for the Jiva (self), but also, naturally the possibility of great pain and disappointment. Contrary to this pattern, the teaching from the Bhagavad Gita, urges you to turn your back on the fruits, and never work for the fruits, nor fall into apathy and indifference, because your actions are unfruitful. Will this be possible for the Jiva at all? Can the Jiva live up to these injunctions?

A : Obviously, the renunciation of the fruits of actions is natural for the *sthitha prajnya*, this is in fact how he acts. The truth is that he never falls into apathy and inaction, arising from despondency. The *Jiva*, if it has already acquired some little maturity, can attempt to turn away from the fruits. It may fail in the first few attempts, and thus, by attempting to live up to this, the *Jiva* has the possibility of making its *self*, 'void' where the fruits are concerned. Make also the *self* void, where the desire for inaction is concerned, in a moment of despondency. However in this, desire for inaction, there may be no spontaneity.

Most significantly, by coming on the path of *self* - Knowing and that followed by Self - Realization, the *Jiva* need not struggle, these admirable selfless qualities will automatically arise in the *sthitha prajnya*.

26. The *Atma* is untainted, like *Akash*

Yathā sarva-gataṁ saukṣmyād ākāśaṁ n'opalipyate |
Sarvatr'āvasthito dehe tathā'tmā n'opalipyate ||

- **Bhagavad Gita XIII.32[26]**

"Just as the all pervading *akash*, because of its subtlety is untainted by anything, so this *Atman*, though residing in all bodies as the 'I' is never tainted by any impurity."

Q : *Is this Atma imperishable and incorruptible, as J. Krishnamurti often says?*

A : Yes, this is indeed the *Atma*, because the *Atma* is on a plane, outside time and space.

Q : *Thus, the Atma of a criminal, or a cheat, is also ever blemishless and pure?*

A : Yes, It always is. However the consciousness is awfully polluted in such asuric individuals and all spiritual practices are always only intended to purify the polluted consciousness.

27. *Parabrahma*: 'Very Far but Very Near'

Bahir antaś ca bhūtānām acaram caram eva ca |
Sūkṣmatvāt tad avijñeyam dūrastham c'āntike ca tat ||

- **Bhagavad Gita XIII.15[26]**

Parabrahma, is within and without all beings, both living as well as non-living. For the reason of His subtlety, i.e., He cannot be 'seen & understood, like all other sense objects'; we may say, He is very, very far, although in reality He is very, very near.

Q : *So, it is only the inconceivable Parabrahma, who is imperceptible, isn't it, not certainly the Atma?*

A : You are the *Atma*, It is the essence of your unrecognized being, underlying all your becoming, and you will know that if you are a true seeker. It is the 'conscious presence', that you are, to use the special vocabulary of Nisargadatta Maharaj. This *Atma*, which we are, is fortunately 'That', the unknowable Supreme Being, *Parabrahma*, so it is only the *Parabrahma*, whom we will never know. The *Atma* we also cannot know as a physical sensory object, since, the *Atma* is the living subject, timeless and spaceless.

Q : *So, firstly, the subtlety of the Parabrahma, secondly the unknowability of the Parabrahma, and thirdly, the Parabrahma not being accessible to sensory perceptions-are these the three concomitant factors, which come together and give the false impression that He is very very far, when He is actually the Atma itself, our timeless and spaceless being?*

A   : Yes, only three factors, 'conspire together' to create the illusion that the *Parabrahma*, 'That' is very very far, when the opposite is true. So, to look for the *Parabrahma* in an entity, orther than the *Atma,* is to give room for illusions.

---

28. Correct Perception of that *Bhagavan*

Yo māṁ paśyati sarvatra sarvaṁ ca mayi paśyati |
tasyāhaṁ na praṇaśyāmi sa ca me na praṇaśyati ||

- Bhagavad Gita VI.30[23]

He who sees Me everywhere, and sees every thing in Me, he never becomes separated from Me, nor do I become separated from him.

Q   : *Can we understand this sutra from the Bhagavad Gita, using 'Atma tattva', or the nature of the Atma, as it has been taught to us?*

A   : And what would be your way of understanding this *sutra*?

Q   : *As the Atma is in every created object, whether it is a stone, insect or a Sage or a building, so 'That' is also everywhere, because the Atma is 'That' only. As the whole world exists in us, on the canvas of the Self, the Atma, surely the whole world, exists in Him only. And when these are true, the sloka is also true.*

A   : Good logic, and this ought to give that very imp *intellectual conviction* which has been strongly emphasized by Adi Sankaracharya.

29. 'Everywhere, only the Self Appears'

Sarva-bhūta-stham Ātmānaṁ sarva-bhūtāni c'Ātmani |
īkṣate yoga-yukt'Ātmā sarvatra sama-darśanaḥ ||

- **Bhagavad Gita VI.29[23]**

When one is yoked to the *Atma* by *yoga* he sees the *Atma* abiding in all beings and all beings in the *Atma*; he sees the same everywhere.

Q : *We are reiterating the same truth again and again in slightly different ways, so as to rub out our conditioning which is born of sensory perception and which therefore is erroneous. In the sciences it has been discovered that 'the senses are liars and deceivers'. Is it not the same discovery in the field of religion also?*

A : Here too, sensory perceptions turn out to be anything but the truth, because what is a subjective universe and a pattern formation on the canvas of the Self, has turned topsy turvy due to sensory perception and we have come to believe that the universe is an objective reality that exists apart from us. Here we may note that not only the senses are liars and deceivers, as in the sciences, but language itself is a fantastic illusion, because the duality in consciousness and the body centered nature of the *Jivas* is fully incorporated into our language and the pronouns of the first person, second person and third person. Nothing which we discover by sitting in the throne of the *Atma* has ever become part of our language. The moment we open our mouth, we have to basically speak something which is full of illusion and this is not any different from a drunken man blabbering something which is at complete variance with the truth. The sciences are not disenchanted with the language, as sages in the religious field are, because sciences study and observe the physical world which is the world of duality. Hindusim in its farther reaches, namely *Advaita* mostly has all the discoveries made from the throne of the *Atma* to be shared, but these cannot be shared through the dualistic language, unless both the speaker and the listener have gone beyond duality.

---

30. *Siva-Sakti Sutra*

यावत्संजायते किंचित्सत्त्वं स्थावरजङ्गमम् ।
क्षेत्रक्षेत्रज्ञसंयोगात्तद्विद्धि भरतर्षभ ॥

॥ १३ ॥ २६ ॥

Yāvat saṁjāyate kiñcit sattvaṁ sthāvara-jaṅgamam |
Kṣetra-kṣetrajña-saṁyogāt tad viddhi Bharata'rṣabha ||

- **Bhagavad Gita XIII.26[26]**

Sankara: This is the basis of *Vastu shastra*. The *Vastu purusha* in *Vastu shastra* is the *Sivatva*, the *Atmatva* in every building and in every object of creation. The *sutra* basically says, that every created object is a combination of *Siva & Sakti*. *Siva* is the subtle presence of the Supreme Being, 'That', as *Atma* of the object, and this is in no way different from your *Atma* or my *Atma*. In this sense, every object, whether it is animate or inanimate has an *Atma* and this *Atma* is the same as ours. *Sakti* can be weak or *Sakti* can be strong. When spiritual people prepare sacred objects, such as the *vigrahas* in temples, or gem pendants, they usually empower these sacred objects with *mantric* energy, which is *Sakti*. This *Sakti* in infused into the sacred object, carrying the *samkalpa*, thus investing the sacred object with the specific power to do whatever spiritual function it is supposed to do. *Siva* or *Atma* are the same in all objects whether they are sacred or not. *Sakti* alone is the variable. These *sutras* must be correctly memorized and by repeating them, the consciousness will come to dwell on their meaning and they will get internalized this way.

31. Clear Pond : Waters of the *Atma*

Clear Pond/Lake = 'Waters of the *Atma*',
'Witnessing' Bird = Seat of Feeling *per se.*

Sankara: The above pond or lake of clear water is being used as a metaphor for pure feeling, which is completely bereft of every possible contamination of sensory objects. This is so new to us, this state of utter purity, that we may not be able to grasp the significance of all this, without a direct experience of such pure feeling, not, for something, some idea or person, opr thing, but rather, pure feeling *per se,* without any association with an animate or inanimate sensory object. To know deeply and grasp this rather esoteric theme of feeling *per se,* divested of every association, verbal, or sensory, we will do well to go to the work of the master Sri J. Krishnamurti. He is seen discussing this theme, with a seeker who had come to talk to him, regarding the importance of having 'simplicity in life'. I shall reproduce their conversation, to bring the significance of this theme into full relief.[44]

Krishnamurti: Have you ever tried to stay with the feeling?

Seeker: 'What do you mean by staying with the feeling?'

Krishnamurti: You stay with the feeling of pleasure, don't you? Having tasted it, you try to hold on to it, you scheme to continue with it, and so on.Now, can one stay with the feeling which the word 'simplicity' represents?

Seeker: 'I don't think I know what that feeling is, so I can't stay with it.'

Krishnamurti: Is there the feeling apart from the reactions aroused by that word 'simplicity'? Is there the feeling separate from the word, the term, or are they inseparable? The feeling itself and the naming of it are almost simultaneous, aren't they? The word is always put together, made up, but the feeling is not; and it is very arduous to separate the feeling from the word.

Seeker: 'Is such a thing possible?'

Krishnamurti: Is it not possible to feel intensely, purely, without contamination? To feel intensely *about* something - about the family, about the country, about a cause - is comparatively easy. Intense feeling or enthusiasm may arise through identifying oneself with a belief or ideology, for example. Of this one knows. One mauy see a flock of white birds in the blue sky and almost faint with the intense feeling of such beauty, or one may recoil with horror at the cruelty of man. All such feelings are aroused by a word, by a scene, by an act, by an object. But is there not an intensity of feeling without an object? And is not that feeling incomparably great? Is it then a feeling or something entirely different?

Seeker: 'I am afraid, I don't know what you are talking about, sir. I hope you don't mind my telling you so.'

Krishnamurti: Not at all. Is there a state without cause? If there is, then can one feel it out, not verbally or theoretically, but actually be aware of that state? To be thus acutely aware, verbalization in every form, and all identification with the word, with memory, must wholly cease. Is there a state without cause? Is not love such a state?[44]

----

32. In the 'New Life', by abiding in the *Atma*, you deal with all Challenges in Life.

In the *new life* you learn to function like an amphibian, like a tortoise, getting back to the waters (rolling back the *Atma* into itself)-from the field of the body and the field of consciousness) and again re-entering the field of the body and field of consciousness-like we all do at daybreak. In this *new life*, there is an ineffable mystery, no sense of separation, intelligence is at once and there is a constant calmness, you have become a perfect stranger to sorrow, and fear.

Sankara: We have been so habituated to functioning with thought, divisiveness, planning and cunning calculation, that, any suggestion that one can indeed live life with very little of all this, may sound very frightening in the beginning. In truth, when the *Jiva's* complex baggage of planning, cunning calculation, is entirely discarded, we become extremely light and therefore highly sensitive, innocent, intelligent and vulnerable to life. Contrary to our perception, which is born of fear of losing all our baggage, the new life is incomparably easier, with none of the concern for the future and the agony of constant planning. Then, as the master Krishnamurti has said, 'then you don't have to take care of life, life will take care of you'. Especially so, because, throwing away your burdensome individuality, you have settled into a solidarity and harmony with the whole movement of life. This turns out to be an 'enviable' blessing, not at all, a life of weakness and dependence on the world and on its mercies.

---

33. As the *Atma*, you live like an Amphibian
- 'Retreating and Re-entering' the field of the body and consciousness.

In this picture, the body of the man stands for the *Atma* which has incarnated. Man has two options: Either he can abide as the *Atma* in the *Atma* (like a turtle in the river), Or, he can come 'on land', namely into the field of the body and consciousness. Previously, he did not know the joy of renouncing, being a purely, 'land animal'. His life was then utterly dry. As the *Atma*, he knows he is immortal, and that he is having a dream in which he has woken up!

Sankara: The metaphor of this 'amphibious man' illustrates the ability of the *sthitha prajnya*, to effortlessly enter the consciousness country, as and when challenges, call for this. Unlike the *Jiva,* who is perpetually beset with fruitless thinking and negative anticipations, because of fear; the *sthitha prajnya*, keeps a safe distance from thought and divisiveness, as he abides in the *Atma* as the *Atma*. Far from suffering from any incapacity in thinking, the *sthitha prajnya*, approaches all challenges in life through the silence of *prajnya*, through the negation of thought and through his 'seeming weakness' of innocence! The *Jiva* perpetually suffers from an inner blindness and weariness, because of excessive dissipative thinking, whereas, the *sthitha prajnya*, functions, much more efficiently, because, he is free of the burden of thought and calculation. *Thus, he becomes an adept in the art of spiritual living.*

----

34. Agamas : Atma Sakshatkara

1. "Though considering himself the Self, He desires to attain that *Siva*, the Supreme Self, *as one apart. Whoever contemplates on Siva, thus in delusion, will not attain Sivahood by such contemplation – know this.*

2. "'*Siva* is other than I; I am other than *Siva*' – uproot this attitude of differentiation. 'I indeed am *Siva*' – this conviction that is non-dual, ever practice".

- *Siva Mahadeva* speaking to His son,
Guha in the work called '*Atma Sakshatkara*' [14]

Q : *These two quotations from an Agama text Atma Sakshatkara raise two important questions. The first question is Shivoham is a mantra used by Advaitins and Shaivaits and is very renowned. How many Hindus who recite this mantra hundreds and thousands of times, have taken up the important question as to what their equation with Siva is? Do they consider themselves at the Atmic level to be the same as Siva? Do they have the courage to take this stand?*

Secondly, a sadhana of 'Shivoham' done without any consideration of our dualistic equation with Siva, what will its fruits be? Will they be confused, because we are ourselves confused?

A : You have asked many questions. Answer to the first question is - There are a few rare dare devils who are audacious enough to claim this absolute equality with *Siva* at the *Atmic* level. This audaciousness does not negate their humility, because this comes from a profound understanding. In the absence of this audacity, that they are one with *Siva*, the *sadhana* of the *Siva mantra*, '*Sivoham*' may not bear the desired fruit of *moksha*, it may bear some other fruit depending on the maturity of the seeker and his specific *samkalpa*. Usually the people who are seekers of *moksha* are audatious and are dare devils. Without this dare devilry you may not be able to make it, unless the Divine unexpectedly comes in pursuit of you, as in the case of Sri Ramana Maharshi.

The mechanical chanting of *Sivoham* which is done with a lot of devotion in India is not the essence of this *mantra sadhana*. The essence is soaking in the audacious thought and feeling, may be for many months that your *Atma* is *Siva* and endlessly wondering about it. If the *mantra sadhana* is taken up after the ground has been tilled and the seeds have been sown, then the fruit of *moksha* may appear. Otherwise the fruit may not be spectacular.

---

35. No Outer *Moksha* Signs

"He who has attained *Brahman*, cannot be distinguished from other men of the world, either in their dress, or in their behavior. He bears no external signs."

- **Mahabharata, quoted in the *Ashtavakra Gita*[37]**

Sankara: To many devotees and seekers, this verdict from *Ashtavakra Gita* will be shocking, because we carry our own idiotic impressions of how a person who has crossed over will look like, and how he will talk, etc. A great master is one, who will make a declaration at the very beginning that, 'I have no special treasure, which you do not also possess. The only difference between me and you is that I may know the meaning and significance of the treasure, namely the *Atma* or 'That' and you may not as yet know the meaning and significance. Apart from this distinction, there is absolutely no difference between a master and a seeker or a disciple'. In fact more or less these are the words of the master Sri Nisargadatta Maharaj. More *sadhakas* and seekers approach a master with the belief which they have as a *Jiva,* that the master has some enormous treasure and that, they should be fortunate enough to get a piece of that. With the beggar's mentality, people come to see a master. This at best can be a pain to the master. The master wants to engage in a dialogue. You should go to a master to ask questions and to learn, instead we go to admire, we go to seek recognition from him, we go for his blessings which we already have. To dispel this Himalayan *maya*, the retreat started with an admonition supported by Sri Ramana Maharshi himself, which I shall now repeat, since we have come to the end of the retreat.

'Seeking' for Self - Realization is absurd:

Your Thought: "All these masters are Self - Realized, they are in possession of a priceless wealth, call it *Atma* or Self. *I do not have this wealth, I am trying*!"

This is utterly wrong, this thought is your enemy, since you are at the core, only the *Atma.*

"As the Self of a person, who tries to attain Self - Realization is not different from him *and as there is nothing other than or superior to him to be attained by him,* Self - Realization is only the Realization of one's own nature."

-Sri Ramana Maharshi[14]

----

36. The Danger of Desire After Realization

"Even after knowing that substance (the *Atman*), powerful desire, which is 'beginningless' and in the form of 'I am the doer and enjoyer' does not die. It remains there. What can be done with that? You must do away with that desire carefully, because lessening of that desire is freedom. That should be done, even after Realization."

- 'Viveka Chudamani' of Adi Sankaracharya[43]

Sankara: These are the words of Adi Sankaracharya, in his classical work on *Jivanmukti*, namely, *Viveka Chudamani* (Crest-Jewel of Discrimination). There are many key words in this quotation to which we ought to pay very close attention. So, let us look at these important words, one by one. Firstly, we are warned that, that even if we have succeeded in *sravana, manana and nidhidhyasana*; we should never exult, in the euphoric thought that 'we have arrived'. In fact, the sages know that, it is a misfortune, if such a thought were to arise, in the aftermath of *nidhidhyasana* (abidance in the *Atma*). This may be shocking to seekers and *mumukshus*, who have a tendency to look upon masters and *Jivanmuktas*, as though, they have attained to such perfect state, which offers absolute guarantee, against spiritual falls. However, *mumukshus* and seekers need never despair, for there is an antidote, for the poison of *maya*. It is eternal vigilance and perpetual awareness.

The second bombshell falling on the heads of seekers and *mumukshus* is the unwelcome news that, such a desire, is by nature 'beginningless', and results in the feeling of being an 'agency'. Why does the great Adi Sankaracharya, declare this desire to be 'beginningless'? He does so, because, it came home to him, that *maya*, is ever a concomitant of *Brahman* and follows *Brahman*, like a shadow. He must have discovered this with absolute clarity and also finding that the scriptures, which are the wisdom of countless sages, reiterate the same truth; he is seen here boldly enunciating this shocking truth. It means that, this *maya*, was ever in the 'beginning', indeed, if it were legitimate for us to suppose, such a beginning.

The third bombshell is that this 'serpentine' desire (slimy, slippery and surreptitious), *'does not die, but remains there'*. This means that it has 'eternal life' and that, it is even the Divine Plan, that this desire be indeed there, as if, it was Divinely intended to pollute the perfection of *Jivanmukti*! Adi Sankaracharya, therefore gives us a timely warning that we should never entertain the false hope that, after *Jivanmukti*, we will be ushered into a veritable heaven, one in which, the evil of selfish desire, will never touch us! This is really disappointing news for people still in *maya*, those, who mistake their conception of *Jivanmukti*, for the real *Jivanmukti*.

In Ch. III, topic 10, we discussed the myeterious snakes, slithering and crawling on the body of *Siva*. In that context, we had interpreted the snakes to be expressions of *kundalini sakti*, the energy of the Primal Mother *(Adi Sakti)*. If we pause to consider the real meaning of the snakes again, we will see that all the snakes around *Siva's* body, are really the energetic pulsations of the Divine Mother *(Adi Sakti)*. *Kundalini* in the *nadis* and *chakras* is only one expression of *Adi Sakti*. Another expression is what Adi Sankaracharya alludes to in this *sutra* in *Viveka Chudamani*. Namely, that this 'beginningless desire' and this sense of *self*, which has been the central theme in this retreat, is also verily, after all, a pulsing expression of the same *Adi Sakti*. We thereby arrive at the absolutely liberating insight, that, beyond the taming, calming and silencing of the *self*; we ought not to attempt anything, beyond this, *as such a thing, as complete extinction of the self, will not happen at all, as it goes against the mandate of Adi Sakti, as exemplified in Viveka Chudamani.*[43]

The fourth bombshell is that the *Jivanmukta*, must part company with the swarm of desires, and this is done through *vairagya* or renunciation. Without this *vairagya* or renunciation, *Jivanmukti* will lack lustre and will also most probably reverse itself-again, something very provocative to the seekers and *mumukshus*, still caught in *maya*.

The fifth and last bombshell is that after *Jivanmukti*, there is continuation of *sadhana*, built on the bedrock of detachment or *vairagya*. All these five bombshells, may be regarded as the secrets of *moksha*, given to us by Bhagavan, Sri Adi Sankaracharya.

----

37. Supreme Importance of Regular Meditation

"Meditation must be practiced without any break. When the mature mind is absorbed in *Brahman* (that is, in 'I am ness'), then comes *samadhi* - the state that is free from all doubts. And then naturally one becomes the enjoyer of eternal bliss. By this *samadhi*, all desires and the knots of the heart are destroyed as well as all actions, internally and externally. And without any effort on the part of the individual, comes the manifestation of the Self *(Atman)*. Simultaneously comes the destruction of mind and desires, and the realization of the Self."

- 'Viveka Chudamani'[43]

Sankara: In this *sutra*, pertinent to *Jivanmuktas*, further *sadhana* is enjoined, of continuous abidance in *Atma*, without a break, then ensues, *Samadhi*, which is being introduced as a state of equanimity, bereft of all doubts. By *Samadhi*, Adi Sankaracharya is referring to *Nirvikalpa Samadhi*, which is known to give total liberation. Unless and until *Nirvikalpa Samadhi* happens, the full glory of the *Atma* will not be revealed, this is the import of the *sutra*. Thus, *Nirvikalpa Samadhi*, is pointed to as the final destination of this inward journey, beyond the milestone of *Jivanmukti*.

This marks the completion of our 'Tat Tvam Asi' meditative journey, for the sake of Self - Realization, but through *self* - Knowing.

Seventh Day (Chapter -VII), 2nd 'Tat Tvam Asi' Meditation

Subtler Discovery of Union of the *Atma* with *Parabrahma*

Conclusive Meditation

Aum Tat Sat

Bibliography and Notes

[1]   Giri, Sri Swami Yukteswar. *The Holy Science*. 8th Indian Ed.1963. Yogoda Satsanga Society of India, Calcutta, 1990.

[2]   Emeneau, M. B. *The Journal of the American Oriental Society*. 1955. Vol. 75, No: 3, (July-Sept), Pgs. 145-153. The theme of his discourse on that occasion was 'India and Linguistics'.

[3]   Ratiocination, means, go through logical processes, reason, especially using syllogisms. *The Illustrated Oxford Dictionary*, 1998.

[4]   Leggett, Trevor. *Sankara on the Yoga Sutras*. 1992. Translated with commentary from the Sanskrit original. Motilal Banarasidass, Delhi, India.

[5]   Tapasyananda, Swami. *Srimad Bhagavad Gita*. 1984. Ch. III, Sloka 26. Translated from Sanskrit with commentary. The President of Sri. Ramakrishna Math, Chennai, India.

[6]   Lokeswarananda, Swami. *Mundaka Upanishad*. 1994. Pgs. 95-99. Translated from the Sanskrit original with commentary and notes based on the ancient commentary of Adi Sankaracharya. The Ramakrishna Mission Institute of Culture, Calcutta, India.

[7]   Tapasyananda, Swami. *Srimad Bhagavad Gita*. 1984. Ch. II, Slokas 29, 47, 50 and 54-72. Translated from the Sanskrit original with commentary.The President of Sri. Ramakrishna Math, Chennai, India. Cited in this work in Ch. II, topic 38; Ch. III, topic 34; Ch. V, topics 4, 19, 23, 24, 28, 29 and 31; Ch. VI, topics 8 and 12; Ch. VII, topic 25.

[8]   Krishnamurti, J. *The Awakening of Intelligence*. 1973. Part XI, Pgs. 509-538. Conversations between: J. Krishnamurti and Professor David Bohm. Victor Gollancz Ltd., London, UK. Cited in this work in Ch. V, topic 3.

[9]   Krishnamurti, J. *Krishnamurti to Himself (His Last Journal)*. 2009. Pgs. 29-30. Krishnamurti Foundation India (KFI), Chennai, India.

[10]   Ibid., Pgs. 51-52; 62-63.

[11]   Bhagavadpada, Sankara. *Sri Ramana Maharshi's Moksha*. Reprinted 2012. Yogi Impressions Books Pvt. Ltd., Mumbai, India.

[12]   Narasimha, Swami, B.V. *Self-Realization*. 2002. Pgs. 17-18 (Sri Ramana Maharshi's 'death experience'). Sri Ramanasramam, Tiruvannamalai, India.

[13]   Krishnamurti, J. *Meditations*. Selections made by Evelyne Blau, Reprinted, 2013. Pgs. 8-9. KFI, Chennai, India. Cited in this work in Ch. I, topic 5; Ch. II, topics 18, 48 and 49; Ch. III, topics 1 and 36; Ch. IV, topics 13 and 32; Ch. V, topic 1.

[14]   *The Collected Works of Ramana Maharshi*. Pgs. 53, 130, 161, 196 and 270. Ninth Revised Edition, 2004. Sri Ramanasramam, Tiruvannamalai, India. Cited in this work in Ch. I, topic 6; Ch. VI, topic 32; Ch. VII, topics 2, 8, 16, 17, 34 and 35.

[15]   Karapatra, Swami. *Advaita Bodha Deepika*. Reprinted, 2000. Pg. 32. Sri Ramanasramam, Tiruvannamalai, India.

[16]   Dikshit, Sudhakar S. Ed. by. *I Am That. Talks with Sri Nisargadatta Maharaj*. Translated from the Marati original by Maurice Frydman. Reprinted, 1993. Pgs. 29 and 34. Chetana Pvt. Ltd. Mumbai. Cited in this work in Ch. I, topic, 23; Ch. II, topic 21; Ch. III, topic 9; Ch. IV, topic 3.

[17]   Powell, Robert. Ed. by. *The Ultimate Medicine. As prescribed by Sri Nisargadatta Maharaj.* 1996. Pg. 134. Motilal Banarasidass Publishers Pvt. Ltd., Delhi, India. Cited in this work in Ch. I, topic 28.

[18]   Ibid., Pg 161. Cited in this work in Ch. I, topic 29; Ch. II, topic 25.

[19]   Krishnamurti, J. *Meditations*. Selections made by Evelyne Blau. Reprinted 2013. Pgs. 8, 9. Krishnamurti Foundation India (KFI), Chennai, India. Cited in this work in Ch. I, topic 34; Ch. III, topic 21.

[20]   Rajagopal, D. Ed. by. *Commentaries on Living. From the Notebooks of J. Krishnamurti.* 1976. Pgs. 104 -105. Victor Gollancz Ltd., London, UK. Cited in essence, in this work in Ch. I, topics 40-43. The verbatim ref. could not be traced.

[21]   Powell, Robert. Ed. by. *The Ultimate Medicine.* As prescribed by Sri Nisargadatta Maharaj. 1996. Pg. 205. Motilal Banarasidass Publishers Pvt. Ltd., Delhi, India. Cited in this work in Ch. II, topic 2; Ch. III, topic 2.

[22]   Lokeswarananda, Swami. *Svetasvatara Upanishad.* 1994. Translation of the Sanskrit original with commentary and notes, based on the ancient commentary of Adi Sankaracharya. The Ramakrishna Mission Institute of Culture, Calcutta, India. Cited in this work in Ch. III, topic 28; Ch. VII, topics, 22, 23 and 24.

[23]   Tapasyananda, Swami. *Srimad Bhagavad Gita.* 1984. Ch. VI. Slokas 5, 7, 29 and 30. Sri Ramakrishna Math, Madras - 600 004, India. Cited in this work in Ch. III, topic 35; Ch. V, topic 8; Ch. VI, topic 23; Ch. VII, topics 28 and 29.

[24]   Tandavaraya, Swami. *Kaivalya Navaneetham.* Translated from the original Tamil and recommended to the devotees coming to his asrama by Bhagavan Sri Ramana Maharshi.

Sri Ramanaramam. Tiruvannamalai, India. Cited in this work in Ch. III, topic 45; Ch. IV, topics 23 and 25; Ch. VI, topic 7.

[25]   Aiyer, Narayanaswami, K. *Laghu Yoga Vasishtha*. 1975. Third Ed. Trans from the Sanskrit original. The Adyar Library and Research Centre, Chennai, India. Cited in this work in Ch. IV, topic 27.

[26]   Tapasyananda, Swami. *Srimad Bhagavad Gita*. 1984. Ch. XIII. Slokas, 7, 9, 12, 15, 22, 26 and 32. Sri Ramakrishna Math. Chennai, India. Cited in this work in Ch. II, topics, 29 and 30; Ch. IV, topics 29, 30 and 31; Ch. VI, topics, 9, 15 and 30; Ch. VII, topics, 26, 27 and 30.

[27]   Powell, Robert. Ed by. *The Ultimate Medicine*. As prescribed by Sri Nisargadatta Maharaj. 1996. Pg. 84. Motilal Banarasidass Publishers Pvt. Ltd., Delhi, India. Cited in this work in Ch. III, topic 38; Ch. IV, topic 6.

[28]   Ibid., Pg. 196. Cited in this work in Ch. III, topic 42.

[29]   Ibid., Pg. 191. Cited in this work in Ch. III, topic 43.

[30]   Ibid., Pg. 144. Cited in this work in Ch. IV, topic 28.

[31]   Deekshitulu, A.S., and Sundara Ramiah. *Atma Bodha*. English translation and commentary on Adi Sankaracharya's Sanskrit work. Verse. 2. E-book from www.geetadeeksha.com Cited in this work in Ch. II, topic 6.

[32]   Krishnamurti, J. *The First and Last Freedom*. Reprinted 2016. Ch. IX, Pgs. 62, 65. KFI, Chennai-600 028, India. Cited in this work in Ch. II, topic 23.

[33]   Powell, Robert. Ed by. *The Ultimate Medicine*. As prescribed by Sri Nisargadatta Maharaj. 1996. Pgs. 160-161. Motilal Banarsidass Publishers Ltd. Delhi, India. Cited in this work in Ch. II, topic 25.

[34]   Ibid., Pg. 191. Cited in this work in Ch. III, topic 44.

[35]   Dikshit, Sudhakar S. *I Am That-Talks with Sri Nisargadatta Maharaj*. 1993. Pg. 382. Translated from the Marati original by Maurice Frydman. Cited in this work in Ch. V, topics 25, 26 and 27.

[36]   Cohen, S. S. *Guru Ramana. Memories and Notes*. 1993. 6th Ed. Pg. 89. Sri Ramanasramam, Tiruvannamalai, India. Cited in this work in Ch. V, topic 32.

[37]   Nityaswarupananda, Swami (Ramakrishna Mission). *Ashtavakra Gita*. 2001. Pg. 156. Translated into English and also Kannada, from the Sanskrit original. Sri Ramanasramam, Tiruvannamalai, India. Cited in this work in Ch. V, topic 13; Ch. VI, topics 15, 19, 20, 22 and 25; Ch. VII, topics, 7 and 35.

[38]   Dikshit, Sudhakar, S. *I Am That-Talks with Sri Nisargadatta Maharaj*. Reprinted 1993. Pgs. 439-440. Translated from the Marati original by Maurice Frydman. Chetana Pvt. Ltd., Mumbai, India. Cited in this work in Ch. VI, topic 21.

[39]   Swahananda, Swami. *Vedanta Panchadasi of Sri Vidyaranya Swami.*1967. Ch. III, Sutra 20. Sri Ramakrishna Math, Chennai, India. Cited in this work in Ch. VI, topic 24; Ch. VII, topic 9.

[40]   Tapasyananda, Swami. *Srimad Bhagavad Gita.* 1984. Ch. VII, Sloka 27. Sri Ramakrishna Math, Chennai, India. Cited in this work in Ch. VI, topics 10 and 11.

[41]   Sankaranarayanan, P. *Viveka Chudamani of Sri Adi Sankaracharya.* 1988. English translation and commentary on the Sanskrit original. Slokas 255 and 256, Pgs. 269 and 270. Bharatiya Vidya Bhavan, Kulapati K. M. Munshi Marg. Mumbai-400 007, India. Cited in this work in Ch. VII, topics 4 and 5.

[42]   Dikshit, Sudhakar, S. *I Am That-Talks with Sri Nisargadatta Maharaj*. Reprinted 1993. Pg. 34. Chetana Pvt. Ltd., Mumbai, India. Cited in this work in Ch. VII, topic 6.

[43]   Turiyananda, Swami. Translated from the Sanskrit original. *Viveka Chudamani*. 1987. Slokas 362 and 363. Sri Ramakrishna Math, Chennai, India. Cited in this work in Ch. VII, topic 36 and 37.

[44]   Rajagopal, D. Ed by. *Commentaries on Living, Third Series. From the Notebooks of J. Krishnamurti.*2004. KFI, Chennai, India.Pg.370. Cited in this work in Ch. VII, topic 31.

[45]   Tapasyananda, Swami. *Srimad Bhagavata* (in four volumes). 1980. Trans from the Sanskrit original, with a detailed general Introduction. Vol. II. Pgs. 311-344. Sri Ramakrishna Math, Chennai. The *devas-asuras* model is sourced here, in the Bhagavata Purana. Cited in this work in Ch. III, topic 16.

[46]   Ramana, Maharshi. Sri. *Upadesa Saram*…. Sri Ramanasramam, Tiruvannamalai, India. Cited in this work in Ch. V, topic 13.

Sources of the Photographs and Pictures

1.   'The Two 'Tat Tvam Asi' Birds' (Ch. I, topic 17; Ch. II, topics 20 and 31; Ch. Topic 4; Ch. V, topic 5); https://in.pinterest.com/hamahjones1994/nanday_conure/

2.   'Water Contaminated by Algae' (Ch. I, topic 19; Ch. III, topic 7; Ch. IV, topic 10; Ch. V, topic 6); www.organicearthsolutionsllc.com/lake-pond-restoration.html/

3.   'A Model of the *Jiva* with *Maya*' (Ch. I, topic 18; Ch. II, topic 47; Ch. III, topic 5; Ch. IV, topics 11 and 24); www.vanislewater.com/how-deal-pond-algae/

4.   'Water without Contamination by Algae' (Ch. I, topic 20; Ch. II, topic 32; Ch. III, topic 8; Ch. IV, topic 12; Ch. V, topic 7); www.diversservices.com/Retention-Detention-Pond-Clean-Out/

5.   'The *Jiva* as a Lonely Wanderer in the Memory-Lane' (Ch. I, topic 37); www.alamy.com/stock-photo/cobble-stones.html/

6.   '*Jiva* says, 'this is my wife', 'my husband'' (Ch. II, topic 13); www.lightscamerabollywood.com/vidya-balan-wedding/

7.   'The Dance of *Siva & Sakti*' (Ch. III, topic 10; Ch. V, topic 14; Ch. VII, topic 18) is from the book by Harish Johari, *Tools for Tantra*.1983. Inner Traditions India. One Park Street, Rochester, Vermont 05767, USA.

8.   'The Divine *(Siva & Sakti)* Govern our Destiny' (Ch. III, topic 16); www.sanatansociety.org/indian_epics_and_stories/the_churning_of_the_ocean.htm

9.   'Untamed *Sakti* Dominating *Siva*' (Ch. III, topic 34; Ch. VI, topic 8) is from the book by Heinrich Zimmer. *Myths and Symbols in Indian Art and Civilization*. Edited by Joseph Campbell. Plate 69. Bollingen Series/ Princeton University Press. USA. 1972.

10. 'Tamed *Sakti-Sthitha Prajnya's* Consciousness' (Ch. III, topic 35; Ch. V, topic 8) is from the book by Heinrich Zimmer. *Myths and Symbols in Indian Art and Civilization*. 1972. Plate 34. Edited by Joseph Campbell. Bollingen Series/ Princeton University Press. USA.

11. 'The Caterpillar *(Jiva)* will 'Metamorphose' into the Butterfly *(Atma)*' (Ch. V, topic 16); http://amazingdata.com/the-metamorphosis-of-butterflies/

12. 'Consciousness is the Prison, Something External'(Ch. V, topics 25, 26 and 27); www.waldeneffect.org/blog/Chick_hatching_photos/

13. 'M. C. Escher's Drawing Hands' (Ch. VII, topic 15); is the art work of the renowned Dutch painter M. C. Escher; https://en.wikipedia.org/wiki/Drawing_Hands/

Sanskrit Glossary

Aastika:	The term applies to those individuals and those schools of Hindu philosophy, who accept the *Vedic* authority regarding ultimate reality and accept also the principle of the *Atma*.
Adharma:	That which is a violation of *dharma* or virtue.
Advaitic path:	The spiritual path to *moksha*, based on understanding the *Jiva (self)* and the *Atma*, one in which, right from the very beginning, duality is 'not recognised', and it is taught that the purified *Jiva* alone is *Atma* and *Brahman* (Divine). The paths taught by Adi Sankaracharya, Ramana Maharshi, Nisargadatta Maharaj and J. Krishnamurti.
Ahankara:	*Ahankara* is the ingredient or faculty in consciousness, whose function is to 'manufacture' and create *a sense of self*. Aham is *self* and *kara* is the making of the *self*.
Ahimsa:	The prefix 'a' in Sanskrit denotes negation. *Himsa* is cruelty or violence, so *ahimsa* is the negation and eschewing of violence. Spiritual ideal adopted by Mahatma Gandhi during India's freedom struggle.
Amanaska Yoga:	By *Yoga*, is meant traditionally, the union or yoking into the Divine, which is understood to be the bedrock of our agitated consciousness. *Amanaska* means negation of the *manas* or individual consciousness. So, *Amanaska Yoga* would mean, complete calming and silencing of consciousness, whereupon our unity with the Divine is revealed.
Anatmavada:	The Buddhist view and certain materialistic schools of Hindu philosophy which refute the reality and existence of the *Atma,* are considered to be *Anatmavadins* (they uphold the view that there is no *Atma* or Soul).
Antaratma:	Inner *Atma*, with emphasis placed on the kernel of our being, namely the *Atma*.
Anumanta:	Means, sanctioner, the authority or 'Power Wielder' who sanctions. Refers to the Supreme Lord, in Bhagavad Gita, Ch. XIII, *Sloka*, 22.

Apadhbandhava:	'A close relative *(bandhu)* who in times of danger or distress *(apadh)*'comes to our rescue is referred to by this name. Name, applied to the Divine as *Vishnu*, in the Hindu world - as He comes to our rescue in times of distress.
Apeethakuchaambal:	This is the special name of the Divine mother, who is the consort of *Arunachaleswara* in the Tiruvannamalai Temple. The etymology of *Apeethakuchaambal* is the Divine mother of un-suckled breasts (her son *Muruga* was not suckled by Her, but by six other foster mothers). This is according to the legend of *Arunachaleswara*.
Artha and Kama:	*Artha,* one of the four goals of human life in Hindu society. Goal or pursuit of: wealth, status, power, achievement. *Kama* is aspirations, desires. Sometimes *kama* is wrongly understood as sexual desire. *It is every kind of aspiration and desire.* *Artha and kama* are goals which go together. *Kama*, like *artha* is one of the four goals of human life.
Arunachala/ Arunachaleswara:	*Aruna* means red, fiery (this fire element is what gives *Jnana* or Illumination). *Achala* means unmoving, therefore a mountain. So *Arunachaleswara* is the sacred mountain in Tiruvannamalai which is considered to be *Siva* Itself, and which therefore blesses with *Jnana* or Illumination.
Ashtanga Yoga:	The *Yoga* of eight limbs *(Ashta anga)*, systematized by *Maharishi Patanjali*.
Ashtavakra Gita:	One of the Hindu classics on *moksha*, the fourth goal of human life. It is in fact a *moksha shastra*, an *Advaitic* teaching given by the Sage *Ashtavakra* to *Janaka Maharaj*, an ancient Hindu king.
Asmita:	The taint of the human individuality and self-hood, sourced in the feeling that 'one exists as a separate individual' and as a body.
Atma anusandana:	This is a means to *nidhidhyasana*, which is abidance in the *Atma*. By enquiry into our root nature *(Atma anusandhana)*, we will come to discard the false identity of ourselves, as our thoughts and feelings and in this way, come to take our *asana*, or our 'resting place' in the *Atma*, as the *Atma* (this is *nidhidhyasana*).
Atma sakti:	This is the mysterious power which the *Atma*, as the imperceptible inner Self, i.e., as *Siva*, can switch on, through a *samkalpa*. The 'tip

of the iceberg of the *Atma'* is 'I am ness', or the, 'conscious presence'. *Sakti* means energy. *Sakti* is in time, *Siva* is timeless.

Atma:	Pronounced as *Aatma* - is subtle the witnessing awareness in man. It is awareness, as Sri J. Krishnamurti refers to it, or the 'conscious presence', as Sri Nisargadatta Maharaj puts it; or as the pure 'I', or Self, as Sri Ramana Maharshi, referred to it. It is obviously outside time and space. It is the purest form of the 'I' Consciousness, because it is the ultimate perceiving subject. It can never be known as an 'object', as It is our true Self. Represented by the witness Bird, in the metaphor of the two 'Tat Tvam Asi' Birds. *Atma* is the *Siva* in us. *Atma* and *Paramatma* (Supreme *Atma*) are used interchangeably in the spiritual literature of India.
Atmajnana:	Realization *(Jnana)* of the Self *(Atma)*. Here, it must be understood that realization means an irreversible understanding of the reality and nature of the *Atma*, and a conviction that one is perpetually in abidance in that *Atma*.
Atmavada:	The Hindu conviction or *darsana*, which upholds the reality and existence of the *Atma*, the non-dual Self, as enunciated in the Bhagavad Gita, *Upanishads and Brahma sutras*.
Atmavichara:	*Vichara* is enquiry or investigation, so this term means enquiry into the nature of the *Atma*, the Self.
Avang manasa gochara:	Not reachable by thinking, by analysis, by the intricate use of words and language.
Avatar:	Incarnation of the Divine, meaning the Divine has descended to earth and taken a human form. In truth, every insect, animal, human is an incarnation of the Divine only, but the *Avatar* is one who has this realization and helps humanity to know and understand the Divine.
Avidya:	Nescience, or ignorance. Meaning ignorance of the existence of the Divine, and the way we are connected to the Divine.
Bhagavad Gita:	One of the three canonical Hindu spiritual texts. It is a *shastra* in *dharma and moksha*, which are the two spiritual goals of the Hindus. Teaching given by *Bhagavan* Sri Krishna to his disciple *Arjuna* on the battle field of *Kurukshetra* (Mahabharata War), roughly around 3500 BCE.

Bhagavata Purana:	Maharshi Vyasa is the author, it is the Hindu ancient history of how God *Vishnu* incarnates, from age to age. *Purana* is 'ancient' (history).
Bhaktavatsala:	'One who has affection *(vatsalya)* for the devotee *(Bhaktha)*'. Applied to the Divine, as *Vishnu*.
Bharta:	'Supporter', referring to the Supreme Lord in Bhagavad Gita, Ch. XIII, *Sloka*, 22.
Bhokta:	'Enjoyer', referring to the Supreme Lord in Bhagavad Gita, Ch. XIII, *Sloka* 22.
Brahma Tat Tvam Asi:	In *Advaita Vedanta*, the *darsana* (world-view), expounded by Adi Sankaracharya; 'Tat Tvam Asi' is the final realization, that one is in essence, 'That', *Parabrahma*. *'Brahman'* is also used to represent the same *Parabrahma*; so 'Brahma Tat Tvam Asi' (occurring in Viveka Chudamani, Adi Sankaracharya's work), signifies that, 'Thou Art, That Brahman'.
Brahma:	In the Hindu *Puranas* (ancient Hindu spiritual texts, much mythologized), *Brahma* is the deity for creation. *It is not that there are three separate deities for creation (Brahma), preservation (Vishnu) and destruction (Siva).* Rather, the same Godhead has all the three functions and the intellect wanting to understand this clearly has assigned one deity for each function!
Brahma:	The Hindu deity in the Hindu *Puranas*, invested with the function of Divine creation. Along with *Vishnu* and *Siva*, the other greater Lords, in charge of Divine preservation and Divine destruction, constitute the Hindu trinity of *Brahma-Vishnu-Maheswara*. *In truth, there are no three gods, but only the self-same, one Divine essence and Godhead, involved in all three functions.*
Brahman:	Absolute Godhead or the unmanifest Divine, as spoken of in the Upanishads (one of the three Hindu canonical spiritual sources). Understood to be the totality of the cosmic manifestation, as well as the unmanifest Divine. The root is *'Brih'* meaning vast or infinite.
Brihadaranyaka Up.:	*Brihad* is that which is vast and large and *aranya* is forest. So an Upanishad which arose in a vast forest. Again deals with *Atma vidya* and *Brahma vidya*, namely knowledge of *Atma* and *Brahman*.
Buddhi:	One of the four faculties and functions of the human consciousness. It is the power of analytical reasoning, or rational thought and

484

intellect. However, in the Bhagavad Gita the same word is used to signify intelligence, which is different from the intellect. For example, in the Bhagavad Gita expression *Buddhi yoga,* by *Buddhi,* is meant intelligence.

Chakras:	The nerve-plexuses and junctions along the spinal cord, standing for the various wheels of consciousness and corresponding to the higher and subtler planes of consciousness. In *Tantra yoga,* one meditates on these *chakras,* as visual patterns, with the intention to activate them, and awaken *Kundalini.*
Chitta shuddhi:	It is the purification of the *chitta* or purity of the *chitta* reached by taming and pacifying the *ahankara* and purifying the feeling and understanding faculty of the *manas* and also quietening the faculty of the intellect, *buddhi.* It must be noted that here, by *chitta,* is meant all inner organs, *manas, buddhi, ahankara* and *chitta.* The same word *chitta* is also used with an entirely different meaning, as in what follows.
Chitta:	*Chitta* is one of the four faculties and functions in consciousness. However, it is the basic 'matrix' of human consciousness. It is the 'matrix' of *Sakti,* the *Atma* being *Siva.* Important ingredients in *chitta,* are like 'islands floating in the sea': they are *buddhi* the intellect, *ahankara* (*self* or the ego) and *manas* the faculty of feeling and perceptual understanding.
Dakshinamurti:	One of the classical manifestations of *Siva,* as the silent teacher of *moksha. Murti* means manifestation and *Dakshina* means *Atmic* Intelligence, so *Dakshinamurti* means *Siva* as the great teacher, embodiment of *Atmic* intelligence, who imparts moksha through understanding.
Darsana:	Literally, meaning a vision, stands for a philosophical system or world-view, that is arrived at as a result of mystic insights and experiences on the one hand and an intelligent and systematized formulation by intuition of the illumined on the other.
Dasa:	A major astrological season or cycle of time in *Vedic* Astrology.
Devas and *Asuras:*	*Devas* and *asuras* are *puranic* conceptions (ancient Hindu spiritual conceptions), they are the cosmic benefic *(devas)* and cosmic malefic *(asuras)* life energies. They have their origin in *Sakti* who arises from *Siva* and she is called *Adi Sakti,* i.e., the primal Divine energy. The

devas are represented by the functional benefic planets and the *asuras* are represented by the functional malefic planets in *Vedic* astrology.

Dhanvantari: Name of the Hindu god of Ayurvedic medicine, *Avatar* of *Vishnu*.

Dharma: *Dharma* means that which is stable and that which supports and it is the moral law, moral conduct, moral order and virtue in thought, word and deed which arises from the perception of unity of all life. *Dharma* is the first of the four cardinal goals of life in Hindu society

Dvaita: A Hindu *darsana* or world-view (philosophy), that takes for granted the duality between the perceiving subject and the perceived object and builds a Divine-centered world-view, based on this experiential dualistic perception.

Dwapara yuga: *Yuga* means age or cosmic cycle. In Sri Yukteswar Giri's model of the chronology of the *yugas,* in each cosmic cycle *(maha yuga)* of 24,000 yrs, a certain segment of time has the quality of *dwapara.* During this period, the bull of *dharma* stands only on two of its four feet. During such a *yuga, dharma* or virtue is reduced to 50% of its original presence. We are now in the ascending *dwapara yuga.*

Ganesha: *Ganesha* is the first Hindu deity who represents the *Atmic* nature of all living being, humans in particular, in the Hindu world-view. Therefore represents the witness consciousness and the pure 'I' without any associations.

Guru: A God - Realized or Self - Realized spiritual master in the Hindu tradition, who serves as an embodiment of the Divine light, leading us from darkness to light and who enjoys full freedom to expound the truth of the Self or *Atman*, or God, in manner, he or she has realized. The *guru* is not obliged to adhere to any one tradition *(sampradaya)*, as it is with an *acharya*.

Gurukula ashrama: An *ashrama* is the home and abode of a spiritual master, or *rishi* and his family. Usually a peaceful abode and a seat or centre for spiritual learning.

Gurupatni: Spouse of the *guru*.

In terms of content and chronology, *Vedas* are the well-preserved corpus of ancient Sanskrit compositions, which have been recognized to be the oldest well-spring of religious *suktas* (hymns), as well as of historical records of the *Vedic Aryans*. Some *Vedic* scholars hold the view that the classification of the *Vedas* into four distinct parts, the *Rig, Yajur, Sama* and *Atharva*, date back to 3700 BCE-their real genesis may be of ever greater antiquity. The oldest among the *Vedas* is the *Rig Veda*, which consists of some ten books, covering 1028 *suktas* (hymns) and 10,552 mantras. Hinduism, which is the world's oldest living religion, stands firmly upon the bedrock of the *Vedas*.

Isvara: *Isvara* is the supreme controller in *Dwaita*. In *Advaita*, when the Absolute reality is perceived from a state of *avidya* or spiritual ignorance (duality); the *self (Jiva)*, experiences the Absolute reality as *Isvara* or God; i.e., as the Supreme Being, other than itself.

Jiva: *Jiva* is the human sense of *self* or 'living individuality' which is nothing but the Divine *Atma* shrouded by *maya*, the web of illusions (explained in the 'algae man' metaphor in the retreat). So at the core, the *Jiva* is the *Atma*. Nevertheless the *Jiva* is in profound ignorance and sorrow because of *maya*.

Jivanmukti/ Jivanmukta: *Jivanmukti* is liberation of the *Atma* from the clutches of *maya* (illusion). The *Atma* got entangled in *maya* because of creation, so *Jivanmukti* is the disentanglement of the *Atma* from the debilitating and corrupting influence of *maya*. *Jivanmukta* is one who has become free of *maya*, so he is liberated. *Mukti* means liberation and *mukta* means the liberated one.

Jivatma: It is the same as *Jiva*, but the emphasis reminds us that the core of the *Jiva* is the *Atma*, so it is the human *self*, which thinks itself to be a mere individual because of the beclouding *maya*.

Jnana yoga: *Jnana* is understanding and wisdom. *Jnana yoga* is Self - Realization through learning, understanding, contemplation and enquiry. It is a path to *moksha*.

Jyotish: *Jyotish* is the *Vedic* understanding of how the Divine life energies, govern and drive our life in all aspects. The Divine is the life-giving Light *(Jyoti)*. This mathematical understanding of the imperceptible Divine Source resulted in *Vedic* astrology, which is also called *Jyotish*. The function of *Jyotish* is to help us understand the Divine will in our life and to see how this Divine will shapes the whole of our life.

Kala-chakra:	The wheel of time, *kala* is time, *chakra* is wheel. Hindu sages understood happenings in society, according to the cycles of time, called the *yugas*.
Karma:	In the Hindu view of life, *karma* is the connection between cause and effect, in so far as, human thought, word and deed are concerned. Every thought, word and deed has a consequence and these 'seeds' and their causal consequences constitute *karma*. *Karma* can be auspicious or inauspicious. *Punya karma* is auspicious *karma*, *papa karma* is inauspicious *karma*, as it causes suffering.
Karmadyakshaha:	Dispenser of the fruits of *karma*. Namely the Divine, in the unmanifest aspect, as *Parabrahma*.
Karunakara:	'One who showers compassion or mercy'. Applied to the Divine.
Kshetra:	Means, field. In chapter XIII of the Bhagavad Gita, this refers, very specifically to the 'inner field' of consciousness *(antah karana)*, as *manas* (feelings), *buddhi* (reasoning faculty), *ahankara (self)* and *chitta* (flowing movement of consciousness, including, memory, dreams, sub-consciousness, etc.).
Kshetrajna:	Refers to the observing Intelligence, or perceiving Intelligence, or knowing Intelligence. It perceives the *kshetra*, or the field of consciousness. It is obviously, the *Atma*, the birthless and deathless, life-giving Divine seed in all of us.
Kundalini:	The coiled up, hidden and dormant energy of the Divine Mother *(Sakti)*, lying dormant in the nerve plexus at the bottom of the spine *(muladhara chakra)*.
Maheswara:	*Maha* is the Supreme, *Isvara* is Lord, so, *Maheswara* is supreme Lord. Refers to *Siva*, or in *Vedanta*, *Parabrahma* or *Brahman*.
Manana:	Contemplation and understanding of the teachings.
Manas:	There are three independent faculties in the 'matrix' of *Sakti* called *chitta*. *Manas* is one of them. It is the faculty of understanding and feeling. It is more intimately connected to the *Atma* than *buddhi* and *ahamkara* which are the other two faculties. Some people equate *manas* with 'mind' (another name for consciousness), but in our terminology 'consciousness' is really, *chitta*, with the three faculties embedded in it. It is sometimes forgotten that *manas* is the faculty of

feeling and understanding. Feeling and understanding are the essence of *manas*.

Mantra sadhana:	The spiritual practice *(sadhana)* of chanting a specific *mantra*, with a specific spiritual *samkalpa* (intention) in view.
Mantra:	Something (a word, a *sutra*, a principle), which liberates *(trayate)* the mind, when one dwells upon it. *Manana* is contemplation.
Maya:	An aspect of the power of the manifestation of the Divine *(Sakti)*, that makes us perceive duality, or separation between the *self* and another, whereas, from the state of *moksha*, duality is seen to be a sensory appearance only, bereft of any substance. Etymologically, the word means, that *(ya)* which we are not *(ma)*, namely, the body, etc.
Meenakshi kalyanam:	*Meenakshi* is one of the manifestations of the Divine Mother *(Adi Sakti)* and this *kalyanam* is the 'marriage' and returning home of *Sakti* to *Siva*, Her Lord and Master So *Meenakshi kalyanam* is one representation of *moksha*. It is not to be understood as a marital union between a god and a goddess.
Moksha shastra:	*Shastra*, or authoritative scriptural text on *moksha*.
Moksha:	*Moksha* is the fourth and the last goal in the human drama. The word means liberation and freedom. Freedom from all illusions *(maya)* and freedom from all bondages, freedom from the past and freedom from the future, freedom from ignorance and all sorrow as well.
Mrityunjaya mantra:	The *mantra* which secures victory *(jaya)* over death *(mrtyuhu)*. 'Mrtyunjaya' is one of the names of *Siva*. *Siva* in a *puranic* episode, vanquished death and bestowed immortality *(moksha)*.
Mula-avidya:	'Root Ignorance', as *mula* means root, and *avidya* is 'primordial ignorance'. This primordial ignorance, takes the form of an inability to know oneself, or 'believing' that one is obviously the body, and this inability to know our true nature is due to *maya*, which is also a Divine creation. In Christianity, this is called original sin, which commences with the fall from innocence into duality, the world of 'me and you'.
Mumukshus:	Seekers who are in search of *moksha*.
Mundaka Up.:	*Mundaka* means 'clean shaven'. So probably an Upanishad which emphasises renunciation and detachment from the body.

489

Naastika: The term applies to such individuals and such schools of philosophy, which have deviated from the *Vedic* tradition. Buddhism, Jainism and other materialistic philosophies are considered to be *Naastika.*

Nadis: Modern research has established the existence of the *primo vascular system*, which is a very subtle network of energy channels, permeating the entire body. The *nadis* are therefore fine pathways, along which *prana* or the life energy flows to the various organs of the body.

Navamsha Div Chart: *Navamsha* means the *amsa* (division) of the ninth *(nava)* house of the *Rasi* Chart. Most important of all the sixteen divisional charts. If the *Rasi* chart is the body, the *Navamsha* divisional chart (DC) is like the spinal cord of that body. This is the essence or the 'fruit' of the *Rasi* Chart. It also shows the spiritual nature of the soul, and to what an extent, this can be discovered and manifested in life.

Nidhidhyasana: Abidance in the *Atma*, the kernel of our consciousness. This is possible only by negation of our thoughts and feelings, which do not belong to us, which are of a peripheral nature. Yet, in our nescience, we mistake ourselves and think that we are these thoughts.

Nirguna bhakti: *Bhakti* or devotion to the Divine in the *nirguna*, formless and unmanifest aspect. This is the seventh and highest level of devotion.

Nivritti: Spiritual life, away from worldly pursuits, intended for *mumukshus* and serious seekers. *Nir* means without or negation, *vritti* means mode of life.

Papa karma: *Papa karma* is the *karma* which is connected to inauspicious consequences arising from inauspicious thought, word and deed. *Papa* means sinful.

Parabrahma: The *Vedantic* term for unmanifest *Siva Mahadeva,* the unmanifest Divine, the unknowable, imperceptible, yet the Father and Mother of all creation.

Paramatma: The Supreme *(Para)* Self *(Atma)*. Referring to *Parabrahma,*

Prajnya: *Jnya* means to know or to understand, here the knowing and understanding is in the context of grasping the truth of the Divine, in Its ultimate unmanifest aspect. *Prajnya* means the most excellent form of knowing and understanding the truth which comes as a blessing to seekers, who are rooted in the *Atma. So prajnya is intelligence, or rather Atmic intelligence. Ramana Maharishi calls it the intelligence of the enlightened.*

Prajnya:	*Atmic* intelligence, intelligence, which is awareness, which is coincident with *Prajnya* or awareness.
Pralaya:	Cosmic dissolution after each *maha yuga*.
Prasada:	'Gracious gift or blessing from the Divine', is the essential meaning. Also refers to an offering to God, master, *Avatar*, Deity, and thereafter distributed to the devotees, as a token of the blessings of the Divine. It is gladly accepted and eaten, as it is, by intention, the repository of the blessings of the Divine-in some worshipped form.
Pratyahara:	Withdrawal of the senses from the sense objects, part of the *yogic* discipline, necessary for *moksha*.
Pravritti:	Life of extroversion, which is natural in the spheres of *artha and kama*. It is the opposite of *Nivritti* (life of introversion).
Punya karma:	*Punya karma* is auspicious *karma*, when auspicious thought, word and deed lead to auspicious consequences.
Puranas:	*Purana* means, ancient. Historical spiritual-historical texts of ancient Hindus, dating back some 5000 yrs, but certainly not in the sense of Western chronological history. The 'history' of the Hindus, though not entirely faithful to space-time happenings and reality, on account of its mythological, philosophical, religious and spiritual ingredients; has more inspirational and didactic value, rather than, as texts that accurately portray purely historical events.
Purusharthas:	The goals *(artha)* of man *(purusha)* in Hindu society, namely, *dharma, artha, kama, moksha*.
Rasi Chart:	*Rasi* means zodiac, spanning the twelve zodiacal signs. The birth chart of an individual, showing the planetary positions on the *Rasi* chart, at the time and place of birth. It is a diagram or chart.
Rishis:	Hindu sages.
Sadhaka:	Seeker, or one who does *sadhana*, or spiritual practice.
Sadhana:	Spiritual practice of some kind, especially when it is done in a serious and concerted manner over a long period of time.

Sakhaya:	From the two Upanishads mentioned in the retreat. Refers to the two 'Tat Tvam Asi' birds. Means, very much alike, kindred.
Sakshi:	The *Atma* as the completely indifferent and detached 'witness'.
Sakti:	The dynamic aspect of *Siva,* considered feminine, which creates all formful manifestations and thus stands for His Divine power - in contrast to His timeless transcendental state of Divine Being, considered to be masculine. However, this *Sakti* aspect of *Siva* is intrinsically inseparable from His unmanifest state of Divine Being.
Samadhi:	*Samadhi* is a state of the human consciousness or 'I', whereby the *yogi* is well-established in awareness, or the pure 'I', to such an extent that nothing in the outside world or in consciousness is a distracting influence any more. Such a *yogi* becomes capable of paying attention to the whole movement of life, without his attention ever wavering. The word is also used to describe sometimes a trance state, where the *yogi* has sunk so deeply within himself or herself that, he/she becomes dead to the outside sensory world. Generally, in *samadhi,* the awareness is wide awake, implying *prajnya* is in full relief as well. Consciousness is naturally in all such states, 'whole and well integrated'. Thus the *sthitha prajnya* is obviously in the state of *samadhi.*
Samkalpa:	*Samkalpa* is intention. *Samkalpa* can be made by the *Jiva* which is in ignorance or the *samkalpa* can arise from the *Atma,* in which case it is a Divine emanation.
Samskaras	A deeply buried impression, lying in the sub-conscious mind, and emanating from there, from time to time as a *vasana*. Think of it as a 'sea-animal or complex' which has life and which lies at the bottom of the ocean, and which under certain circumstances, comes floating to the surface, into the consciousness, and which may later also vanish, sink down and make itself invisible, etc.
Sannyasis:	Those who either physically or mentally, move away from the customary materialistic pursuits of life and dedicate themselves to the fourth and last goal of life, *moksha,* may be called *sannyasis.* Thus, even householders, as well as, naturally, renunciants, may be in essence, *sannyasis,* depending on their inner disposition.
Sapta svaras:	The seven *(sapta)* basic notes *(swaras)* of classical music.

Sat-Chit-Ananda:	*Sat* is absolute Truth, That which eternally exists, namely *Atma* and *Brahman*. The Divine in its unmanifest form, beyond space and time. *Chit* is awareness, its face in the human consciousness. *Ananda* is pure and uncaused joy. Joy which is not pleasure, that is generally sourced in some sensory gratification.
Sathya yuga:	The bygone *yuga* of truth *(satya)*, characterized by 100% *dharma* or moral virtue. From, 11,501, BCE to 6701, BCE, according to Ref [1]. A span of 4800 yrs.
Satsang:	Association and in the company of spiritual and wise people.
Satyagraha:	One of the ideals of Mahatma Gandhi during India's freedom struggle. Means tenacious conformity or adherence *(graha)* to truth *(satya)*.
Saucha:	Cleanliness, inner and outer, necessary in *Yoga*.
Sayuja:	From the *Svetasvatara* and the *Mundaka* Upanishads, referring to the two 'Tat Tvam Asi' birds. Means, the two birds, though seemingly two separate entities, are nevertheless, yoked together, or united.
Self (Paramatma):	A synonym for *Atma*, with the emphasis on its Sovereignty. Because the *Atma* is one with Godhead, this *Atma* is also the *Paramatma*.
self:	The English name for *Jiva*. Sometimes it is perceived of as being the very core of *Jiva*, one then speaks of the *Jiva's self*. We can use the expression either way. Sri J. Krishnamurti has thrown the greatest light on the working of the *self*, which is actually *ahankara*, which is one of the three faculties embedded in *chitta*, the 'matrix' of consciousness.
Shraddha:	Faith in the Divine.
Siva & Sakti:	*Siva* is the absolute Godhead, beyond time and space. Etymologically means peace and the abode of all the Infinite excellences seen in the manifested world. *Sakti* is an auspicious emanation from *Siva*. Though She arises from the ground of *Siva*, She has a great deal of autonomy so, She is called *Svathantriya Sakti*, to emphasize her independence. This independence of *Sakti* places her on an equal footing with *Siva*. *Sakti* is in time and *Siva* is timeless. *Sakti* is perceptible to the senses and *Siva* is unknowable and imperceptible.

Sloka:	A poetic structure of verses in Sanskrit works with four *padas* (quarters), using the well-known metre *(chandas)* called *Anushtub*. Used in the epics, *Ramayana* and *Mahabharata*. Ideally designed for chanting or singing in a rhythmic fashion.
Sravana:	Hearing the teachings.
Sthambhana:	Withholding, suspension, cessation.
Sthapatya Veda:	The systematized Hindu *shastra* of temple architecture and temple sculptures. It is Divine-centric, hence called *Veda*.
Sthitha Prajnya:	The term *sthitha prajnya* is used in the Bhagavad Gita. *Sthitha* means stable. So *sthitha prajnya* is the one in whom, *prajnya* (the *Atmic* intelligence), which has been awakened has become steady, rock-like and stabilized.
Sunyata:	In Buddhism, the Ultimate Ground is conceived to be the Great Void, the 'Vacuum of Quantum Field Theory'. Sanskrit name is *Sunyata*, meaning, the great Nothingness.
Sutra:	*Sutra* is a principle or natural law or a string as in a beaded necklace where all the beads are strung on the same one string. The natural law or principle is likened to many beads strung on a string, because just as a string holds all the beads together, the principle *(sutra)* accounts and holds together, all the hundreds and thousands of natural happenings, and events.
Svatantriya Sakti:	The adjective, points to Sakti's utter independence *(svatantriyata)*. This is the reason, it is not enough to discover *Siva* alone. One must also discover and acknowledge the complementary half, namely *Sakti*, as She is, an independent Power.
Svetasvatara Up.:	*Sveta* is white. *Asva* is horse, so the adjective means a white horse. Every Upanishad teaches *Atma vidya* and *Brahma vidya*. *Atma* is the Pure 'I' Consciousness in man and *Brahman* is Godhead, the Absolute-also sometimes called *Parabrahma*.
Swabhava:	Intrinsic nature.
Tat Tvam Asi:	'Tat' refers to *Parabrahma*, 'That'. 'Tvam' refers to yourself and 'Asi' means 'are'. So this is a *maha vakya* from the *Chandogya* Upanishad, which means you, in your *Atmic* essence, are verily, the *Parabrahma*. Thus, 'Tat Tvam Asi' means, 'That thou art'.

Treta yuga:	The bygone *yuga* of 75% truth and moral virtue. From 6701 BCE to 3101 BCE. A span of 3600 yrs.
Upadrashta:	Used in the Bhagavad Gita, Ch. XIII, *Sloka* 22. Means, close witness.
Upanishad (Up.):	Whole body of Hindu scriptures considered to be the crown of the *Vedas*. There are about hundred or two hundred Upanishads and the etymology of the word is - a teaching which is received by sitting at the feet of the master.
Vanaprastha:	Refers to the third stage of life in ancient Hindu society. Its purpose was to make the transition from a full involvement in worldly life *(grihasthasrama)* to spiritual seclusion and renunciation *(sannyasrama)* smooth and without any sense of shock. It took the form of withdrawal from all worldly responsibilities by retreating into the woods *(vana)*, as this afforded the necessary solitude and peaceful environment for pursuing the contemplative life as a prelude to complete renunciation.
Vasanas:	Past-life impressions and tendencies, as, 'fragrances' carried over into the present life. *Vasanas*, can be of various kinds, manifesting as attachment to body, to property, to knowledge, to specific people, to wealth, etc.
Vastu shastra:	*Shastra* means authoritative study of, a subject. *Vastu shastra* would therefore be the classical study of architecture, based on the cosmic life energies, such as the Bio-Electro Magnetic (BEM) fields and how they influence, positively and negatively, human life and habitation.
Vasudaiva kutumbakam:	From the *Maha* Upanishad, meaning, 'the world as one family, or the earth as one family'.
Vedanta:	Means, the limit or the pinnacle of the *Vedas*, namely the *Vedasiras*, the crown of the *Vedas*, or the Upanishads.
Vedas:	Has its origin in the Sanskrit verb, *vid*, to know. Thus *Vedas*, in so far as its esoteric and spiritual dimension is concerned, refers to knowledge of a certain mystical and *yogic* nature. Such knowledge must have become available to sages, *yogis*, when they plumbed the depths of their consciousness during meditations, or when they received the blessings of the Divine in the form of intuitive revelations.
Vedasiras:	The crown *(siras)* of the *Vedas*, namely the Upanishads.

Vedic astrology:	The knowledge systems of the Hindus were all Divine-centric, so they were called *Vedic*, this or *Vedic* that. *By Vedic, we should really understand, knowledge of anything, understood in a Divine-centric way.* *Vedic* astrology *(Jyotisha)* is thus a Hindu, Divine-centric system of knowledge, that comprehends, the totality of human life from birth to death, by mathematically analysing the same, as due to the complex interplay of nine cosmic life energies, that are represented by the orderly movement of seven planets, plus two nodes of the Moon, namely, *Rahu and Ketu.*
Visishtha Advaita:	The world-view *(darsana)* or philosophy propounded by the *Vaishnava acharya,* Sri Ramanujacharya. It is 'qualified monism'.
Viveka Chudamani:	'Crest jewel of discriminative knowledge', a veritable *moksha shastra,* written by Adi Sankaracharya. A work on Self - Realization.
Yoga sutras of Patanjali:	One of the canonical *moksha shastras*, the crowning goal in the text is *Kaivalya* (Self - Realization) or *moksha*. Attributed to Maharishi Patanjali. Roughly 5000 BCE.
Yuga:	A cosmic cycle of time of the order of thousands of years, governing the rising and falling of civilizations, as understood by the Hindu sages.

———————————

Made in the USA
Monee, IL
10 November 2019